LANGUAGE DIVERSITY
Problem or Resource?

A Social and Educational Perspective on Language Minorities in the United States

Sandra Lee McKay and Sau-ling Cynthia Wong, Editors

NEWBURY HOUSE PUBLISHERS
A division of Harper & Row, Publishers, Inc.
Cambridge, New York, Philadelphia, San Francisco, Washington, D.C.
London, Mexico City, São Paulo, Singapore, Sydney

Sponsoring Editor: Leslie Berriman
Production Coordinator: Cynthia Funkhouser
Cover Design: 20/20 Services Inc.
Compositor: TCSystems
Printer and Binder: Malloy Lithographing Inc.

NEWBURY HOUSE PUBLISHERS
A division of Harper & Row, Publishers, Inc.

Language Science
Language Teaching
Language Training

Language Diversity: Problem or Resource? A Social and Educational Perspective on Language Minorities in the United States

Library of Congress Cataloging in Publication Data

Language diversity, problem or resource?

Bibliography: p.
1. Linguistic minorities—United States.
2. Multilingualism—United States. 3. Language and education—United States. 4. Language policy—United States. 5. Language planning—United States.
I. McKay, Sandra. II. Wong, Sau-ling Cynthia.
P119.315.L34 1988 401′.9′0973 88-1450
ISBN 0-06-632608-7

Printed in the U.S.A.
63-26086

First printing: March 1988
91 90 89 88 9 8 7 6 5 4 3 2 1

To Jer, Jerry, and Michael

—S. L. M.

To Huan-Hua and C.
—S. C. W.

Contents

Preface

The language situation of the United States is fraught with contradictions. The English language is so universally recognized that many Americans believe it to be the official language—and certainly most act as if it already were—but nothing in the Constitution designates it as such. When we open our borders to immigrants and refugees from all over the world, proficiency in English is not stipulated as a condition for entry; once admitted, however, the newcomers often find themselves facing social, economic, and political consequences of their lack of mastery of the language. Many of our policy-makers claim to espouse cultural pluralism; at the same time, linguistic pluralism, its twin, is frequently treated as if it were a problem created for the Anglophone majority by burdensome minorities. As a nation without an explicitly articulated language policy, we generally look to the schools as our major vehicles of language planning; yet resources for developing effective language education programs are often scarce.

Since the liberalization of immigration laws in 1965, with the demographic composition of the nation undergoing a radical transformation, the ambiguities inherent in the American language situation have been growing more visible. As the schools experience an influx of language minority children, it becomes increasingly apparent that language teaching and learning are not merely matters of pedagogy or individual endeavor; rather, what happens in school is intimately related to what happens in the surrounding community. Without a clear understanding of the social context in which the various immigrant language minorities operate, efforts to aid children in their language education may well prove misdirected or even counterproductive.

This book aims to provide a social and educational perspective on contemporary immigrant language minorities, especially those large, fast-growing Hispanic and Asian groups whose presence is felt strongly in the schools. It is addressed primarily to preservice and in-service teachers of English, whether in language arts, bilingual education, or English as a second language classrooms. We hope that the information and perspectives offered in this book can help create a better understanding of language minority students in a larger context than the classroom or school.

In putting together this volume, we start from several premises. First, we believe that the linguistic diversity of the United States is a valuable resource rather than a problem, and that the emphasis in our current language education practices—curtailing mother tongue maintenance among immigrants and then providing foreign language programs for Anglophone monolinguals (many of whom are former bilinguals)—is, to say the least, wasteful. Language resources, like natural resources, should be wisely conserved and developed. Secondly, we believe that language minorities in this country, regardless of their ethnic origin and length of residence here, have a dual right: to gain proficiency in English through meaningful educational programs, and to maintain their native languages in their family and community life. Further, an enlightened language education policy should recognize that these two processes, rather than being antagonistic, are in fact interdependent. Finally, we believe that while the schools can do a great deal to help language minorities attain their potential for participation in American society, there are limits to the powers of language education. The philosophical commitment of the entire community to what Richard Ruíz terms a "language-as-resource" perspective, accompanied by economic support, is necessary before a more coherent and far-sighted language policy can be implemented through the schools. At the moment, when the national mood is dominated by nativist sentiments, whether such a reorientation is forthcoming may be doubtful, but it is a goal worth bearing in mind and working for.

The educational authorities in many states have created handbooks designed to familiarize teachers and administrators with the linguistic and cultural background of language minority children. Typically, a handbook on a group would list features of the ethnic language that contrast with English, as well as aspects of the culture that might explain the children's "different" behavior in American classrooms. This book differs in a crucial way from such works. We believe that the linguistic and cultural background of individual learners is but a part (often a minor part) of the language situation of a group, and that it is often more important to see the group functioning as a minority in a complex network of social attitudes, economic activities, and political power. Although readers of this volume will still be able to obtain information on the linguistic and cultural background of specific minority groups, either through discussion in the text or through references to sources, our emphasis is on the overall context of language acquisition and maintenance. Hence the reader will find more space devoted to information on immigration history and demographic data, which are areas traditionally considered peripheral to the concerns of language teachers.

Several major sets of questions are explored in this book. The first concerns the language policy, language heritage, and current linguistic composition of the United States. To what extent can the United States be called a multilingual nation, and to what extent can it be called an Anglophone one? What kinds of dynamics determine the constantly shifting relationship between multilingualism and English dominance? What has our historical policy been toward English and other tongues spoken on our soil? How has immigration policy interacted with language policy? What changes in America's linguistic picture have been wrought by the 1965 immigration reform? The second set of questions focuses on the most numerous and fastest-growing immigrant language minorities since 1965. Who are they and who were their forebears? Historically, how have each group and its language been perceived and treated in the United States? What are the demographic, sociocultural, and linguistic characteristics of the group? How have these characteristics affected the way its members use language—both English and their ethnic language—and what are the prospects for the acquisition of the former and the maintenance of the latter? The final set of questions pertains to education. What relevant theoretical constructs are available to help us understand the processes of language acquisition and maintenance by immigrant language minorities? What educational alternatives exist for promoting widespread proficiency in English as well as strengthening language resources? How do they compare to each other? To what extent are language minorities entitled to various types of language education services?

To examine the above questions, the volume is organized into four sections. The first section provides the conceptual framework that underpins the collection, the terms in which the varied material in this text might be coherently understood. The second section sketches out a historical overview of multilingualism in the United States and documents the current state of language diversity. The third section analyzes in depth the language situation of seven immigrant language minorities: three Hispanic and four Asian. The last section explores the educational implications of language diversity from the perspectives of language acquisition theory, pedagogy, and law.

In determining which language minorities to include in this section, we have relied on contemporary immigration demographics. According to Waggoner (Table 3.2), immigrants from countries where Asian and Pacific Island languages are spoken, and those from countries where Spanish is spoken, currently make up the two largest categories of language minorities. From the former category, we have selected the four fastest growing groups for detailed coverage: Vietnamese, Filipinos, Chinese, and Koreans. As for the latter, although Central and South American immigrants are a large and growing group, there is little available research on them due to the newness of the influx. As a result, we have decided to focus on Mexican Americans, Puerto Ricans, and Cuban Americans.

With the exception of Ruíz's paper in the first section, from which the conceptual terms of this book are drawn, all the chapters have been specifically written for the collection. The discussion questions in the "Exploring the Ideas" and "Applying the Ideas" sections following each chapter are provided by the editors. We are grateful to all our contributors for their insightful work; in a most literal sense, this volume would not have been possible without them. We would like to take this opportunity to thank them not only for sharing their professional expertise so generously, but also for making our experience of editing the volume such a pleasant one. We would also like to thank our reviewers, Susan Caesar, Lydia Stack, and Jean Ramirez, for their constructive suggestions. A special thanks is due to Leslie Berriman for her interest in and support of this project. Stan Yogi, Angela Pao, David Palumbo-Liu, and Kathy Lo, who provided prompt and meticulous assistance in the preparation of the manuscript, deserve special appreciation. Finally, we would like to thank our families for their patience and understanding while we completed the manuscript.

The Authors

Sandra Lee McKay received her Ph.D. from the University of Minnesota in applied linguistics. Presently she is Professor of English at San Francisco State University, where she teaches English as a second language methods and materials development and sociolinguistics. She has trained English teachers in Guatemala, Uruguay, South Africa, China, Hong Kong, and Hungary on Fulbright and U.S.I.A. grants. Her publications include numerous articles and several books on composing and reading in a second language such as *Composing in a Second Language, At the Door,* and *Writing for a Specific Purpose.*

Sau-ling Cynthia Wong is Assistant Professor in the Asian American Studies Program, Department of Ethnic Studies at the University of California, Berkeley. A native of Hong Kong, she holds a Ph.D. in English and American literature from Stanford University and a Master's degree in teaching English as a foreign language/second language from San Francisco State University. Her professional interests include teaching composition to Asian American students, issues in language acquisition and maintenance for Asian Americans, Asian American literature, and Chinese immigrant literature.

Choung Hoang Chung received a Master's degree in education from the University of San Francisco and a Master's degree in art and photography from Lone Mountain College. Presently he is a doctoral candidate in education at the University of San Francisco and is on the faculty of the Asian American Studies Program at the University of California, Berkeley, and at San Jose State University. He is also a research specialist for the Multifunction Resource Center, a project funded by the U.S. Department of Education. His research interests center on language use, language maintenance, and language acquisition within the Vietnamese community.

Rosita G. Galang is Associate Professor of Credential and Master's programs in bilingual education and teaching English as a second language in the School of Education at the University of San Francisco. She served as lecturer at the Summer Institute for Advanced Educational Research on Asian Americans at Berkeley (1979), Boston (1980), and Hawaii (1981) and was president of the California Association for Asian Pacific Bilingual Education and the National Association for Asian and Pacific American Education. She is coauthor of *Assessment of Filipino-Speaking Limited English Proficient Students with Special Needs* (Special Education Resource Network, 1986) and *Handbook for Teaching Filipino Speaking Students* (California State Department of Education, 1986). She obtained her Master's degree in teaching English as a second language at the University of Hawaii and her Ph.D. in linguistics from Ateneo de Manila University–Philippine Normal College Consortium.

Ofelia García and **Ricardo Otheguy** are specialists in bilingualism and bilingual education. Both were born in Cuba and now teach in the Bilingual Education Program at the City College of New York. Ofelia García has published in the areas of sociolinguistics and the education of language minorities. She has conducted joint research with Joshua A. Fishman on written Spanish in the United States and biliteracy in ethnic schools. Ricardo Otheguy is a linguist who has done research on Spanish grammar and semantics. He has also studied Spanish in the United States, as well as African survivals in New World Spanish. His publications include "Thinking about Bilingual Education: A Critical Appraisal," published in the *Harvard Educational Review*. García and Otheguy have coauthored a number of articles on the sociolinguistic and socioeducational situation of Cuban Americans.

Bok-Lim C. Kim has taught social work in Korea and the United States for 28 years. She was formerly Associate Professor of Social Work, School of Social Work, University of Illinois, Urbana (1969–1979). Her research and publications (four books and many journal articles) focus on the adjustment and adaptation of Asian immigrants in the United States and on cross-cultural counseling. She is an active advocate for Asian women who married American servicemen overseas. Currently she combines private practice psychotherapy with research consultation and workshops on cross-cultural psychotherapy.

Mary McGroarty, Ph.D., Stanford, 1982, is Assistant Professor in the TESL/Applied Linguistics program at the University of California, Los Angeles. She has worked in several language education programs and has trained teachers in the United States and abroad. Her research and teaching interests include theoretical and pedagogic aspects of bilingualism, the nature of language skills, and cultural influences on language learning and teaching. She has published in the *TESOL Quarterly* and the *NABE Journal*.

Jean Molesky teaches in the Native American Studies Program, Department of Ethnic Studies at the University of California, Berkeley. Previously she taught English as a second language at San Jose City College and with Metropolitan Adult Education in San Jose. She has published several articles on Central Americans in exile in *World Immigration, Creation,* and *The Witness* and is the author of the *White Paper on the Immigration and Con-*

trol Reform Act of 1986: Recommendations for Effective Implementation. Currently she is writing a novel on recent immigrants to California.

Richard Ruíz received degrees in Romance Languages and Literatures at Harvard College and in Anthropology and Philosophy of Education at Stanford University. He was a member of the Department of Education Policy Studies at the University of Wisconsin–Madison for 9 years. Currently, he teaches courses in language planning and policy studies and in the foundations of education at the University of Arizona.

Guadalupe Valdés is a sociolinguist who specializes in the study of English/Spanish bilingualism. She has carried out extensive research on Mexican Americans over the past 14 years, focusing on code-switching and language choice in bilingual communities, language and the development of reading, language use within newly arrived Mexican families, and language needs of minorities in the courtroom. This research was carried out in the New Mexico/Texas/Chihuahua border of which she is a native. Currently, Valdés is Professor of Education at the University of California, Berkeley.

Dorothy Waggoner is a specialist on language minority statistics and bilingual education. She helped develop the language questions for the 1980 Census as part of a federal government interagency committee on race and ethnicity for the Census. Since the Census data have become available she has been involved in various projects to use the information to monitor the status of minorities in the United States and to document their special needs. Her Ph.D. was obtained in applied linguistics at Georgetown University.

Ana Celia Zentella, born and raised in the South Bronx, New York City, received a Ph.D. in Educational Linguistics from the University of Pennsylvania. Her dissertation, " 'Hablamos los dos. We speak both': Growing up Bilingual in El Barrio," won First Place in the Outstanding Dissertations Competition sponsored by the National Advisory Council on Bilingual Education (1982). She is Associate Professor in the Department of Black and Puerto Rican Studies, Hunter College, and is on the doctoral faculty of the Linguistics Program, Graduate Center, City University of New York. Her research interest in Spanish–English code-switching has led to studies of this phenomenon in Philadelphia, East Harlem, bilingual classrooms in the Bronx, and high schools in Puerto Rico. Currently she is studying language behavior and attitudes of the four largest Spanish-speaking groups in New York City: Puerto Ricans, Dominicans, Cubans, and Colombians. This research is supported by a Rockefeller Foundation Minority Scholars Grant.

Part I

LANGUAGE AS RESOURCE: A CONCEPTUAL FRAMEWORK

The article by Richard Ruíz, "Orientations in Language Planning," provides the conceptual framework for this text. In the chapter, Ruíz delineates three social orientations toward languages and their role in society: language-as-problem, language-as-right, and language-as-resource. Each of these orientations is related to a particular constellation of language attitudes that helps to determine what the legitimate approaches to languages are within the society. Ruíz argues that a language-as-resource orientation offers the United States a variety of social, economic, and political benefits.

CHAPTER

1

Orientations in Language Planning

Richard Ruíz
University of Wisconsin-Madison

Basic orientations toward language and its role in society influence the nature of language planning efforts in any particular context. Three such orientations are proposed in this paper: language-as-problem, language-as-right, and language-as-resource. The first two currently compete for predominance in the international literature. While problem-solving has been the main activity of language planners from early on (language planning being an early and important aspect of social planning in "development" contexts), rights-affirmation has gained in importance with the renewed emphasis on the protection of minority groups. The third orientation has received much less attention; it is proposed as vital to the interest of language planning in the United States.

*Bilingual education is considered in the framework of these orientations. Many of the problems of bilingual education programs in the United States arise because of the hostility and divisiveness inherent in the problem- and rights-orientations which generally underlie them. The development and elaboration of a language-resource orientation is seen as important for the integration of bilingual education into a responsible language policy for the United States.**

Source: Richard Ruíz. 1984. Orientations in Language Planning. *NABE Journal.* *8*(2):15–34. Reprinted by permission of the publisher.

* Research for this paper was supported partly by a Rockefeller Foundation Fellowship in the Social Sciences. I am also grateful to Andrew Cohen and Alicia Oman for useful suggestions and encouragement.

There are few conceptual models or principles which serve to orient the language planning literature. After 15 or so years of trying to delimit and elaborate the field, we have not moved far beyond the point of adapting basic typologies like that of Haugen (1966) or Neustupný (1970) to new field situations; many of the very important early works, with titles like "Some comments on . . ." and "Toward a definition of . . .", intended as starting points to the international debate on the nature and uses of language planning, still await integration into a more comprehensive theory.

Some notable exceptions to this contention come to mind: Neustupný's (1970) policy-cultivation distinction; Kloss' (1969) discussion of corpus and status planning; McRae's (1975) territoriality-personality principles; and Tollefson's (1981) notions of centralized and decentralized language planning have emerged as important approaches to the basic issues of the field. However, there is still another level of conceptual integration in which orienting models are lacking; what is needed are meta-models which would serve to focus attention on the nature of the basic concepts with which language planning specialists work. It is in considering that kind of question that we can assess the usefulness of any particular model or language plan.

ORIENTATIONS

In this paper, the concept of *orientations* is proposed as a heuristic approach to the study of basic issues in language planning. *Orientation,* as it is used here, refers to a *complex of dispositions toward language and its role, and toward languages and their role in society*. These dispositions may be largely unconscious and prerational because they are at the most fundamental level of arguments about language; yet, the argument here is that an important role of the metatheoretician of language planning is to make these orientations obvious. One way to do this is to discover them in policies and proposals which already exist; another is to propose or advocate new ones. Both of these are attempted in this chapter.

Orientations are basic to language planning in that they delimit the ways we talk about language and language issues, they determine the basic questions we ask, the conclusions we draw from the data, and even the data themselves. Orientations are related to *language attitudes* in that they constitute the framework in which attitudes are formed: they help to delimit the range of acceptable attitudes toward language, and to make certain attitudes legitimate. In short, orientations determine what is thinkable about language in society.[1]

An example of how planners holding different orientations come to different policy positions will serve as a preliminary illustration of the importance of this concept. Tauli (1974) writes from an orientation which he would call "language as a means"; in the same argument he refers to language as a "tool." He contends that as tools some languages can be more useful than others, and that this usefulness is measurable.

> From the fact that language is a means follows that a language and its components can be evaluated, altered, corrected, regulated, improved, and replaced by others and new languages and components of a language can be created at will. Thus all languages or the components of a language, as constructions, words or morphemes, are not equal in efficiency in every respect. The efficiency of a language or a component of a language as a means of communication can be evaluated from a point of view of economy, clarity, redundancy, etc. with objective scientific often quantitative methods. (Tauli 1974:51)

From this basic idea of "language-as-means" Tauli generates a definition of language planning as "the methodical activity of regulating and improving existing languages or creating new common, regional, national or international languages" (1974:56). He goes on to propose the development of super-languages, which he calls "interlanguages," which would serve the communications needs of many different language communities. As evidence for the need of such interlanguages, he cites what he calls the "highly irrational" translation procedures of international bodies, and the difficulties of scientists in reading work in a variety of languages. "The ideal situation would be that all people all over the world who need to communicate with the people who have another mother tongue learn the same interlanguage as a secondary language (1974:66)."

Others, proceeding from an orientation which Kelman (1972) might call "language as sentimental attachment," would be reluctant to create language policies from such a strictly "instrumental" point of view. After all, language is an important aspect of self-expression and self-identification; the value of these considerations must be measured by standards other than those of efficiency, clarity, redundancy, and others like these. Language policies based on these criteria can have devastating social consequences.

> Since language is so closely tied to group identity, language-based discrimination against the group is perceived as a threat to its very existence as a recognizable entity and as an attack on its sacred objects and symbols. The issue is no longer merely a redistribution of power and resources, but it is self-preservation of the group and defense against genocide. The conflict becomes highly charged with emotion and increasingly unmanageable. Genocide, after all, is not a matter for negotiation but for last-ditch defense. (Kelman, 1972: 199–200)

It is precisely for these kinds of reasons that some nations have conferred official status on previously subordinate indigenous languages; no one can suggest reasonably that it was for reasons of efficiency that Malaysia recently declared Malay an official language for government and education.

It is this sort of consideration, as well, at the basis of much of the advocacy for bilingual education in the United States. In the international sphere, the problems of mutual intelligibility that Tauli bemoans are, from this orientation, merely technical; it is worth the effort to try to solve them on their own terms if the only other alternative is the abandonment of ethnic language.

In the following pages, two orientations in language planning are described which have had a significant impact on policy formulation; these two, called "language-as-problem" and "language-as-right," are healthy competitors in the planning literature (though as suggested above, advocates of each position may not recognize at what level their disagreement lies). A third is proposed, called "language-as-resource," which, although suggested by a number of others before, has benefitted from almost no conceptual elaboration at all. It is recommended as a potentially important redirection for language planning. At the same time, one should realize that these are competing but not incompatible approaches (here, the comparison to Kuhn's "paradigm" breaks down): while one orientation may be more desirable than another in any particular context, it is probably best to have a repertoire of orientations from which to draw.

Language-as-Problem

The bulk of the work of language planners and those who have written in the field of language planning has been focused on the identification and resolution of language problems (Neustupný, 1970; Rubin and Shuy, 1973; Fishman, 1975). Karam, in reviewing the work of Haugen, Rugein and Jernudd, and Fishman, concludes that "the terms reviewed [for language planning] refer to an activity which *attempts* to solve a language problem" (1974:105). Fishman himself delimits language planning as "the organized pursuit of solutions to language problems, typically at the national level" (1974a:79;1975). Karam even implies that language problems are a necessary ingredient to any language planning at all. "Theoretically, wherever there is a communication problem concerning language, language planning is possible (1974:108)." Mackey suggests that language problems are inherent in the multilingual situation: "the more languages there are to choose from, the more complex the problems tend to become" (1979:48).

There are probably many reasons for this focus. One of the most obvious is that language planning activities have been carried out in the past predominantly in the context of national development, as Fishman points out:

> The sociology of language planning tends to be largely the sociology of organized change processes vis-a-vis non-Western languages. The focus on the non-West is related to a corresponding focus on "newly developing" entities. (1975:84)

Neustupný's (1970) examples of language problems—code selection, standardization, literacy, orthography, language stratification—suggest overwhelmingly a development context, as well.[2] In a frame-work so constituted, one must conclude that language is merely another of the problems of modernization.

Given this context, the emphasis on language problems is perhaps reasonable. This also may be a partial explanation of the lack of conceptual models in language planning: early specialists were interested less in the conceptual articulation of an academic area of research than in the treatment of practical and immediate field problems of policy-makers.

There are other explanations, as well, for the preponderance of problem-oriented language planning approaches. One of these certainly must be the unique sociohistorical context of multilingual societies. In the United States, for example, the need for language training of large numbers of non-English speaking Americans coincided, in the late 1950s, with a general societal concern for the disadvantaged. The importance of this coincidence lies in language issues becoming linked with the problems associated with this group—poverty, handicap, low educational achievement, little or no social mobility. The sorts of programs designed in the 1960s to address these socially undesirable conditions treated language as an underlying problem. Thus, the Bilingual Education Act (BEA) of 1968 and the state statutes on bilingual education which have followed start with the assumption that non-English language groups have a handicap to be overcome; the BEA, after all, was conceived and formulated in conjunction with the War on Poverty. Resolution of this problem—teaching English, even at the expense of the first language—became the objective of school programs now generally referred to as transitional bilingual education.

There is ample evidence that this connection of non-English language heritage and bilingualism with social problems has become entrenched in popular thought. Consider this passage from *U.S.* v. *Texas* (1971), in which Judge Justice delimits the Mexican American group.

> Mexican American students exhibit numerous characteristics which have a causal connection with their general inability to benefit from an educational program primarily designed to meet the needs of so-called Anglo Americans. These characteristics include "cultural incompatibilities" and English language deficiencies—two traits which immediately and effectively identify those students sharing them as members of a definite group whose performance as norm habitually will fall below that of Anglo American students who do not exhibit these traits. It would appear, therefore, . . . that it is largely these ethnically-linked traits—albeit combined with other facts such as poverty, malnutrition, and the effects of past educational deprivation—which account for the identifiability of Mexican American students as a group . . . (del Valle 1981:1)

This is a remarkable statement; for the purposes of the court, the Mexican American group has been identified on the basis of a number of criteria—all of them negative. Language is one of those. This statement is almost equivalent in its effects to another contained in a recent controversial report on the effectiveness of bilingual education programs.

> [E]ducational policy makers should recognize the complexity of the needs of language-minority children. The source of their educational difficulties may warrant the types of approaches that have been developed in compensatory education programs (smaller class sizes, more individual attention, more structured curricula, etc.) for other children from economically disadvantaged backgrounds. (Birman and Ginsburg 1981:12)

Again, there is here an implicit understanding that economic disadvantage is inherent in the language-minority situation (the key word in the passage is ''other'').

Perhaps these examples suggest another explanation for the linking of language-minority persons with social problems; this explanation would be less arbitrary than those we have offered thus far, since it points to a central tendency, an essential tension, in all social systems: in any society, a sociolinguistic darwinism will force on us the notion that subordinate languages are problems to be resolved. That is why, as Fishman (1978) says, it is the speakers of the ''little'' languages who are thought to need bilingualism: ''they'' need ''us.''

> Whether it is General Motors or the American Federation of Teachers or the Interethnic Brotherhood of Deracinated Intellectuals, the pious view is advanced that ''proper'' monolingualism is the only sane solution to poverty, backwardness, and powerlessness. If only all those wild little people out there would speak English . . . , they could solve all their problems. (1978:45)[3]

Maintenance of a subordinate first language and bilingualism involving one of those ''little languages'' is therefore associated in a pre-rational way with intellectual limitation, linguistic deficiency (always defined from the perspective of English-speakers [Lawerence 1978:310]), provincialism, irrationalism, disruption, so that ''the escape from little languages is viewed as liberating, as joyful, as self-fulfilling, as self-actualizing (Fishman 1978:47).''

This attitude obscures the current debate over whether transitional or maintenance-oriented bilingual programs are the more desirable. The question has already been decided: if the programs are acceptable at all, they are only to the extent that they are effective as transitions. Notice in the second sentence of this passage the obvious indifference to language loss:

> Underlying this paper is the assumption that the ultimate goals of bilingual education programs are to learn English and keep up with English-speaking peers in subject matter. While bilingualism per se is a laudable and worthwhile outcome, we judge benefit in terms of English acquisition and subject matter learning. The 1978 amendments embodied this assumption. (Birman and Ginsburg 1981:5n)

If these comments are suspect because of the attitudes of the authors toward bilingual education (see Gray's criticism in Babcock, 1981), they are not inconsistent with the views of even those who are thought to be in favor of the program generally. Shirley Hufstedler, Secretary of Education in the Carter Administration, sees the goals of bilingual education as exactly those two cited by Birman and Ginsburg, though her concern is as much the program regulations established following *Lau* v. *Nichols* (1974) as the 1978 BEA. As to the question of language loss, her response is that "the Lau regulations are *not* designed to maintain any language or subculture in the United States (Hufstedler 1980:67)."

The transition-maintenance controversy has been kept alive by a few dedicated advocates of language maintenance like Fishman and Hernández-Chávez, but even they concede that, in practice, alternatives to transitional language programs in the public schools are not viable ones (Hernández-Chávez, 1978). Again, it is as if nothing else is thinkable. This emphasis on transition, and the problem-orientation to language for which it stands, has been embodied in federal and state legislation from the beginning. The original BEA made poverty a requirement for eligibility in bilingual programs, and although this was dropped in the 1974 version, it remains a popular notion that bilingual education is for the poor and disadvantaged. The state statutes reinforce this attitude. The Massachusetts law is called "Transitional Bilingual Education"; the Wisconsin Statute is located in the state code in the chapter on "handicapped children," and proceeds to define the target population on that basis (see Ruíz, 1983). Even in California, where the code is considered more progressive than most, the transitional quality of the programs is obvious from the language of the Education Code (Section 5761):

> A primary goal of such programs is, as effective and efficiently as possible, to develop in each child fluency in English so that he may then be enrolled in the regular program in which English is the language of instruction. (AB 1329, Chapter 576: 1978)

The major declarations of the courts, as well, do nothing to encourage anything other than transition.[4] Hufstedler herself says that the essential purpose of the Lau Regulations is to identify the best services for treating English-limited students and "to determine when those services are no longer needed and the students can be taught exclusively in English (1980:66)."

Perhaps the perception most compelling—the connection of language and language diversity with social problems—is that multilingualism leads ultimately to a lack of social cohesiveness; with everyone speaking their own language, political and social consensus is impossible. This view is implicit in Hufstedler's statement:

> Cultural diversity is one of America's greatest strengths. We could not suppress it if we would; and we should not suppress it if we could. But unity is also America's strength. And the ability of every citizen to communicate in our national language is the keystone of unity. (1980:69)

Hufstedler creates a false distinction between diversity and unity; it is based, as Fishman (1978:43) points out, on the identification of unity with uniformity; it becomes, as well, an important element in the justification of monolingualism as an ideal. Whether or not the distinction is false, the conviction is strongly held nonetheless, possibly at a level beyond argument; President Reagan's rejection of maintenance programs as "absolutely wrong and against the American concept"[5] seem to strike a chord resonating deep in the U.S. consciousness.

The orientation that language is a social problem to be identified operationally and resolved through treatments like transitional bilingual education may be more pervasive than we think. Whether the orientation is represented by malicious attitudes resolving to eradicate, invalidate, quarantine, or inoculate,[6] or comparatively benign ones concerned with remediation and "improvement," the central activity remains that of problem-solving. And, since language problems are never merely language problems, but have a direct impact on all spheres of social life (Karam, 1974: 108), this particular orientation toward language planning may be representative of a more general outlook on cultural and social diversity.

Language-as-Right

Alan Pifer has written that "bilingual education has become the preeminent civil rights issue with Hispanic communities (1975:5)." Pousada, as well, sees the current efforts on behalf of bilingual education for Hispanics as "a result of the civil rights movement (1979:84)." These statements are representative of a strong movement, both within the United States and internationally, which would advocate consideration of language as a basic human right. How can language be fitted into a general conception of rights? What is meant by those who construe language as a right?

Several researchers give examples of language rights. For del Valle

(1981), the right to "effective participation in governmental programs" has several aspects: provision of unemployment insurance benefits forms in Spanish for Spanish monolinguals; bilingual voting materials like ballots and instructional pamphlets; and interpreters.[7] Hernández-Chávez adds to these the right to the use of ethnic language in legal proceedings and the right to bilingual education (1978:548n); he also mentions other things which a language-minority community might demand, like the use of the dominant language in the media, medical services, and in commercial contracts, but it is not clear that he offers these as examples of rights. Macías suggests two kinds of language rights: "the right to freedom from discrimination on the basis of language" and "the right to use your language(s) in the activities of communal life (1979:88–89)." More specifically, the Committee on the CCCC Language Statement (1978) affirms "the right of students to their own language," by which is meant primarily whatever *variety of English* the students happen to speak. Also in the domain of education, Zachariev proposes as his Seventh Principle of Language Policy that mother tongue instruction is an inalienable right (1978:271).

The wide range of statements proposed as language rights is explained in part by the pervasive nature of language itself: since language touches many aspects of social life, any comprehensive statement about language rights cannot confine itself to merely linguistic considerations. By extension, this means that discrimination as to language has important effects in many other areas, as several writers assert.

> Deprivations resulting from language discrimination may be devastating for skill acquisition. Language barriers have all too often worked to frustrate and stifle the full development of latent capabilities. When people are deprived of enlightenment and skill, their capabilities for effective participation in all other value processes are correspondingly diminished. (McDougal, Lasswell, and Chen 1976: 155; see also del Valle, 1981).

It is not only access to formal processes like voting, civil service examinations, judicial and administrative proceedings, and public employment which are influenced; the right to personal freedom and enjoyment is also affected.[8] It is for this reason that an exhaustive list of language rights is difficult to compile.

The development and persistence of the rights-orientation is influenced by several factors. One of the most important is the nature of the U.S. legal system, in which the protections provided for minority groups are central (Lamb 1981:13; Burke 1981: 166). A host of language-related cases—*Meyer* v. *Nebraska* (1923), *Yu Cong Eng* v. *Trinidad* (1925), *U.S.* v. *Texas* (1971), and *Lau* v. *Nichols* (1974), among others—have served to highlight the importance of the protection, more specifically, of *language*-minority groups in U.S. law, as well (Leibowitz 1971; Teitelbaum and Hiller 1977). It seems, however, that the basis of those protections and the nature of the entitlements which flow from them are still a source of some confusion. For example, some would contend that there is a connection between national origin and language; that, in fact, Congress and federal agencies have acted in a variety of ways based on an acknowledgement of that connection; discrimination on the basis of language, therefore, violates basic constitutional guarantees (del Valle 1981). Other arguments deny such a connection (see the discussion in *Garcia* v. *Gloor* [1980]). These sorts of confusions indicate that the debate on the legal status of language rights may continue indefinitely.

Another factor contributing to the emergence of a language-rights orientation is the concern for rights on a trans-national level (Van Dyke 1976; McDougal, Lasswell, and Chen 1976; Buergenthal 1977; Zachariev 1978; Macías 1979). The charters of the League of Nations and, later, the United Nations, included the first significant protection of minority groups in the trans-national community; other internationally recognized documents like the Universal Declaration of the Rights of Man and the Helsinki Final Act contain important statements on language-based discrimination. Zachariev, using many of these documents for support, puts language rights in the larger context of human and educational rights; he sees the necessity of linking language planning with social and educational planning:

> La planification linguistique est partie intégrante de la planification sociale et économique d'une société donnée. Par conséquent, la formulation d'une politique linguistique à l'école et al réalisation des droits linguistiques s'insèrent dans une vision globale d'un projet de société et dans le cadre d'un système éducatif national correspondant (1978:271).

Along with this general concern with human rights and the protection of minority groups, a most important development has been the emergence of ethnic researchers as prime movers in the effort to affirm language-identification as both a legal entitlement and a natural endowment. The kinds of arguments that have carried so much weight in other areas of discrimination have been adopted for language issues. Indeed, major ethnic agencies like the Mexican American Legal Defense and Education Fund (MALDEF) and the Centro de Estudios Puertorriqueños have devoted a great deal of their resources to resolving the legal status of language rights. One expects that these efforts will only intensify as the non-native-English-speaking population continues to grow and other issues, like the persistent question of the status of Puerto Rico, become less easily ignored. The clear implication of all of this is that the language-as-right orientation in language planning can only gain in importance.

What should be our attitude toward this orientation? To be sure, the importance of the legal argument in U.S. society is not be denied. It is essential that for short term protections and long term guarantees, we be able to translate the interests of language-minority groups into rights-language; agencies like MALDEF should receive our support for performing this valuable service.

Yet, one cannot deny the problems of this approach. The most important of these could be that terms included in the legal universe of discourse do not incline the general public toward a ready acceptance of the arguments. Terms like "compliance," "enforcement," "entitlements," "requirements," and "protection" create an automatic resistance to whatever one is talking about. Their use creates confrontation.

Confrontation, of course, is what the legal process is all about. More generally, rights-affirmation is also confrontation, since the nature of a full-fledged right is that it is not a mere "claim-to" something but also a "claim-against" someone (Feinberg 1970).[9] Even common-sense justifications of non-compliance do not go unchallenged: "Plaintiffs should be allowed to probe the validity of any defense made on the basis of administrative burden, and, courts should weigh such burdens as against the rights involved and available alternatives (del Valle 1981:2)." This atmosphere creates a situation in which different groups and authorities invoke their rights against each other: children vs. schools; parents vs. school boards; majority vs. minority groups; some minority groups vs. others; state rights vs. federal authority; and so on. In the case of language rights, for example, the controversy could be seen as one where the rights of the few are affirmed over those of the many.

Under these circumstances, a widespread response is non-compliance. Ignoring federal regulations, like those following *Lau,* for example, continues to be a common practice in which school districts engage with impunity, for the most part: a variety of factors conspire to make enforcement almost totally ineffective (Pousada 1979:89). Legal manipulation is another way of avoiding compliance, and it has a long history. Sapiens, for example, cites the arguments of the California State Attorney General in 1930 that Chicanos were Indians; this identification was important for social policy toward Chicanos because of the state law permitting the segregation of Indians (1979:77).[10] See, also, González' contention that Judge Justice in *U.S.* v. *Texas* (1971) declared Title VI—where one must show the *effect* of discrimination-and the Fourteenth Amendment—where one must show *intent*—"coextensive." This particular maneuver, if successful, could mean that language discrimination cases would be harder to bring forward (NIME 1981:6–7).

Other problems haunt the language-rightists: How does one delimit the affected class? (Macías 1979: 91, 98) How important is the criterion of *numerosity,* mentioned by each Justice giving an opinion in *Lau,* and clearly the deciding factor for at least one of them? (Carter, Brown, and Harris 1979:300; del Valle 1981:2; Pousada 1979:90). How are rights-claims to be articulated, given that some are more "immediate" than others? (Macías

1979:89) How are allegedly incompatible rights dealt with? For instance, while some see an "inherent inconsistency" between bilingual education requirements and desegregation orders (Burke 1981:167; Glazer 1983), others deny the inconsistency (Pousada 1979:90; Arias, 1979). How are rights-standards at different levels (international, national, state, personal) integrated? (Macías 1979:90) How are rights which are conceptualized in different forms (e.g., individual vs. group rights) reconciled? (Williams 1981: 62)

These are not simple questions. It is important to recognize that their formulation is peculiar to a rights-orientation: they are not of the sort that would emerge from a problem-orientation. Thus, one would expect answers to *those* questions to be sought in the universe of discourse appropriate to rights. Certainly, consideration of language rights must remain a central activity of language planners, as William suggests:

> . . . before detailed language policies are formulated, it behooves us to question the relationship between language planning and language rights and to suggest the manner in which planning can realize the fulfillment of individual and group based rights. (1981:62)

One might also consider, however, whether a rights-orientation, given the problems it faces, is sufficient as a way of addressing our language planning needs. Yet another language planning perspective is proposed in the following pages.

Language-as-Resource

After reviewing several well-known typologies of language planning, Thompson concludes that another, a "resources-oriented typology may provide a more suitable approach" for language planning in the United States (1973:227). He goes on to sketch a few ideas of what would be involved in this approach. These are not developed very extensively in his brief report, though his work can be considered a good starting point for the elaboration of such a typology. (Compare, as well, Karam's [1974:113] characterization of the work of Jernudd and Das Gupta.) Greater development of a language-resources approach to language planning has not been forthcoming, possibly because of the sort of intractability perceived by Fishman: "language is certainly an odd kind of resource for current cost-benefit theory to handle, precisely because of the difficulty in measuring or separating 'it' from other resources (1974a:83)."

As a justification for turning to other approaches in language planning, this criticism is weak. It is as applicable to others, as well: a language "problem" is no easier to distinguish from other "problems," for example (in another place, Fishman recognizes this [1974b:261]). A closer look at the idea of language-as-resource could reveal some promise for alleviating some of the conflicts emerging out of the other two orientations: it can have a direct impact on enhancing the language status of subordinate languages; it can help to ease tensions between majority and minority communities; it can serve as a more consistent way of viewing the role of non-English languages in U.S. society; and it highlights the importance of cooperative language planning. Let us now turn to a consideration of language-resource planning.

Among observers of language use in the United States, there is almost unanimous agreement that this country has a great deficiency in language capability (Keller and Roel, 1979; President's Commission on Foreign Language and International Studies 1979; Simon, 1980a, 1980b; Thompson, 1980; Tsongas, 1981).[11] Not only are we not developing language skills in the population to any great extent; we are doing almost nothing to encourage non-English language maintenance. The result could well be a pattern of language loss over just a few generations (Hernández-Chávez, 1978). The variety of proposals to remedy this situation indicates the urgency with which these issues have been approached recently in the literature.

Thompson (1980), for example, places his emphasis on the development of more and better language skills. He recommends a national teacher training program, longer sequences in language classes, development of better language aptitude measures, and a diversification of school approaches—including "bilingual-schools-for-all-Americans" and international high schools. The report of the President's Commission on Foreign Language and International Studies (1979) includes similar recommendations, and adds specific ones related directly to schools and universities. Among other things, the reestablishment of language requirements at the university level (the exact form of which was the subject of some controversy—see Rep. Fenwick's dissent in the addendum) is singled out as an important step influencing offerings throughout the educational system. Simon (1980b) is also concerned with the development of greater language capability, especially because of its usefulness in the areas of foreign affairs and international trade.

Development, obviously, is an important aspect of any resources-oriented policy, but what is missing in these proposals is a direct concern with resource *conservation;* what is worse, there seems to be no acknowledgment of the fact that existing resources are being destroyed through mismanagement and repression. This is true even where language communities are recognized as important reservoirs of language skills:

> Because of our rich ethnic mix, the United States is home to millions whose first language is not English. One of every 50 Americans is foreign born. We are the fourth largest Spanish-speaking country in the world. Yet almost nothing is being done to use these rich resources of linguists

to train people in the use of a language other than English (Simon 1980b:33; cf. Thompson 1973:227)

The irony of this situation is that language communities have become valuable to the larger society in precisely that skill which the school has worked so hard to eradicate in them! "National programs in the past have tended to encourage the study of foreign languages in the schools while at the same time discouraging continued study of languages represented by those ethnic minorities (Rudolph Troike, in Thompson, 1973:229)." Consider, for example, Eddy's (1979) report of a national survey showing overwhelming support for offering foreign language courses in schools and universities, and considerable support for *requiring* such study. This is all true in a country where non-English speakers are *expected* to lose their first language (Macías, 1979:96), and have suffered considerably and directly when that expectation was not fulfilled (see the discussion of school-language discriminatory practices in Ruíz, 1983). How is this explained? Could it be that the nature of the prevailing problem-orientation allows this seeming-contradiction as a basic tenet? After all, it is the "world standard" languages which one is expected to learn in school for personal enrichment or international understanding or foreign service, not the inferior vernaculars spoken by ethnic groups. For them, the best course would be to forget their "little" language, with the hope that one day they will be able to relearn it in a more acceptable form in school.

This is the way things are. But the situation could be different. A fuller development of a resources-oriented approach to language planning could help to reshape attitudes about language and language groups. In what way is language a resource? We can start with the common arguments for the benefits of language capability. Those of most interest involve trans-national considerations. Military preparedness and national security are issues which receive immediate attention; Tsongas, in fact, suggests to those concerned with language capability and training that "we must phrase the debate in terms of American interest and national security" (1981:115; cf. President's Commission on Foreign Language and International Studies 1979 and the discussion on Conant in Valverde and Brown 1978:287). Also prominent is the importance of language skills for diplomatic functions: Thompson argues that language is an important aspect of "enlightened leadership" in foreign policy (1980:47), and Gwertzman (1977) and Wooten (1977) record an embarrassing incident in Poland created by the inadequate language skills of the State Department.

Other trans-national concerns are also central to the new efforts at reviving language training in the U.S. In an economically interdependent world, Fishman claims that "English monolingualism is bad for business (1978:46);" he is seconded by Dugan (1981), Pincus (1980), Simon (1980a), and Valverde and Brown (1978). Keller and Roel see linguistic diversity as an important part of the future of international communications: "In the process, the United States may be forced to reshape its system of communications as an integral, rather than dominant, component of a world language and information system (1979:110)."

Not all arguments in favor of language training are of this sort. We have now, for example, a considerable body of literature on the positive effects of multilingual capacity on the social and educational domains. Timpe's (1979) study showed a relationship between declining ACT scores and decreased foreign language study. We are only now starting to see, on the domestic scene, the long-term effects of our incipient monolingualism. Kessler and Quinn (1980) show how improved conceptual skills in science are also related to multilingual ability. Hernández-Chávez (1978) holds that bilingualism can aid in general concept learning and skill (especially reading) development.

More generally, others argue for the social value of language competence. Lambert considers it important for the "deparochialization" of the student (in Thompson, 1973:228). By this he seems to be saying, along with Sharp (1978:3), that language study creates an awareness in students "that their own way of thinking and living is not the only reasonable possible one; and that some cultures are often keenly perceptive in areas in which others are short-sighted." Drake considers that bilingualism might help in blunting intergroup conflict and in making ethnic communities "better equipped to cope with . . . modernity (1978:10)." Keller and Roel (1979) are critical of U.S. mass media, which are largely ineffective in making the population aware of foreign cultures; greater access to non-English language communities would help.

Language planning efforts which start with the assumption that language is a resource to be managed, developed and conserved would tend to regard language-minority communities as important sources of expertise. Not only could language-competent community members be used to train others; the whole community itself could afford multilingual opportunities for language students. For example, students of Japanese being prepared for foreign service could benefit from an internship in a Japanese community center in San Francisco sponsored by the State Department. This would begin to address several problems. It would help to give students a more "natural" language training experience; it would give balance to language training programs dominated by written language (Pincus [1980] shows that spoken language training is generally poor, and Garvin [1974] implies that written language is the common focus of most language planning); it would help with any status problems the language and the community might have; and it would give something back to the community by encouraging the persistence of language maintenance institutions like community centers. This sort of consideration demonstrated in language plans can only contribute to a greater social cohesion and cooperation. On the question of affording that benefit, the language-as-problem orientation offers no hope; the rights orientation has had mixed results.

CONCLUSION

To be sure, a resource orientation in language planning is not without its problems, and the development of a more comprehensive model based on it is a matter for consideration elsewhere. For now, however, perhaps the best approach would be to encourage the compilation of a strong literature with an emphasis on language as a resource; this could create an atmosphere where language planning is seen as important in social planning. As it stands at present, the assumption of English monolingualism as the only acceptable social condition means that most people will see language planning as a meaningless activity (cf. Bailey, 1975:156). Practically speaking, this implies a reluctance to acknowledge the importance of alternative linguistic behavior; ultimately, as in other parts of the world, this leads to social conflicts which, if ignored, can have disastrous effects (Deutsch, 1975:7).

What is proposed in this paper is that language planning can benefit from a variety of approaches, and that in some circumstances some approaches are better than others. This is a call for the articulation of a new orientation in which language issues are framed and language attitudes developed. This orientation holds promise for a kind of cooperative language planning effort rarely seen anywhere. Indeed, in the United States, any meaningful language planning may not be possible without it.

EXPLORING THE IDEAS

1. Ruíz maintains that the three orientations—language-as-problem, language-as-right, and language-as-resource—while competing approaches, are not incompatible.

Do you agree with Ruíz that the three orientations are compatible? For example, in an employment context, how might the fact of being bilingual be viewed as a problem, as a right, and as a resource?

2. Ruíz cites Fishman's theory that the language-as-problem orientation is based on the belief that if minority groups would only "speak English . . . they could solve all their problems."

Do you see the acquisition of English as the key to language minority members' social acceptance and mobility? If so, why? If not, what other factors play a role in their social acceptance and mobility?

3. Ruíz argues that Hufstedler's idea that the key to our national unity rests in a shared language is based on a false distinction between unity and diversity.

Do you think national unity is primarily dependent on a shared language? If so, why? If not, what social, economic, and political conditions could enable diverse language groups in a nation to feel a sense of national unity even though they lack a common language?

4. Ruíz maintains that the legal discourse surrounding the language-as-right orientation, such as "compliance" and "enforcement," creates an automatic resistance to whatever one is talking about, yet language minorities have found it important to pursue the legal guarantees of language rights.

Given the potentially negative effect of legal discourse, what are the advantages of having laws to protect the language rights of minority groups and what are the advantages of specifying these rights in legal language?

5. Ruíz points out that while many Americans support the study of foreign languages in the school, they do not support the maintenance of immigrant languages.

What do you think are some explanations for this apparently paradoxical attitude toward linguistic diversity?

6. Ruíz lists several possible benefits of linguistic pluralism, such as increased national security, better diplomatic relations, increased business, improved international communication, and social and educational gains.

For each category, list one or two concrete situations in which linguistic pluralism would be an asset.

7. Ruíz concludes that a "resource orientation in language planning is not without its problems."

What do you see as some limitations of a language-as-resource orientation?

APPLYING THE IDEAS

1. Ruíz points out that various international documents such as the charters of the League of Nations and the United Nations, the Universal Declaration of the Rights of Man, and the Helsinki Final Act recognize the language rights of minorities.

Research the issue of language rights in international law; you might want to begin with Macías (1979), cited by Ruíz.

2. Ruíz maintains that the atmosphere surrounding the language-as-right orientation encourages different groups to invoke rights against each other.

Investigate the provisions of the 1965 Voting Rights Act and its 1975 amendment. How might different language minority groups invoke rights against one another in terms of their access to bilingual ballots? Is there any way of avoiding this situation?

3. In 1986, the State of California passed the following proposition regarding an official state language.

English as the Official Language of California
Initiative Constitutional Amendment

Section 1. Section 6 is added to Article III of the Constitution to read as follows:

SEC. 6. (a) Purpose.

English is the common language of the people of the United States of America and the State of California. This section is intended to preserve, protect and strengthen the English language, and not to supersede any of the rights guaranteed to the people by this Constitution.

(b) English as the Official Language of California.

English is the official language of the State of California.

(c) Enforcement.

The Legislature shall enforce this section by appropriate legislation. The Legislature and officials of the State of California shall take all steps necessary to insure that the role of English as the common language of the State of California is preserved and enhanced. The Legislature shall make no law which diminishes or ignores the role of English as the common language of the State of California.

(d) Personal Right of Action and Jurisdiction of Courts.

Any person who is a resident of or doing business in the State of California shall have standing to sue the State of California to enforce this section, and the Courts of record of the State of California shall have jurisdiction to hear cases brought to enforce this section. The Legislature may provide reasonable and appropriate limitations on the time and manner of suits brought under this section.

Section 2. Severability

If any provision of this section, or the application of any such provision to any person or circumstance, shall be held invalid, the remainder of this section to the extent it can be given effect shall not be affected thereby, and to this end the provisions of this section are severable.

First, carefully examine the wording of the amendment to determine how the provision could be enforced and what problems might arise in interpreting the provision. Then, either investigate which other states have similar provisions in their constitution or find out the present status of the English-only amendment (the proposed constitutional amendment to make English the official language).

4. Ruíz cites Fishman's dictum that "English monolingualism is bad for business."

Contact a large multinational corporation such as IBM to find out the corporation's language policies. Does the corporation actively seek to hire bilingual employees? Does the corporation have any program to develop the language skills of its employees?

NOTES

1. Readers will recognize the similarities of "orientations" to other concepts current in language planning and social science more generally. Heath's (1977) idea of "language ideology" seems very close; the brevity of the discussion of this concept there makes me reluctant to claim a perfect match, however. Kuhn's (1970) "paradigm" is a reasonable comparison, though his claims for it (especially his criterion of incommensurability) are larger than what is proposed here for orientation. Perhaps the best comparison is that of Boulding's (1956, 1959) "image," especially as he might have focused it on language ("the image of language") in the way he did on other aspects of social life. Most interesting in his discussion is the way he sees the "image" determining the range of possible behavior: "people whose decisions determine policies and actions of nations do not respond to the 'objective' facts of the situation, whatever that may mean, but to their 'image' of the situation. It is what we think the world is like, not what it is really like, that determines our behavior (1959:120)."

2. These problems are associated with the "policy" approach to language planning, which Neustupný says prevails in developing societies. Neustupný also lists other problems (correctness, efficiency, style, etc.) aligned with a "cultivation" approach predominant in modern nations. This latter concern seems less central to the work of language planners, with some notable exceptions (e.g., Haugen).

3. Fishman's cutting ridicule is aimed at Noel Epstein's analysis of bilingual education (1977).

4. In *Lau* v. *Nichols* (414 U.S. 563 [1974]), for example, Justice Douglas states that "no specific remedy is urged upon us." Still, this decision relied heavily on the 1970 HEW regulations (35 Fed. Reg. 11595) which held that any program for this population "must be designed to meet these language skill needs as soon as possible and must not operate as an educational deadend or permanent track."

5. See *The Washington Post,* March 4, 1981, and the discussion in Ruíz, 1983.

6. This term was suggested by Jim Cummins.

7. Del Valle's comments are most relevant to Puerto Ricans, who are citizens of the United States and who live in a commonwealth where Spanish is the official language. The legal argument for provision of materials in the non-English dominant language for this group is perhaps more compelling than it would be applied to other groups.

8. Del Valle discusses *Hernández* v. *Erlenbusch* (1974), where a tavern rule against non-English language use at the bar abridged the "rights of Spanish-speaking patrons to buy, drink, and enjoy what the tavern had to offer on an equal footing with English-speaking patrons (1981:2)."

9. Mere "claims-to" certain benefits or guarantees (fair housing, freedom from employment discrimination, etc.) could constitute what Feinberg would call a "manifesto right." Presumably, clear and purposeful action on the claim could not be taken until the identification of whomever were denying or inhibiting the guarantee. The

presence of a valid ''claim-to'' and a valid ''claim-against'' constitutes a ''full-fledged right.'' See the discussion of this adapted to ethnicity and language in Ruíz, 1983.

10. cf. *Gong Lum* v. *Rice,* 275 U.S. 78 (1927), where orientals were taken to be ''negroes''; and *Ross* v. *Eckels,* 434 F. 2d 1140 (5th Cir. 1970), where Chicanos were not differentiated from whites for desegregation purposes: combining Chicanos with Blacks would therefore constitute minimum compliance.

11. But, see Pincus (1980:82ff), whose report for the Rand Corporation found ''no general market shortage'' of language-trained specialists; he recognizes, however, that ''market shortage'' is not necessarily the same as ''need.''

REFERENCES

Arias, M. Beatriz (1979). Desegregation and the rights of Hispanic students: the Los Angeles case. *Evaluation Comment* 6 (1): 14–18.

Babcock, Charles R. (1981). Studies disavow U.S. focus on bilingual education. *The Washington Post* September 29

Bailey, Charles-James N. (1975). The new linguistic framework and language-planning. *Linguistics 158:*153–157

Birman, Beatrice F. and Alan L. Ginsburg (1981). *Addressing the Needs of Language-Minority Children: Issues for Federal Policy*. Mimeo. Oct. 5

Boulding, Kenneth E. (1956). *The Image: Knowledge in Life and Society*. Ann Arbor: University of Michigan Press

Boulding, Kenneth E. (1959). National images and international systems. *Conflict Resolution 3:*120–131. June

Buergenthal, Thomas, ed. (1977). *Human Rights, International Law, and the Helsinki Accord.* Montclair, New Jersey: Allanhead, Osmun & Co.

Burke, Fred G. (1981). Bilingualism/biculturalism in American education: an adventure in Wonderland. *The Annals of the American Academy of Political and Social Sciences 454:* 164–177. March

Carter, David G., Frank Brown, and J. John Harris III (1978). Bilingual/bicultural education: a legal analysis. *Education and Urban Society X* (3): 295–304. May

Committee on the CCCC Language Statement (1978). Students right to their own language. In: *A Pluralistic Nation: The Language Issue in the United States,* edited by Margaret A. Lourie and Nancy Faires Conklin. Rowley, Massachusetts: Newbury House Publishers. 315–328.

del Valle, Manuel (1981). Hispanics' language rights and due process. *New York Law Journal 186* (22):1–2. July

Deutsch, Karl W. (1975). The political significance of linguistic conflicts. In: *Multilingual Political Systems,* edited by Jean-Guy Savard and Richard Vigneault. Quebec: Les Presses de l'Université Laval.

Drake, Glendon (1978). Ethnicity, values and language policy in the United States. *NABE Journal III* (1):1–12. Fall

Dugan, J., Sanford (1981). World languages and trade opportunities. *Foreign Language Annals 14* (4 & 5): 287–292.

Eddy, Peter A. (1979). Attitudes toward foreign language study and requirements in American schools and colleges: results of a national survey. *ADFL Bulletin 11* (2):4–9. November

Epstein, Noel (1977). *Language, Ethnicity, and the Schools: Policy Alternatives for Bilingual-Bicultural Education.* Washington, D.C.: Institute for Educational Leadership

Feinberg, Joel (1970). The nature and value of rights. *Journal of Value Inquiry* 4:243–257.

Fishman, Joshua A. (1974a). Language modernization and planning in comparison with other types of national modernization and planning. In: *Advances in Language Planning,* edited by Joshua A. Fishman. The Hague: Mouton. 79–102.

Fishman, Joshua A. (1974b). Language planning and language planning research: the State of the art. In: *Advances in Language Planning,* edited by Joshua A. Fishman. The Hague: Mouton. 15–33.

Fishman, Joshua A. (1975). Some implications of 'the International Research Project on Language Planning Processes (IRPLPP)' for sociolinguistic surveys. In: *Language Surveys in Developing Nations: Papers and Reports on Sociolinguistic Surveys,* edited by Sirarpi Ohannessian, Charles A. Ferguson, and Edgar C. Polome. Arlington, VA.: Center for Applied Linguistics. 209–220.

Fishman, Joshua A. (1977). Social science perspective. In: *Bilingual Education: Current Perspectives* (vol. 1: Social Science). Arlington, Va.: Center for Applied Linguistics. 1–49.

Fishman, Joshua A. (1978). Positive bilingualism: some overlooked rationales and forefathers. In *Georgetown University Round Table on Languages and Linguistics 1978,* edited by James E. Alatis. Washington, D.C.: Georgetown University Press. 42–52.

Garvin, Paul L. (1974). Some comments on language planning. In: *Advances in Language Planning,* edited by Joshua A. Fishman. The Hague: Mouton. 69–78.

Glazer, Nathan (1983). The school and the judge. In *Ethnicity, Law, and the Social Good,* edited by W. A. Van Horne. Milwaukee: American Ethnic Studies Coordinating Committee.

Gwertzman, Bernard (1977). Interpreter's gaffes embarrass State Department. *New York Times* December 31

Haugen, Einar (1966). *Language Conflict and Language Planning: The Case of Modern Norwegian.* Cambridge: Harvard University Press

Heath, Shirley Brice (1977). Social history. In: *Bilingual Education: Current Perspectives* (Vol. I: *Social Science*). Arlington, Va.: Center for Applied Linguistics. 53–72.

Hernández-Chávez, Eduardo (1978). Language maintenance, bilingual education, and philosophies of bilingualism in the United States. In: *Georgetown University Round Table on Languages and Linguistics 1978,* edited by James E. Alatis. Washington, D.C.: Georgetown University Press. 527–550.

Hufstedler, Shirley M. (1980). On bilingual education, civil rights, and language minority regulations. *NABE Journal V* (1): 63–69. Fall

Karam, Francis X. (1974). Toward a definition of language planning. In: *Advances in Language Planning,* edited by Joshua A. Fishman. The Hague: Mouton. 103–124.

Keller, Edward and Ronald Roel (1979). Foreign languages and U.S. cultural policy: an institutional perspective. *Journal of Communication 29* (2): 102–111. Fall

Kelman, Herbert C. (1972). Language as an aid and barrier to involvement in the national system. In: *Advances in the Sociology of Language,* Vol. II, edited by Joshua A. Fishman. The Hague: Mouton. 185–212.

Kessler, Carolyn and Mary Ellen Quinn (1980). Positive effects of bilingualism on science problem-solving abilities. In: *Georgetown University Round Table on Languages and Linguistics 1980,* edited by James E. Alatis.

Kloss, Heinz (1969). *Research Possibilities on Group Bilingualism: A report.* Quebec: International Center for Research on Bilingualism.

Kuhn, Thomas S. (1970). *The Structure of Scientific Revolutions.* Chicago: University of Chicago (International Encyclopedia of Unified Science).

Lamb, Charles M. (1981). Legal foundations of civil rights and pluralism in America. *Annals of the American Academy of Political and Sciences 454:*13–25. March

Lawrence, Gay (1978). Indian education: why bilingual bicultural? *Education and Urban Society X* (3): 305–320. May

Leibowitz, Arnold (1971). *Educational Policy and Political Acceptance: The Imposition of English as the Language of Instruction in American Schools.* Arlington, Va.: Center for Applied Linguistics

Macías, Reynaldo F. (1979). Language choice and human rights in the United States. In: *Georgetown University Round Table on Languages and Linguistics 1979,* edited by James E. Alatis. Washington, D.C.: Georgetown University Press. 86–101.

Mackey, William F. (1979). Language policy and language planning. *Journal of Communication 29* (2):48–53. Spring

McDougal, Myres S., Harold D. Lasswell, and Lung-chu Chen (1976). Freedom from discrimination in choice of language and international human rights. *Southern Illinois University Law Journal 1:*151–174.

McRae, Kenneth D. (1975). The principle of territoriality and the principle of personality in multi-lingual states. *Linguistics 158:* 33–54.

National Institute for Multicultural Education (NIME) (1981). *Interview with Dr. Josue González.* (Unabridged edition). Mimeo. June 25

Neustupný, J. V. (1970). Basic types of treatment of language problems. *Communications 1:* 77–98.

Pifer, Alan (1979). *Bilingual Education and the Hispanic Challenge* (the Report of the President). Reprinted from *The Annual Report.* New York: The Carnegie Corporation

Pincus, John (1980). Rand meets the President's Commission: the life cycle of a non-event. *Annals of the American Academy of Political and Social Science 449:* 80–90. May

Pousada, Alicia (1979). Bilingual education in the U.S. *Journal of Communication 29* (2): 84–92. Spring

President's Commission on Foreign Language and International Studies (1979). *Strength Through Wisdom: A Critique of U.S. Capability* (A report to the President). Washington, D.C.: U.S. Government Printing Office

Rubin, Joan and Roger Shuy, eds. (1973). *Language Planning: Current Issues and Research.* Washington, D.C.: Georgetown University Press.

Ruíz, Richard (1983). Ethnic group interest and the social good: law and language in education. In *Ethnicity, Law, and the Social Good,* edited by W. A. Van Horne. Milwaukee: American Ethnic Studies Coordinating Committee.

Sapiens, Alexander (1979). Spanish in California: a historical perspective. *Journal of Communication 29* (2): 72–83. Spring

Sharp, John M. (1978). Foreign language as a means of introduction to the study of minority group cultures in the United States. In: *Problems in Applied Educational Sociolinguistics: Readings on Language and Culture Problems of United States Ethnic Groups,* edited by Glenn E. Gilbert and Jacob Ornstein. The Hague: Mouton. 1–8.

Simon, Paul (1980a). Foreign language study: political, economic, and social realities. *Foreign Language Annals 13* (5):355–358

Simon, Paul (1980b). The U.S. crisis in foreign language. *Annals of the American Academy of Political and Social Science 449:*31–44.

Tauli, Valter (1974). The theory of language planning. In: *Advances in Language Planning,* edited by Joshua A. Fishman. The Hague: Mouton. 49–67

Teitelbaum, Herbert and Richard J. Hiller (1977). The legal perspective. In: *Bilingual Education: Current Perspectives* (Vol. 3: Law). Arlington, Va.: Center for Applied Linguistics

Thompson, Richard T. (1973). Language resources and the national interest. In: *Georgetown University Round Table on Languages and Linguistics 1973,* edited by Kurt R. Jankowsky. Washington, D.C.: Georgetown University Press. 225–231.

Thompson, Richard T. (1980). New directions in foreign language study. *The Annals of the American Academy of Political and Social Science 449:* 45–55.

Timpe, Eugene F. (1979). The effect of foreign language study on ACT scores. ADFL Bulletin 11 (2): 10–11.

Tollefson, James W. (1981). Centralized and decentralized language planning. *Language Problems and Language Planning 5* (2): 175–188.

Tsongas, Paul E. (1981). Foreign languages and America's interests. *Foreign Language Annals 14* (2): 115–119.

Valverde, Leonard A. and Frank Brown (1978). Equal educational opportunity and bilingual-bicultural education: a socioeconomic perspective. *Education and Urban Society X* (3): 277–294.

Van Dyke, Vernon (1976). Human rights without distinction as to language. *International Studies Quarterly 20* (1):3–38.

Williams, Colin H. (1981). The territorial dimension in language planning: an evaluation of its potential in contemporary Wales. *Language Problems and Language Planning 5* (1): 57–73

Wooten, James T. (1977). Carter in Warsaw on six-nation tour. *The New York Times,* 1:4. Dec. 30

Zachariev, Z. (1978). Droits linguistiques et droits à l' éducation dans les sociétés plurilingues. *International Review of Education XXIV* (3): 263–272.

Part II

A HISTORICAL PERSPECTIVE ON LANGUAGE DIVERSITY IN THE UNITED STATES

From the time of the first settlers, language diversity has been central to the American experience; perhaps no other country in the world has had so many tongues represented within its boundaries. At the same time, the United States is also a predominantly English-speaking nation where a common language has been universally accepted in the absence of legal coercion. This surprising duality can be said to define the overall sociolinguistic situation in which language minorities function.

The chapters in this section were written to provide a historical perspective from which to view language minorities in the United States today. In the first chapter, Jean Molesky presents a conceptual framework for understanding the changes undergone by various languages in the United States, especially immigrant languages. She traces major events in immigration and settlement history that have helped to shape the "American linguistic mosaic," illustrating the processes of language maintenance and language shift by focusing on selected groups. She also explores how contemporary, post-1965 immigrant language minorities resemble or differ from their earlier counterparts. In the second chapter, Dorothy Waggoner presents information on the numbers and language characteristics of minority children and adults in the 1980s. She also discusses the problems of accurately estimating the number of limited English-proficient individuals in the country. Her figures on language minorities include updates of the 1980 Census and are made available in print form for the first time in this volume. There may be minor discrepancies between her data and the estimates cited by other contributors in this volume.

CHAPTER

2

Understanding the American Linguistic Mosaic: A Historical Overview of Language Maintenance and Language Shift

Jean Molesky

INTRODUCTION

Linguistically, what kind of nation is the United States? This apparently simple and innocuous question is likely to elicit surprisingly diverse, often emotional, answers. Supporters of the recent English-only movement[1] might depict the United States as a nation Anglophone by right but threatened by Babel-tongued immigrants from abroad and by disloyal ethnolinguistic minorities at home (e.g., Henry 1983; Will 1985); contrasts might be drawn between the linguistic homogeneity of the United States and the dangerous heterogeneity of places like Canada or India. Many scholars, on the other hand, consider multilingualism to be not an aberration but a basic fact of American sociolinguistic history, of which the contemporary scene is simply a continuation (Fishman et al. 1966; Kloss 1977; Ferguson and Heath 1981; Conklin and Lourie 1983; Waggoner, this volume); the idea of a ''pure'' Anglophone population subsequently corrupted by intruders is thus more myth than reality. The proverbial man or woman in the street, if queried, might describe the United States as an English-speaking nation or a multilingual one, depending on where, when, and how the question is asked.

The United States is indeed both a linguistically diverse nation and an English-speaking one, if the latter term is taken to mean the undisputed dominance of English in public life. The complex current language situation in the United States is the result of intertwining developments in immigration, settlement, and policy-making. In this chapter, I will attempt to sketch out a conceptual framework for understanding the vicissitudes undergone by various languages, especially immigrant languages; to trace major events and examine major groups in settlement and immigration history which have helped shape language diversity in the United States; and to explore how contemporary ethnolinguistic minorities resemble or differ from earlier immigrants.

A brief note on terminology is in order before we proceed. The word "immigrant" presupposes the existence of a receiving society to which the alien attaches himself or herself. The immigrant is not, then, someone who populates a region void of original inhabitants or creates a new society and lays down the terms of admission for others. Rather, an immigrant is the bearer of a foreign culture to one already established (Higham 1955:6). Although, in one sense, the American "colonists" (see below) may be said to be "immigrants" relative to native Americans (American Indians), in this paper, the term *immigrant* is reserved for those migrating into the United States after the nation had been established (Kloss 1977:11). The term does not include people forcibly incorporated into the host society, such as the Africans brought in as slaves. However, for convenience of reference, the many refugees who have sought political asylum in the United States will be considered under this category in this chapter even though the involuntary nature of their departure from the home country distinguishes them from typical immigrants who emigrate without coercion.

FACTORS AFFECTING LANGUAGE MAINTENANCE AND LANGUAGE SHIFT

Although data from American ethnic groups have never been collected systematically to help us understand language maintenance and language shift (Fishman 1980:629), and although language shift has been more widely studied than language maintenance (which may contribute to a somewhat biased overall linguistic picture), some researchers have examined ethnolinguistic minorities in the United States and attempted to identify factors and patterns that affect both processes (Haugen 1956; Kloss 1966; Fishman 1966, 1980; Glazer 1978; Weimer 1980; Conklin and Lourie 1983; see also Anderson 1979 on Canada). A survey of their concepts will help us understand various historical facts about American multilingualism in a coherent manner.

Table 2.1 from Conklin and Lourie (1983) provides a useful, though by no means exhaustive, overview of the many variables that determine whether an ethnolinguistic group, especially one in an immigrant setting, will preserve or lose its native language. The categories are more or less self-explanatory. However, it is important to note that researchers differ in their emphasis. Depending on which factors one chooses to single out and elaborate upon, theories attempting to explain the same language maintenance and shift phenomena may look very different.

Glazer (1978), for example, because his analysis is based mainly on the nineteenth century European immigration experience, stresses complex and elusive sociocultural factors more than Conklin and Lourie. According to Glazer, which social classes from the home country are represented in an immigrant group helps to determine the success of language retention. If the full spectrum of social classes take part in immigration, allowing for ethnic language schools, publications, and other cultural entities to flourish, the ethnic language is more likely to be retained. (However, sometimes there may be a rift between earlier and later immigrants from the same language group who represent different social classes and educational backgrounds.) The degree of ideological mobilization associated with language maintenance is also singled out by Glazer for discussion: if a group emigrates because of religious, political, or cultural oppression, members will cling to their national language more than if they have emigrated to improve their economic situation. Those who see their stay in the United States as temporary, whether for economic or political reasons, will maintain native language facility longer and move over to English more slowly.

Finally, Glazer asserts that American civilization itself may be a potent countermaintenance force. Mass, free education teaches almost all the children English, as well as the superiority of English over the language their parents spoke. Mass culture, too, teaches English and creates images favorable to English speakers. The political system makes it possible for immigrants to participate in political processes; hence retention of their ethnic tongues is made less necessary or attractive. Whether minority political participation has been as full as Glazer suggests is open to question, but his description of the powerful pull exerted by mainstream American culture is, on the whole, sound.

Most researchers seem to agree that economic factors have an important effect on language retention and language shift. Conklin and Lourie's table cites "social and economic mobility" as an issue; Glazer notes that shift to English provides access to education and therefore escape from unskilled, low-paying jobs (1978:40–41). Dorian writes that "if some other language [than the ethnic language] proves to have greater value, a shift to

Table 2.1. FACTORS ENCOURAGING LANGUAGE RETENTION AND LANGUAGE LOSS

Language retention	Language loss
Political, social, and demographic factors	
Large number of speakers living in concentration (ghettos, reservations, ethnic neighborhoods, rural speech islands)	Small number of speakers, dispersed among speakers of other languages
Recent arrival and/or continuing immigration	Long, stable residence in the United States
Geographical proximity to the homeland; ease of travel to the homeland	Homeland remote and inaccessible
High rate of return to the homeland; intention to return to the homeland; homeland language community still intact	Low rate or impossibility of return to homeland (refugees, Indians displaced from their tribal territories)
Occupational continuity	Occupational shift, especially from rural to urban
Vocational concentration: employment where co-workers share language background; employment within the language community (stores serving the community, traditional crafts, homemaking, etc.)	Vocations in which some interaction with English or other languages is required; speakers dispersed by employers (e.g., African slaves)
Low social and economic mobility in mainstream occupations	High social and economic mobility in mainstream occupations
Low level of education, leading to low social and economic mobility; *but* educated and articulate community leaders, familiar with the English-speaking society and loyal to their own language community.	Advanced level of education, leading to social and economic mobility; education that alienates and Anglifies potential community leaders
Nativism, racism, and ethnic discrimination as they serve to isolate a community and encourage identity only with the ethnic group rather than the nation at large	Nativism, racism, and ethnic discrimination as they force individuals to deny their ethnic identity in order to make their way in society
Cultural factors	
Mother-tongue institutions, including schools, churches, clubs, theatres, presses, broadcasts	Lack of mother-tongue institutions, from lack of interest or lack of resources
Religious and/or cultural ceremonies requiring command of the mother tongue	Ceremonial life institutionalized in another tongue or not requiring active use of mother tongue
Ethnic identity strongly tied to language; nationalistic aspirations as a language group; mother tongue the homeland national language	Ethnic identity defined by factors other than language, as for those from multilingual countries or language groups spanning several nations; low level of nationalism

Table 2.1 (*continued*)

Language retention	Language loss
Emotional attachment to mother tongue as a defining characteristic of ethnicity, of self	Ethnic identity, sense of self derived from factors such as religion, custom, race rather than shared speech
Emphasis on family ties and position in kinship or community network	Low emphasis on family or community ties, high emphasis on individual achievement
Emphasis on education, if in mother-tongue or community-controlled schools, or used to enhance awareness of ethnic heritage; low emphasis on education otherwise	Emphasis on education and acceptance of public education in English
Culture unlike Anglo society	Culture and religion congruent with Anglo society
Linguistic factors	
Standard, written variety as mother tongue	Minor, nonstandard, and/or unwritten variety as mother tongue
Use of Latin alphabet in mother tongue, making reproduction inexpensive and second language literacy relatively easy	Use of non-Latin writing system in mother tongue, especially if it is unusual, expensive to reproduce, or difficult for bilinguals to learn
Mother tongue with international status	Mother tongue of little international importance
Literacy in mother tongue, used for exchange within the community and with homeland	No literacy in mother tongue; illiteracy
Some tolerance for loan words, if they lead to flexibility of the language in its new setting	No tolerance for loan words, if no alternate ways of capturing new experience evolve; too much tolerance of loans, leading to mixing and eventual language loss

(*Source:* Conklin, N. and M. Lourie. 1983. *A Host of Tongues*. New York: The Free Press.)

that other language begins'' (1982:47). Fishman's (1980:630) statement of this idea is the most forceful:

> Social mobility is a crucial element in language shift among American immigrant groups, not so much because it increases contact (even intimacy) with ''outsiders,'' but primarily because it dislocates previous status and role relations in the immigrant family. . . . In the context of the powerful participatory reward system that America has traditionally made available to so many of its inhabitants, few immigrant (or other minority) ethnicity reward systems have been able to remain aloof from or impervious to it. Those non-English-speaking populations who were

> outside the national system (for example, most American Indians, Mexican Americans, Puerto Ricans, and small self-isolating groups such as the Hutterites or Amish) retained their non-English mother tongues.

Last, but by no means least, one must consider the role played by language policy in the retention or loss of minority languages. Although, as Fishman (1980:629) points out, explicit legal encouragements or restrictions do not necessarily affect the *intragroup* use of the ethnic language, language policy does play a role in affecting the public fortunes of minority languages. A brief historical survey of U.S. language policy will enable us to understand better how multilingualism and English dominance interact.

A PARADOX IN U.S. LANGUAGE POLICY

As soon as one attempts to characterize the language situation of the United States from a broad historical perspective, a curious paradox presents itself: surprisingly for a nation of such size and demographic complexity, the United States does not have a comprehensively conceived and clearly promulgated language policy (Keller 1983:253), yet it has been quite successful in maintaining itself as an English-speaking polity. Kloss (1977:283) notes:

> [T]he non-English ethnic groups in the United States were anglicized not *because of* nationality laws which were *unfavorable* toward their language but *in spite of* nationality laws relatively *favorable* to them. Not by legal provisions and measures of the authorities, not by governmental coercion did the nationalities become assimilated, but rather by the absorbing power of the highly developed American society (original italics).

Thus America has been able to "[produce] *without* laws that which other countries, desiring a culturally unified population, were not able to produce *with* laws" (Glazer 1978:34; original italics).

The relatively weak role played by overt legal coercion on language use is not an unqualified blessing to language minorities. Heath and Mandabach (1983:101) note that, in a country with merely "an unwritten [language] 'policy' which is the legacy of English history," defining language rights for linguistic minorities would be quite a formidable task:

> Restrictions on the use of languages other than English have been imposed through the unwritten laws of institutions. *Laws* perceived as violating basic national values, i.e., restricting basic freedoms, can be contested as unconstitutional; to contest unwritten laws or *norms of behavior* would be much more difficult (original italics).

The Constitution itself makes no mention of an official language, although there is an implicit recognition of English in that the document is written in that language (Leibowitz 1984:59), and subsequently English has been used as the language of government "more or less as a matter of course" (Wagner 1981:37). While "the question of how precisely early national leaders perceived issues relating to linguistic freedom and cultural diversity will, no doubt, remain open" (Heath 1977:273), Heath argues that the decision not to grant official status to English was a matter of policy (Heath 1977, 1981). It was based partly on the British tradition of resistance to government interference in language choice (Heath and Mandabach 1983:88–92), partly on the need for the new nation to attract immigrants (Marshall 1986:9–10; see also Fuchs 1983:294–296 and Leibowitz 1984:26–27), but most importantly on the spirit of liberty guiding the founding of the new nation (Heath 1976:9–10; see also Fuchs 1983:310).[2]

The silence of the Constitution on language matters has two opposing ramifications. One is that it encourages tolerance of linguistic diversity and allows "room" for legal concepts protecting the language rights of minorities to evolve over time (see Wong, "Educational Rights of Language Minorities," this volume). On the other hand, the lack of explicit guidelines on language issues in the Constitution also means that interpretations of language rights for minorities may be made conservatively, leaving "room" for restrictionist arguments. These two contrasting consequences have been observed throughout American history. Kloss (1977:285) calls them, respectively, the "American bilingual tradition" and the "one country, one language" tradition; they correspond to "cultural pluralism" (Kallen 1915) on the one hand and "Anglo conformity" (Gordon 1964) on the other (Leibowicz 1985:539–542).

As a result of the tension between these two traditions, language minorities not only have to contend daily with social pressures on the use of their ethnic languages, but during periods of national stress or crisis—typically characterized by economic depression, hostility against foreign powers, xenophobia, and uncertainty over the assimilative and regenerative powers of the body politic—they are also confronted with explicit and direct intrusions of language-related legislation into their lives. Throughout U.S. history, periods of tolerance for linguistic diversity have alternated with periods of linguistic restrictions on or even persecution of "newcomers."[3] especially if the "newcomers" are visibly "different," non-Anglophone, non-Northwest-European immigrants. Multilingualism and English supremacy can be said to exist in a highly unstable, dynamic relationship.

APPROACHING THE AMERICAN LINGUISTIC MOSAIC

Because immigration is not only fundamental to the establishment of the nation but has also in fact been a continuous process reaching into the present, the linguistic composition of the American population is in constant flux, making it difficult to give a concise historical account of the American language situation without imposing artificial segmentations.

An obvious way to impart order is to divide language groups by their settlement history, such as Kloss (1977; modified in Kloss 1986:172) and Conklin and Lourie (1983:3–59) have done. Thus we might think of (1) "indigenous" or pre-Columbian languages, which include Native American (Amerindian), Eskimo, and precolonial Pacific languages; (2) "colonial" languages: the languages of "old settlers" who came to North America in about the same period before the founding of the United States; and (3) "immigrant" languages spoken by groups entering the United States after the nation had been established.

However, organizing a historical review by such categories alone has its problems. Many languages are both "colonial" and "immigrant" and thus will not fit ready generalizations: Spanish is a notable example. Moreover, as will be seen, "immigrant languages" is too broad a term to capture fine differences between ethnolinguistic groups and between periods of immigration, in particular, between the "Great Wave" of immigration during the 1880–1920 period and the post-1965 influx. In this chapter, a more flexible framework will be adopted to bring out what I consider salient features of the American linguistic mosaic.

INDIGENOUS LANGUAGES[4] AND THEIR SUBSEQUENT DEVELOPMENT

Nowhere is the multilingual heritage of the United States more striking than in the case of Native American languages—and nowhere is the effect of a policy of suppression more tragically apparent.

On the American continents, over 1,000 languages and dialects can be verified for the period just preceding European contact (Ruhlen 1987:6). Anthropologists and linguists have found many relationships between Indian languages in North and South America, which implies that the languages have branched off from a common parent stock or from several language groups. Though estimates vary widely (Hagan 1961:2; Ruhlen 1987:6), one might with good reason assume that there were 30–40 million (Ruhlen 1987:6) Native peoples on the North American continent at the end of the fifteenth century. But as European contact began, Native people were drastically reduced in numbers by wars, disease, and encroachments of settlers onto their ancestral lands, and Native languages were forced to shift in favor of the intrusive English language.

Systematic linguistic subjugation was not a universal policy among colonists, who showed different emphases in their treatment of Native Americans. Spanish exploration parties established a string of outposts in the

Southwest and along the Pacific coast, often with missions intent upon "domesticating" and "civilizing" the "Indians." Their aim was to bring about a rapid and thoroughgoing transformation of the Native Americans. The Native Americans were to be hispanicized not only in religion but also in social organization, language, dress, work habits, and virtually every other aspect of their lives (Rawls 1984:14). In contrast, the French, who established fur trading outposts in the Great Lakes region and then proceeded down the Ohio and Mississippi rivers, saw the Native Americans as allies for their fur trading and did not colonize them; rather, they developed close military and economic ties with various tribes. It was the English colonists who attempted most forcibly to assimilate the Native Americans: if the latter could be taught to read and write English, count, and farm, they could be "civilized." However, the Native peoples proved resistive both to assimilation and to enslavement, and were therefore steadily exterminated or driven westward.

Language policy toward the Indians was an integral part of a policy of conquest and dislocation of the Native population. As the settlers demanded more land for farming, President Andrew Jackson decreed expulsion of all remaining major tribes to the west of the Mississippi River in the Indian Removal Act of 1829 (Conklin and Lourie 1983:8). From 1830 to 1850, Indians were forced to evacuate from their homelands and dumped into new territories; an indication of the enormity of this dislocation was the fact that, on the famed "Trail of Tears," when tribes were force-marched to resettle in Indian Territory (now the state of Oklahoma), 25 percent died along the way. In 1850, the U.S. government began the Reservation Policy, isolating the Indians in parcels of reserved lands where they would be "Americanized" (Rawls 1984:142).

To accomplish the federal government's policy of turning the Native peoples into patriotic, disciplined, God-fearing, English-speaking farmers, Christian missionaries were sent in to convert Indians, and teachers were hired to school them in the English language, American patriotism, and manual and agricultural skills. In 1880, off-reservation boarding schools, run in paramilitary fashion, were set up for the same purpose: children were rounded up and forced to attend. In these boarding schools, they were punished and humiliated for the use of their Indian languages, through corporal punishment, school jailings, and head shavings (Hagan 1961:134–137). As a result, Indian languages were severely eroded in the last half of the nineteenth century, along with the traditional family structure and culture. By 1920, at the lowest point of tribal population, only 400,000 Indians remained. Most tribal communities had lost much of their culture and language; alcoholism, suicide, poor nutrition, a high infant mortality rate, and poverty marked reservation life (Hagan 1961:146–156).

The erosion of Indian languages was not arrested when federal policy changed. Thirty years later, as a major alternative to Indian rural poverty and another attempt at assimilation, the federal government designed the Relocation Program. Indians who would move to select urban areas were promised housing, job training, employment, and transportation to the city; however, these uprooted migrants, deprived of tribal supports, lacked skills to survive in the cities. Over the years, this has further weakened the use of Native languages.

The contemporary language situation of Native Americans is not encouraging. There are now an estimated 2.5 million Native Americans in North America; of the 300 recognizably separate Native American languages and dialects still extant, only roughly 40 percent have more than 100 speakers. Tribes with the most active use of their languages include the Eskimos (40,000–50,000 speakers) in the Northwest; the Apache, Hopi, Pueblo (10,000–15,000 each), and Navajo (89,000) in the Southwest; the Cherokee (10,000) in the Southeast; and the Lakota (10,000–15,000) on the Plains. In the case of approximately 55 percent of these languages, the remaining speakers are of advanced age (Chafe 1962:162–179).[5] These facts imply that many Native American languages are likely to disappear with the death of the current speakers.

Fortunately, in the last two decades, various tribes have reasserted the right to their own cultures and languages. Many tribes, building on the idea that self-worth, confidence, and cultural identity are important for education, have taken advantage of Title VII funds for bilingual education. So while some tribal languages are being lost, others are being maintained and encouraged (Conklin and Lourie 1983:8).

THE "COLONIAL" LANGUAGES AND THEIR SUBSEQUENT DEVELOPMENT

The "colonial" languages are the languages of the "old settlers" who came to North America during the general period before the establishment of the United States as a nation; Fishman et al. (1966:23) identify them as English, Spanish, French, German, Russian, Swedish, and Dutch, but the last three did not survive as colonial languages (except in a few isolated pockets) for an appreciable length of time after the mother countries lost control of their colonial holdings. The term "colonial language" is not to be taken as absolutely distinct from and exclusive of "immigrant language"; the same language can be both, evolving according to a complex set of social, cultural, economic, and political variables. A brief look at the developments undergone by the four major colonial languages will help to clarify how the processes of language maintenance and shift operate in a historical context.

The Case of English

The story of how English-speaking colonists founded the nation is familiar to most American readers and need not be repeated here. What is less well known is that, for a long time in the colonial and early national periods, the ascendency of the English language was by no means a foregone conclusion. In fact, from 1776 to around the mid-nineteenth century, multilingualism was accepted as a common, even desirable, phenomenon befitting a nation of immigrants; few fears were expressed about the potential threat of multilingualism to national unity (Heath 1977; Fuchs 1983:294–296; Leibowitz 1984:26–28). Eventually, English was able to displace the established indigenous languages as well as take precedence over other colonial languages for a number of reasons. English had the benefit of numbers; of concentration and control of urban life, education, and entry into service occupations; and of legal protection. It dominated the avenues of social mobility, and the ideological and organizational institutions (Fishman 1980:630).

The importance of English as a common language was greatly reinforced by massive immigration from Ireland in the nineteenth century. Between 1820 and 1854, some 4 million Irish arrived in the United States (Commons 1967:67). The first immigrants from Ireland, before the famines of the 1830s and the 1840s, were predominantly Protestant settlers of Scottish ancestry. But by the mid-1800s, general poverty, crop failure, and massive famines forced the Celtic Irish, of Catholic background, to emigrate. The bulk of immigrants were from rural communities. Most settled in ports of debarkation in Boston and New York or found work building roads, canals, and the railroad, or in coal mines.

The history of how Irish immigrants and their descendents have fared in the United States illustrates the interaction of language with other social factors. Being impoverished, poorly educated, and religiously "different" (Catholic), the Irish immigrants were discriminated against (Fuchs 1983:300); in this they were no different from many "newcomers" in the history of this nation. However, the Irish had a distinct advantage in adapting to life in the New World: the majority of them were English speakers. In addition, the Irish had a strong sense of identity and cohesion stemming from foreign oppression in their native land, as well as a history of having maintained underground religious and political organizations there. These social factors augmented their linguistic congruence with the ruling group; thus they were soon able to make historic inroads in municipal politics, the Catholic Church hierarchy, union leadership, and journalism, despite heavy prejudice from American nativists (Sowell 1981:40).

As we will see, because of a number of domestic factors as well as international events, the English language was eventually to become unrivaled in the United States.

The Case of French

The contrasting fortunes of English and French demonstrate some of the variables of language retention and loss discussed earlier.

French colonists claimed Louisiana in 1682 (Louisiana was purchased by the United States in 1803). Because French speakers, like the English colonists, came "under the auspices and protection of an official plan of French colonization," the French language was initially in a strong position (Gilbert 1981;261). However, it should be remembered that actual French immigration was very limited during the colonial and early republican periods. Besides, the Protestant Huguenots who fled religious persecution were assigned by the French to English-speaking areas such as New England, and were quickly absorbed (Gilbert 1981:260–261). Thus French did not become an important competitor of English as a possible common language in the new nation.

The largest numbers of French-speaking immigrants entered as late as after the Civil War; they came from Canada as sojourners in response to the lure of the booming New England mill towns (Fishman 1966:24). As "cyclical migrants," they swarmed to the mill towns during periods of prosperity and returned home in periods of depression; gradually, an increasing proportion remained in "the States" (Commons 1967:98). Due to the group's proximity to Francophone Canada, its continuing poverty and strong ethnic identification, and the establishment of French language churches, schools, presses, and radio broadcasts, French Americans have been able to retain their ethnic language in the New England area (Conklin and Lourie 1983:20).

In Louisiana, because French continued to fulfill a religious and educational function (Gilbert 1981:261), the language was also well retained. Today, Louisianan speakers of French are mostly native-born and include descendants of the original French settlers; descendents of the Acadians, who brought their own brand of French called Cajun when they were expelled from their Canadian homeland in 1755; and descendents of the West Africans imported to work on plantations, who speak Louisiana French Creole, a combination of French and West African languages (Conklin and Lourie 1983:19).

However, in the national picture, despite often favorable stereotypes of French speakers and the prestige of French as a language of culture, French has not been maintained as well. With the xenophobic restrictions against *all* foreign language teaching following World War I (see below), French declined in prominence. Over time, French has turned from a colonial language into a "school language"; enrollments in French classes tend to fluctuate according to such factors as American attitudes toward France and the perceived value of studying French. Today, the future of French "lies almost entirely in [its] function as [a] foreign [language], not as first or second languages" (Gilbert 1981:271).

The Case of German

Much more dramatically than the case of French, the case of German illustrates how social factors interact with language policy to influence the vicissitudes of a minority language.

Although introduced on a large scale during colonial days and often labeled as a "colonial language," German was not the language of a colonial power on the continent. In other words, unlike the officially sponsored English and French speakers, early German settlers were "outcasts from the home country, not colonial representatives" sent out to establish a New Germany (Gilbert 1981:260). Thus it would be more accurate to describe the status of German as a colonial–immigrant amalgam.

The Germans who emigrated during the early eighteenth century settled in Pennsylvania. By the time of the American Revolution, Pennsylvanian Germans—also called Pennsylvanian Deutsch or Dutch—constituted a third of the population of Pennsylvania. Fear of German ascendency caused Benjamin Franklin to write:

> Those who come hither are generally the most stupid of their own nation. . . . [A]s few of the English would understand the German language and so cannot address them either from the press or pulpit, it is almost impossible to remove any prejudices they may entertain. . . . Not being used to liberty, they knew not how to make a modest use of it (cited in Heath 1981:9–10).

As Heath observes, this kind of statement illustrates a trend that we are to see repeatedly:

> throughout the history of the United States, whenever speakers of varieties of English or other languages have been viewed as politically, socially, or economically threatening, their language has become a focus for arguments in favor of both restrictions of their use and imposition of Standard English (Heath 1981:10).

Though Pennsylvanian Germans preferred to remain aloof from their English and Scotch–Irish neighbors, the movement for American independence forced them into contact with the English-speaking population. After the Revolution, Pennsylvania was a bilingual state; German language newspapers were printed in New York, Pennsylvania, and Boston (Conklin and Lourie 1983:29). But the political subordination of Germans to English speakers was clear (Gilbert 1981:260). By 1815, the vast majority of colonial Germans had merged culturally and linguistically into Anglo-American society. Only members of strict, traditional religious sects such as the Amish and Old Order of Mennonites have continued to use the old language in self-imposed isolation (Conklin and Lourie 1983:29).

After renewed large-scale immigration from Germany started in 1820 (Schlossman 1983:142), the fate of the German language in the United States took another turn. During the nineteenth century, the Germans were, at any given time, either the largest or second largest immigrant group (after the Irish), and were the numerically dominant non-English-speaking group (Schlossman 1983:142). The numerical dominance was favorable to language maintenance. This was further helped by the geographic concentration of the German immigrants in the Midwest, often in isolated, rural areas. Even in cities like Milwaukee, Buffalo, New York, Baltimore, and Cincinnati, as well as in the state of Texas, "the Germans did not mingle much with the American population," and German residential patterns involved "minimal neighborhood contact" (Sowell 1981:57–58).

Besides demographic factors, cultural factors were favorable to ethnic language retention. Although most Germans were peasants and day laborers, from 1848 to 1880 a large number of highly cultured German intellectuals emigrated. At the time, according to Glazer, the United States was in fact "culturally underdeveloped" compared to Europe (Glazer 1978:36). Thus it was natural for German linguistic maintenance efforts to flourish.

The German language was maintained by the German press and ethnic clubs (Thernstrom 1973:131), and, most importantly, by schools. Not only were there parochial schools using German, but the newly established public school system, out of the need to attract immigrant children, also sometimes offered German instruction (Heath 1981:13; Schlossman 1983:145). The one-room, one-teacher rural schools throughout the Midwest used German quite extensively, while urban public schools offered limited German instruction (Schlossman 1983:144). By 1910, the total number of persons who spoke German natively may well have been around 9 million (Fishman et al. 1966:213). No other northern European non-English language has been spoken by as large a proportion of U.S. residents.

However, the outbreak of World War I brought a general aversion to everything "German." In fact, even prior to the war, a "war psychology" stemming from various U.S. military ventures had already created a general distrust of multilingualism and suspicion toward "foreigners" (Marshall 1986:12), while the normal processes of acculturation had already begun to erode German language and culture (Fuchs 1983:299). In reaction to xenophobia, many German Americans were forced to drop traditional loyalties, secular German associations felt obliged to dissolve, and the teaching of German was forbidden in many private and public schools. By 1923, 34 states had passed laws requiring that the teaching in elementary schools be in English (Leibowitz 1984:40).

Though the English-medium laws were struck down as unconstitutional in 1923 and 1927, the damage had already been done not only to German maintenance but also to foreign language education in general (Gilbert 1981:165). Public bilingual education was not be attempted again until the

1960s. By that time, "among the descendants of the 9 million or so German-speakers who lived on American soil in 1910, at most 50,000 of those under eighteen years of age still [spoke] German natively" (Fishman 1966:248). Data from a 1975 survey show an extremely rapid shift to English among German-ancestry individuals; for example, only 3 percent of the 1975 German mother-tongue claimants still used German as their individual language in German-speaking households, 26 percent used English in German-speaking households, while the rest, 71 percent, lived in monolingual English households. Today, like French, German is primarily a "school language" whose popularity shifts according to various social factors; its importance as a first or second language is very limited (Gilbert 1981:269, 271).

What Heath and Mandabach (1983:101; see above) see as a disturbing potential for oppression in America's "informal" language policy is clearly demonstrated in the history of German in America. Gilbert (1981:262) comments on the ban on German in the period around World War I:

> The concerted and speedy action to drop German, which was taken in unison by independent local and state school boards across the country, is truly frightening. An educational decree issued from a centralized dictatorship could have hardly done it better.

The Case of Spanish

Of the four major colonial languages, except for English with its de facto official status, Spanish is the one that has survived most robustly. Today it has the largest number of speakers among non-English minorities; Waggoner (Table 3.8), using 1980 Census data, estimates that over 11,000 people aged 5 and older speak Spanish at home. The present numerical dominance of Spanish speakers is the result of both intergenerational retention and immigration.

Spain, America's oldest colonial power, at various times had controlled almost all of the territory west of the Mississippi and in Florida. Spanish settlers established the first permanent colony in Florida in 1565; Florida was permanently annexed to the United States in 1820. Santa Fe was established in 1609, followed by other settlements in the Southwest. Central and eastern Texas was settled in the mid-1700s. In the eighteenth century, the Spanish settled California in response to Russian and English activity on the Pacific coast. However, with the westward movement of immigrants to California, the Gold Rush of 1848, and the defeat of Mexico in the Mexican–American War, Spanish influence quickly declined in California (Lavender 1972:65).

Spain's decline as a world power and racial mixing in the Western Hemisphere have changed the prestige of the Spanish language in the last two centuries. But as Conklin and Lourie (1983:15) point out, several factors have ensured the continuance of the Hispanic influence in these early settlement areas. As members of the oldest European culture in these areas, Hispanics were more resistant to Anglo assimilation than were members of other cultures who arrived late; the proximity of the southwestern United States to Mexico and of the southeastern United States to the Spanish-speaking Caribbean islands reinforced the Spanish language and culture.

Although intergenerational retention of Spanish in the old settlement areas has been widespread, it is important to emphasize that, without continued immigration, Spanish would not have attained the numerical strength and visibility it has today. The massive immigration from Mexico, Puerto Rico, Cuba, and Central America in this century has reinforced the maintenance of Hispanic culture and language (see below).

THE GREAT WAVE OF IMMIGRATION 1880–1920

The American linguistic mosaic continued to be changed by immigration after the colonial and early national periods. Besides the flood of Irish (4 million) and Germans (5.2 million) from 1820 to midcentury (Commons 1967:67) discussed above, from 1865 to 1875 came another 3.5 million, mostly from England and the Scandinavian countries (Dinnerstein and Reimers 1977:12). The majority of the Swedes and Norwegians settled in isolated rural communities in the Midwest, preserving their languages through ethnic churches and newspapers, but also gradually adapting to Anglophone society by sending their children to public schools (Haugen 1956:30). The total size of the immigration wave from 1820 to 1890 was about 15 million (Bouvier and Gardner 1986:8). In addition, the Chinese entered in large numbers as laborers between the Gold Rush and the Chinese Exclusion Act in 1882 (on the eve of which they numbered 100,000; see Lyman 1970:68). They formed a notable exception to the mostly northwestern European immigrants of the mid- to late nineteen century.

The characteristics of American immigration underwent a dramatic change in the last decades of the nineteenth century. In the 40 years between 1880 and 1920, approximately 23 million immigrants from the southern and eastern European nations crossed the Atlantic to start a new life in the United States. These newcomers added to the already diverse American population many linguistic and cultural ingredients that had been only meagerly represented up to that point. Between 1896 and 1917, 60 percent of the new arrivals came from Russia, Austria–Hungary, Italy, and Greece. From 1899 to 1919, about 2.3 million Italians migrated; all but 400,000 came from poverty-stricken southern Italy and Sicily. In 1880 there were an estimated

900,000 Jews in the United States; during the next 20 years 2 million Jews arrived, most of them driven by persecution from Russian and eastern Europe. By the turn of the century there were 2 million Poles in the United States, who, along with Lithuanians, Czechs, Slovaks, Croatians, and Hungarians, migrated with the hope of a better future (Rosenblum 1973:70). It has been estimated that, between 1905 and 1914, an average of over a million people annually crowded past immigration inspectors (Kessner and Caroli 1982:9).

Because the majority of the immigrants during the "Great Wave" were darker-skinned peoples of southern and eastern Europe, were "foreign-speaking, strange-looking, poor, and often illiterate," and tended to concentrate in the cities (Fuchs 1983:300), they were highly visible (Leibowitz 1984:30). In this they were different from the English-speaking Irish immigrants, as well as the skilled and geographically relatively dispersed German and Scandinavians coming before them. In addition, their entry coincided with the progressive closing of the frontier and the beginning of an American labor movement (Fuchs 1983:301). Thus their presence gave focus to strong nativist sentiments, and, as we will see, language issues often came to the fore in national debates concerning the direction to be taken by the United States and the nature of "Americanness."

FACTORS AFFECTING THE LANGUAGE MAINTENANCE AND LANGUAGE SHIFT OF IMMIGRANTS DURING THE "GREAT WAVE"

The linguistic picture of the immigrants who arrived during the "Great Wave" is incredibly complex. In a chapter of this length, one cannot hope to give a comprehensive account. A more feasible approach is to apply the concepts discussed in the theoretical section of this chapter to some of the ethnolinguistic groups represented, so that we can better understand how the dynamic relationship between multilingualism and English supremacy was constantly modified. Weimer (1980) points out that most characteristics affecting a community's language use are double-edged: for example, the high education of immigrants may help ethnic language maintenance by fostering self-respect and interest in bilingual schooling; at the same time, it may encourage economic mobility and thus accelerate ethnic language loss. This is a useful idea to bear in mind as we examine the specific factors contributing to both ethnic language retention and shift to English. Furthermore, it should be remembered that there are rarely pure textbook examples of a single factor at work; more often than not, factors interact with each other, creating subtle and complex situations.

Economic Motivation

Earlier in this chapter, it was suggested that economic factors are intimately related to language maintenance and loss. Separate from the importance of economic mobility in encouraging language shift, Glazer (1978:40) points out the role played by economic motivation for immigration. People who emigrate primarily to improve their economic condition tend to shift to English more readily than those who emigrate to escape political, religious, or cultural persecution in their homeland.

In examining the immigrants during the 1880–1920 period, we will find that economic motivation for emigration was very strong in many ethnic groups. In the southern and eastern European areas where the immigrant originated, population growth had outpaced arable land and nonagricultural work opportunities. This condition was exacerbated by the traditional land tenure system, which awarded the family plot to the eldest son or divided it among the male children; by the oppression of large landowners on tenant farmers and landholding peasants; and by the advent of the industrial revolution, which bankrupted cottage industries. Severely impoverished, the peasantry of southern and eastern Europe set out for both South and North America (Krickus 1976:56). Immigration was touted as a solution for the Old World's problems by agents hired by American companies and states, who scoured the heartland of Europe, promising to uprooted peasants jobs, high wages, and a carefree, independent life in the New World (Taylor 1971:16). The fact that so many immigrants during the "Great Wave" came to the United States for a better life was conducive to their adoption of the new country's language and culture.

However, economic motivation can also work against shift to English under some circumstances. A large percentage of the 1860–1920 immigrants were "sojourners," who came to the United States for the explicit purpose of earning enough money to return home and buy land or set up a business. The U.S. Immigration Report of 1911 (the Dillingham Commission Report) estimated that two-fifths of the new immigrants returned to Europe after a relatively short period, with one-fifth of those who returned doing so after 5 years or less in the United States (Portes and Bach 1985:31). Repatriation encouraged retention of the ethnic language and slowed acquisition of English. Sojourner repatriation was counteracted to some extent by the fact that relatively cheap third-class passage across the Atlantic allowed people to come back to the United States if they wanted to. The Dillingham Commission estimated that one-third of the immigrants who returned to Europe eventually came back (Portes and Bach 1985:31). This back-and-forth population movement helped maintain the ethnic language as well as the "sojourner mentality" (Rosenblum 1973:17).

Ideological Mobilization: Churches, Schools, Community Organizations

Another issue to consider concerning ethnic language maintenance and loss is the degree of ideological mobilization associated with a group's language, as both Glazer (1978) and Conklin and Lourie (1983) have pointed out. Immigrant groups fleeing religious and ethnic persecution and seeking refuge in America are more likely to retain their languages as a symbol of their group identity and historical continuity. This factor can be seen at work among the immigrants of the "Great Wave."

At the end of the nineteenth century, as the specter of nationalism spread throughout Europe, ethnic minority populations—Greeks and Bulgarians living under Turkish rule; Poles, Lithuanians, and Jews in the Russian Empire; and Slovaks, Croats, and Serbs in the Austro-Hungarian Empire—were vulnerable to discrimination at the hands of their majority neighbors. In some areas local languages were forbidden, newspapers suppressed, and intellectuals and political activists imprisoned, exiled, or even executed. As a result, thousands emigrated to the United States (Krickus 1976:61). The single largest group among eastern Europeans to flee persecution was the Jews. Pogroms in Southern Russia, the Ukraine, and Poland forced entire families, in some cases even entire villages, to set out for the New World.

Once in the New World, immigrants fleeing persecution established places of worship as well as community organizations to preserve their heritage and sense of belonging; these institutions, often intimately linked, were favorable to ethnic language maintenance. One example of this situation is the St. Stanislaus Kostka Parish in Chicago in the 1920s, which was the home of 140 organizations: mutual aid societies, women's organizations, youth groups, and cultural associations (Krickus 1976:81). Religious cohesion was particularly strong when the religion was a national one associated with the historical trials and current struggles of a people. In the case of the Poles, Czechs, and Italians, for example, immigrants rallied around the ethnic churches against the Anglophone, Irish Roman Catholic hierarchy, demanding priests who spoke their own languages. Ethnic organizations provided a familiar environment where immigrants could retrieve their sense of cultural identity. As Thomas and Znaniecki (1984:253) note:

> Their aim is to preserve the cultural stock brought by the immigrants to this country—language, mores, customs, and historical traditions—so as to maintain the racial solidarity of Poles as an ethnic group, independent of their political allegiance and of any economic, social or political bonds which may connect each of them individually with their American milieu.

Language functioned prominently in such efforts at group self-preservation.

Once again, as in the case of economic factors, escape from persecution as a motive for immigration can sometimes work in a way opposite to the usual effect. Thus the Jewish immigrants, who fled extreme persecution, often acquired English readily because they never intended to return: America would become their new home (Sachar 1958:240–260). Acquisition of English and preservation of the ethnic language were not mutually exclusive but existed side by side.

A similar dual emphasis can be observed in the case of parish schools established by immigrants, which were another important agent of ideological mobilization as well as ethnic language maintenance. In Polish parish schools, for example, which were usually established immediately after the completion of the church or even before, both Polish and English were used as teaching languages, though the proportion varied in different schools.

> Whereas the children who go to public schools become completely estranged from their parents, if these are immigrants, the parish school . . . prevents the estrangement because it inculcates respect for these traditional values and for the nation from which they came. (Thomas and Znaniecki 1984:252–253)

Cultural preservation, not isolation from the Anglophone majority, was the aim. Thus while the first-generation southern and eastern European immigrants encouraged children in the use of their native languages, they also instilled in their children the need to acquire English.

Patterns of Settlement

Another important factor affecting ethnic language maintenance and shift is the size and geographical concentration of a group. The formation of "language islands" would facilitate ethnic language retention; dispersal would undermine it.

Though immigrants were mostly of peasant stock, in America their "livelihood would come more commonly from mine and mill than from tilling the soil" (Ehrlich et al. 1979:54). Immigrants during the 1880–1920 period tended to be concentrated in industrial centers. Arriving in the United States with little money, finding soaring land prices and massive American farms, and lacking occupational skills, the immigrants were drawn to the Northeastern industrial areas where the demand for unskilled labor, however poorly paid, promised them a livelihood. Many newcomers joined friends and relatives who were already established in the New World. Industrial centers in Massachusetts, Connecticut, New Jersey, New York, Pennsylvania, Ohio, and Illinois absorbed the newcomers.

"Language islands" were often formed when newcomers from the same language background congregated for mutual assistance and cultural security. This took place both in smaller industrial and mining towns dominated by particular ethnolinguistic groups, and in large cosmopolitan areas with various ethnic enclaves. The former condition was more favorable to language maintenance. For example, Polish immigrants, who found employment in smaller textile towns in the Northeast, the stockyards of Chicago, the mill towns of Akron and Youngstown, and the coal mines of Illinois, Minnesota, Michigan, and Pennsylvania, were quite successful at retaining the Polish language because of the weakness of cosmopolitan influences. In contrast, in large urban centers, despite the formation of enclaves like "Little Italy," there was typically much mixing of immigrant groups from diverse backgrounds, so that the acquisition of the language and culture of the host society was facilitated. Urbanization was widespread among immigrants during the 1880–1920 period. It is estimated that by 1910, 72 percent of all foreign-born Americans lived in urban areas (Taylor 1971:171–182). About 80 percent of the Italians settled in East Coast cities; close to 90 percent of the Jewish immigrants claimed cities for their new homes, with the Lower East Side of New York City functioning to draw new immigrants into the Jewish community; Lithuanians settled in Chicago (Sowell 1981:78; Portes and Bach 1985:40–41). Under such conditions, ethnic language maintenance and the shift to English took place side by side.

Class Structure and Dynamics Within the Ethnic Community

Glazer (1978) suggests that the social class background of immigrants has an important bearing on language retention and shift. It makes a difference to the survival of the ethnic language whether an entire social spectrum or only a small segment immigrated, and also, in the former case, how the classes interacted with each other. The case of Jewish American immigrants in the 1880–1920 period illustrates the complex operation of this factor.

Unlike their contemporaries who were mainly of the peasant class, Jewish immigrants during this period represented all sectors of the community (Sachar 1958:240–260). The inclusion of intellectuals facilitated the creation of ethnic language schools, publications, and cultural societies. The newcomers, many of whom were merchants, settled on the Lower East Side of New York City, peddling wares, opening small shops, and working in factories owned by German Jews. They quickly learned the English language, business and occupational skills, and the "ways" of the new society. Taken as a group, the Jewish immigrants learned the new language and acculturated rapidly, succeeding in various industries and sending their children to city colleges and later to universities. Overall, the success of the Jewish immigrants at both language retention and shift to English can be attributed in no small degree to a history of learning survival strategies involving quick acquisition of the language of the host society.

NATIVISM AND LANGUAGE ISSUES

During the earlier expansionist period in American history, the languages of minorities were not a major issue tied to concepts of citizenship or patriotism: when the United States acquired southern and western territories, through purchase or conquest, thousands of non-English-speaking people became American citizens without controversy (McFadden 1983:6). However, during and after the "Great Wave" of immigration, public interest in and debate on language issues intensified; multilingualism began to be seen as threatening to the welfare of the nation, and English supremacy was increasingly promoted. An analysis of this process would confirm Heath's dictum that "ideological or political views about the status of a particular language may arise in response to issues which have no direct or necessary relation to language" (1981:10).

The public agitation for restrictions on immigrant languages during this period had very clear economic roots. While the immigrants supplemented a scarce domestic labor market and furnished the bulk of the manpower for the industrialization of the United States, they did so by filling the bottom positions of the industrial labor market. It was in the interest of employers to confine them to the worst jobs with low salaries and under incredibly harsh conditions. Immigrant workers were repeatedly hired as strikebreakers in mines and factories during this period and thus became a powerful tool for employers against the American Federation of Labor and other labor organizations. Economic competition also intensified because of the closing of the frontier. As a result, these visibly "different" immigrants became both symbols and agents of the widening gap between capital and labor (Portes and Bach 1985:35). Since, as Deutsch (1975:7; cited in Marshall 1986:14) notes, "language is an automatic signaling system, second only to race in identifying targets for possible privilege or discrimination," the linguistic differences of the immigrants easily became the focus of a widespread nativist, antiforeigner, anti-immigrant movement.

During the 1860–1920 period, nativists were outspoken and made highly visible efforts to "save the American standard of life"; organizations such as the Immigrants Resistance League linked the new immigration to the growth of slums and the high incidence of crime, disease, and insanity. Sentiment continued to grow for a more general ban that would regulate both the number and quality of the new arrivals. In response to public agitation against immigrant participation in American life, an English requirement for naturalization (that the petitioner for citizenship be able to sign in his or her own handwriting and to speak English) was instituted in 1906, and a literacy requirement for immigration (that the immigrant be able to read and comprehend some language or dialect) was passed in 1917 (Leibowitz 1984:37). Though these laws were specifically about language, they shared the same nativist, anti-immigrant spirit as the many exclusionary laws passed against further immigration, such as the 1882 Chinese Exclusion Act and the 1907–1908 Gentlemen's Agreement curtailing Japanese entries.

AMERICANIZATION AND ENGLISH LANGUAGE EDUCATION

In a nativist atmosphere, the English language became increasingly associated with "being American" and "being patriotic." Teaching immigrants to replace their ethnic language with English only was considered an effective means of inculcating correct American values.

President Theodore Roosevelt was one of the most prominent and articulate spokesmen of the idea that being a "hyphenated American" was indefensible, and that lack of proficiency in English could be equated to lack of patriotism. He asserted that "the man who becomes completely Americanized . . . and who 'talks United States' instead of the dialect of the country which he has of his own free will abandoned is not only doing his plain duty by his adopted land, but is also rendering to himself a service of immeasurable value." He also stated:

> I want to make as strong a plea as I possibly can against hyphenated Americans of every kind. . . . I am an unflinching believer in and supporter of our common school system . . . in which the exercises shall be conducted in English and the children are taught to speak United States (both quotations cited in Wagner 1981:40).

"Education," declared a New York high school principal, "will solve every problem of our national life, even that of assimilating our foreign element" (Higham 1955:235). With a similar faith in education, but often with different orientations, many civic-minded groups made efforts to teach immigrants English as part of a process of adjustment and assimilation. In the 1890s, humanitarians initiated settlement houses in which English was taught; one example is Hull House established by Jane Addams for immigrant workers (Krickus 1976:94). At the same time, patriotic hereditary societies, such as Daughters of the American Revolution, the Sons of the Revolution, and the Colonial Dames, fearing that newcomers would threaten the American way of life, set up programs of patriotic education to indoctrinate foreigners with loyalty to America and to the English language (Higham 1955:236). "Teach them English and the natal cord which nourished their foreign ways in the U.S. would be severed" (Krickus 1976:94). Larger

American cities created evening classes for English for immigrants. In 1879, New York City had 1,376 foreigners enrolled in English classes; by 1905, there were 36,000 (Higham 1955:379). By 1909 Chicago had 13 percent of its total non-English-speaking population enrolled in adult school. The Detroit Board of Commerce began a massive civic campaign in 1915 to get non-English-speaking foreigners into night school (Higham 1955:379).

Private employers sometimes joined in this effort to inculcate patriotism through teaching English. One well-known case is the Ford English School set up by Henry Ford, which employees were required to attend before or after work 2 days a week. The first English words immigrant auto workers learned were "I'm a good American" (Krickus 1976:95; Higham 1955:244).

American nativism and linguistic chauvinism came to a head when World War I set off a nationwide witch-hunt against bilinguals, paced by Theodore Roosevelt's words:

> The events of the past three years bring us face to face with the question whether in the present century we are to continue as a separate nation at all or whether we are to become merely a huge polyglot boarding house and counting house in which dollar-hunters of twenty different nationalities scramble for gain, while each really pays his soul-allegiance to some foreign power (cited in Haugen 1956:109).

As noted in the section above on the development of the German language, World War I created a xenophobic mood against German Americans that eventually affected all endeavors at foreign language education and cultural preservation. Not only German but also other major foreign language newspapers declined, especially the Yiddish, Italian, and Scandinavian ones (Dinnerstein and Reimers 1977:143). By 1919, 15 states had passed legislation stating that English must be used at all public and private gatherings; in Iowa the governor proclaimed that only English could be used in public gatherings, including telephone conversations (Krickus 1976:96).

World War I significantly altered the structure of the American economy and the role of immigrants; after the war, restrictive immigration laws were passed to control the number and racial distribution of immigrants. In 1921, the United States established the Quota Law, which set the first numerical constraints on European immigration by limiting them to approximately 355,000. Some 60 percent of the quotas went to northwestern European countries (Bouvier and Gardner 1986:11). The final restrictive legislation was passed in 1924, with the National Origins Act. As implemented in 1929, this allotted 82 percent of a maximum of 150,000 annual immigrants from the Eastern Hemisphere to countries of northwestern Europe, 16 percent to southeastern Europe, and 2 percent to all others. Totally barred from entry were all "aliens ineligible for citizenship," which effectively excluded all Asians (Portes and Bach 1985:48).

CONTEMPORARY IMMIGRATION AND ITS IMPACT ON THE LANGUAGE SITUATION OF THE UNITED STATES

The Americanization debate and the concomitant language controversies subsided with the immigration restrictions of 1924. When the Great Depression set in, the United States was "sufficiently uninviting so that even those countries with high quotas, such as Great Britain, failed to use them," and in 1932, at the lowest point in immigration since 1831, "total emigration actually exceeded total immigration by 290 percent" (Fuchs 1983:302).

World War II brought about some important changes in American attitudes toward foreigners and foreign languages. Not only did some relaxation in immigration legislation occur as a result of American involvement in World War II, such as the 1946 War Brides Act and the 1948 Displaced Persons Act (Fuchs 1983:302–303), but also, in general, the unprecedented exposure of Americans to foreign cultures overseas, America's new role as international superpower, and a new awareness of language as a "national defense [resource]" (Fuchs 1983:302; Marshall 1986:20), all worked to diminish the effects of nativism.

In 1965 the United States abandoned the quota system that for nearly half a century had preserved the overwhelmingly northern European character of the nation. The Immigration Act of 1965 abolished the national origins quota system and discrimination against Asians. It raised the annual quota for Eastern Hemisphere immigration to 170,000, with no more than 20,000 to come from any one country, and placed a ceiling of 120,000 per year on total Western Hemisphere immigration. Its principal effect was to change the basis for preferential admission from national origin to, first, family reunification, and, second, occupational skills. This new law has caused the largest influx of immigrants since the turn of the century, constituting a new "Great Wave" every bit as momentous as its predecessor. Only this time, unlike those coming during the 1880–1920 "Great Wave," the newcomers have arrived not from the Old World but from the Third World, mainly Asia and Latin America. From 1955 to 1964, half of the new immigrants were born in Europe, but in the next decade the figure declined to less than one-third. Immigration from Asia, which was less than 2 percent of the total in 1950, accounted for 50 percent in 1980. African immigration, insignificant to begin with, has been expanding rapidly. Immigration from Canada is down sharply while that from the Caribbean is on the increase (Portes and Bach 1985:52). This enormous migration is rapidly and permanently changing the texture of American society. Table 2.2, with its accompanying Figures 2.1 and 2.2, dramatically illustrates this shift in demographics, which in turn has radically altered the linguistic composition of the nation.

The rest of this chapter will provide a brief overview of the main compo-

Table 2.2. LEGAL IMMIGRATION TO THE UNITED STATES, ACCORDING TO REGION OF LAST RESIDENCE: 1820–1985

Percent of total

Intercensal decade	Total number	Europe total[a]	North and West Europe[b]	South and East Europe[b]	Asia[c]	Africa	Americas total[d]	Canada	Latin America[e]	Mexico
1820–1830	151,824	70.1	67.9	2.2	—	—	7.9	1.6	6.2	3.2
1831–1840	599,125	82.7	81.7	1.0	—	—	5.6	2.3	3.3	1.1
1841–1850	1,713,251	93.2	92.9	0.3	—	—	3.6	2.4	1.2	0.2
1851–1860	2,598,214	94.4	93.6	0.8	1.6	—	2.9	2.3	0.6	0.1
1861–1870	2,314,824	89.2	88.1	1.1	2.8	—	7.2	6.6	0.5	0.1
1871–1880	2,812,191	80.8	76.2	4.5	4.4	—	14.4	13.6	0.7	0.2
1881–1890	5,246,613	90.3	78.8	11.5	1.3	—	8.1	7.5	0.6	f
1891–1900	3,687,564	96.4	60.6	35.8	2.0	—	1.1	0.1	1.0	f
1901–1910	8,795,386	91.6	46.1	45.5	3.7	0.1	4.1	2.0	2.1	0.6
1911–1920	5,735,811	75.3	25.3	49.9	4.3	0.1	19.9	12.9	7.0	3.8
1921–1930	4,107,209	60.0	32.5	27.0	2.7	0.2	36.9	22.5	14.4	11.2
1931–1940	528,431	65.8	38.6	26.7	3.0	0.3	30.3	20.5	9.7	4.2
1941–1950	1,035,039	60.0	49.9	9.8	3.1	0.7	34.3	16.6	14.9	5.9
1951–1960	2,515,479	52.7	39.7	12.7	6.1	0.6	39.6	15.0	22.2	11.9
1961–1970	3,321,677	33.8	18.3	15.4	12.9	0.9	51.7	12.4	38.6	13.7
1971–1980	4,493,314	17.8	6.7	11.0	35.3	1.8	44.1	3.8	40.3	14.2
1981–1985	2,864,406	11.4	5.4	6.0	47.8	2.6	37.5	2.1	35.4	11.7
1985	570,009	11.1	5.3	5.7	46.4	3.0	38.8	2.0	36.7	10.7
Total 1820–1985	52,520,358	69.8	47.2	22.5	8.8	0.4	20.0	8.0	11.8	4.9

(*Source:* Bouvier, L. and R. Gardner. "Immigration to the U.S.: The Unfinished Story." POPULATION BULLETIN, Volume 41, No. 4 (Washington D.C.: Population Reference Bureau, 1986, page 8.) Reprinted by permission.

Data: U.S. Immigration and Naturalization Service (INS), *1984 Statistical Yearbook* (Washington, D.C.: 1986) Table IMM 1.2, and unpublished data for fiscal year 1985 (October 1, 1984–September 30, 1985).

[a] Includes all of present-day U.S.S.R., except 1931–1950, when U.S.S.R is divided into European U.S.S.R. and Asian U.S.S.R.

[b] Through 1901–1910, North and West Europe includes Austria-Hungary. After 1901–1910, Austria included in North and West Europe, Hungary in South and East Europe. Immigrants recorded as "Other Europe" (57, 182 altogether through fiscal year 1984) are omitted from these two regions as shown in this table.

[c] Asia according to INS definition, includes Southwest Asia, e.g., Iraq, Israel, Syria, Turkey.

[d] Includes Canada and Latin America (see next note).

[e] Includes Mexico, Caribbean, Central America, South America.

[f] No record of immigration from Mexico, 1886–1893.

Note: A dash (—) indicates less than .05 percent.

nents of this "new immigration"—Asian and Hispanic immigration; note parallels and contrasts between the current influx with the previous "Great Wave"; and relate demographic changes to changes in the linguistic composition of the United States over the last two decades. The immigration history of groups covered in this volume—the Mexican Americans, Puerto Ricans, and Cuban Americans; and the Chinese, Filipino, Korean, and Vietnamese Americans—will not be covered in detail here; readers are referred to the chapters on those groups. Other selected groups that may serve to illustrate the processes of language retention and loss will be discussed.

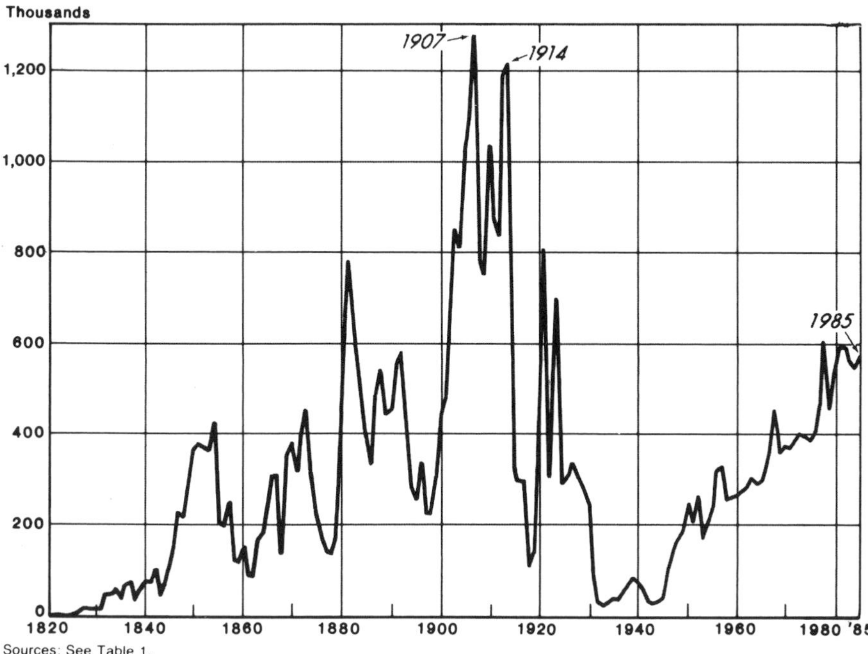

Figure 2.1. Legal immigration to the United States: 1820–1985. (*Source:* Bouvier, L. and R. Gardner. "Immigration to the U.S.: The Unfinished Story." POPULATION BULLETIN, Volume 41, No. 4 (Washington D.C.: Population Reference Bureau, 1986, page 10.) Reprinted by permission.

Asian Immigration

Until 1961, most Asian nations had annual quotas of only 100 and the Asia–Pacific Triangle had a ceiling of 3,000. In 1965, Asian immigrants totalled 20,583, about 5 percent of the total. But by the late 1970s, Asian immigration had increased sixfold and accounted for over 40 percent of the newcomers (Reimers 1985:93). China, the Philippines, India, Korea, and Vietnam were among the leading nations sending people to America.

As a result of this massive Asian immigration, the already great linguistic diversity of the United States is being further reinforced. It is not known exactly how many Asian languages are represented by the post-1965 immigrants, but they include not only various Indian dialects but also

> Philippine languages (Austronesian), the Mon-Khmer languages, the Miao and Yao languages, the various Chinese dialects and languages, Korean, Japanese, and Vietnamese. Among just one small group of recent immigrants, the so-called "montagnards" of southern Vietnam, there are tens of different native languages (Li 1983:4).

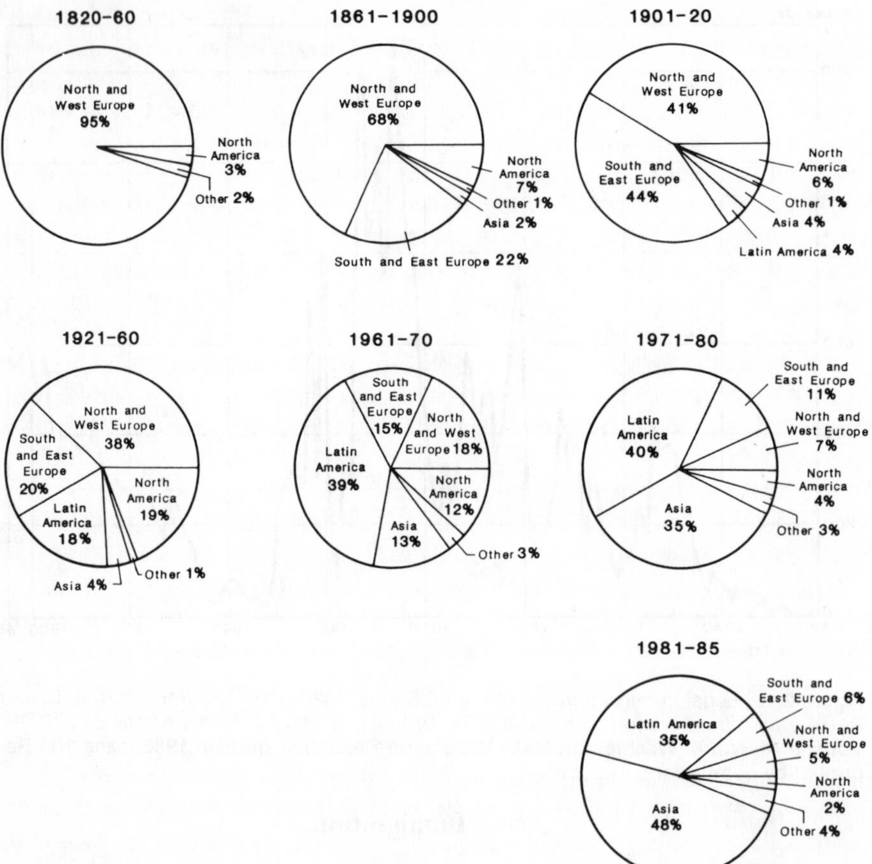

Figure 2.2. Legal immigrants admitted to the United States, by region of last residence: 1820–1985. (*Source:* Bouvier, L. and R.Gardner. "Immigration to the U.S.: The Unfinished Story." POPULATION BULLETIN, Volume 41, No. 4 (Washington D.C.: Population Reference Bureau, 1986, page 16.) Reprinted by permission.

This has had a huge impact on the schools, but, at the same time, the linguistic resources of the United States have been greatly enhanced. In addressing the language needs of Asian immigrants, the public education system needs to take into account the salient demographic characteristics of the Asian population: high concentration in certain geographical areas, rapid rate of growth, relative unpredictability of demographic changes (due to the refugee population), and heterogeneity of background (Wong 1987).

While the 1965 changes in immigration quotas instituted both occupational skill and family reunification preference categories, immigration from Asia often shows an interaction between the two. A typical example is for professionals to enter first, and then send for relatives on the family reunification basis. This pattern is seen in the case of medical professionals—doctors and nurses, and, to a smaller extent dentists, pharmacists, and other medical workers—from the Philippines, Korea, and India. Many settled in large cities like Los Angeles, Chicago, and New York, taking less desirable jobs in inner city hospitals. After establishing themselves, they would send for family members. For example, of the total quota for the Philippines, by 1978, those entering under the occupational preference category had declined to about 17 percent, while those entering under family reunification categories accounted for 80 percent (Reimers 1985:108). Ironically enough, the emphasis on family reunification written into the 1965 law was intended by supporters as a means of preventing a large-scale influx of Asians, the reasoning being that, given the small number of Asians then residing in the United States (less than 1 percent of the total population), it would be relatively harmless to allow their relatives to enter (Reimers 1984:30–48; cited in Wong 1987).

If we compare the conditions causing recent Asian immigration with those responsible for the "Great Wave" of 1880–1920, we will see both similarities and differences. According to Reimers (1985:97), one important "push" factor is that American wages and standards of living are considerably higher than throughout Asia, while many Asian nations experience poverty, hunger, and deprivation. This differential has made the United States an attractive destination for immigration. (Japan, whose economy grew at a rapid rate, accordingly sent very few emigrants to the United States and constituted a major exception to the Asian pattern.) In addition, the unstable political and social conditions or uncertain political future in some Asian areas, such as the Philippines or Taiwan, have created apprehensiveness among many residents and prompted an exodus. These factors are comparable to those that "pushed" European immigrants across the Atlantic a century ago.

There are, however, some significant differences between the old and new immigration. While among a few 1880–1920 ethnic groups, such as the Germans or the Jews, a full spectrum of social classes was represented in the United States, the majority of the immigrants came from impoverished rural backgrounds and provided the unskilled labor for American industrialization. In fact, even the predecessors of the current Asian immigrants fit into this pattern: the Chinese railroad builders and Filipino, Japanese, and Korean agricultural laborers who came in the nineteenth century were typically young men of peasant background who provided the cheap labor needed by the developing nation. In contrast, the post-1965 Asian immigration is much more diverse, consisting of both the unskilled and the highly skilled. Because of occupational preference categories and opportunities for higher education in the United States, many educated middle-class people from Asian countries have emigrated. In nations such as India, the Philippines, and Korea, many professionals have found that their skills are not in high demand, whereas the United States offers them better wages and working conditions. Thus there has been a "brain drain" alongside the emigration of less highly trained workers.

A perhaps even more important condition accounting for immigration, which did not exist during the 1880–1920 period, was the unprecedentedly extensive penetration of the United States military, economy, and culture into Asia during and after World War II. The postwar outreach of American military forces into the Philippines, Korea, the Samoan Islands, and Southeast Asia has heightened people's awareness of the United States and contributed to their subsequent emigration. The cultural and economic penetration into these nations has brought American goods and companies. Books, newspapers, movies, magazines, records, and radio programs tell of American events and life. Cultural and economic bridges have already been built into these countries; the availability of modern transportation has made emigration possible.

Refugees from Southeast Asia

Finally, not to be overlooked in accounting for the influx of Asians was the U.S. involvement in Vietnam in the 1960s and 1970s, which created waves of refugees from Vietnam, Cambodia, and Laos. In fact, in 1980 the United States established the Refugee Act, admitting a greater number of refugees into this country. The Act was an attempt to solve the problem of refugee admissions once and for all. The definition of "refugee" was broadened to conform to United Nations guidelines: persons suffering persecution or with a well-founded fear of persecution because of political opinion, membership in a particular social group, race, ethnicity, nativity, or religion. Refugee numbers were removed from the overall immigrant quota (which was then reduced to 280,000 in 1980 and 270,000 thereafter), and were to be determined yearly by the President in consultation with Congress (Bouvier and Gardner 1986:4).

This group of newcomers are forced from their homelands by very different factors from those motivating the other Asians who are "voluntary" immigrants. The influx of Southeast Asian refugees offers some parallels with the nineteenth century immigrants fleeing political, religious, or ethnic persecution in the Old World; however, in the current case, the influx is a direct result of U.S. policy in the region.

The Vietnamese refugees, whose language situation is discussed elsewhere in this volume (see chapter by Chung), will not be covered in this chapter. However, besides the approximately 1 million Vietnamese who have found refuge in the United States since 1975, thousands of refugees from Laos and Cambodia have sought a new life in this society. Laos became a Communist state in December 1975 and anti-Communist leaders fled, including those who had led a clandestine army of Hmong hill tribesmen financed by the Central Intelligence Agency (CIA). Thousands of Cambodians fled the bloodbath begun by Pol Pot's Khmer Rouge regime and then the Vietnamese invasion of Cambodia in 1978. Many of the refugees of this first wave were members of the middle-class and political elites, though most represented a cross-section of the population. After 1978 many of the refugees were ethnic Chinese, along with Cambodian peasants and Laotian tribesmen (Reimers 1985:181).

Some preparation for their new life in the United States was provided these newcomers in refugee camps; typically, they would receive some English as a second language instruction as well as introduction to American culture and lifestyle while they lived in a UN-sponsored camp in Thailand and waited for sponsorship in their new country. However, once in the United States, many still suffered shock and maladjustment. Most of the refugees have undergone traumatic experiences of war and dislocation and suffered the loss of family members and property. Emotionally taxing life experiences such as these may interfere with the process of linguistic and cultural adjustment.

The case of the agricultural Lao tribespeople, such as the Hmong and the Mien, illustrates some factors affecting the language maintenance and shift of refugees. Having always lived in closely knit clans under a tribal leader, they continue to live this way upon relocating to the United States. Many of the Hmong have followed their clan leader out of urban areas into agricultural areas, where they might have a life more similar to that in their own country. These tribespeople typically had had little formal education and were without a written language until the 1960s. Such a background, added to the community's frequent geographical isolation from the larger society, has made the acquisition of English, either informally or through schooling, difficult. The third and probably the most important factor is that these refugees come with severe emotional losses and lasting scars. That pain is compounded by being overwhelmed by the differentness in the host society, the difficulty in finding gainful employment, and constant worries about family members left behind. All this makes the burden of learning English tremendous. Yet the refugees also realize that the possibility of returning home is remote, and that the United States is their home now. Often the children begin acquiring English first, paving the way for a transition to a new life for their families.

Hispanic Immigration

The single largest language minority in the United States is the Hispanics of various backgrounds, who made up 14.6 percent of the national population at the time of the 1980 Census. Of these, 60 percent were Mexican, 10 percent Puerto Rican, 10 percent Cuban, and 20 percent Central or South American (Reimers 1985:137). Hispanics are concentrated in the Southwest, Texas, Florida, California, and New York. Because of their number and concentration, as well as widespread misconceptions about the nature of their language use, they have become the focus of much public debate on language and the main target of the recent English-only movement.

Immigrants from Mexico, Spanish-speaking Caribbean countries, and South and Central America have migrated north for economic and political reasons at different times. Some, like many Mexicans or Puerto Ricans (Bonilla and Campos 1981:152), are either "cyclical migrants," crossing and recrossing the border in response to fluctuating economic opportunities in industry, construction, or agriculture; or "sojourners" who return home after working in the United States for a period of time. Others, like the Colombians and Venezuelans, come, usually to stay, for greater economic opportunities. More recently, political refugees from Chile and Central America have tried to find safety within these borders. In the late 1970s and early 1980s, civil war broke out in Guatemala, El Salvador, and Nicaragua. Most of these refugees who fled north, usually to Texas and California, were political refugees, who stayed with the hope of returning to their home country soon.

As the three chapters on Hispanics in this volume (by Valdés, Zentella, García and Otheguy) will demonstrate, the Hispanics are by no means a monolithic group, but are in fact highly diverse in terms of origin and nativity, physical appearance, immigration history, socioeconomic background, occupation, education, geographical distribution, cultural practices, and language use characteristics; the subpopulations are often isolated from each other. Of these variables, nativity is the most significant in determining language. Subgroups vary in the percentage of native- and foreign-born. Based on 1976 language data, Veltman (1983:47) estimates that

> [n]early all persons of Cuban ancestry were born outside the United States, while nearly four in five Puerto Ricans and two in three "Other Hispanics" were also foreign born. Only the Chicano group contains a majority of native born persons of Spanish mother tongue, nearly five in eight persons having been born in the United States.

Because of the annexation of formerly Mexican territories by the United States during the nineteenth century, a large number of Hispanic Americans are not only not immigrants, but also can trace their roots back to times before English speakers settled on their land. The 80,000–100,000 Spanish speakers inhabiting the Southwest before the 1848 Treaty of Guadalupe–Hidalgo did not cross the border—the border crossed them. This contrasts greatly with the Hispanic newcomers, who enter as foreigners to an established nation. Thus the language situations of the Hispanic subgroups are necessarily varied. In Veltman's words (1983:47), "students of the Spanish language group should exercise caution before assuming too much homogeneity based on a common language."

Nevertheless, it is undeniable that unlike the recent Asian immigrants who are grouped together by geographical origin and often by skin color but speak mutually unintelligible languages (sometimes even the dialects within a country are mutually unintelligible), the Spanish-speaking segment of the Hispanics does share a common language. This fact has given Hispanics the image of being a unified minority and created a fear among the uninformed that Spanish is well on its way to superseding English as a common language in the United States.

It is also true that taken as a group, Spanish speakers have been very language-retentive. Apart from the historical status of Spanish as a colonial language and the geographical proximity of the American Southwest and Southeast to Spanish-speaking areas (discussed in an earlier section of this chapter), we can identify many factors contributing to language maintenance that are familiar from our discussion of European immigration during the 1880–1920 period. Many Hispanic immigrants are sojourners and (especially for agricultural workers) cyclical immigrants. The relative ease and affordability of modern travel have made back-and-forth movement more common than in the age of steamship and railroad travel. In addition, concentration in "barrios" or ethnic enclaves is widespread, facilitating intragroup interaction in the ethnic language. Spanish speakers are among the most severely excluded from economic participation in the United States; shift to English has therefore been retarded by low social mobility and limited economic rewards. Ideological mobilization through language is particularly strong in situations where racism and discrimination are felt acutely. For example, the Puerto Ricans are U.S. citizens who can freely migrate back and forth; however, whereas in their homeland the Puerto Ricans have been socialized into an expectation of being treated as citizens, on the mainland they quickly realize that they are treated as foreigners (Moore and Pachon 1985:46). This consciousness of being a minority discriminated against by a hostile, English-dominant world reinforces the retention of Spanish. Finally, for political refugees like those from Cuba and Central America, the ethnic language is a symbol of their past and their struggles and therefore tends to be retained; this is particularly true if they have any hope of returning to their homeland.

Despite these conditions fostering language retentiveness, Hispanics are not impervious to the English language, as many English-only proponents have charged. In this, again, Hispanics do not show any new pattern that one cannot recognize from America's historical experience with immigration. Veltman (1983:54) notes that "there is no evidence which would suggest that immigrants in [the Spanish] language group resist the adoption of the English language as the principal language of use." What distinguishes the Spanish language group from the other language minorities (except the Navajos) "is not the lower rates of anglicization which has been found," but rather "the fact that anglicization more frequently takes the form of English bilingualism" (i.e., more frequent than a complete shift to English monolingualism; Veltman 1983:90). "Spanish is retained largely because of the continuing in-migration of monolingual Spanish speakers" (Larmouth 1987:49); thus a singling out of Hispanics by curtailing their language would only "increase a risk which is at present minimal—a risk of disenfranchising a significant number of people, perhaps sufficiently to give rise to the very disunity that we fear" (Larmouth 1987:55).

CONCLUSION

From this overview of precolonial to present times, we can see how the American linguistic mosaic has been changing in response to various historical factors, in particular immigration, in complex processes in which factors affecting both language maintenance and language shift interact with each other.

Two decades after the liberalization of immigration laws in 1965, the United States is again entering a period of nativism, with a concomitant upsurge of public interest in language issues masking concern over the changing demographics, domestic development, and world role of the United States. America's defeat in the Vietnam War, years of economic recession, intense economic competition from abroad, and a general awareness of the nation's declining influence as a world leader have all contributed to a renewal of nativist sentiments. As occurred after World War I, English speakers demand legislation restricting immigration (the Immigration Reform and Control Act was passed in 1986) as well as promoting the supremacy of English.

Is the post-1965 immigration so different from earlier immigration as to justify fears of some impending national disaster? Certainly differences do exist, but they do not significantly alter the basic language situation of the United States, which, as we have seen, is that of a multilingual nation in which English nevertheless plays a universally recognized dominant role. Moreover, technological innovations, new to the twentieth century, that may reinforce ethnic language maintenance also function to preserve the ascendency of English. For example, modern means of transportation and mass media technology, which allow immigrants to keep in close touch with their homelands and their ethnic languages, are also a potent means of disseminating the English language and American culture throughout the world.

Perhaps the current negative reaction many nativists have to recent immigrants is a function of perceived differences. As we have seen, "newcomer'' is a relative concept, and so is ''difference'': in comparison to the Protestant English speakers, the Catholic Irish immigrants were intruders; but to English speakers in general, the southeastern European immigrants were foreign. Now, in comparison with the immigrants during the 1880–1920 ''Great Wave,'' who were at least from the Old World, contemporary Asian and Hispanic immigrants are threateningly alien, bringing a bewildering variety of languages and swelling the ranks of a single, historically well-established minority language, respectively.

Commenting on recent immigration, Bouvier and Gardner (1986:46) observe:

> One thing is clear: The nation's ethnic composition is again changing dramatically. This is an opportunity and a challenge. As one writer puts it: ''America is a country that endlessly reinvents itself, working the alchemy that turns 'them' into 'us'. That is the American secret: motion, new combinations, absorption. The process is wasteful, dangerous, messy, sometimes tragic. It is also inspiring.''

The following chapters of this book will address the question of how the ''alchemy that turns 'them' into 'us' '' has been and will be shaping the language situation of new immigrant groups.

EXPLORING THE IDEAS

1. Molesky's article contains Conklin and Lourie's comprehensive table on factors encouraging language retention and language loss.

Select one particular minority language group, either one discussed in the article or one with which you are familiar, and discuss the group in terms of each of the categories included in the table.

2. According to Heath and Mandabach, cited in Molesky, the United States imposes restrictions on minority language use not through an explicit policy but ''through the unwritten laws of institutions'' or ''norms of behavior.''

What are some ways in which members of a linguistic minority may feel ''unwritten'' restrictions on the use of their ethnic language? What factors in American society (both historical and contemporary) make it possible to have linguistic conformity without legal enforcement? Why do Heath and Mandabach say it is harder to change silent codes of linguistic behavior than to challenge written laws curtailing the language rights of minorities?

3. The need to attract new immigrants from diverse nations is cited by several scholars as one of the reasons early national leaders decided against making English the official language of the United States.

Over the last two centuries, American's need for immigrants has clearly undergone many changes, both in scope and in nature. Do you think the United States' language policy should be determined, at least in part, by its immigration policy? Why or why not?

4. Molesky notes that, throughout U.S. history, "periods of public debate over language rights for linguistic minorities have also been periods of insecurity in the national mood."

Why do you think there is such a strong connection between public debates on language and insecurity in the national mood? Another way of phrasing the question is: Why does public interest in language issues subside when the national mood is confident? Can you find specific examples of nativist sentiments in contemporary American society?

5. According to Molesky, many of the immigrants who came at the end of the nineteenth century were members of ethnic minority groups who left their homeland because of oppression by the majority culture. Furthermore, they tended to be young and unskilled laborers, many of whom were coming only as sojourners.

Discuss how each of these factors could have affected the late nineteenth century immigrants' language retention and language loss.

6. Molesky notes that the "new immigrants" of the early 1900s became the scapegoats for social problems. The sheer number of newcomers and the fact that they were ethnically different led many Americans to view them as the root of all social problems.

What parallels exist with the "new immigrants" of the present day? Do you see any evidence of recent newcomers being viewed as the source of social ills?

7. Molesky refers to the fact that by 1919 15 states had passed legislation that stated that English must be used at all public and private gatherings. The current English-only movement is also attempting to legislate the use of English.

What social factors in the early twentieth century and at the present time do you think are contributing to the perceived need to legislate the use of English?

APPLYING THE IDEAS

1. Many Americans assume that it is "natural" for immigrants to lose their ethnic languages and shift to the indigenous one(s). However, in the world context, sometimes the indigenous languages are displaced.

Research examples of language shift in both these directions. Compare and contrast them with the situation in the United States. Then compile a list of possible factors that can determine the outcome of contact between an indigenous language and an immigrant language.

2. Molesky points out that with several immigrant groups, such as the French and the Germans, language maintenance efforts were aided by the establishment of ethnic presses.

Select several ethnic newspapers available in your area. For each newspaper find out when it began, how large its present circulation is, and how this compares with its earlier circulation. Carefully examine one issue of each newspaper to determine in what contexts English is used and in what contexts the minority language is used.

3. As Molesky notes, to obtain citizenship, an applicant must demonstrate a basic level of proficiency in English.

Contact the Immigration and Naturalization Service branch in your community to investigate how candidates for naturalization are tested for English proficiency. Find out what support services exist to help minority applicants prepare for the test.

NOTES

1. While the beginning of the English-only movement is difficult to date precisely, we might consider 1981 (when S. I. Hayakawa introduced the first of a series of proposed constitutional amendments to make English the official language of the United States) and 1983 (when U.S. English, a national organization to promote the status of English, was founded) as marking its rise in national visibility.

2. This view is challenged by Gerda Bikales, executive director of U.S. English (Bikales 1986:78–79); however, she has not provided new evidence concerning views on language rights in the early national period.

3. The term is, of course, relative, and ultimately political and economic power rather than length of residence determines who would be perceived as "newcomers" with no claim to the land. The colonists were newcomers from the point of view of Native Americans; Anglos were newcomers relative to the French speakers in Louisiana and the Spanish speakers in the Southwest; yet the popular expectation has been for these older groups to conform to English speakers. Irish Catholics were once the target of much restrictive legislation but have now largely blended into the dominant group. Fuchs (1983:293) sees American national identity as being defined in a combination of ideological, cultural–linguistic, racial, and class terms; "newcomers" are those who do not fit into the implicit definition of national identity at a given moment in history.

4. Only "Amerindian" languages will be discussed in this section.

5. These 1962 figures are the most recent systematic estimates available (personal communication, Professor Leanne Hinton, Department of Linguistics, University of California, Berkeley).

REFERENCES

Anderson, A. B. 1979. The survival of ethnolinguistics. In H. Giles and B. Saint-Jacques, eds., *Language and Ethnic Relations*. New York: Pergamon Press.

Bikales, G. 1986. Comment: the other side [on Marshall 1986]. *International Journal of the Sociology of Language* 60, 77–85.

Bonilla, F. and R. Campos. 1981. A wealth of poor. *Daedalus* 110.

Bouvier, L. and R. Gardner. 1986. Immigration to the U.S.: The unfinished story. *Population Bulletin*. 41:4 (November).

Chafe, W. L. 1962. Estimates regarding the present speakers of Native American Indian languages. *International Journal of American Linguistics* 28, 162–191.

Commons, J. R. 1967. *Races and Immigrants in America*. New York: August M. Kelley Publishers.

Conklin, N. F. and M. A. Lourie. 1983. *A Host of Tongues*. New York: The Free Press.

Deutsch, K. A. 1975. The political significance of linguistic conflicts. In J. Savard and R. Vigeault, eds., *Les États Multilingues*. Cited in Marshall 1986:14.

Dinnerstein, L. and D. Reimers. 1977. *Ethnic Americans: A History of Immigration and Assimilation*. New York: New York University Press.

Dorian, N. 1982. *The Loss of Language Skills*. Rowley, MA: Newbury House.

Ehrlich, P. R., L. Bilderbeck and A. H. Ehrlich. 1979. *The Golden Door: International Migration, Mexico and the United States*. New York: Ballantine.

Ferguson, C. A., and S. B. Heath, eds. 1981. *Language in the USA*. Cambridge: Cambridge University Press.

Fishman, J. A. et al. 1966. *Language Loyalty in the United States*. The Hague: Mouton Press.

Fishman, J. A. 1980. Language maintenance. In S. Thernstrom, ed., *Harvard Encyclopedia of American Ethnic Groups*. Cambridge, MA: Harvard University Press, 629–637.

Fuchs, L. H. 1983. Immigration, pluralism, and public policy: the challenge of the *pluribus* to the *unum*. In M. M. Kritz, ed., *U.S. Immigration and Refugee Policy: Global and Domestic Issues*. Lexington, MA: Lexington Books.

Gilbert, G. G. 1981. French and German: a comparative study. In C. A. Ferguson and S. B. Heath, eds., *Language in the USA*. Cambridge: Cambridge University Press. 257–272.

Glazer, N. 1978. The process and problems of language maintenance: An integrative review. In M. A. Lourie and N. F. Conklin, eds., *A Pluralistic Nation: The Language Issue in the United States*. Rowley, MA: Newbury House. 32–42.

Gordon, M. M. 1964. *Assimilation in American Life: The Role of Race, Religion and National Origins*. New York: Oxford University Press.

Hagan, W. T. 1961. *American Indians*. Chicago: University of Chicago Press.

Haugen, E. 1956. *Bilingualism in the Americas: A Bibliography and Research Guide*. University of Alabama, American Dialect Society 26 (November).

Heath, S. B. 1976. A national language academy? Debate in the new nation. *International Journal of the Sociology of Language* 11, 9–43.

Heath, S. B. 1977. Language and politics in the United States. In M. Saville-Troike, ed., *Linguistics and Anthropology: Georgetown University Roundtable on Languages and Linguistics 1977*. Washington, D.C.: Georgetown University Press.

Heath, S. B. 1981. English in our language heritage. In C. A. Ferguson and S. B. Heath, eds., *Language in the USA*. Cambridge: Cambridge University Press. 6–20.

Heath, S. B. and F. Mandabach. 1983. Language status decisions and the law in the United States. In J. Corbarrubias and J. A. Fishman, eds., *Progress in Language Planning: International Perspectives*. Berlin: Mouton. 87–105. (Originally published in 1978 by Washington: National Institute of Education.)

Henry III, W. A. 1983. Against a confusion of tongues. *Time* June 13, 30–31.

Higham, J. 1955. *Strangers in the Land: Patterns of American Nativism, 1860–1925*. New Brunswick, NJ: Rutgers University Press.

Kallen, H. M. 1915. Democracy versus the melting pot. *The Nation* Feb. 15, and 18, 1915. Revised version reprinted as *Culture and Democracy in the U.S.* New York: Boni and Liveright, 1924.

Keller, G. D. 1983. What can language planners learn from the Hispanic experience with corpus planning in the United States? In J. Cobarrubias and J. A. Fishman, eds., *Progress in Language Planning: International Perspectives*. Berlin: Mouton Press. 253–265.

Kessner, T. and B. B. Caroli. 1982. *Today's Immigrants: Their Stories*. New York: Oxford University Press.

Kloss, H. 1966. German-American language maintenance efforts. In Fishman et al, eds., *Language Loyalty in the United States*. The Hague: Mouton Press. 206–252.

Kloss, H. 1977. *The American Bilingual Tradition*. Rowley, MA: Newbury House.

Kloss, H. 1986. Comment [on Marshall 1986]. *International Journal of the Sociology of Language* 60, 169–175.

Krickus, R. 1976. *Pursuing the American Dream: White Ethnics and New Populism*. Bloomington, IN: Indiana University Press.

Larmouth, D. W. 1987. Does linguistic heterogeneity erode national unity? In W. A. Van Horne and T. V. Tonnesen, eds., *Ethnicity and Language*. Milwaukee, WI: University of Wisconsin System Institute on Race and Ethnicity. 37–57.

Lavender, D. 1972. *California: Land of New Beginnings*. Lincoln, NE: University of Nebraska Press.

Leibowicz, J. 1985. The proposed English language amendment: Shield or sword? *Yale Law and Policy Review* 3:2, 519–550.

Leibowitz, A. H. 1984. The official character of language in the United States: Literacy requirements for immigration, citizenship, and entrance into American life. *Aztlan* 15:1, 25–70.

Li, C. 1983. The basic grammatical structures of selected Asian languages and English. In M. Chu-Chang, ed., *Asian- and Pacific-American Perspectives in Bilingual Education: Comparative Research*. New York: Teachers College Press, Columbia University, 3–30.

Lyman, S. 1970. *The Asian in the West*. Social Science and Humanities Publication No. 4. Reno, NV: Western Studies Center, Desert Research Institute, University of Nevada System.

Marshall, D. F. 1986. The question of an official language: Language rights and the English Language Amendment. *International Journal of the Sociology of Language* 60, 7–75.

McFadden, B. J. 1983. Bilingual education and the law. *Journal of Law and Education* 12:1, 1–27.

Moore, J. and H. Pachon. 1985. *Hispanics in the United States*. Englewood Cliffs, NJ: Prentice-Hall.

Portes, A. and R. C. Bach. 1985. *Latin Journey*. Berkeley, CA: University of California Press.

Rawls, J. J. 1984. *Indians of California: A Changing Image*. Norman, OK: University of Oklahoma Press.

Reimers, D. M. 1984. South and East Asian immigration into the United States: From exclusion to inclusion. *Immigrants and Minorities* 3:1, 30–48.

Reimers, D. M. 1985. *Still the Golden Door: The Third World Comes to America*. New York: Columbia University Press.

Rosenblum, G. 1973. *Immigrant Workers*. New York: Basic Books.

Ruhlen, M. 1987. Voices from the past. *Natural History* 96:3, 6–11.

Sachar, H. M. 1958. *The Course of Modern Jewish History*. New York: Dell Publications.

Schlossman, S. L. 1983. Is there an American tradition of bilingual education? German in the public elementary schools, 1840–1919. *American Journal of Education* 91 139–186 (February).

Sowell, T. 1981. *Ethnic America*. New York: Basic Books.

Taylor, P. 1971. *The Distant Magnet*. London: Eyre & Spotteswoode.

Thomas, W. I. and F. Znaniecki. 1984. *The Polish Peasant in Europe and America*. Chicago, IL: University of Illinois Press.

Thernstrom, S. 1973. *The Other Bostonian*. Cambridge, MA: Harvard University Press.

Veltman, C. 1983. *Language Shift in the United States*. Berlin: Mouton Press.

Wagner, S. T. 1981. America's non-English heritage. *Society* 19, 37–44.

Weimer, W. P. 1980. Factors affecting native language maintenance. In R. V. Padilla, ed., *Ethnoperspectives in Bilingual Education Research,* Vol. 2: *Theory in Bilingual Education*. Ypsilanti, MI: Bilingual/Bicultural Education Program, East Michigan State University, 35–46.

Will, G. F. 1985. In defense of the mother tongue. *Newsweek* July 8, 78.

Wong, S. C. 1987. The language needs of school-age Asian immigrants and refugees in the United States. In W. A. Van Horne and T. V. Tonnesen, eds., *Ethnicity and Language*. Milwaukee, WI: University of Wisconsin System Institute on Race and Ethnicity. 124–159.

CHAPTER

3

Language Minorities in the United States in the 1980s: The Evidence from the 1980 Census

Dorothy Waggoner

INTRODUCTION

The United States is a multilingual country. One person in seven in the United States either speaks a language other than English at home or lives with family members who do. In New Mexico nearly half the population belongs to a language minority group. In Hawaii more than a third do. In four other states, at least one in four people is a member of a language minority group. These people are predominantly native-born. More than two-thirds of all language-minority people, and nearly three out of five of the people who speak languages other than English at home, identified in the 1980 Census, were born in the United States.

In the 1980 Census, household respondents reported that 23.1 million people speak languages other than English at home. They reported that 9 million other people who only speak English at home lived in families in which one or more family members speak languages other than English and that there were 2.6 million children under age 5 one or both of whose parents speak a non-English language. Language minority people numbered 34.6 million out of a total United States population of 226.5 million in 1980.

Since 1980, more than 2.7 million people have legally emigrated to the United States from countries in which languages other than English are spoken. An unknown number of other people have entered the United States without documentation, fleeing political turmoil in their home countries or seeking, as immigrants have always sought, a chance for a better economic life. These immigrants have added to the numbers of language minority people in the United States. They and their children enrich the language resources of the United States.

This chapter will discuss the various concepts that have been and continue to be used to document cultural and linguistic diversity in the United States in decennial censuses. It will then examine the information about language minorities in the United States provided by the 1980 Census of Population and the information from the Immigration and Naturalization Service (INS) on post-1980 legal immigrants from countries in which languages other than English are spoken. Working from the Census data, it will investigate the language backgrounds, geographic distribution, nativity, and current language usage of language minorities in the United States. It will discuss their age and sex distribution and make some inferences about the relative language maintenance and language shift of the various groups based upon who speaks the non-English language and who only speaks English at home, the proportion of language minority families in which all family members speak the non-English language (the linguistically homogeneous families), and the self-ratings of English-speaking ability of members of the various groups. Finally, it will discuss the implications of the findings for bilingual education and other special educational programs in U.S. schools in the 1980s.

Sources and Reliability of the Census Data

The source of the language minority data in this chapter is the 1980 Census of Population. The Census language data are contained in *1980 Census of Population, Volume 1, Characteristics of the Population, Chapter D, Detailed Population Characteristics,* Part 1 of which is the *U.S. Summary* (Bureau of the Census 1984a) and Parts 2 to 52 of which are the parts for the individual states and the District of Columbia (Census 1983b). Data on race and ethnicity are contained in *Chapter C, General Social and Economic Characteristics* with parts similar to those of Chapter D for the *U.S. Summary,* the states, and the District of Columbia (Bureau of the Census 1983a).

The language questions asked in the 1980 Census were contained on the long form of the Census, which was completed by about 18 percent of households nationwide. The estimates were derived from the responses of this sample, not all U.S. households. Thus, the estimated numbers may vary from the numbers that would result had the same questions been asked for every household on the short form of the Census, which was completed by 100 percent of households. The possible variation of the numbers estimated from a sample of the total population from the "true" numbers realized from a count of the total population is called the standard error. It is greater, proportionally, the smaller the size of the group estimated.

The Census Bureau provides complete descriptions of the methodology used in the Census and tables of standard errors, as well as formulas and factors for calculating standard errors for given characteristics, such as language usage and ability to speak English (see Bureau of the Census 1984a:C-1-D-9). Applying the standard error formula and the factor for language usage to the estimated total number of language minority people in the United States in 1980—34.6 million—yields a "true" number of such people of between 34,598,000 and 34,675,000 at the 95 percent level of confidence (plus or minus two standard errors). By the same process, we can be 95 percent certain that the "true" number of Japanese language minority people—estimated to be 542,000—is between 536,000 and 547,000.

Information gained from decennial censuses, whether collected from all households or from a sample of households, is subject to various kinds of other potential errors. If households or certain types of individuals are missed, there will be an undercount. One group that probably was not completely counted in 1980, with a resulting underestimate of language minority people, consists of workers and others who have entered the United States without work permits, visas, or other legal documentation. The Bureau of the Census believes that about 2 million of these people were included in the 1980 Census counts (Warren and Passel 1983). Unknown numbers of other undocumented immigrants were missed.

Another type of nonsampling error that may lead to underreporting or overreporting of certain characteristics results from sociopsychological factors. If the respondents belong to a minority group, their responses to questions in surveys and censuses may be influenced by the position or perceived position of that group in the broader society. Their responses may be influenced by the extent to which they believe that the information is personal and privileged. Responses to questions about language behavior are especially sensitive. Respondents may be unwilling to provide information about the non-English languages used at home. They may feel that it is somehow un-American to admit that they speak languages other than English in the United States or they may consider that, as an Asian immigrant once put it, "it would be impolite to say that you didn't speak the language of the country which had received you." Respondents may be reluctant to provide information about the ability of household members to speak the national language.

Responses to questions in surveys and censuses are influenced by the way in which the information is gathered. In its monthly Current Population Survey (CPS) in November, 1979, the Census Bureau tried out the 1980 Census language questions. The data were gathered largely in telephone interviews. Respondents reported to CPS interviewers that 18 million people, aged 5 and older, speak languages other than English at home (Census 1982:14). Four months later, the respondents to the Census, who recorded their answers in the privacy of their homes and mailed the forms to the Bureau, reported that 23.1 million people, aged 5 and older, spoke languages other than English at home. Ninety-three percent of the difference between these two estimates is accounted for by the increase in the numbers of people reported to speak English very well or well. When respondents were asked about the language usage of these people in the CPS interviews, they reported that they only spoke English at home.

A discussion of the advantages and problems of using data from national censuses for sociolinguistic study is contained in Lieberson (1966).

Sources of the INS Data

The data on legal immigrants since 1980 come from the *Statistical Yearbooks* of the INS for fiscal years 1980, 1981, 1982, 1983, 1984, and 1985. INS provides complete counts of the immigrants admitted each year by country of birth and age. It does not collect any information about language background or usage. Therefore, countries of birth in which languages other than English are spoken are used as a surrogate measure of the language background of immigrants and the totals vary accordingly. Except in the case of people born in Canada, the numbers of immigrants from bilingual or multilingual countries have not been allocated by language spoken. This results in an undercount for certain groups of countries. For example, if they could be allocated by language, some Swiss immigrants would be added to the French-speaking, German-speaking, and Italian-speaking totals; Belgian immigrants would be divided between French-speaking and Dutch-speaking countries. The numbers of Canadian immigrants have been allocated between the totals for English-speaking and French-speaking countries because the 1980 Census provides the percentage of people born in Canada who speak a language other than English—presumably French—at home (Census 1984b). Use of the country of birth as a surrogate for language background can also result in an overcount if the language background of immigrants is not that associated with their countries of birth. A case is that of some immigrants from Vietnam who are ethnic Chinese and speak a Chinese language.

Based on the assumption that the number of immigrants who arrived between April 1, when the Census was taken, and September 30, 1980, was the same as the number who arrived between October 1, 1979, and March 31, 1980, the data for fiscal year 1980, October 1, 1979, to September 30, 1980, were divided in half. The numbers of immigrants who arrived in the United States during fiscal years 1980 to 1985 have been averaged by year of age to produce estimates of the numbers of post-Census immigrant children, aged 5–17, and adults, aged 18–64, in 1985.

INFORMATION ON CULTURAL AND LINGUISTIC DIVERSITY IN DECENNIAL CENSUSES

The concept of language minority is only one of several used to identify cultural and linguistic diversity in American society in decennial censuses. Some of these concepts are discussed in this section. The relationship of the concepts used in the 1980 Census to each other is expressed in Figure 3.1.

Race, Ethnicity, and Nativity

Race and nativity are the traditional indicators of cultural or ethnic diversity in decennial censuses. Racial/ethnic groups overlap with groups identified by their language characteristics but are not identical. Thus, 716,000 people identified themselves as racially Japanese in the 1980 Census; 542,000 people, 336,000 of whom speak Japanese at home, belonged to the Japanese language minority group in 1980. There were 6.9 million people who claimed Italian ancestry; 2.6 million people belonged to the Italian language minority group, 1.6 million of whom use Italian at home. Japanese language minority people were not necessarily of Japanese race, nor were Italian language minority people necessarily of Italian ancestry, although probably most, in both cases, were.

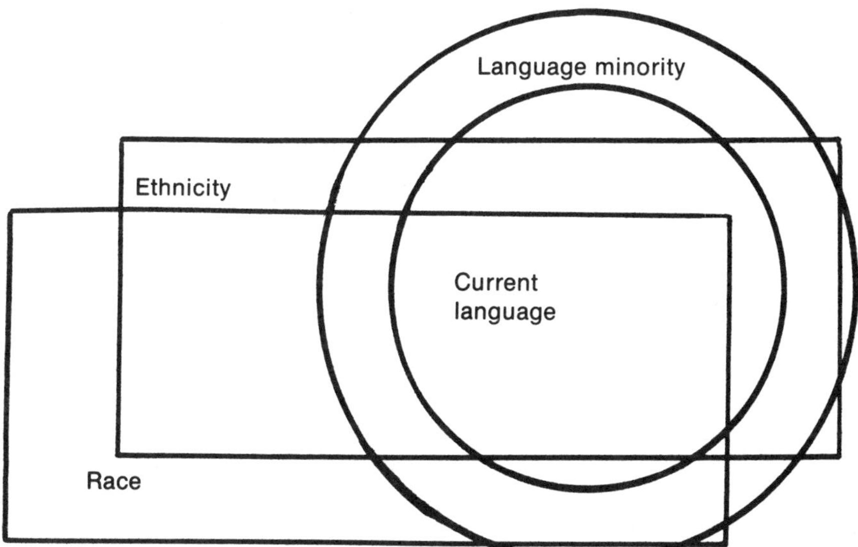

Figure 3.1. Relationship of concepts of cultural and linguistic diversity to each other.

Questions on race go back to the beginning of the Census in 1790, when a count was taken of the number of "free white males of 16 years and upward," "free white males under 15 years," "free white females," "all other free persons" and "slaves" (Bureau of the Census 1979:8). In early censuses, the census taker identified the race of the people being enumerated. Since 1960, when Census forms were mailed to households for the first time and household respondents were expected to answer the questions in writing, responses to the race question have been based upon self-identification (Levin, McKenney and Berman 1984). All of the 1980 Census forms contained a question asking the household respondents to identify each member of the household as white, black or Negro, Japanese, Chinese, Filipino, Korean, Vietnamese, Indian (American), Asian Indian, Hawaiian, Guamanian, Samoan, Eskimo, Aleut, or Other. As in past decennial censuses, the responses to this question provide identifiers for information about the Asian and Pacific Islander, American Indian, Eskimo, and Aleut racial groups comparable to that about the white majority and blacks in the 1980 Census (Bureau of the Census 1983a).

Ethnicity, usually meaning European ethnicity, was traditionally identified through the use of questions concerning the nativity of individuals and their parents, that is, whether they were born in the United States or in a selected foreign country (see Bureau of the Census 1973). This limited the size of the ethnic groups to estimates of the size of the foreign stock: the numbers of foreign-born people and the people with foreign-born or mixed foreign-born and native-born parentage. It did not identify native-born people of native-born parentage with loyalty to their national origins or ancestry. In 1980 a new question was introduced: "What is this person's ancestry?" Responses to this question on the 1980 Census sample form provide identifiers used in the comparisons of the characteristics of selected European ancestry or ethnic groups with those of the racial groups identified through responses to the race question (Bureau of the Census 1983a).

Because of the importance of information on the Hispanic population, as the largest ethnic minority group in the United States, the Census added a Hispanic self-identification question to the 1970 Census form sent to five percent of households nationally. It began gathering information on Hispanics on a regular basis, using a standard self-identification question, early in the 1970s, as described in the Current Population Report, *Persons of Spanish Origin in the United States: March 1973* (Bureau of the Census 1974). In the 1980 Census a separate question, "Is this person of Spanish/Hispanic origin or descent?" with response options for Mexican, Mexican American, or Chicano; Puerto Rican; Cuban, and other Spanish/Hispanic was included on all Census forms. Most of the information provided for the white majority and for blacks in 1980 Census publications is also provided for persons of Spanish origin with the stipulation that they may be of any race.

Mother Tongue

The traditional source of information about linguistic diversity in the United States is the mother tongue question: "What language was spoken in this person's home when he or she was a child?" It was first asked in 1910. Because it was assumed that only immigrants or their children maintained non-English mother tongues in the United States, the question was not asked of the entire population until 1940. In that year 21.8 million white people reported non-English mother tongues. In 1970, when it was asked again for the entire population, 30.3 million people of all races reported non-English mother tongues (Waggoner 1981:498). Since the mother tongue question does not provide information on current usage and does not appear to lead logically to information on the number of people who may have difficulties in English, it was decided to substitute questions on current language usage in the 1980 Census. The mother tongue question and the 1980 Census language questions were asked in the November 1979 CPS. In November, 1979, 32.4 million people, aged 14 and older, reported non-English mother tongues and 15.4 million in the same age group reported that they currently speak non-English languages at home (Bureau of the Census 1982:14).

Because the 1980 Census did not ask the mother tongue question, counts of language minorities from the 1980 Census do not include estimates of the number of people with non-English mother tongues who currently speak only English and live in families or households in which only English is spoken. By rights these people are members of language minority groups and should be included. Moreover, if their acquisition of English was influenced by home environments in which English was spoken infrequently or imperfectly and their educational opportunities were limited, some of them may experience difficulties with English and should be included in groups with special educational needs related to their language backgrounds. Estimates of the number of people who no longer speak their non-English mother tongues and live in English monolingual environments, whether or not they have limited English proficiency, cannot be derived directly from the 1980 Census.

Current Language Usage Questions

As indicated above, questions on current language usage were substituted for the mother tongue question in the 1980 Census. These questions, on the sample form, were as follows:

13a. Does this person speak a language other than English at home?
0 Yes 0 No, only speaks English—skip to 14

b. [If yes] What is this language?
c. How well does this person speak *English?*

0 Very well	0 Not well
0 Well	0 Not at all

The numbers of people who speak languages other than English at home—home speakers of non-English languages—can be directly estimated from the responses to questions 13a and b. By combining the responses for people in a given family or a given household, the numbers of people who belong to language minority groups or people with non-English language backgrounds (defined as people who speak languages other than English at home plus adults and children who only speak English at home living in families or in households in which one or more other people speak languages other than English at home,) can also be estimated from the responses to questions 13a and b. Use of the household as the unit of analysis produces a somewhat larger estimate. By counting English speakers in language minority families, there were 34.6 million language minority people in the United States in 1980. By counting English speakers in language minority households, there were 35.3 million language minority people. In this chapter, the language minority population is defined as people who speak non-English languages at home and English speakers who live in families in which one or more family members speak non-English languages, except in the discussion of language minorities by nativity, when they are defined as including English speakers in households in which one or more household members speak non-English languages.

English-Speaking Ability and Limited English Proficiency

The responses to the English-speaking ability question in the 1980 Census yield direct estimates of the minimum number of people who do not speak English at all, but not necessarily all of them, for the reasons cited in the section on the sources and reliability of the census data. They also make possible the construction of a measure of relative English-speaking ability of the groups of home speakers of various languages—the index of relative English-speaking ability (IRESA)—as follows: 600 points were allowed for each "very well" response, 400 for each "well" response, 200 for each "not well" response, and no points for each "not at all" response, and the results were averaged. The maximum IRESA is 600. The IRESAs and the proportions of non-English speakers in the various groups are used in this chapter to examine the potential relative need of the various groups for special educational programs such as bilingual education or English as a second language. They are also used as a part of the examination of the evidence for language maintenance and language shift.

Although the responses to the English-speaking ability question yield minimum estimates of the numbers of people in the United States who do not speak English at all and make possible the construction of the IRESAs, they do not yield estimates of the total numbers of language minority children and adults who have special needs related to their language backgrounds and proficiency in English. In addition to the mitigating factors in the use of census language data already cited, there are a number of specific reasons why estimates of the numbers of home speakers of non-English languages who speak English less than very well, as identified in the 1980 Census, are not the same as estimates of the numbers of language minority children and adults with limited English proficiency (LEPs). These are: (1) The question was not asked for everyone who is potentially limited in English proficiency. It was only asked for people who speak languages other than English at home. There are people who speak only English in language minority families who have difficulties with English related to their language backgrounds. Moreover, as indicated above in the discussion of the mother tongue question, some people with non-English mother tongues who no longer speak them and who now live in monolingual English-speaking environments may also have difficulties in English. (2) Respondents were only asked to rate English-speaking ability. English-speaking ability is only one of the language skills subsumed in the concept of English proficiency. Individuals who are proficient in English not only speak and understand English but also read and write the language. Reading and writing skills are crucial in school success or effective performance in all but the very lowest-level unskilled jobs. (3) If the household respondents rating their own and others' English-speaking ability are themselves speakers of English as a second language, they may be unable to determine how well the children and other adults speak English with native English speakers. They may have limited opportunities to observe the other household members interacting with native English speakers. (4) Estimates of the numbers of LEP people must be related to some objective standard of the degree of proficiency needed to succeed in school programs taught entirely in English or to achieve one's economic or social potential in English-speaking society. Estimates of the numbers of LEP people must be based upon objective testing with results correlated to a criterion measure.

Bilingualism

Bilingualism has been defined by Ferguson and Heath as "the use of two languages by the same person (individual bilingualism) or by the same social group (group, institutional, or societal bilingualism)" (1981:527). Using this definition, individuals identified in the 1980 Census who speak languages other than English at home and have some degree of ability to speak

English may be said to be bilingual. Similarly, all of the language minority families and households in which both English and a non-English language are spoken are bilingual. However, since the Census did not ask about ability to speak languages other than English, much less about literacy in other languages or in English, bilingual individuals, defined as those with proficiency in two languages or with an equal command of two languages, cannot be identified in the Census.

LANGUAGE MINORITIES IN THE UNITED STATES

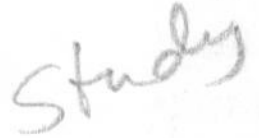

The Origins of Multilinguality

There are two main origins of multilinguality in the United States: (1) non-English-speaking populations already living in territories acquired by the United States and (2) voluntary immigration. Native Americans, Hispanics, and perhaps some French populations fall into the first group. Speakers of English and other European languages, such as German, Swedish, and Dutch, who settled on the eastern seaboard in the colonial period; speakers of these and other European languages, who emigrated in the nineteenth century and the first half of the twentieth century; and speakers of Asian languages, many of whom are recent arrivals, are members of the second group.

Native Americans inhabited this continent before Europeans colonized it. The 1980 Census data show that, despite all of the efforts to suppress them and their languages in the 200 years since the establishment of the United States, American Indians and Alaska Natives are more numerous today than they have been in earlier periods and they still speak some of the languages of their ancestors. Spanish-speaking populations became a part of the United States with the annexation of Texas in 1845, the territory that became the states of New Mexico, Colorado, Arizona, Utah, Nevada, and California 3 years later at the end of the Mexican War, and the island of Puerto Rico at the end of the Spanish–American War in 1898. The descendents of these populations have been joined by Cubans who began to come to the United States in large numbers after Fidel Castro took power in Cuba in 1959 and by other Spanish-speakers who have emigrated recently from Mexico, the Caribbean, and Central and South America. As shown by the 1980 Census data, the Spanish-speaking population is growing faster than the English-speaking majority population. French-speaking populations became a part of the United States with the Louisiana Purchase in 1803. They also came to United States territory as immigrants both before and after the American Revolution. Although the French-speaking group is the largest language minority group after Spanish, French-speaking families do not appear to be passing the language on to many of their children.

People from Europe predominated among immigrants until the end of the Second World War. From the time the INS began keeping records in 1820 until after the Civil War, the majority of immigrants were from English-speaking countries—the United Kingdom and Ireland—and the remainder were from Germany and northern Europe. In the 1880s, when more than 5 million people arrived here, nearly two-thirds were from non-English-speaking European countries, predominantly Germany and other northern European countries, and almost all the rest were from the English-speaking countries. During the decade of the greatest immigration in our history—the first decade of this century when nearly 9 million people arrived—more than four out of five immigrants were from non-English-speaking European countries. The majority of European immigrants from non-English-speaking countries were from eastern and southern Europe. Only 12 percent of the total immigrants were from English-speaking countries; 6 percent were from other areas of the world: Asia, Latin America, and the Caribbean.

Since the end of the Second World War, the character of immigration to the United States has changed. People from Latin America and the Caribbean began to constitute sizable proportions beginning in 1951. After the repeal of the Asian exclusion laws in the 1960s, Asians became a significant and increasing proportion of the total immigration. In the decade immediately preceding the Census, 1971–1980, 4.5 million people legally emigrated to the United States. Of these, 1.8 million (40 percent) came from Latin America and the Caribbean; 1.6 million (35 percent) came from Asian countries; fewer than a million altogether came from non-English-speaking European countries and from the United Kingdom, Ireland, Canada, and Newfoundland (INS 1982:2–4). The presence of these immigrants is reflected in the size of the various language minority groups identified in the 1980 Census and in their characteristics.

Language Minority Groups in 1980

According to the 1980 Census, there were 34.6 million language minority people in the United States in 1980. They constituted 15 percent of the total population: one person in seven. Of them 7.9 million were school-age children, 20.6 million were adults, and 2.6 million were children under age 5, all of whom lived in families in which they or other people spoke a language other than English at home. In addition, there were 3.5 million home speakers of non-English languages not living with family members.

The largest language-minority group are Spanish-speaking persons. Fifteen and a half million people—nearly 45 percent of all language minority people—belonged to this group in 1980. The French, German, Italian, and

Polish groups each had at least 1 million members. In all, 30 language minority groups in the United States in 1980 had at least 100,000 members each.

The majority of children, aged 5–17, in language minority families live in Spanish-speaking families. In 1980, the 4.2 million children of Spanish language background constituted 52 percent of the 7.9 million school-age children living in language minority families identified in the Census. No other group had as many as 1 million school-age children. There were 685,000 children in French-speaking families, 594,000 in German-speaking families and 437,000 in Italian-speaking families. There were between 100,000 and 200,000 children each living in families in which Filipino languages, Polish, Native American languages, Chinese languages, or Greek and Portuguese are spoken.

Data on the various language minority groups in the United States in 1980 are shown in Table 3.1.

Immigration Since 1980

The shift in immigration patterns has continued since 1980. Among the 3.1 million people who emigrated between April 1, 1980, when the Census was taken, and September 30, 1985, the largest group (43 percent or 1.3 million people) consisted of people born in countries in which Asian and Pacific Island languages are spoken. The second largest group and the largest from a single language background consisted of people born in Spanish-speaking countries: 824,000 or 26 percent. Fewer than 800,000 people altogether emigrated legally from English-speaking countries and countries in which other European languages are spoken.

There were at least 100,000 immigrants each from countries in which six Asian languages or related groups of Asian languages are spoken: Vietnam, the Philippines, Chinese-speaking countries, Korea, countries speaking Asian Indian languages, and Laos. The 257,000 immigrants from Vietnam doubled the potential size of the Vietnamese language minority; the 182,000 immigrants from Korea added nearly half again as many potential members of the Korean language minority, and the 222,000 immigrants from Chinese-speaking countries increased the potential size of the Chinese-speaking language minority group by 29 percent. The largest group from a non-Asian or Pacific Island country consisted of 88,000 immigrants born in countries in which Arabic is spoken. They increased the potential size of the Arabic language minority by 28 percent.

More than half a million school-age children have legally emigrated to the United States from non-English-speaking countries since the 1980 Census. Nearly 300,000 of them were born in countries in which Asian or Pacific Island languages are spoken. Three in ten were born in Spanish-speaking countries; one in ten was born in a country in which another European language is spoken. Among working-age adults, 46 percent were born in countries in which Asian and Pacific Island languages are spoken, 30 percent in Spanish-speaking countries, and 13 percent in countries in which other European languages are spoken.

Table 3.2 presents the information about people who immigrated legally to the United States between April 1, 1980, and September 30, 1985.

Geographic Distribution of Language Minorities

Language-minority people are widely distributed throughout the United States. They live in every state. In 1980, there were 41 states with at least 100,000 each. However, two-thirds of the 1980 language minority population lived in eight states: California, New York, Texas, Illinois, Florida, New Jersey, Pennsylvania, and Massachusetts.

Nearly seven million language minority people lived in California in 1980. Four and a half million lived in New York and 3.8 million in Texas. Illinois, Florida, New Jersey, Pennsylvania, and Massachusetts were home to at least a million each.

Of the 7.9 million school-age children in language minority families in 1980, 1.6 million lived in California, 1.1 million in Texas, and 926,000 in New York. Altogether, 16 states each had at least 100,000 school-age children living in language-minority families in 1980.

Table 3.3 shows the information on the estimated size of language minority groups in the various states and the District of Columbia in 1980.

Proportions of Language Minority Adults and Children

Language minorities are significant proportions of the population in six states, four of them in the Southwest. The most multilingual state is New Mexico, where people with non-English language backgrounds, predominantly Spanish-speaking or Native American, constituted nearly half the population in 1980. Language minorities constituted more than a third of the population in Hawaii. They constituted at least a quarter of the population in California, Arizona, Texas, and New York. In all, at least one person in ten in more than half the states and the District of Columbia in 1980 either spoke a language other than English at home or lived with family members who did. Figure 3.2 displays these proportions graphically.

One in six children, aged 5–17, in the United States comes from a non-English-language background. In New Mexico, more than half of school-age children had language minority backgrounds in 1980. A third or more of children in Hawaii, California, Arizona, and Texas had language minority backgrounds. In all, in 29 states and the District of Columbia the proportion

Table 3.1. ESTIMATED NUMBERS OF LANGUAGE-MINORITY PEOPLE IN THE UNITED STATES, BY AGE GROUP, ENGLISH OR NON-ENGLISH LANGUAGE (NEL) SPOKEN AT HOME, AND LANGUAGE: 1980 (NUMBERS IN THOUSANDS)

		People living in language minority families[a]							
			Aged 5–17			Aged 18 and older			
Language	Total	Children <5[b]	Total	Speak English	Speak NEL	Total	Speak English	Speak NEL	Other home speakers of NELs
Total	34,637	2,562	7,948	3,466	4,482	20,616	5,549	15,067	3,511
Spanish	15,548	1,537	4,164	1,284	2,879	8,472	1,610	6,862	1,375
French	2,937	147	685	468	218	1,776	772	1,004	328
German	2,834	120	594	401	193	1,773	727	1,046	348
Italian	2,627	86	437	285	152	1,871	637	1,233	233
Polish	1,285	31	166	123	43	916	310	606	172
Chinese languages	769	58	152	37	115	476	44	432	84
Filipino languages	713	70	168	104	63	423	64	359	52
Greek	548	33	108	42	66	361	71	290	46
Japanese	542	26	98	65	33	358	114	244	59
American Indian or Alaska Native languages	512	54	155	66	89	262	59	203	41
Portuguese	480	34	103	36	67	307	57	249	35
Yiddish	430	16	41	22	20	290	76	214	83

Korean	384	40	95	36	60	224	42	182	25
Asian Indian languages	321	41	67	24	43	188	12	175	25
Arabic	312	32	64	26	38	179	37	142	38
Hungarian	266	8	37	25	12	186	55	131	36
Dutch	252	13	52	36	16	159	54	105	27
Vietnamese	250	27	75	14	61	122	15	107	27
Russian	232	10	34	15	20	152	34	117	36
Serbo-Croatian	211	10	35	16	19	146	35	110	21
Czech	194	5	26	21	5	134	46	87	29
Norwegian	184	5	26	19	7	120	48	72	34
Ukrainian	168	6	22	12	10	121	28	92	19
Swedish	163	5	22	15	7	103	43	60	33
Slovak	141	2	15	12	3	106	40	66	19
Armenian	127	6	20	7	13	89	14	75	12
Persian	138	10	24	7	17	76	14	63	28
Thai	127	17	31	11	21	66	14	52	13
Finnish	111	3	16	13	3	74	26	48	19
Lithuanian	104	2	11	8	3	73	21	52	17
Other languages	1,726	108	404	216	188	1,015	428	587	198

[a] Families in which one or more family members speak a non-English language at home.
[b] Children whose parents, one or both, speak a language other than English at home.
Note: Detail may not add to total because of rounding.
Source: 1980 Census of Population (Bureau of the Census 1984a).

Table 3.2. **ESTIMATED NUMBERS OF IMMIGRANTS ADMITTED TO THE UNITED STATES BETWEEN APRIL 1, 1980, AND SEPTEMBER 30, 1985, BY AGE GROUP IN 1985 AND COUNTRY OR GROUP OF COUNTRIES OF BIRTH WHERE SPECIFIC LANGUAGES ARE SPOKEN**

Country(ies) of birth	Total	Children 5 to 17 in 1985	Adults 18 to 64 in 1985
Total	3,130,000	639,000	2,236,000
Born in English-speaking countries[a]	380,000	86,000	271,000
Born in Spanish-speaking countries[b]	824,000	173,000	597,000
Born in countries in which other European languages are spoken	338,000	55,000	255,000
Haiti	47,000	9,000	36,000
Soviet Union	45,000	8,000	30,000
Germany and Austria	40,000	6,000	31,000
Poland	39,000	6,000	31,000
Portuguese-speaking countries[c]	39,000	8,000	27,000
French-speaking countries[d]	24,000	4,000	18,000
Italy[e]	21,000	3,000	16,000
Greece	19,000	2,000	15,000
Romania	18,000	3,000	13,000
Yugoslavia	9,000	1,000	7,000
Dutch-speaking countries[f]	8,000	1,000	6,000
Czechoslovakia	6,000	1,000	4,000
Sweden	5,000	1,000	4,000
Hungary	4,000	*	3,000
Denmark and Greenland	3,000	*	2,000
Norway	2,000	*	2,000
Finland	2,000	*	1,000
Other countries[g]	9,000	1,000	7,000
Born in countries in which Asian and Pacific Island languages are spoken	1,339,000	293,000	913,000
Vietnam	257,000	75,000	170,000
Philippines	242,000	43,000	167,000
Chinese-speaking countries[h]	222,000	38,000	158,000
Korea	182,000	39,000	117,000
Countries in which Asian Indian languages are spoken[i]	167,000	25,000	127,000
Laos	104,000	32,000	64,000
Kampuchea	71,000	21,000	45,000
Thailand	28,000	9,000	15,000
Japan	22,000	2,000	19,000
Afghanistan	12,000	3,000	9,000
Indonesia	6,000	1,000	4,000
Burma	5,000	1,000	4,000
Malaysia	5,000	1,000	4,000
Singapore	2,000	*	2,000
Other countries[j]	11,000	2,000	9,000
Born in other countries	248,000	32,000	201,000
Countries in which Arabic is spoken[k]	88,000	13,000	70,000

Table 3.2. *(Continued)*

Country(ies) of birth	Total	Children 5 to 17 in 1985	Adults 18 to 64 in 1985
Iran	68,000	8,000	56,000
Israel	18,000	4,000	13,000
Turkey	12,000	1,000	9,000
East African and Subsaharan African countries	58,000	7,000	50,000
Other countries[l]	3,000	*	2,000

* Fewer than an estimated 1,000 children.

[a] Anguilla, Antigua–Barbuda, Australia, The Bahamas, Barbados, Belize, Bermuda, British Virgin Islands, Canada (79.5% of total), Cayman Islands, Dominica, Grenada, Guyana, Ireland, Jamaica, Montserrat, New Zealand, St. Christopher–Nevis, St. Lucia, St. Vincent-Grenadines, Trinidad-Tobago, Turks and Caicos Islands, and the United Kingdom.

[b] Argentina, Bolivia, Chile, Colombia, Costa Rica, Cuba, Dominican Republic, Ecuador, El Salvador, Guatemala, Honduras, Mexico, Nicaragua, Panama, Paraguay, Peru, Spain, Uruguay and Venezuela.

[c] Brazil, Cape Verde, and Portugal.

[d] Canada (20.5% of total), France, French Guiana, Guadeloupe, Martinique, and Monaco.

[e] Includes San Marino.

[f] Netherlands, Netherlands Antilles, and Surinam.

[g] Albania, Andorra, Belgium, Bulgaria, Estonia, Gibraltar, Iceland, Latvia, Liechtenstein, Lithuania, Luxembourg, and Switzerland.

[h] China, Hong Kong, and Taiwan.

[i] Bangladesh, India, Nepal, Pakistan, and Sri Lanka.

[j] Bhutan, Brunei, Fiji, French Polynesia, Kiribati, Macau, New Caledonia, Niue, Pacific Island Trust Territories, Papua New Guinea, Solomon Islands, Tonga, Tuvalu, Vanuatu, and Western Samoa.

[k] Algeria, Bahrain, Egypt, Iraq, Jordan, Kuwait, Lebanon, Libya, Malta, Morocco, Oman, Qator, Saudi Arabia, Sudan, Syria, Tunisia, United Arab Emirates, Yemen (Aden), and Yemen (Sanaa).

[l] Cyprus and unknown or unreported countries of birth.

Note: Detail may not add to total because of rounding.

Sources: U.S. Department of Justice, Immigration and Naturalization Service (1980, 1981, 1982, 1983, 1984, and 1985).

of children who speak non-English languages at home or live in families in which non-English languages are spoken was at least one in ten in 1980.

Table 3.4 shows the estimated numbers of language minority populations and school-age populations as proportions of the populations of the various states and the District of Columbia in 1980.

Nativity of Language Minorities

The language minority population in the United States is predominantly native-born. Nearly three out of five of the people, aged 5 and older, who lived in language minority households in 1980, were born in one of the 50 states, the District of Columbia, Puerto Rico, or another outlying area. Of these 32.7 million people, 22.6 million were native-born and 10.1 million were foreign-born. There were 5.5 million language minority people who had emigrated to the United States prior to 1970 and 4.6 million who had emigrated in the decade immediately preceding the 1980 Census.

Table 3.3. ESTIMATED NUMBERS OF LANGUAGE-MINORITY PEOPLE IN THE UNITED STATES, BY AGE GROUP, ENGLISH OR NON-ENGLISH LANGUAGE (NEL) SPOKEN AT HOME, AND STATE: 1980 (NUMBERS IN THOUSANDS)

		People living in language minority families[a]							Other home speakers of NELs
			Aged 5–17			Aged 18 and older			
State	Total	Children <5[b]	Total	Speak English	Speak NEL	Total	Speak English	Speak NEL	
Total	34,637	2,562	7,948	3,466	4,482	20,616	5,549	15,067	3,511
California	6,915	624	1,640	591	1,049	3,943	734	3,208	708
New York	4,514	304	926	323	603	2,753	589	2,163	531
Texas	3,802	391	1,052	258	794	2,086	310	1,775	274
Illinois	1,805	137	392	161	231	1,090	285	804	186
Florida	1,634	87	310	110	200	1,053	227	826	183
New Jersey	1,594	100	336	134	203	1,022	264	758	136
Pennsylvania	1,293	60	253	143	110	841	328	513	140
Massachusetts	1,074	56	215	110	105	679	203	475	124
Michigan	954	53	204	125	79	596	215	381	101
Ohio	914	50	203	118	85	572	228	345	89
Arizona	727	74	200	72	127	397	77	320	57
Louisiana	699	44	174	125	49	425	146	279	56
Connecticut	637	35	133	63	69	406	120	286	64
New Mexico	618	62	170	60	109	341	47	294	45
Colorado	475	37	120	74	46	268	81	188	49
Washington	452	33	103	58	46	260	95	165	55
Wisconsin	438	22	90	57	33	266	108	158	61

Maryland	415	24	96	51	45	257	96	161	38
Virginia	392	27	95	53	42	229	91	138	41
Indiana	381	26	95	53	42	225	93	132	35
Minnesota	374	18	76	52	24	223	94	129	57
Hawaii	360	23	72	44	29	233	64	169	32
Georgia	277	18	71	44	27	163	81	82	25
Missouri	270	16	64	40	24	162	75	87	29
North Carolina	273	17	68	43	26	162	85	78	26
Oregon	227	17	52	30	22	128	49	78	30
Rhode Island	224	11	43	24	18	147	42	105	24
Oklahoma	212	17	53	33	20	120	49	70	22
Maine	187	10	42	30	13	114	35	79	21
Kansas	185	14	43	26	17	107	42	65	21
Utah	184	21	49	32	17	98	38	60	17
Tennessee	179	11	46	29	17	107	58	50	16
Iowa	174	10	40	25	15	102	47	55	22
South Carolina	157	10	42	27	15	91	49	42	14
New Hampshire	153	7	33	24	9	95	32	63	17
Alabama	152	9	39	25	14	92	51	41	12
Kentucky	132	9	34	21	12	78	42	36	12
Nebraska	124	8	26	18	9	74	30	44	16
Nevada	121	8	27	16	11	71	25	47	14
North Dakota	119	5	24	21	4	73	25	48	16
Mississippi	100	7	28	18	10	58	31	27	7
Idaho	88	9	23	13	9	46	18	29	10
Arkansas	85	6	22	14	8	51	26	25	7

(Continued)

Table 3.3. *(Continued)*

		People living in language minority families[a]							
			Aged 5–17			Aged 18 and older			
State	Total	Children <5[b]	Total	Speak English	Speak NEL	Total	Speak English	Speak NEL	Other home speakers of NELs
South Dakota	84	6	20	13	7	48	16	32	11
West Virginia	81	4	19	12	6	51	26	25	7
Alaska	74	7	20	10	10	40	11	28	8
Montana	71	5	16	11	5	42	17	24	8
District of Columbia	70	3	12	6	6	36	13	23	19
Vermont	58	3	13	10	4	36	15	21	7
Delaware	55	3	13	7	5	33	14	19	5
Wyoming	51	5	13	9	4	28	11	18	5

[a] Families in which one or more family members speak a non-English language at home.
[b] Children whose parents, one or both, speak a language other than English at home.
Note: Detail may not add to total because of rounding.
Source: 1980 Census of Population (Bureau of the Census 1983b, 1984a).

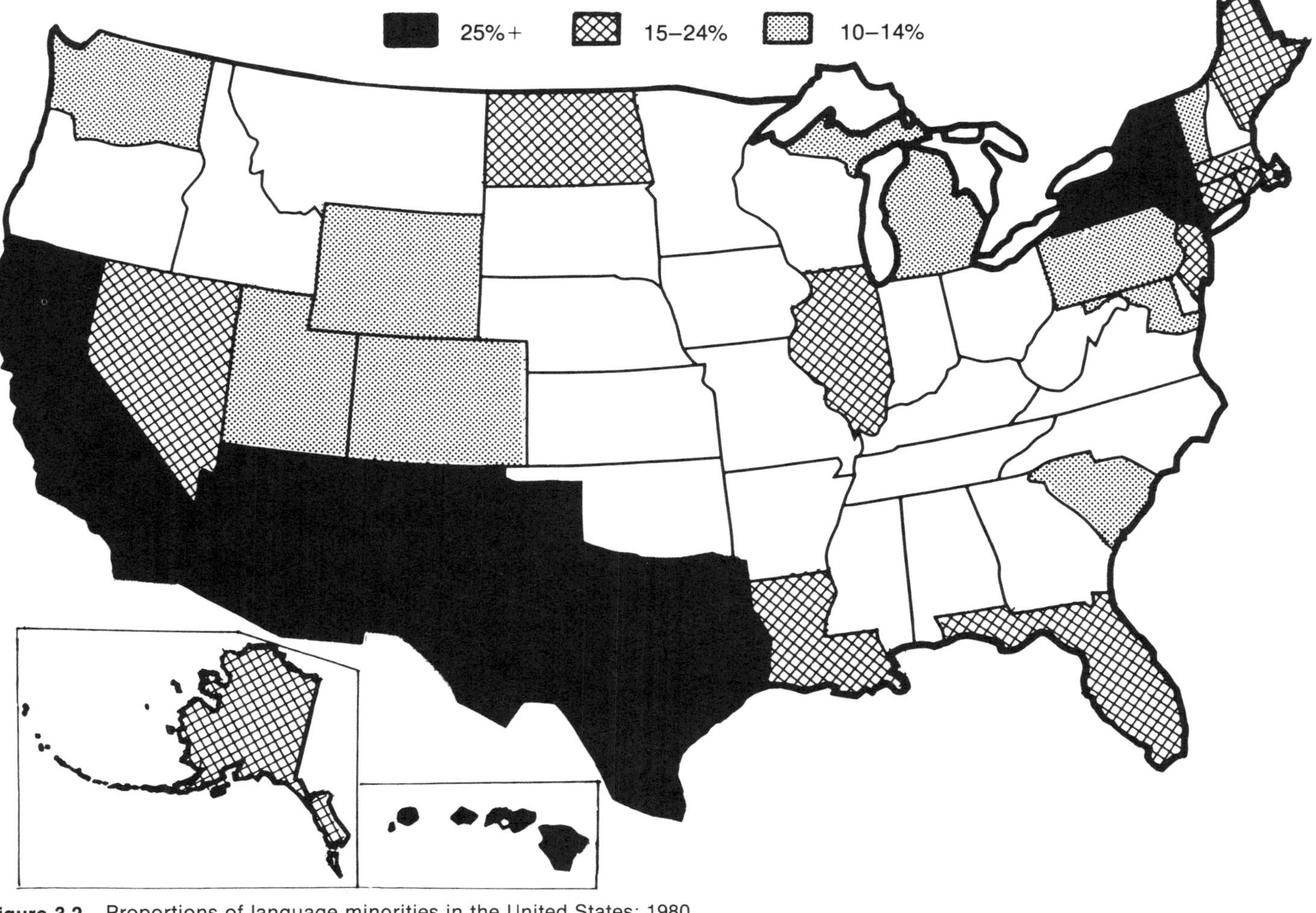

Figure 3.2. Proportions of language minorities in the United States: 1980

Table 3.4. ESTIMATED TOTAL POPULATION AND SCHOOL-AGE POPULATION AND NUMBERS AND PROPORTIONS OF LANGUAGE MINORITIES[a], BY STATE: 1980 (NUMBERS IN THOUSANDS)

State	Total population			Population, aged 5–17		
	Total	Language minority[a]	Proportion	Total	Language minority[a]	Proportion (%)
Total	266,546	34,637	15.3	47,494	8,034	16.9
New Mexico	1,302	618	47.5	303	171	56.4
Hawaii	964	360	37.4	198	73	36.9
California	23,637	6,915	29.3	4,685	1,665	35.5
Arizona	2,715	727	26.8	579	202	34.9
Texas	14,218	3,802	26.7	3,143	1,062	33.8
New York	17,546	4,514	25.7	3,560	936	26.3
Rhode Island	947	224	23.7	187	43	23.0
New Jersey	7,360	1,594	21.7	1,531	339	22.1
Connecticut	3,106	637	20.5	639	134	20.9
Massachusetts	5,734	1,074	18.7	1,155	216	18.7
Alaska	401	74	18.5	92	20	21.9
North Dakota	652	119	18.2	137	25	18.0
Florida	9,738	1,634	16.8	1,795	316	17.6
Maine	1,123	187	16.7	244	42	17.4
Louisiana	4,202	699	16.6	972	175	18.0
New Hampshire	920	153	16.6	196	33	16.9
Colorado	2,887	475	16.5	594	122	20.5
Illinois	11,418	1,805	15.8	2,407	395	16.4
Nevada	799	121	15.1	160	28	17.3
Utah	1,460	184	12.6	350	50	14.4
South Dakota	690	84	12.2	148	20	13.4
Vermont	511	58	11.4	110	13	12.2
District of Columbia	638	70	11.0	109	12	10.8
Pennsylvania	11,856	1,293	10.9	2,380	255	10.7
Washington	4,128	452	10.9	834	105	12.5
Wyoming	469	51	10.8	101	13	12.6
Michigan	9,254	954	10.3	2,068	205	9.9
Maryland	4,214	415	9.8	896	96	10.8
Wisconsin	4,703	438	9.3	1,013	90	8.9
Idaho	943	88	9.3	214	23	11.0
Minnesota	4,073	374	9.2	867	77	8.9
Delaware	594	55	9.2	125	13	10.1
Montana	786	71	9.0	167	16	9.8
Oregon	2,629	227	8.6	526	53	10.1
Ohio	10,790	914	8.5	2,308	204	8.8
Nebraska	1,569	124	7.9	325	27	8.2
Kansas	2,362	185	7.8	469	44	9.3
Virginia	5,343	392	7.3	1,114	96	8.6
Indiana	5,486	381	7.0	1,201	96	8.0
Oklahoma	3,023	212	7.0	623	53	8.6
Iowa	2,912	174	6.0	606	41	6.7
Missouri	4,912	270	5.5	1,011	64	6.4

Table 3.4. *(Continued)*

	Total population			Population, aged 5–17		
State	Total	Language minority[a]	Proportion	Total	Language minority[a]	Proportion (%)
Georgia	5,459	277	5.1	1,236	72	5.8
South Carolina	3,120	157	5.0	706	43	6.0
North Carolina	5,878	273	4.7	1,256	69	5.5
West Virginia	1,949	81	4.2	414	19	4.5
Tennessee	4,588	179	3.9	975	46	4.7
Alabama	3,892	152	3.9	868	39	4.5
Mississippi	2,519	100	3.9	602	28	4.7
Arkansas	2,285	85	3.7	496	22	4.5
Kentucky	3,658	132	3.6	802	34	4.3

[a] People living in families in which one or more members speak a non-English language at home and people who speak non-English languages at home not living with family members.

Note: Percentages calculated on unrounded numbers.

Sources: 1980 Census of Population (Bureau of the Census 1983b, 1984a).

Nativity and home language usage are closely related. Foreign-born people are much more likely than native-born people to speak non-English languages at home. In 1980, 97 percent of the adults and 90 percent of children who were foreign-born continued to speak the languages of their homelands in their U.S. households. In contrast, among people born in this country, 63 percent of adults and only half of the children spoke a non-English language.

Recent immigrants are more likely to live in language minority households than people who have been in the country at least 10 years, but time in the United States does not appear to affect the home language usage of those who continue living in such households. In 1980, 86 percent of the 1970–1980 immigrants, but only 65 percent of the pre-1970 immigrants, lived in language minority households. Ninety-six percent of the pre-1970 immigrants and 97 percent of the recent immigrants in language minority households in 1980 continued to speak the languages of their homelands.

Information on the nativity of the U.S. population, aged 5 and older, and of the language-minority population, defined as people who speak languages other than English at home and people living in households in which one or more other people speak non-English languages, is contained in Table 3.5.

Language Usage in Language-Minority Families

Language usage in language-minority families is related to age. Adults are more likely than children to speak non-English languages at home. The proportions of each group in comparison to the proportions who speak only

Table 3.5. ESTIMATED NUMBERS OF PEOPLE IN THE UNITED STATES, AGED 5 AND OLDER, BY LANGUAGE CHARACTERISTICS, AGE GROUP, NATIVITY, AND PERIOD OF IMMIGRATION OF THE FOREIGN-BORN: 1980 (NUMBERS IN THOUSANDS)

			Language minority (LM) population						
				Aged 5 to 17			Aged 18 and older		
Nativity and period of immigration	Total	Speak English in all-English environment[a]	Total	Total	Speak English in LM households[b]	Speak NEL	Total	Speak English in LM households[b]	Speak NEL
Total	210,247	177,503	32,745	8,123	3,555	4,568	24,621	6,130	18,492
Native-born	196,388	173,754	22,634	6,893	3,437	3,456	15,741	5,867	9,874
Foreign-born	13,859	3,749	10,110	1,230	118	1,112	8,880	263	8,617
Immigrated before 1970	8,520	3,024	5,496	199	36	164	5,296	202	5,094
Immigrated 1970-1980	5,340	725	4,614	1,030	82	948	3,584	61	3,523

NEL, non-English language.

[a] People who speak only English at home in households in which no one speaks a non-English language at home and people who speak only English at home not living in households as defined by the Census Bureau.

[b] People who speak English in households in which one or more people speak a language other than English at home.

Note: Detail may not add to total because of rounding.

Source: 1980 Census of Population (Bureau of the Census 1984a).

English and the extent of difference between the proportions of adults and the proportions of children who speak the non-English languages are measures of the extent to which certain language groups are maintaining their mother tongues and passing them on to the younger generation, while others are shifting to English.

Table 3.6 shows the proportions of children and adults in language-minority families who speak their home languages at home, according to language group. Overall, nearly three-quarters of the adults and 56 percent of the children spoke non-English languages at home in 1980. The home language usage of adults varied from 91 percent in families in which Chinese languages are spoken to 56 percent in French-speaking families. The usage by children varied from 81 percent in Vietnamese-speaking families to 16 percent in Finnish-speaking families. Based on these findings, no language group will fail to lose some ground in the next generation, but those in which two-thirds or more of the children speak the home language are obviously in a better position to maintain the language than those in which fewer, proportionally, speak their parents' language. Without new currents of immigration, those in which only a bare majority of adults speak the languages and in which half as many or fewer, proportionally, of children do so are in danger of dying out.

Homogeneity of Language Minority Families

Another measure of language maintenance and language shift is the proportion of language minority families in which all family members speak the non-English language and no one speaks only English. Children from linguistically homogeneous families are more likely than children raised in families in which some people speak only English to come to school dominant in their mother tongues. They are also more likely to establish families in which their own children will learn the non-English language. As a group, in 1980, about the same number of language minority families were bilingual as were linguistically homogeneous but there was considerable variation among the language groups, ranging from three-quarters of Chinese-speaking families to a quarter of French-speaking families. These findings reinforce many of those with regard to comparative proportions of children and adults who speak the home language in language minority families. The numbers of language minority families of the various language groups and the proportions that are linguistically homogeneous are presented in Table 3.7.

Home Speakers of Non-English Languages

One in ten people in the United States speaks a language other than English at home. In 1980, there were 23.1 million home speakers of non-

Table 3.6. PROPORTIONS OF CHILDREN AND ADULTS WHO SPEAK NON-ENGLISH LANGUAGES IN LANGUAGE MINORITY FAMILIES, BY LANGUAGE: 1980

	Children, aged 5–17	Adults, aged 18+
Total	56.4	73.1
Vietnamese	81.1	87.7
Chinese languages	75.7	90.8
Persian	69.2	82.2
Spanish	69.1	81.0
Thai	65.6	78.4
Armenian	65.0	84.6
Portuguese	65.0	81.1
Asian Indian languages	64.2	93.1
Korean	62.6	81.1
Greek	61.1	80.3
Arabic	59.1	79.6
American Indian or Alaska Native languages	57.4	77.5
Russian	57.2	77.4
Serbo-Croatian	55.4	75.9
Yiddish	48.4	73.8
Ukrainian	44.7	76.4
Filipino languages	37.5	84.9
Italian	34.8	65.9
Hungarian	33.9	70.4
Japanese	33.7	68.2
German	32.5	59.0
French	31.8	56.5
Dutch	30.9	65.8
Swedish	30.1	58.4
Lithuanian	30.0	71.5
Norwegian	26.1	59.9
Polish	25.9	66.2
Czech	20.6	65.3
Slovak	17.0	62.4
Finnish	16.2	65.0
Other languages	46.6	57.8

Source: 1980 Census of Population (Bureau of the Census 1984a).

Table 3.7. ESTIMATED NUMBERS OF LANGUAGE MINORITY FAMILIES[a] IN THE UNITED STATES, BY LANGUAGE AND PROPORTION OF FAMILIES IN WHICH ALL MEMBERS SPEAK THE NON-ENGLISH LANGUAGE AT HOME: 1980

	Total	Proportion homogeneous (%)
Total	8,722,000	48.7
Chinese languages	187,000	76.0
Asian Indian languages	82,000	73.0
Vietnamese	50,000	71.4
Armenian	34,000	65.9
Persian	34,000	63.5
Portuguese	125,000	63.0
Spanish	3,655,000	61.5
Greek	147,000	58.3
Russian	65,000	58.1
Arabic	74,000	57.3
Korean	97,000	55.8
Ukrainian	49,000	54.0
Serbo-Croatian	61,000	53.1
Thai	30,000	51.8
Yiddish	127,000	51.7
American Indian or Alaska Native languages	106,000	50.0
Lithuanian	30,000	46.3
Filipino languages	162,000	46.2
Hungarian	79,000	44.6
Polish	375,000	39.4
Japanese	148,000	38.6
Italian	745,000	37.5
Czech	57,000	36.4
Slovak	42,000	34.9
Finnish	32,000	34.4
Dutch	68,000	33.0
Norwegian	53,000	27.8
German	770,000	27.5
Swedish	46,000	27.0
French	759,000	24.2
Other languages	431,000	30.5

[a] Families in which one or more family members speak a non-English language at home.

Source: 1980 Census of Population (Bureau of the Census 1984a).

English languages aged 5 and older. Nearly half of these people (48 percent or 11.1 million) speak Spanish. At least a million and a half each speak Italian, German, or French. In all, there were 26 languages spoken by at least 100,000 people in their homes in 1980. These data are displayed in Table 3.8.

Age Distribution of Home Speakers of Non-English Languages

The age distribution of the people who speak languages other than English at home is the most direct indication available from the 1980 Census of the extent to which children are learning the languages of their families or, conversely, that the languages are mostly spoken by older people and are dying out among people presently living in the United States. Age distribution reflects the immigration histories, fertility rates, and language usage patterns of the various groups of home speakers of non-English languages. Foreign-born people in general are older than native-born people; recent immigrants, however, are younger and their age distribution is related to the reasons why they have emigrated. Groups that come seeking economic opportunities are mostly young adults and adults in their prime working years, and they may be primarily male. Groups that come as a result of political upheaval in their home countries may include whole family groups with children and older family members. Young adult immigrants form families with American-born children who will be raised, for the most part, in families in which the languages of the home countries are spoken. Language minority groups with higher than average fertility rates are increasing as proportions of the total U.S. population. Children in those groups would constitute increasing proportions of the school-age populations in the states in which they are concentrated, even with no immigration.

The age distribution of the various groups in 1980 is displayed in Table 3.9, in which the data in Table 3.8 are given in percentages rearranged by proportion of school-age children in each language group. It will be noted from this table that the proportion of school-age children speaking non-English languages in 1980 ranged from a third of Vietnamese speakers to fewer than 3 percent of Slovak speakers.

A quarter of the foreign-born people in 1980 emigrated to this country before 1950; another 14 percent emigrated during the decade 1950–1959 (Census 1984a). These people came mostly from the European countries that had supplied the vast majority of immigrants during the great periods of immigration in the nineteenth century and the first half of this century (INS 1982:2-5). They are represented among the home speakers of Yiddish, Swedish, Norwegian, Slovak, Czech, Finnish, and Lithuanian, at least 40 percent of whom were aged 65 and older in 1980. School-age children in these groups, and among speakers of Polish, Hungarian, and Ukrainian, consti-

Table 3.8. ESTIMATED NUMBERS OF PEOPLE, AGED 5 AND OLDER, WHO SPEAK LANGUAGES OTHER THAN ENGLISH AT HOME, BY AGE GROUP AND LANGUAGE: 1980 (NUMBERS IN THOUSANDS)

Language	Total	Age group				
		5–17	18–24	25–44	45–64	65+
Total	23,060	4,568	3,146	7,095	4,978	3,273
Spanish	11,116	2,952	1,913	3,756	1,847	648
Italian	1,618	147	112	302	543	515
German	1,587	192	166	401	404	424
French	1,551	223	204	467	398	259
Polish	821	41	35	120	344	281
Chinese languages	631	114	83	251	129	53
Filipino languages	474	63	50	225	88	48
Greek	401	66	46	118	118	55
Portuguese	352	68	42	109	87	46
Japanese	336	34	29	110	119	45
American Indian or Alaska Native languages	333	93	54	104	56	27
Yiddish	316	19	13	33	77	174
Korean	266	60	33	132	33	8
Asian Indian languages	243	44	25	147	23	5
Arabic	218	37	44	84	36	17
Vietnamese	195	64	35	73	18	4
Hungarian	179	11	10	33	64	62
Russian	173	19	14	46	43	51
Serbo-Croatian	150	19	10	37	47	38
Dutch	148	16	15	40	45	33
Czech	122	5	4	18	43	53
Ukrainian	121	9	9	24	47	32
Norwegian	112	6	6	15	28	57
Persian	107	18	31	44	19	3
Armenian	101	14	11	26	29	21
Swedish	100	7	6	15	20	52
Slovak	88	2	2	7	34	42
Thai	85	22	13	45	4	1
Lithuanian	73	3	3	10	26	30
Finnish	69	3	2	10	25	29
Other languages	973	197	126	294	193	162

Note: Detail may not add to total because of rounding.
Source: 1980 Census of Population (Bureau of the Census 1984a).

Table 3.9. AGE DISTRIBUTION(%) OF PEOPLE, AGED 5 AND OLDER, WHO SPEAK LANGUAGES OTHER THAN ENGLISH AT HOME, BY LANGUAGE: 1980

		Age group				
Language	**Total**	**5–17**	**18–24**	**25–44**	**45–64**	**65+**
Total	100.0	19.8	13.6	30.8	21.6	14.2
Vietnamese	100.0	33.1	18.2	37.7	9.0	2.0
American Indian or Alaska Native languages	100.0	27.8	16.1	31.3	16.8	8.0
Spanish	100.0	26.6	17.2	33.8	16.6	5.8
Thai	100.0	25.3	15.4	53.1	5.0	1.1
Korean	100.0	22.4	12.5	49.4	12.6	3.1
Portuguese	100.0	19.2	11.9	31.0	24.8	13.0
Chinese languages	100.0	18.1	13.2	39.8	20.5	8.4
Asian Indian languages	100.0	18.0	10.2	60.2	9.5	2.1
Arabic	100.0	16.9	20.0	38.5	16.6	8.0
Greek	100.0	16.4	11.3	29.3	29.3	13.6
Persian	100.0	16.4	29.3	41.3	10.1	2.9
French	100.0	14.4	13.2	30.1	25.6	16.7
Armenian	100.0	13.7	11.1	25.4	29.1	20.7
Filipino languages	100.0	13.3	10.6	47.6	18.5	10.0
Serbo-Croatian	100.0	12.5	6.8	24.6	31.0	25.0
German	100.0	12.1	10.5	25.2	25.5	26.7
Russian	100.0	11.2	7.9	26.7	24.7	29.6
Dutch	100.0	11.1	9.9	26.7	30.2	22.2
Japanese	100.0	10.0	8.7	32.6	35.4	13.3
Italian	100.0	9.1	6.9	18.6	33.6	31.8
Ukrainian	100.0	7.8	7.3	19.8	38.5	26.6
Hungarian	100.0	6.1	5.4	18.2	35.9	34.5
Yiddish	100.0	6.1	4.0	10.4	24.5	54.9
Norwegian	100.0	5.7	4.9	13.5	25.1	50.8
Polish	100.0	5.0	4.3	14.7	41.9	34.2
Swedish	100.0	6.9	5.9	15.4	19.9	51.8
Lithuanian	100.0	4.5	4.7	13.9	35.3	41.5
Czech	100.0	4.2	3.6	14.3	34.9	43.1
Finnish	100.0	3.8	3.3	15.1	35.7	42.2
Slovak	100.0	2.6	2.2	7.9	39.3	48.1
Other languages	100.0	20.3	12.9	30.2	19.8	16.7

Note: Detail may not add to 100.0% because of rounding. Percentages calculated on unrounded numbers.

Source: 1980 Census of Population (Bureau of the Census 1984a).

tuted fewer than 10 percent, thus reinforcing the findings on the proportions of children who speak the non-English languages in language minority families and the proportions of such families that are linguistically homogeneous. Children are not learning these languages and few will form bilingual families of their own.

Asian people did not begin to constitute substantial proportions of the immigration stream until the 1960s. In 1980, nearly three out of five of the people who identified themselves as Asians or Pacific Islanders were born abroad (Bureau of the Census 1984a). The other two-fifths were their children, many of whom are being raised in linguistically homogeneous families. Among the recent immigrant groups are most of the speakers of Vietnamese, and many of the speakers of Thai and Korean. Children constituted a third of Vietnamese speakers, a quarter of Thai speakers, and 22 percent of Korean speakers in 1980. People in the oldest age groups of these populations are notably lacking. Most people are young adults or adults in their prime working years. As indicated by the data on proportions of children and adults who speak the languages at home and on proportions of linguistically homogeneous families, these languages are being passed on to the majority of foreign-born and American-born children.

People from the Caribbean and Latin America began to constitute a substantial proportion of the immigrant stream in the 1950s and the largest proportion in the 1960s. Nearly half a million people emigrated legally from Mexico alone between 1961 and 1970 and more than 600,000 between 1971 and 1980 (INS 1982:4). Nevertheless, Hispanics in the United States are largely American-born. They are the children and grandchildren of Hispanic populations in the old Southwest and elsewhere and they are Puerto Ricans whose home island has been a part of the United States since 1898. Among the people who identified themselves as Hispanic in the 1980 Census, fewer than three in ten were born in foreign countries. Rather than their immigration history, the second factor mentioned at the beginning of this section needs to be considered in relationship to the age distribution of Spanish speakers, that is, fertility rates.

Hispanics have larger families than the white majority population. In 1980, 27 percent of the total Hispanic population, or 31 percent of the population aged 5 and older—the universe of home speakers of languages other than English—was aged 5–17. In contrast, 20 percent of the total white population and 21 percent of the population aged 5 and older, was school-age. Among Spanish-speakers, 27 percent were school-age children in 1980, which is fewer than would be expected from the proportion of youngsters among Hispanics as a whole but still considerably more than among the majority population. These data indicate that while some children in Spanish-speaking families speak only English, the numbers of school-age Spanish-speaking children are growing faster, proportionally, than the numbers of majority children. Even without additional immigration from Spanish-speaking countries, children with these characteristics form an increasing proportion of the population entering U.S. schools.

The age distribution of people who speak American Indian or Alaska Native languages reflects the higher than average fertility rates of these groups, almost all of whom are American-born. School-age children constituted 28 percent of the total group of people who identified themselves as American Indians or Alaska Natives in 1980 and 31 percent of those aged 5 and older, which is the age group of home speakers of non-English languages. They constituted 28 percent of the speakers of Native American languages. This is fewer, proportionally, than would be expected from the proportion among Native American people generally but more than among the majority. Thus, as in the case of Spanish-speaking children, Native American children who speak their home languages are increasing as a proportion of the school population in the states in which they are concentrated.

Gender of Home Speakers of Non-English Languages

The proportions of all home speakers of non-English languages who are girls and women are similar to the proportions of English speakers who are girls and women. As in the normal demographic situation, women slightly outnumber men, and boys slightly outnumber girls. However, there are striking differences among the language groups. Among the aging populations of speakers of the European languages cited in the previous section—Slovak, Swedish, Lithuanian, Yiddish, Czech, Polish, Finnish, Norwegian, and Hungarian—and among speakers of French and German, the overall populations are predominantly female, and many of the women are in the oldest age group. Speakers of Japanese and Korean also have higher than "normal" proportions of women, which is perhaps explained by the marriages of Japanese and Korean women to American men. In 1980, girls and women constituted 57 and 56 percent, respectively, of all speakers of these languages.

There are anomalies in the gender distribution of home speakers of Persian (Farsi), Vietnamese, Asian Indian languages, and Arabic, which are probably explained by recent immigration patterns. Boys and men outnumbered girls and women in all age groups of Farsi speakers in 1980. They outnumbered girls and women in all but the oldest age group among speakers of Asian Indian languages and Arabic. In 1980, males outnumbered females 1.8 to 1 among people born in Iran, 72 percent of whom had emigrated to the United States in the 5 years immediately preceding the Census. Among people born in India and Pakistan, males outnumbered females 1.2 and 1.7 to 1, respectively (Census 1984b).

Table 3.10 displays the data on the proportions of home speakers of non-English languages who are girls and women.

Table 3.10. PROPORTIONS(%) OF PEOPLE, AGED 5 AND OLDER, WHO SPEAK LANGUAGES OTHER THAN ENGLISH AT HOME WHO ARE GIRLS AND WOMEN: 1980

Language	Total	Age group				
		5–17	18–24	25–44	45–64	65+
Speakers of non-English languages, total	52.5	49.8	49.1	51.3	54.0	59.8
Slovak	60.1	43.5	48.6	56.4	57.8	64.1
Lithuanian	58.8	52.2	52.2	54.2	56.5	63.8
Swedish	58.8	50.4	54.7	61.3	56.2	60.7
Yiddish	57.7	46.9	45.3	50.2	58.3	61.0
Japanese	57.4	51.0	49.8	55.3	62.7	58.0
Czech	57.3	45.3	50.3	50.5	55.2	63.0
Polish	57.3	49.6	50.7	53.1	56.2	62.3
Finnish	57.1	49.4	47.6	55.3	53.8	61.9
Korean	56.3	48.4	56.3	60.1	52.9	67.1
French	56.2	53.8	53.5	54.6	56.2	63.6
Norwegian	56.1	50.4	52.1	55.1	52.3	59.2
German	55.6	49.8	48.9	54.3	56.2	61.5
Hungarian	55.6	48.1	47.5	50.9	54.5	61.9
Italian	54.2	49.9	49.3	50.3	53.5	59.6
Russian	54.2	47.2	48.3	49.4	55.4	61.9
Ukrainian	54.2	50.5	49.4	53.0	55.3	56.0
Dutch	53.8	50.5	50.3	55.2	51.6	58.5
Filipino languages	53.6	49.4	52.6	57.9	56.1	35.4
Thai	52.6	49.1	50.5	54.4	56.5	60.4
Serbo-Croatian	52.4	48.6	51.8	49.1	51.5	58.8
Armenian	52.3	48.5	44.7	49.8	52.6	61.6
Portuguese	51.6	49.3	49.4	50.5	52.3	58.6
American Indian or Alaska Native languages	51.1	49.8	49.8	51.1	53.0	54.1
Spanish	51.1	50.0	49.2	50.8	52.9	57.4
Greek	50.2	49.6	48.0	48.4	49.8	57.6
Chinese languages	49.3	46.8	49.3	50.4	48.7	51.4
Vietnamese	47.1	46.0	43.0	49.1	47.8	62.6
Asian Indian languages	45.3	49.1	49.8	43.9	40.5	54.7
Arabic	41.4	47.7	32.7	37.0	47.3	59.2
Persian	37.2	43.8	33.6	34.9	24.4	49.2
Other languages	52.2	48.5	47.7	49.2	55.6	61.6

Source: 1980 Census of Population (Bureau of the Census 1984a).

Relative English-Speaking Ability and Nativity

As explained in the first section of this chapter, it is not possible to derive estimates of the numbers of people with limited English proficiency from the 1980 Census. However, the responses to the English-speaking ability question can be used to compare the relative acquisition of English-speaking skills of various groups through comparison of the indices of relative English-speaking ability (the IRESAs) and the proportions of people who do not speak English at all.

The proportions of people who do not speak English at all are strongly related to nativity and to length of residence in the United States. As shown in Table 3.11, recent immigrants are more likely than immigrants who have lived in this country at least 10 years not to speak English at all. In 1980, they were more than two and a half times as likely as pre-1970 immigrants and nine times more likely than native-born home speakers of languages other than English not to speak English.

The relationship between the IRESAs and nativity and time in the United States is not so clear, especially if they are examined separately for children and adults. Foreign-born school-age children who speak non-English languages at home are likely to have acquired considerably better speaking skills in English than foreign-born adults, especially those children

Table 3.11. RELATIVE ENGLISH-SPEAKING ABILITY OF HOME SPEAKERS OF LANGUAGES OTHER THAN ENGLISH, AGED 5–17 AND 18 AND OLDER, AND PROPORTIONS OF HOME SPEAKERS OF LANGUAGES OTHER THAN ENGLISH OF ALL AGES, BY NATIVITY AND PERIOD OF IMMIGRATION OF THE FOREIGN BORN: 1980

Nativity and period of immigration of the foreign born	Index of relative English-speaking ability[a]		Proportion of non-English speakers of all ages
	Aged 5–17	Aged 18+	
Total, home speakers of non-English languages	484	460	5.3
Native-born population	503	518	1.7
Foreign-born population immigrated before 1970	533	435	5.9
Foreign-born population immigrated between 1970 and 1980	405	332	15.4

[a] Calculated from the responses to the Census question "How well does this person speak English?", as follows: 600 points were allowed for each "very well" response, 400 for each "well" response, 200 for each "not well" response and no points for each "not at all" response; the results were then averaged. The maximum numbers of points is 600.

Source: 1980 Census of Population (Bureau of the Census 1984a).

who arrive at age 7 or earlier. In contrast, native-born children who speak languages other than English at home are somewhat less skilled in speaking English than their parents and they are considerably less skilled than foreign-born children who emigrated as young children. Foreign-born children are likely to acquire strong skills in their mother tongues, either before they come to the United States or in closely knit linguistically homogeneous families after emigration. For this reason they appear to be better prepared to learn English, as predicted by the theory that language development in the native language is essential to successful acquisition of a second language in children (Cummins 1981).

The data on the relative English-speaking ability and the proportions of non-English speakers among native-born and foreign-born speakers of non-English languages are shown in Table 3.11.

Relative English-Speaking Ability of Home Speakers of Various Languages

There are two reasons for examining relative English-speaking ability and the proportions of non-English speakers among the various language groups: (1) They are indicators of the relative potential need for special educational programs, such as bilingual education or English as a second language; and (2) they can serve as negative measures of language shift. While individuals who acquire proficiency in English do not necessarily abandon their mother tongues—they may choose to be bilingual—individuals who lack speaking and other skills in English cannot shift to English. Table 3.12 shows the IRESAs and the proportions of people who do not speak English at all for each language group.

Speakers of Vietnamese, Thai, Korean, and Chinese languages (these are groups with many recent immigrants) have the lowest IRESAs and some of the largest proportions of non-English speakers among the language groups examined. Among the European language groups, Russian and Portuguese speakers also have low IRESAs and high proportions of people who do not speak English at all. These groups are candidates for programs in which they and their children will have opportunities to develop English skills sufficient to realize their educational and economic objectives in the English-speaking majority society.

Spanish speakers not only have a low IRESA as a group but they also have one of the highest proportions of people who do not speak English at all. Moreover, the 938,000 Spanish-speaking people who did not speak English in 1980 constituted more than three-quarters of all non-English-speaking people identified in the Census. The Spanish language background population must continue to be the major focus of special language-related programs.

Table 3.12. RELATIVE ENGLISH-SPEAKING ABILITY OF HOME SPEAKERS OF LANGUAGES OTHER THAN ENGLISH AND PROPORTIONS OF HOME SPEAKERS OF LANGUAGES OTHER THAN ENGLISH WHO DO NOT SPEAK ENGLISH, BY LANGUAGE: 1980

	Index of relative English-speaking ability[a]	Proportion of non-English speakers (%)
Total	465	5.3
Norwegian	547	[b]
Swedish	546	[b]
Dutch	541	[b]
German	537	0.3
Finnish	532	[b]
French	527	0.7
Yiddish	527	0.7
Czech	525	[b]
Asian Indian languages	518	1.7
Slovak	518	[b]
Polish	508	1.2
Hungarian	502	0.8
Lithuanian	502	0.9
Filipino languages	495	1.0
Italian	493	1.9
Greek	486	2.5
Ukrainian	486	1.3
Arabic	481	2.4
Serbo-Croatian	476	2.0
Persian	467	2.2
American Indian or Alaska Native languages	464	4.5
Armenian	453	5.3
Japanese	452	2.2
Spanish	434	8.4
Portuguese	420	9.5
Russian	419	6.8
Chinese languages	403	8.9
Korean	400	4.9
Thai	366	10.2
Vietnamese	356	8.5
Other languages	406	2.0

[a] Calculated from the responses to the Census question "How well does this person speak English?", as follows: 600 points were allowed for each "very well" response, 400 for each "well" response, 200 for each "not well" response and no points for each "not at all" response; the results were then averaged. The maximum number of points is 600.

[b] Base number fewer than an estimated 1,000 persons.

Source: 1980 Census of Population (Bureau of the Census 1984a).

The groups of mostly aging speakers of European languages—Norwegian, Swedish, Finnish, Yiddish, and Czech, plus Dutch, German, and French—have the highest IRESAs. Very few speakers of these languages have failed to learn English. They are bilingual by choice.

Although many of them are recent immigrants, speakers of Asian Indian languages and Filipino languages also have high IRESAs and include few non-English speakers. By continuing to speak the languages of their homelands in the United States and to teach them to their children, they are not neglecting English but are maintaining bilingualism. In both cases, English is the second language and it is an important language of higher education in the countries from which these people come. Highly educated people are emigrating from India and the Philippines. In 1980, the average age of 1970–1980 immigrants from these countries was 30. A large majority had graduate degrees. Some may have made the switch to English even before emigrating. In 1980, 10 percent of the 1970–1980 immigrants spoke only English at home and two-thirds of the Indian English speakers and a third of the Filipino English speakers already lived in all-English environments (Census 1984a). Immigrants from India and the Philippines who speak only English and live in monolingual English environments are not included in the counts of language minority people.

IMPLICATIONS OF THE FINDINGS

The United States is a multilingual country and it is continuing to receive immigrants from all parts of the world, who add to the multiplicity of language backgrounds in our population. The 1980 Census identified 34.6 million language minority people. There were 30 language minority groups representing single languages or groups of related languages with at least 100,000 members each. Since then, 2.7 million people have legally emigrated from all countries in which languages other than English are spoken. The total potential language minority population is now at least 37.4 million.

The largest language group consists of Spanish speakers and people in families in which Spanish is spoken. People with Spanish language backgrounds constituted nearly 45 percent of the total language minority population and children from Spanish-speaking families made up 52 percent of the school-age language minority children in 1980. Since 1980, 824,000 legal immigrants have come to the United States from Spanish-speaking countries to join the 15.5 million Spanish language-minority people who were in the United States in 1980. The Spanish language group is increasing in size, both because Spanish-speaking families are larger than English language majority families and because immigration from Spanish-speaking countries continues.

Hispanics are our nation's largest ethnic minority. In many ways, they are educationally and economically behind the majority mainstream. As indicated by the relative level of English-speaking skills of Spanish speakers and the proportions of non-English speakers found among them in the 1980 Census, language plays a role in the problems of this group. With appropriate programs in which they can develop their English skills and overcome past neglect and inappropriate education, they will eventually make their full contribution to U.S. society.

Immigrants are coming in increasing numbers from Asia. In the 5 years between 1980 and 1985, the potential size of the Vietnamese language minority doubled, that of the Korean group by half again, and other Asian groups grew significantly. Groups of new immigrants from these and other countries need language programs in which they and their children will acquire the English skills needed to succeed in their new home.

The children from linguistically homogeneous families, among the new immigrants and among the older established language groups, are prime candidates for bilingual education programs. We must help them to build upon and continue to develop their skills in their home languages, as well as to acquire and develop their skills in English. But knowledge of other languages and understanding of cultures other than our own are not just resources we should cherish in our native-born and foreign-born language minority populations. They are crucial for all Americans today. Children from English language majority backgrounds should have opportunities to learn second languages and acquire an understanding of other cultures. More programs should be developed in which language minority children share their skills with English-language-background children. These programs are needed not just in the foreign languages traditionally studied in our schools—French, German, Italian, and Spanish—but in Japanese, Chinese, Russian, and Arabic, which are languages we also need to play our role in today's world.

EXPLORING THE IDEAS

1. Waggoner's chapter indicates that there are many gaps in our knowledge of language minorities in the United States because of the types of questions asked in surveys and censuses, the way they are asked, and the way they are answered.

If, for educational policy-making purposes, you were interested in obtaining as accurate as possible an estimate of the number of NEP and LEP individuals in the United States, assuming minimum practical (e.g., budgetary) constraints on your survey project, what kinds of questions would you ask? How would you conduct your survey?

2. At present, only self-reports of the language minorities' English proficiency are available.

What are some of the problems with relying on self-reports when one tries to assess the need for language education services?

3. According to Waggoner's data, the five states with the highest concentrations of language minorities are California, New York, Texas, Illinois, and Florida.

What are some of the reasons—historical, climatic, economic, and other—for this pattern of geographical concentration?

What would be the impact of such concentration on the states? Think in terms of not only new demands made but also new resources created.

4. Waggoner notes that the age distribution in a language minority group reflects, among other things, its immigration history and language use patterns.

Apply Waggoner's statement to analyze two or three of the groups listed in Table 3.8 (preferably including one not covered in this volume.)

APPLYING THE IDEAS

1. In her conclusion, Waggoner suggests that given the changing composition of the U.S. population and changing international relationships, foreign languages other than those traditionally studied in American schools should also be featured in language programs.

In your local community, research the foreign language course offerings in one or more of the following: high schools, community colleges, universities, and commercial language schools. What proportion of the courses are in "traditional" foreign languages? What proportion are in "nontraditional" foreign languages, such as the languages of recent immigrant groups?

Interview the instructor of a course in a "nontraditional" foreign language. Find out why his or her students are taking this course.

2. Waggoner discusses several factors affecting the English proficiency of a language minority member, such as nativity, age of immigration (if foreign-born), home language environment, and others.

Interview an immigrant and write up his or her "language biography," using some of the concepts in Waggoner's chapter.

REFERENCES

Bureau of the Census, U.S. Department of Commerce. 1973. *1970 Census of Population, Subject Reports, National Origin and Language*. PC(2)-1A. Washington, D.C.: U.S. Government Printing Office.

Bureau of the Census, U.S. Department of Commerce. 1974. *Current Population Reports*, Series P-20, No. 264, Persons of Spanish Origin in the United States: March 1973. Washington, D.C.: U.S. Government Printing Office.

Bureau of the Census, U.S. Department of Commerce. 1979. *Twenty Censuses: Population and Housing Questions, 1790–1980*. Washington, D.C.: U.S. Government Printing Office.

Bureau of the Census, U.S. Department of Commerce. 1982. *Current Population Reports,* Series P-23, No. 116, Ancestry and Language in the United States: November 1979. Washington, D.C.: U.S. Government Printing Office.

Bureau of the Census, U.S. Department of Commerce. 1983a. *1980 Census of Population, Volume 1, Characteristics of the Population, Chapter C, General Social and Economic Characteristics, Part 1, U.S. Summary*. PC80-1-Cl. *Parts 2-52* [individual states and the District of Columbia]. PC80-1-C2-PC80-1-C52. Washington, D.C.: U.S. Government Printing Office.

Bureau of the Census, U.S. Department of Commerce. 1983b. *1980 Census of Population, Volume 1, Characteristics of the Population, Chapter D, Detailed Population Characteristics, Parts 2-52* [individual states and the District of Columbia]. PC80-1-D2-PC80-1-D52. Washington, D.C.: U.S. Government Printing Office.

Bureau of the Census, U.S. Department of Commerce. 1984a. *1980 Census of Population, Volume 1, Characteristics of the Population, Chapter D, Detailed Population Characteristics, Part 1, U.S. Summary*. PC80-1-D1. Washington, D.C.: U.S. Government Printing Office.

Bureau of the Census, U.S. Department of Commerce. 1984b. Socioeconomic Characteristics of U.S. Foreign-Born Population Detailed in Census Bureau Tabulations. *United States Department of Commerce News,* October 17, 1984, CB84-179.

Cummins, J. 1981. The role of primary language development in promoting educational success for language minority students. In *Schooling and Language Minority Students: A Theoretical Framework*. Los Angeles: Evaluation, Dissemination, and Assessment Center, California State University, for California State Department of Education.

Ferguson, C. A. and S. B. Heath, eds. 1981. *Language in the USA*. Cambridge: Cambridge University Press.

Immigration and Naturalization Service, U.S. Department of Justice. 1980, 1981, 1982, 1983, 1984, and 1985. *Statistical Yearbook*. Washington, D.C.: INS, U.S. Department of Justice.

Levin, M. J., N. R. McKenney and P. A. Berman. 1984. Uses and interpretation of racial and ethnic data from the U.S. Census. Presented at the annual meeting of the American Statistical Association, Philadelphia, Pennsylvania.

Lieberson, S. 1966. Language questions in censuses. *Sociological Inquiry,* Spring: 262–279.

Waggoner, D. 1981. Statistics on language use. In C. A. Ferguson and S. B. Heath, eds., *Language in the USA*. Cambridge: Cambridge University Press.

Warren, R. and J. S. Passel. 1983. Estimates of illegal aliens from Mexico counted in the 1980 United States Census. Presented at the annual meeting of the Population Association of America, Pittsburgh, Pennsylvania, April 14–16.

Part III

CONTEMPORARY IMMIGRANT LANGUAGE MINORITIES

For language minorities living in the United States today, the extent and manner of English acquisition as well as of ethnic language retention are affected by a number of shared factors, such as public schooling, economic incentives, and the mass media. Yet each group is, of course, also unique, showing distinctive patterns in linguistic and cultural origin, prior exposure to English and American culture, immigration history, group size and composition, geographic concentration, educational experience, and socioeconomic status within American society. All these factors have a bearing on language use within the community.

All of the chapters in this section were written specifically for this volume. While individual authors may choose to emphasize different demographic or language use characteristics to bring out the uniqueness of the group in question, they all share a conviction that language minority children and adults in the schools and the way they use language cannot be understood apart from the social matrix of their lives.

All of the groups discussed in this section have undergone rapid expansion and transformation as a result of immigration since 1965. However, it should be noted that in several ethnic groups, immigration augments a well-established, native-born, frequently English monolingual population. Thus although the word "immigrant" appears in the title of this section, to avoid a misleading picture of linguistic and cultural homogeneity, it is often necessary to examine the native-born segment as well.

CHAPTER

4

The Language Situation of Mexican Americans

Guadalupe Valdés

TERMINOLOGY AND GROUP IDENTIFICATION

The term "Mexican American" is used to refer to persons of Mexican ancestry who reside in the United States. Segments of this population, however, refer to themselves using a variety of other terms, including Mexican, *mexicano, Chicano, Latino,* Hispanic, and Spanish American. Moreover, some segments of this population (some original residents of northern New Mexico, for example) may claim to have no Mexican (i.e., mixed Indian and Spanish or *mestizo*) ancestry. In this chapter, the term "Mexican American" will be used to include all persons who are of Mexican ancestry and all persons of Spanish origin whose ancestors settled in what had been Mexican-owned territories before the signing of the Treaty of Guadalupe–Hidalgo in 1848.

THE HETEROGENEITY OF MEXICAN AMERICANS

Popular stereotypes of Mexican Americans invariably obscure the fact that no one list of qualities and characteristics can be applied to identify the many different kinds of individuals who can be described by the term "Mexican American." This population is highly diverse in terms of length and area of residence, educational background, occupational activity, religious and political affiliation, family situation, and physical appearance; it includes bilingual speakers of English and Spanish, and monolingual speakers of either language. There are Mexican Americans residing in many different states in the United States, and it is projected that the Mexican-origin population will continue to increase steadily. In March, 1985, there were 16.9 million persons of Spanish origin in the United States, with 10.8 million of these persons self-identifying as Mexican-origin (U.S. Census Bureau 1985).

Many Mexican American families have been here for over a century. Many of them, in fact, preceded Anglo "pioneer" families who settled in the former Mexican territories now known as New Mexico, Colorado, Arizona, Texas, and California.

Other Mexican Americans who emigrated to the United States during the twentieth century have also been here for several generations. According to Burma (1970), immigration from Mexico has occurred during four different phases. The first phase (before 1918) involved a very small number of individuals who generally settled close to the border areas. The second phase (1918–1930) was triggered by a demand for labor in the United States during World War I. The third phase (1930–1942) coincided with the period of the Great Depression and had the effect of reversing the flow initiated in the previous stage. Finally, the fourth phase, the period from 1942 to 1970, was ushered in by a renewed demand for unskilled labor. Burma conjectures that since immigration quotas did not apply, only personal restrictions (disease, illiteracy) were applied when it was desirable to decrease the labor force. He estimates that approximately 1,750,000 persons entered the United States during this fourth phase. Many of these individuals crossed and recrossed the border numerous times, others entered the county illegally, while others entered the United States as *braceros* or contract agricultural workers and remained here for only one or two seasons. Unfortunately, the figures available are inexact in that they reflect the records of legal border crossings for both seasonal and legal immigrants and not those of actual settlement and residence in this country.

Other Mexican Americans have come to this country more recently. Between 1980 and 1985, for example, the increase in the Hispanic population was 16 percent, compared to 3.3 percent for the overall population. The Mexican-origin population had an increase of close to 2 million persons during this same period. This increase reflects not only high birth rates but also a continued influx of immigrants from Mexico.

One very important difference between other immigrant groups and Mexican-origin immigrants, however, is the fact that the latter group is made up of three different kinds of immigrants: (1) permanent immigrants: persons who have come into this country with the intention of making it their permanent residence; (2) short-term immigrants: persons who spend a very short time in this country (an average of 10–12 weeks) and then return to Mexico; and (3) cyclical immigrants: those persons who normally leave their families in Mexico and who return on a fairly regular basis. The presence of these different types of immigrants obviously affects the linguistic climate of the community. For example, short-term immigrants are not in this country long enough to learn English. Thus, they will reside in the community and seek to get along using Spanish as much as they can, often relying on friends and relatives to translate for them or to cue them in to key phrases in English. Cyclical immigrants, on the other hand, often learn more English on each trip they make into this country. Depending on their opportunity for contact with monolingual English speakers, they will quickly pick up whatever English may help them to stay out of the border patrol's hands. Finally, permanent immigrants closely follow the pattern found in other immigrant communities; that is, they will go from being Spanish monolinguals to English monolinguals in four generations (see below).

In the discussion that follows, the reader should keep in mind that even though broad generalizations are being made about Mexican Americans, their communities, and their language use within these communities, these generalizations are not universally applicable to all Mexican Americans. Language use will be affected by numerous factors, such as the density of the population; the number of short-term, cyclical, and long-term immigrants; the history of the community; the relationship between the Mexican American and Anglo populations; and the proximity of the community to the Mexican border.

CHARACTERISTICS OF THE LANGUAGES USED BY MEXICAN AMERICANS

Before one can begin to describe the characteristics of either the English or the Spanish spoken by Mexican Americans, one must begin by describing the use and function of these two languages in Mexican American communities. More specifically, one must begin by describing the nature of these communities and the ways in which they are like and unlike other communities where immigrant groups have settled in the past. In particular, one must understand the nature of bilingualism, the factors that affect the development of proficiency in two languages, and the roles that two languages play in the lives of bilingual individuals. In this section, a number of key concepts will be presented that will then serve as a basis for the discussion of many issues surrounding the study and analysis of the languages used by Mexican Americans in the United States.

Bilingualism: Some Basic Concepts

Elite Bilingualism Versus Natural Bilingualism Bilingualism as an individual phenomenon develops under two different kinds of circumstances. On the one hand, an individual may consciously decide to acquire another language and to pursue the study or learning of this language in either formal (classroom) or informal (actual communicative) contexts. This type of conscious, voluntary bilingualism has been referred to as "elite" bilingualism. Persons who study foreign languages and then seek out contacts with speakers of these languages either abroad or in this country can be said to be elite bilinguals.

On the other hand, "natural" bilingualism occurs when individuals find that their first language (L1) will not suffice to meet all of their communicative needs. In order to participate fully (or simply to survive) in the context in which they find themselves, it becomes necessary for them to acquire a second language (L2) and to use this language in their everyday lives. Natural bilingualism is characteristic of immigrant groups who must learn to use the majority language of the country they reside in and of conquered or colonized peoples whose original national language is displaced by the conquering or colonial language.

Diglossia A situation known as "diglossia" is said to exist when the two languages in a bilingual community take on specialized and complementary functions, so that the first language is used primarily for the home-related spheres of activity, while the second is used for all formal, institutional, and official matters. The former is called the "low" (L) language; the latter, the "high" (H) language (Ferguson 1959). (Note that "high" and "low" are simply technical labels denoting the division of social functions between the two languages; they should not be taken to suggest that one language is "better" than the other.)

The Bilingual Individual The term "bilingual," as used here, describes an individual who has "more than one competence," that is, who can function to some degree in more than one language. When one uses this broad definition of bilingualism, one includes in the company of bilinguals all individuals who have either receptive or productive skills, to whatever degree, in more than one language. For example, one classifies as bilingual an individual who is a native speaker of English and who can read French, but does not speak or understand the spoken French language. Such an individual is said to have receptive skills in written French and to be clearly more "bilingual" than those persons who can have zero skills in a second language. According to this perspective, a bilingual individual is not necessarily an ambilingual (an individual with native competency in two languages), but a bilingual of a specific type who, along with other bilinguals of many different types, can be classified along a continuum. Different types of individuals (all bilingual in language A and language B) might be classified with relation to each other as illustrated in Figure 4.1.

The broad definition of bilingualism used here also rejects the popular notion of a "true" bilingual—an individual who is equally capable in two

monolingual A ———————————————————— monolingual B

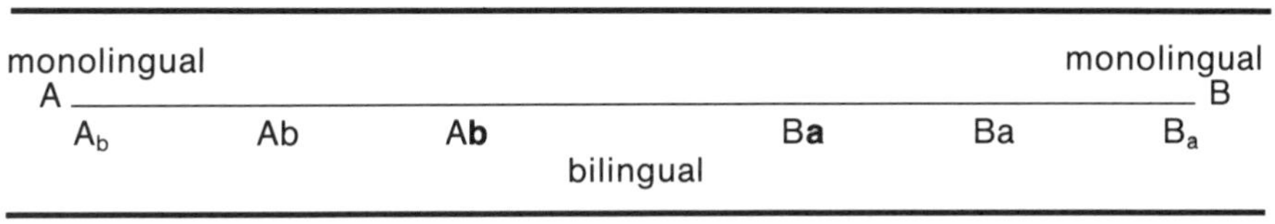

A_b Ab **Ab** **Ba** Ba B_a

bilingual

Figure 4.1. Six individuals with competency in the same two languages (language A and language B) placed on a continuum.

languages—as unrealistic. For a bilingual to be equally proficient in both of his or her languages, he or she would have to balance every experience encountered or carried out in one language with an equivalent experience in the other language. Since this seldom occurs in natural settings, most bilingual individuals' skills vary over a lifetime. Bilinguals may begin, for example, by being dominant in one language, and yet find that their dominance changes over time. Such changes in dominance or relative proficiency will directly reflect the ways in which bilingual persons have used their two languages, the frequency of their interaction with other speakers of each language, the contexts in which the languages are used, and so on.

In sum, bilingualism, rather than being an absolute condition, is a relative one. Bilingual individuals can be both *slightly* bilingual or *very* bilingual and be characterized as having varying degrees of proficiency in their two languages in both the written and oral modes.

Immigrant Bilingualism in the United States: General Characteristics

In the United States, immigrant bilinguals can be said to be natural bilinguals, that is, individuals who find it necessary to acquire English in order to function in American society. They normally learn English by interacting with speakers of this language in the "real world": in the work sphere, in the school context, in the neighborhood, and in all contacts where their first language is not sufficient to meet their communicative needs. Most adult immigrants, however, learn English slowly, acquiring just enough active knowledge of the language to "get by" at the beginning.

According to Fishman (1964), immigrant bilingualism in this country follows a specific pattern which is common to all immigrant groups and which leads to monolingualism in English by the fourth generation. This pattern can be illustrated as follows:

1. *Initial Stage*. Immigrants learn English through their mother tongue. English is used only in those domains (such as work) where the mother tongue cannot be used.
2. *Second Stage*. Immigrants learn more English and can speak to each

other in this language or in their own. Transfer between languages increases, although there is still a dependency on the mother tongue.
3. *Third Stage*. Speakers function in both languages. English appears to be dominant in more and more domains.
4. *Fourth Stage*. English has displaced the mother tongue except for the most intimate or private domains. This stage is the exact reverse of the initial stage.

It is important to note that for all immigrant groups, the process of acquiring English in this country has been similar. Different groups have generally settled in communities where other members of the group had settled previously, and they have used the resources of the community to help them negotiate the system at the beginning. First-generation men have tended to learn some English first because of their need to find employment, while women (if they remain at home) have tended to learn English more slowly or not at all. The second generation, on the other hand, acquires English quite rapidly. Some of these second-generation individuals may speak with an accent and sound foreign, but others speak native-like English indistinguishable from that of monolingual English speakers. Depending upon the unique characteristics of the community or family, second-generation immigrants may be either dominant in the immigrant language or already dominant in English. For the most part, the third generation is primarily English dominant; and, as Fishman has pointed out, fourth-generation immigrants are very seldom still bilingual in the immigrant language.

Mexican American Communities

Mexican Americans have settled in both rural and urban areas, among other *Latino* groups, among other minority groups, and even among mainstream Anglo-Americans. Indeed, in many areas of the country where there are large concentrations of Mexican American people, there appear to be no neighborhoods or city sections that one would identify as Mexican American exclusively or predominantly. In those areas, one might not be able to speak of a Mexican American community; that is, of a community primarily settled by Mexican-origin people who have clustered together in much the same way that other immigrant groups have done upon arriving in the United States. In other areas of the country, however, Mexican American communities are alive and well and growing. In some cases they are made up exclusively of Mexican-origin people, and in other cases they are predominantly made up of Mexican Americans, but include other Latinos as well. These Mexican-origin communities are found both in large cities and in small towns in many parts of the United States. Even though there are differences among them, they are similar enough that one can generalize about their characteristics and about the use of language among the Mexican Americans who live there. The communities that will be described here are representative of many Mexican American communities, both large and small.

Mexican American Bilingualism

Mexican American bilinguals are essentially "natural" bilinguals. They have acquired their second language in a natural context by having to interact with monolingual and bilingual speakers of English in the work or school or neighborhood domains. As might be expected, there are many different types of bilinguals in Mexican American communities.

So varied, indeed, are the different types of English/Spanish bilinguals in Mexican American communities that it is impossible to conjecture about language strengths or weaknesses based on generation, age, schooling, period of residence in this country, or any other such criteria. This is true even though, in general, the "permanent immigrant" segment of the population conforms to Fishman's description of language shift. There are many first-generation Mexican immigrants who acquire English very rapidly, but there are also many who do not. There are many third- and fourth-generation Mexican Americans who are still very fluent in Spanish, but there are also many such Mexican Americans who no longer even understand their original ethnic language. Many individuals will report that their first language was Spanish in such communities; but increasingly, as the Rand Corporation report (McCarthy and Valdez 1985) reveals, Mexican Americans are reporting English as their first language.

It is clear, however, that large numbers of Mexican Americans are, to a greater or lesser degree, bilingual. It is equally clear that, because they *are* bilingual, two languages, English and Spanish, are used in their everyday lives. How they are used and why and what role they play in the community are questions that have been studied at great length by many individuals. In the sections that follow, a general description of this use and of the English and Spanish varieties themselves will be presented.

Language Use

If one were to walk down the street of a typical Mexican American community, and if one were to listen closely as people talked to one another, one could come away with several different impressions. If it happened, for example, that one overheard talk among young people as they walked home after school, one might be convinced that English was the primary language of the community. On the other hand, if one happened to be eavesdropping on two older ladies, their use of Spanish might persuade one that Spanish clearly predominated. A different impression might be obtained if one overheard the conversation of second- or third-generation Mexican Americans in their midtwenties and found that they seemed to use both English and Spanish together, somehow alternating between the two languages after every few words. In that case, one might reach one of two conclusions: that members of the community speak *both* English and Spanish, or that members of the community speak *neither* English nor Spanish (in other words, a hybrid language).

In fact, three of those conclusions would be accurate. For some residents of the community, English would clearly be the dominant and primary language. For other residents of the community, Spanish would still be the primary means of communication. And for still others, both English and Spanish would be perceived as necessary for everyday interaction in the community. On the other other hand, as we will see in the section on code-switching, the idea that speakers alternate between the two languages out of incompetence is inaccurate.

Again, just like many other immigrant communities, Mexican American communities are "diglossic," with English and Spanish taking on specialized functions and associated with certain domains of activity or subject matter. English is the "high" language of prestige; it is the language identified with success and with power. Not only is it the language of the wider surrounding community, but it is also the language in which many "important" things are done: banking, the political process, and all the official institutions that affect the lives of the members of the community. Spanish, on the other hand, is the "low" language of intimacy, the language in which casual, unofficial interactions of the home and the in-group are conducted. In some communities, it is also the language of the church and of the surrounding neighborhood stores. In others, English will have established itself firmly in every domain outside of the home.

The effects of this diglossic relationship can be seen clearly in the ways in which individuals acquire and develop proficiency in each of these two languages. As discussed below, the varieties of Spanish and the varieties of English heard in Mexican American communities reflect not only the social and geographical origins of the population of a specific community but also the degree to which each of these two languages is used or not used in the various domains and contexts within which community members interact with each other.

The Spanish Spoken in Mexican American Communities

The Spanish spoken by Mexican Americans in the United States can be classified as a microvariety or microdialect of Mexican Spanish. This means that Mexican American Spanish is most like the Spanish spoken in Mexico, as opposed to, say, the Spanish spoken in Argentina, in Bolivia, in Guatemala, or in Puerto Rico. It is also a variety of the Spanish spoken in the Americas, rather than a variety of the Spanish spoken in Spain. However, just as the English spoken in Texas or Boston is mutually comprehensible with the English spoken in Georgia, Nova Scotia, South Africa, New Zealand, and London, Mexican American Spanish is mutually comprehensible with every other variety of Spanish spoken in both the Americas and the Spanish peninsula.

Within the last 15 years, much attention has been given by linguists and especially sociolinguists to the study and description of Mexican American Spanish. (For a very complete listing of the types of studies carried out, see Teschner, Bills and Craddock 1975). These studies have confirmed that while this Spanish is indeed very similar to Mexican Spanish, it is also different in several key ways. One of the most important differences has to do with the number of social varieties heard in Mexico in contrast to those heard in Mexican American communities in the United States. In Mexico, the presence of the three principal *normas* or levels of speaking is quite evident. Educated members of the community and persons in positions of power and authority, when speaking formally, use *la norma culta* (the cultivated standard), which is an elevated and somewhat erudite style of speech. These same persons, as well as all persons who may be less educated but who have grown up in urban areas, generally use the popular standard variety or *la norma popular* (a less elaborate and cultivated style) when speaking to each other in ordinary interaction. Finally, persons who have had little access to education and/or interaction with speakers of *la norma popular* use what is termed *la norma rural*. This style of speaking generally sounds rustic to city people and is normally associated with rural lifestyles and backgrounds.

In Mexican American communities, however, while one can still find different styles and modes of speaking, these styles are not identical to those found in Mexico. Indeed, some scholars would argue that because of the diglossic situation, English is used exclusively where *la norma culta* would be used in similar circumstances in Mexico. On the other hand, because there has been a large influx of Mexican-origin people from rural and working class backgrounds into these communities, it is also evident that many features found in the Mexican *norma rural* appear to characterize the speech of large numbers of Mexican Americans.

On the other hand, it should be emphasized that Mexican Americans are not necessarily single-style speakers. Research carried out by Barker (1975) and Elías-Olivares (1976), for example, clearly demonstrated that many speakers are able to alternate between styles, as appropriate, just as they would if they were residing in a monolingual Hispanic country. What is different, then, between such monolingual use of Spanish and the use of the same language in Mexican American communities is the frequency with which each style is heard, the number of speakers who actually control *la norma culta,* the number of speakers who can only alternate between *la norma popular* and *la norma rural,* and the number of speakers whose speech repertoire is made of up of only one Spanish style (*la norma rural*) and yet includes a full complementary set of several English styles appropriate for both informal and formal interactions.

The impression that this different distribution of speech styles or levels makes on the middle-class Latin American person who visits these communities is that, to some degree, the Spanish spoken within them is somewhat limited, less elegant than that heard in monolingual Hispanic countries, more typical of that found in intimate versus formal interactions, definitely most similar to that heard among *las clases humildes* (poor people) in Latin America; and, most importantly, that it is significantly influenced by English language contact. Without denying the importance of this English influence, it cannot be emphasized enough that *excluding features that are found in Mexican American Spanish because of its contact with English,* one cannot find examples of Mexican American Spanish that are not also found in Mexico and in many other areas of the Spanish-speaking world.

The features of Mexican American Spanish that are a result of its contact with English will be described below. For the moment, our concern is with this Mexican American variety of Spanish and with its characteristics when one excludes English contact phenomena. This perspective is an important one because it has often been the case that in writing their descriptions of *Chicano* or Mexican American Spanish, some scholars have not pointed out the fact that the examples they are citing (those that reflect no English influence) are examples of phenomena also found in the rest of the Hispanic world. This has led to many misinterpretations about the nature of Mexican American Spanish. Thus, while it may be useful to review lists of *Chicano* features such as those found in Peñalosa (1980:99), it is important to recall that each of the features and characteristics generally mentioned on the lists that focus on morphology in particular is also typical of, at the very least, rural and/or informal Mexican Spanish. An example of such lists is given in Table 4.1.

In each of the cases in Table 4.1, the items identified as Mexican American are also typical of rural or working class speakers in many areas of the Spanish-speaking world. The use of archaisms such as *truje, asina, caiba, haiga,* for example, has been documented by many Spanish dialectologists (for example, Zamora Vicente 1970). Variations in verb morphology (*puedemos, vivemos, estábanos, hablates*) are also well documented (Oroz 1966; Escobar 1978) as typical of rural speech in many countries. Even Navarro Tomás (1971) lists the substitution of [f] by [x] (*jue* instead of *fue*) and of [u̯e] by [o] (*pos* instead of *pues*) as characteristic of "rustic" speech in his classic study *Pronunciación Española.*

Table 4.1. EXAMPLES OF ITEMS LISTED IN DESCRIPTIONS OF MEXICAN AMERICAN SPANISH

Item labeled Mexican American	"Standard" Spanish Equivalent
vivemos	vivimos
hablates	hablaste
puedemos	podemos
truje	traje
asina	así
caiba	caía
escrebir	escribir
jue	fue
pos	pues
haiga	haya
estábanos	estábamos
váyamos	vayamos

Spanish in Contact with English in Mexican American Communities: How and Why Does English Influence Take Place?

Apart from pointing out its connections with varieties of Spanish used in monolingual Spanish communities, current research on Mexican American Spanish has made clear that what gives this variety its special flavor is the fact that many of its speakers are bilingual. Because many or most of the members of the community use English for a very large part of their everyday lives, the influence or presence of English is often detected in the speech of Mexican Americans when they speak Spanish. Thus, in order to understand Mexican American Spanish, one must be aware not only of its position in relation to other language varieties, but also of how and why it is influenced by English.

English influence on Mexican American Spanish may take several forms, some obvious, some subtle. Briefly, we may distinguish between three ways in which contact with English modifies Spanish: *semantic extension, borrowing,* and *code-switching,* each of which will be discussed in some detail below. It is important to emphasize, however, that to say that Mexican American Spanish is influenced by English does not imply that the language in question has ceased to be Spanish. The fact is that the Spanish spoken in Mexican American communities is *not* a mixed code or a hybrid language that is neither English nor Spanish. Whether used in alternation with English or not, it is clear that all Spanish segments heard among Mexican Americans are unquestionably Spanish, phonologically, morphologically, as well as syntactically.

Semantic Extension The first type of English influence on Spanish, which I will call semantic extension, is rather subtle. Since all the words are in Spanish, there seems, at first glance, to have been no influence from another language.

1. Voy a llevar a la *niñera* a su casa.
   (I'm going to take the babysitter home.)
2. A los perros callejeros se los llevan a la *perrera*.
   (Stray dogs are taken to the dog pound.)

However, upon closer examination, it can be seen that the Spanish words for "babysitter" and "dog pound" have undergone a semantic transformation. Their original meanings were limited to what is normally found in monolingual Spanish-speaking countries. Thus, *niñera* really refers to a servant who lives (or works full-time) in a household and takes care of children, and not to a young person of middle-class background who "sits" with children and charges by the hour. *Perrera* refers to a dog house or even to a female person who takes care of dogs, but not to a dog pound. Few Hispanic countries have such an institution.

Borrowing A more readily detected form of English influence on Mexican American Spanish is borrowing, which is typical of what happens when speakers of a language come into contact with concepts that are new to them and for which they have no available vocabulary. In the following examples of Mexican American Spanish, new words appear to have been created using English base forms and Spanish inflections: nouns are given gender, and verbs are conjugated using the complex Spanish morphological system. English borrowings are known as *anglicismos* in the Spanish-speaking world.

3. Ay te *wacho* (from *watch*).
   (I'll be seeing you.)
4. Tengo que *taipear* esto para la clase.
   (I'll have to type this for the class.)
5. Se esta *liqueando* el *rufo*.
   (The roof is leaking.)

Borrowing is a common result of language contact. For centuries languages have borrowed from one another and have integrated borrowings into their lexical inventory, treating them as if they were native items. For example, English uses terms such as *menu, restaurant, patio,* while Spanish uses *acequia, film, algodón, almohada, canoa.* These examples are all taken from other languages, all integrated into the language, and all used as if they were originally English or Spanish; in the case of Spanish, the borrowed words are accepted by the Real Academia Española. No one suggests that these borrowings distort or seriously threaten either English or Spanish.

Many speakers of Spanish, however, respond negatively to the same process when it occurs in those varieties in contact with English. For this reason, when a speaker creates the term *weldear* from the English base *weld,* and uses it correctly as a conjugated Spanish verb in all its tenses (*yo weldeo, yo weldiaba, yo weldié, ojalá que nosotros weldiemos,* etc.), they see not an integrated borrowing in which the Spanish morphological system is alive and well, but an item they label "Spanglish" and believe is neither English nor Spanish. Even though the Spanish-speaking world reflects the same process in its use of sports terms (*batear* [to bat] and *potear* [to putt]), it appears to be much more suspect in bilingual communities. Somehow, it is assumed that borrowing takes place because speakers are either too lazy or too ignorant to use the "correct" Spanish word.

As was indicated previously, however, the process is not quite that simple. The fact is that languages do not necessarily make the same distinctions; and often there are lexical gaps in one language that will not seem obvious to speakers unless they are exposed to other languages. For example, English makes a distinction between welding and soldering. Spanish has only one term for both: *soldar.* There is, then, a lexical gap in Spanish that becomes evident when a speaker wants to make the same distinction when speaking Spanish that is made in English. The question is: what is the speaker to do given the existing limitations of Spanish? There are a number of choices. These lexical gaps can be filled (1) by using semantic extensions, as in the case of *niñera* and *perrera* discussed above; (2) by borrowing, that is, by using a foreign base and native inflections; or (3) by simply using an unadapted foreign term. In the case of *weld* and *solder,* the choices would involve using *soldar* with the meaning of *weld* and extending its meaning, using the borrowed and adapted new verb *weldear,* or using the unadapted term, as in (6) below, and switching from Spanish to English and back to Spanish.

6. Necesito *weld* esos fierros.
(I have to weld those pieces of metal.)

Whatever choice is made, the point is that reflecting the distinction made by English and not made by Spanish will involve "changing" Spanish to some degree, by adding to it in some way, or by simply switching into the other language. Such changes and borrowings in Mexican American Spanish have been a cause of concern to people who are interested in maintaining language purity. This concern, however, does not take into account the fundamentally dynamic nature of language, or the fact that speakers constantly add to their language in order to talk about new things and experiences.

Indeed, a detailed analysis of such borrowings reveals that rather than capriciously integrating terms, Mexican American Spanish generally responds to specific needs. Often if speakers encounter for the first time concepts with which they were unfamiliar in Mexico, they will create a new word. One individual may use it spontaneously, and in time it will become fully integrated into the local variety. Thus *taipear,* for example, may come to be used, not because there is no equivalent in Spanish, but because speakers may not have had occasion to have been involved with typing and typewriters in their home country, because the word *mecanografiar* has a low frequency, because the term *escribir a maquina* seems too cumbersome, or even because, having heard *taipear* from other speakers in their community, they believe that it is a correct Spanish term.

Because of the sociohistorical context of the interactions between English and Spanish, among Mexican Americans the use of English borrowings is particularly prevalent. This use of borrowings has caused Mexican American Spanish to be stigmatized among monolingual speakers who are increasingly concerned about the impact that English is having on both the culture and language of Latin America. Some feel that the incorporation of *anglicismos* into the language, when there are perfectly good Spanish equivalents, results in a distortion and destruction of the language. These are, however, social and not linguistic judgments. To the degree that Mexican American Spanish continues to use the process of *castellanización,* that is, to the degree that it Hispanicizes those elements that it wishes to use, there is no real destruction or distortion. Even if Mexican American Spanish were to double its vocabulary by using the process of borrowing, it would still be recognizably Spanish. To decide that Mexican American Spanish is no longer pure Spanish because of the presence of these borrowings is, to quote the renowned Latin American linguist Angel Rosenblat (1962), nothing more than misguided linguistic chauvinism.

> . . . And beyond that, what does Castillian (Spanish) purity mean? Castellano (Spanish) is an evolved Latin that adopted elements from Iberian, Visigothic, Arabic, Greek, French, Italian, English, and even elements indigenous to America. How can one speak about Spanish purity, or at what point can we irreversibly set Spanish and pretend that every new contribution is a harmful impurity? This so-called purity is in the final analysis a type of customs house protectionism, of limited linguistic chauvinism which, like all chauvinism, is miserly and impoverishing. (Translated by Valdés)

Code-Switching The third way in which English influence on Mexican American Spanish is manifested is code-switching, which can be defined as the alternating use of two languages at the word, phrase, clause, or sentence level. In the following examples, stretches of unmodified Spanish alternate with stretches of unmodified English:

7. Dijo mi mamá que I have to study.
   (My mother said that I have to study.)
8. Tengo la waist twenty-nine, tengo que reduce.
   (I have a twenty-nine [inch] waist, I have to reduce.)

Code-switching is different from borrowing in that the elements from the other language are used in their original form. No attempt is made to adapt them or to integrate them into the system being used. In other words, each switch into Spanish or English consists of *unchanged Spanish or English words,* and these words are pronounced by the speakers as a native speaker of that language would pronounce them. There is ordinarily a clean break between the two phonemic systems. The following examples show the contrast between borrowing (9), where the English element is incorporated into the Spanish system, and code-switching (10), where the English element is used in its original form:

9. Estábamos *jenguiando* allí en la esquina.
   (We were hanging out there at the corner.)
10. No tengo tiempo ni para estar *hanging out* con los amigos.
   (I don't even have time to be hanging out with friends.)

Frequent code-switching is a very distinctive characteristic of the speech of Mexican American communities. To monolingual speakers of either English or Spanish, code-switching suggests that its speakers speak neither language. Nothing, in fact, is further from the truth. As is the case with borrowing, misunderstandings about how language works in bilingual communities have led to unfair judgments about the language strengths of speakers who use their two languages in this manner. Research on bilinguals and bilingual communities has demonstrated, however, that rather than reflecting weakness, complex code-switching requires that speakers be very proficient in the two languages used.

In the following example, the speaker appears to be using Spanish to recount what happened and English to paraphrase or quote what was actually said; the speaker does not pause before switching from one language to the other, and what is said in one language is not repeated or explained in the other.

11. Y luego me dijo, don't you ever do that again. Y luego yo le dije, well don't think you can tell me what to do. Estaba tan furiosa que I just wanted to walk away. (And then he said, don't you ever do that again. And then I said, well don't think you can tell me what to do. I was so furious that I just wanted to walk away.)

It is clear that code-switching occurs when bilinguals are speaking to each other and not when they are speaking to monolingual speakers of either language. One of the two languages being used can generally be identified as the "base language," although there are times when this base language appears to change within the same interaction. It also appears that when fluent bilinguals speak to each other and code-switch they are able to capitalize on the strengths of *both* languages in order to communicate a broad variety of meanings. By alternating between their languages, bilinguals are able to use their total speech repertoire, which includes many levels and styles and modes of speaking in *two* languages. It is helpful to imagine that when bilinguals code-switch, they are in fact using a twelve-string guitar, rather than limiting themselves to two six-string instruments.

Code-switching, then, has been found to be neither random nor meaningless. Rather, it is a device that can convey important social information ranging from role relationships between speakers to feelings of solidarity, intimacy, and the like. A shift between languages may signal the fact that two bilinguals are shifting their role relationship with regard to one another, that they are changing topics, or that they are responding to the particular characteristics of the setting. It is not unusual, for example, for a bilingual employer and employee to discuss matters relating to business in the language of the work domain, followed by a switch, within the same interaction, to the language of the home or neighborhood for a discussion of personal experiences or social talk.

In the following example, the type of information conveyed by a switch in languages can be seen clearly.

12. Mother: Which dress are you going to wear to the dance, Barbie?
Barbie: The white one.
Mother: (Looking at her 8-year-old son slurping a milkshake nearby) Which one?
Barbie: The one with the puffy sleeves.
Mother: (Interrupting to correct the boy) Leo sientate, mira lo que estas haciendo. Estas tirando todo el milkshake. (Leo, sit down, look at what you're doing. You're spilling all the milkshake.)

A mother is speaking to her adolescent daughter. Her 8-year-old son is playing nearby. The mother becomes more and more impatient with the boy when he fails to respond to her directions. Finally, to emphasize her annoyance (and her parental role), she switches into Spanish. There is no doubt here that the mother controls both English and Spanish. Her switch into Spanish takes place, not because she cannot say the same thing in English, but because she wants to make a specific point. A monolingual English-speaking mother might, under the same circumstances, emphasize the seriousness of the situation to her young son by using his full name to address him and by adopting a harsh tone of voice.

In addition to conveying social information, code-switching can also be used as a personal rhetorical device to add color to an utterance, to emphasize, to contrast, to underscore a context, to create new poetic meanings, and the like. Stylistic code-switching can involve strategies such as the following:

1. Repetition of the same item in two languages: Me tomé toda la cafetera, the whole coffee pot.
   (I drank the whole coffee pot, the whole coffee pot.)
2. The use of one language as the language of narration and the other language as the language of paraphrase:
   Y me preguntó, "Why don't you want to go?" Y pos yo m'hice tonta y le dije, "Why do you think I don't want to go?"
   (And he asked me, "Why don't you want to go?" And well I played dumb and told him, "Why do you think I don't want to go?")
3. The use of items in one language that do not have equivalents of the same strength in the other language:
   He was like muy antipático (very unpleasant) and nobody liked him.

Again, stylistic switching occurs not because speakers lack an equivalent in one of their languages, but because they wish to convey a precise meaning.

Some researchers have also sought to explore the different code-switching styles of bilingual speakers. Preliminary work suggests that certain speakers switch codes to emphasize statements, to paraphrase and narrate, or to convey factual information, while others tend to be natural mimics and adapt the switching patterns of the person to whom they are speaking. Unfortunately, most bilinguals are not aware of the complexity of the strategies they use, and when questioned will often agree with their critics that they switch because it is a sloppy habit, or because they do not know the right words or cannot think of them quickly enough. It has occurred to very few bilingual speakers that such stylistic switching is a reflection of strength rather than weakness.

Evidence to support this last conclusion has been found in the study of code-switching as a rule-governed process. After examining large corpuses of bilingual speech, researchers have concluded that there are definite rules underlying the code-switching process. Work carried out by Timm (1975), Pfaff (1979), Gingràs (1974), Poplack (1980), Wentz and McClure (1975), and others suggests that there are syntactic limits to language alternation within a given sentence. While different scholars appear to disagree about which constraints or limitations apply, it is clear that for a person to code-switch acceptably, he or she must control these constraints. An individual who code-switches between Spanish and English, rather than being alingual, nonlingual, or a speaker of a senseless language mixture, is actually operating within the rules of *both* systems in a uniquely complex manner.

The above sections have presented only superficially the most important aspects of code-switching among bilingual speakers. A number of other factors interact with the processes described here to result in a dynamic linguistic process as yet imperfectly understood. The difficulties of analyzing particular code-switches may be made more evident by Table 4.2, in which a working classification, taken from Valdés-Fallis (1978), is included. These categorizations further emphasize the difficulties of making generalizations about the form or length of such switches and their actual purpose or effect.

In sum, code-switching, particularly when Spanish is the base language, is heard frequently in Mexican American communities. Its use, however, does not imply that speakers are not able to sustain a conversation in this language. While there are indeed many instances when speakers switch to English because of momentary lexical need, many switches are used strategically by speakers to convey important personal and social information.

The English Spoken in Mexican American Communities

In comparison to the research carried out on Spanish as it is used in Mexican American communities, very little work has been undertaken on English as it is spoken among Mexican Americans. Indeed very little research has been carried out even on the varieties of English spoken among monolingual Anglos in those areas of the country in which there are large numbers of Mexican Americans. In spite of this fact, however, one can safely say that the English spoken in Mexican American communities is a microvariety of American English as opposed to, for example, British English or Australian English. It is more difficult, however, to generalize about the specific regional varieties of American English spoken in these communities, and even more difficult to determine to what extent the English spoken by Mexican Americans is truly influenced by Spanish. Put another way, the question is: if one were to walk down the street of a Mexican community in Houston, Texas, for example, would one hear the same Houston, Texas, accent that one hears among Anglos, or would one hear a more general American speech? Would the Houston, Texas, accent be influenced by Spanish? Would the more general American speech also show traces of this influence? To what degree would there be differences among speakers? Would some speak accented English and others not? What would be the difference between individuals who are merely acquiring English and those that are monolingual speakers of the language?

Unfortunately, there are few answers to these questions. The handful of studies that have focused on Mexican American or *Chicano* English have primarily investigated the speech of young children, rather than that of adult Mexican Americans. It is thus difficult to reach conclusions about adult language.

Table 4.2. PRINCIPAL CODE-SWITCHING PATTERNS

Patterns	Definitions	Examples
Switching patterns that occur in response to external factors		
Situational switches	Related to the social role of speakers	Mother uses English to chat with daughters but switches to Spanish to reprimand son.
Contextual switches	Situation, topic, setting, etc., linked to the other language	Students switch to English to discuss details of a math exam.
Identity markers	In-group membership stressed	*Ese bato, órale, ándale pues* used in English conversations, regardless of actual Spanish fluency.
Quotations and paraphrases	Contextual: related to language used by the original speaker	Y lo (luego) me dijo el Mr. Johnson que *I have to study*. (Remark was actually made in English.)
Switching patterns that occur in response to internal factors		
Random switches of high frequency items	Unpredictable; do not relate to topic, situation, setting, or language dominance; occur *only* on word level	Very common words, such as days of the week or colors. Function like English synonyms: gal–girl, guy–fellow, etc. Fuimos al *party* ayer y estuvo tan suave la fiesta.
Switches that reflect lexical need	Related to language dominance, memory, and spontaneous versus automatic speech	Include the "tip of the tongue" phenomenon; item may be momentarily forgotten.
Triggered switches	Due to preceding or following items	Yo lo vi, you know, *but I didn't speak to him.* (Switch is triggered by the preformulation.)
Preformulations	Include linguistic routines and automatic speech	*You know, glad to meet you, thanks for calling, no te molestes, qué hay de nuevo,* etc.
Discourse markers	*But, and,, of course,* etc.	*Este . . . este . . .* yo sí quería ir.
Quotations and paraphrases	Non-contextual: not related to language used by original speaker	He insisted *que no me fuera*. But I did anyway. (Remark was originally made in English.)
Stylistic switches	Obvious stylistic devices used for emphasis or contrast	Me tomé toda la cafetera, *the whole coffee pot*.
Sequential switches	Involve using the last language used by the preceding speaker	Certain speakers will always follow the language switches of other speakers; others will not.

Source: Valdés-Fallis, G. 1978. Code switching and the classroom teacher. *Language in Education: Theory and Practice,* 4:16.

In essence, what most existing studies have provided are lists of Spanish-influenced features found in the speech of young Mexican Americans. Metcalf (1979) describes a number of these studies and includes several listings of usually identified "errors" in the areas of pronunciation, intonation, syntax, and vocabulary. Indeed, there appears to be a fascination with what Fishman (1968) has called "laundry lists," long presentations of instances where Spanish has "rubbed off" on English. For an example of such a list see Table 4.3, taken from several cited in Metcalf (1979).

To some degree, these lists of "errors" can be useful. They have, for example, been used by some linguists to demonstrate that certain features found in the speech of Mexican Americans are, in fact, not products of Spanish interference or transfer, but a direct reflection of the nonstandard English local variety in use in the surrounding community. These lists are not useful, however, if it is assumed that *all* or *most* Mexican Americans exhibit these features in their speech. The fact is that the English spoken by *some* Mexican Americans is indeed a "learner's variety," and is characterized by many instances of direct transfer from Spanish. The English spoken by other Mexican Americans, however, may be very different indeed. It may show no traces of Spanish influence, a few traces of Spanish influence when the speaker is under stress, or even consistent traces of influence at all times.

Not all Mexican Americans can be said to speak English with a Spanish accent, with Spanish intonation, or reflecting Spanish syntax. Indeed, as Gingràs (1972) found, Mexican Americans can be classified as belonging to one of four groups: (1) those whose English is indistinguishable from that of monolingual Anglos in the community; (2) those whose speech has slight divergences from the local Anglo variety, which are probably not detectable by the average person on first contact; (3) those whose speech has moderate divergences from the local variety, all of which are readily apparent to most people; and (4) those whose speech shows clear transfer from the Spanish

Table 4.3. EXAMPLES OF FEATURES SAID TO BE CHARACTERISTIC OF MEXICAN AMERICAN ENGLISH

Pronunciation
- Substitution of *ch* for *sh* (washes replaced by watches)
- Substitution of [f] and [s] for [Θ]: (teef for teeth)
- Replacement of voiced [z] by [s]
- Unaspirated voiceless stops in initial position

Stress
- Stress on both elements of a compound (apple tree)

Syntax
- Use of gerund for infinitive

system and who seem to be in the process of acquiring English. It is, moreover, possible for members of the first three groups to be monolingual speakers of English, that is, persons whose first language was English and who have never spoken Spanish.

Clearly, the kind of English spoken by different individuals within the same Mexican American community is directly related to the types and kinds of English they are in contact with. If there is contact with the local Anglo variety and there is an opportunity for interacting with a peer group of such speakers, Mexican American children will quickly acquire this variety. If, on the other hand, there is little contact between groups, if there are no opportunities for interacting with monolingual Anglo speakers, the result may be quite different. Only other Mexican Americans, who may themselves speak Spanish-influenced varieties of English, will serve as models for those individuals who are acquiring English. It is no wonder, then, that if this is the case, even individuals whose only language is English will speak a variety of this language that seems to suggest they are transferring features from Spanish. No such transfer is occurring, of course, but the impression left with a monolingual Anglo who hears it is that somehow there is something "foreign" about Mexican American English.

The fact that there are large numbers of monolingual English-speaking Mexican Americans in many communities has led some scholars (e.g. Metcalf 1979) to suggest that there is a legitimate variety of English that can be called "*Chicano* English." For Metcalf, *Chicano* English is a variety of English identical to the local Anglo variety, except that it has added a "Spanish accent." He states that it is spoken, not by learners of the language, but by "people whose native language is a special variety of English with a Spanish sound to it" (Metcalf 1979:1).

Other scholars disagree with this classification entirely. Some would argue that Mexican Americans do not have enough contact with Anglos and therefore do not acquire the local variety of English. Thus, they would maintain that, if anything, *Chicano* English is a type of general American or Northern Standard with a Spanish flavor. Other scholars (e.g., Sawyer 1975) reject the entire concept of the existence of a Mexican American variety of English. They argue that the English spoken by Mexican American bilinguals is an imperfect state in the mastery of English, and that it will become more expert from generation to generation.

Until there is more research on the English spoken in Mexican American communities, it will be difficult to defend any of the above positions exclusively. Many questions must be answered that have not been addressed. For example: if we are to describe "Mexican American English" or even to decide if it exists, we must first understand how English was acquired by speakers whose English appears to be indistinguishable from that of monolingual Anglos. Did they interact with Anglos? How soon? How frequently? Did this contact continue over a lifetime? Was there a conscious effort made by Mexican American learners to sound like their Anglo models? What were the results? Is the English variety spoken by these Mexican Americans truly indistinguishable from Anglo English in all contexts? Are there limitations? What are these and where do they appear?

The same types of questions must then be asked about the other three groups of speakers: those whose divergences from Anglo English are not generally noticeable to laymen, those whose divergences are clearly noticeable, and those whose English is obviously colored by transfers from Spanish. We must ask, for example: What are the differences between the first two groups? What is the role of English language models in the acquisition process in each case? Are the slight divergences similar in persons of the same social class, educational background, etc.? What other factors appear to influence the acquisition or use of a Spanish-sounding variety?

Clearly the questions are many and complex. It will take many years before the answers are forthcoming. In the meantime, however, it is evident that what information we do have suggests strongly (1) that Mexican Americans from the same community speak different "kinds" of English; (2) that many Mexican Americans are native speakers of English and are not bilingual; (3) that Mexican Americans can be classified according to the degree to which their English speech diverges from the local Anglo norm; and (4) that the presence of Spanish language elements in a speaker's English does not indicate that the individual is in the process of learning English.

IMPLICATIONS FOR THE TEACHER OF ENGLISH

Mexican American communities are bilingual. Within them, many Mexican American individuals are themselves bilingual. And as bilinguals, they use English and Spanish as appropriate within their specific contexts to carry out different functions and to interact with others.

For the most part, the Spanish and the English heard in these communities will not be identical to that heard among monolingual speakers in other contexts. Spanish will reflect an English influence, primarily in the many borrowings that it uses; and English will reflect a Spanish flavor, particularly in its pronunciation.

What does this mean for English teachers? Clearly the answer depends on what kind of English teachers they are. In this section, a number of suggestions will be presented for two different groups of teachers: teachers of English language arts to fluent bilingual or monolingual Mexican Americans and teachers of English as a second language.

Teaching Fluent English Speakers Who Are Mexican American

For teachers who are involved in teaching language arts to what are supposed to be fluent English speakers, the most important task has to do with learning how to differentiate between actual language limitations and superficial "foreign-sounding" features. As noted previously, Mexican American speakers often have heavy accents in English. It is important that teachers not confuse pronunciation "errors" with lack of control of the language and lack of fluency of expression. The fact that a speaker has an accent does not imply that his or her English is imperfectly learned. Teachers must learn to evaluate overall ability to express ideas in English, instead of focusing primarily on pronunciation. They must recall also that students bring with them what some scholars have described as a legitimate variety of English, a variety that may have a Spanish flavor but that is as valid as any other. Pronunciation, then, should not be corrected, unless the pronunciation of speakers of English from other geographical areas is also being corrected. Pronunciation differences will not interfere with learning to read and write. A grave injustice will be done to students if it is assumed by teachers that they must correct pronunciation *before* they can begin instruction in "real" content.

Creating a positive and rich language environment in the classroom is most important. Teachers must be aware of the need that many children have to hear English from native speakers and to interact with Anglo English-speaking peers. If classes include both Anglos and Mexican Americans, teaching strategies that involve group work and discussion can be most valuable. Assume that students will profit from being exposed to a large variety of styles and levels of language.

Teaching English as Second Language

As noted earlier, English is the language of prestige in all Mexican American communities. It is clear that English is considered important, and that it is expected that every child will become an English speaker. The expectations for adults, on the other hand, are not as clear cut. What normally happens is that those individuals who happen to come into contact with English speakers tend to learn at least some English. Those who do not can spend years in the community without learning much English. They depend on other members of the family to interpret or translate for them. This is particularly true of older immigrant women in Mexican American communities.

The important thing for ESL teachers to remember is that there is no lack of interest in learning English in Mexican American communities. Thus the conclusion to be reached about older people who, after many years, decide to take an English class is not that they refused to learn English before, but rather that for many complex reasons it may not have been possible or feasible for them to study English formally. When such older learners enroll in a class, teachers need to be aware that for some of them a formal class setting is a foreign environment. They may have many fears about their own abilities to learn, which may have to do with their ideas about school, the experiences of others in the community in English classes, their children's success or lack of it in both Mexican and American schools, and the like. Moreover, because there are so many myths in the community about what it is to know a language and how languages are learned, these older learners may be afraid that they cannot learn or that they will never be able to speak. Many of these learners probably have attempted at some point to say something in English, but they might have met with ridicule from family members, even their own children, who, like the surrounding majority community, find heavy accents laughable. For this reason, they probably sell themselves short. They do not realize, for example, that the ability to understand is also a valuable skill and part of "knowing" a language. Many have been convinced, again by family members, of the fact that English is difficult.

The process of teaching such learners clearly begins with sensitivity to fears and scars. If it is apparent that students have very low literacy skills in Spanish, it makes little sense to teach classes in which there is a heavy reliance on written materials. It is perhaps important for such students to learn how to read and write well in their own language and in English, but the role of the ESL teacher in teaching these specific students is to teach English, especially oral English. Oral skills will permit students to function in the surrounding Anglo community. The challenge, then, for the ESL teacher faced with learners who are afraid, who have low literacy skills in their own language, and who may have insecurities about their capacity to learn English is to develop an approach to teaching English that will set students at ease, focus on oral language, and depend minimally on written material.

On the positive side is the fact that because English is spoken so widely in Mexican American communities, it is unlikely that students have zero familiarity with the language. At the very least they will have learned some phrases (which they may repeat shyly), and they may also have developed some listening comprehension skills. The teacher can build on these to boost students' self-confidence.

While many approaches and methodologies are currently in use for the teaching of English, those approaches and methods should be chosen that are most appropriate for developing the kinds of skills students need. This may mean in some cases that a heavy grammatical and analytical approach should not be adopted. This is especially true if, when questioned, students state that their goal in learning English is to get a specific job or to communicate in a specific context. As far as possible, instruction should be tailored to meet students' needs. What this suggests is that a topical or notional/functional syllabus may be most effective because it focuses on specific domains and contexts. By teaching phrases to answer the phone with, for example, and by teaching comprehension of commonly heard telephone talk (e.g., "Is Mary home?" "Is this 223–8879?"), students will quickly be able to use and show off their new skills. This will not be the case if the class has focused on the conjugation of the verb *to be* and has practiced a series of unconnected sentences that cannot be used to say anything real.

In order to keep such learners in class, they must be made to feel comfortable, they must sense that the teacher believes that they *can* learn, and they must feel that they are making *some* progress.

Not all adult learners in the community will fit the above description. Many adult learners from the same community will be very different. They will demand much from the teacher and will feel very comfortable in a class setting. Indeed, they may have selected the class setting because they believe it to be the fastest way of learning English. They will be impatient and will want to progress much faster than is really possible. Teachers can be helpful to these students by identifying contexts in the community in which such students can interact with local Anglos and other English speakers. Often such students must be persuaded to set their books aside and attempt to communicate in the real world.

In comparison to adult learners, younger learners present a different picture. Not only must they acquire English in order to use it in their everyday lives, but they must also acquire the type of school language that will permit them to succeed in an academic setting. It cannot be emphasized enough that such learners especially need to use English for real communication and at the same time be exposed to large amounts of "academic language." How to develop these two levels of language is the real challenge for ESL teachers who work with these young students, especially since there are no real guidelines. For some time in the foreseeable future, ESL teachers must work together with researchers to determine exactly what kinds of formal classroom activities are actually supportive of the development of real-world and academic language proficiency.

Until we have more answers, however, we can merely stress that ESL teachers who wish to become effective teachers for Mexican-origin students cannot hope for easy answers. Learning how to teach these students is not a question of memorizing long lists of possible sources of interference from Spanish. It has long been clear that learners from many different language groups exhibit similar patterns when learning English. It has also been evident that certain errors are simply developmental and will be outgrown, if only learners have the opportunity to interact in English, to hear the language, and to be rewarded by their success in actually communicating with others. A knowledge of how Mexican American communities work and a basic understanding of how bilingualism develops and functions can help teachers decide exactly how they can provide students with instruction directly complementing what they experience in the real world.

CONCLUSION

Language use in Mexican American communities is a complex and fascinating topic. Much can be learned from the study of these communities about the nature of immigrant bilingualism and about language acquisition and language loss. More importantly, much can be learned about the people who live in these communities and about how they struggle to become part of a new world. ESL teachers have much to contribute in helping to make their formal transition into English a less painful process.

EXPLORING IDEAS

1. Valdés notes that "popular stereotypes of Mexican Americans invariably obscure the fact that there is no one list of qualities and characteristics that can be applied to identify the many different kinds of individuals that can be referred to by the term *Mexican Americans*."

What characteristics of Mexican Americans are typically contained in the popular stereotypes of Mexican Americans that appear in the mass media? How might such stereotypes influence the language retention and language loss of the Mexican American community?

2. Valdés refers to the distinction between elite bilingualism and natural bilingualism.

In the United States which type of bilingualism appears to be more valued? What evidence can you cite for your conclusion?

3. Valdés points out that Mexican immigrants are composed of three different kinds of immigrants: permanent immigrants, short-term immigrants, and cyclical immigrants.

How might the fact of having these various kinds of immigrants affect the overall language retention and language loss of Mexican Americans? Do you think having these three types of immigrants will alter Mexican Americans' conformity to the general trend of ethnic groups becoming monolingual by the fourth generation?

4. Valdés states that when one speaks of Mexican American Spanish, excluding features that are caused by its contact with English, the Spanish is most similar to that spoken in rural Mexican areas among the working class.

How might the fact that a Mexican American speaks principally the rural style of Spanish affect his or her interaction with recent middle class, urban Mexican immigrants? How might this fact affect the individual's interaction with a Spanish teacher in a bilingual setting?

5. Valdés cites Gringràs' (1972) contention that Mexican Americans can be classified as belonging to one of four groups: those who speak English indistinguishable from that of monolingual Anglos; those whose speech has a slight divergence from the monolingual Anglos; those whose speech has a moderate divergence from the local standard; and those whose speech shows clear transfer from Spanish and who are learning English.

Do you see these categories as discrete or as a continuum? Do you think an individual might on occasion shift from one category to another? What are some factors in the social setting that could influence this shift?

APPLYING THE IDEAS

1. Valdés defines a bilingual as an individual who can function to some degree in more than one language. One way to determine which language is dominant for an individual is to find out how often and when the individual uses each of the two languages.

In order to determine the degree of an individual's bilingualism, begin by designing a set of questions dealing with language use such as the following.

1. What language do you generally use in talking to your parents? your brothers and sisters? your children? your husband or wife?
2. What language do you generally use at work with your co-workers? your boss?

Next interview a bilingual individual, preferably a Mexican American, to determine where this individual would fall on the continuum depicted in Figure 4.1.

2. Valdés notes that Mexican Americans are a diverse community composed of people of various ages and economic and educational backgrounds who have settled in both rural and urban areas throughout the United States.

Investigate the diversity of the community by consulting data from the 1980 Census on such items as the age, geographical distribution, and educational and economic level of Mexican Americans.

3. Valdés provides examples of several types of English-Spanish code-switching and points out that many studies have been conducted on English-Spanish code-switching.

Research code-switching in the Mexican American community by consulting the sources listed in the article as well as other available sources. Pay particular attention to the rules that govern code-switching and the typical reasons for code-switching.

4. Valdés includes in Table 4.2 a taxonomy of principal code-switching patterns that occur in response to both external and internal factors.

If you are bilingual, gather examples of code-switching among members of your community. Then try to categorize these examples according to Valdés' taxonomy.

SUGGESTED READINGS

Hernández-Chavez, E. A., D. Cohen, and A. F. Beltramo, eds. 1975. *El Lenguaje de los Chicanos*. Arlington, VA: Center for Applied Linguistics. (This book is one of the first major collections of readings on Chicano discourse.)

Peñalosa, F. 1980. *Chicano Sociolinguistics: A Brief Introduction*. Rowley, MA: Newbury House Publishers. (Although this book is out of print, it is the most concise presentation of Chicano language from a sociolinguistic perspective that exists.)

Amastae, J. and L. Elías-Olivares, eds. 1982. *Spanish in the United States: Sociolinguistic Aspects*. Cambridge: Cambridge University Press. (The editors have gathered both new and old articles on the social and educational aspects of Chicano language.)

Sánchez, R. 1983. *Chicano Discourse: Socio-historic Perspectives*. Rowley, MA: Newbury House Publishers. (This book is a study of Chicano language from a social and pragmatic perspective. Sánchez begins with a historical review of the social and economic reality of the Chicano community and then proceeds to discuss the patterns of communication within the community.)

REFERENCES

Barker, G. 1975. Social functions of language in a Mexican American community. In E. Hernández-Chavez et al., eds. *El Lenguaje de los Chicanos: Regional and Social Characteristics of Language Used by Mexican Americans*. Arlington, VA: Center for Applied Linguistics.

Burma, J. H. 1970. *Mexican Americans in the United States: A Reader*. Cambridge, MA: Schenkman.

Elías-Olivares, L. 1976. *Ways of Speaking in a Chicano Community: A Sociolinguistic Approach*. Unpublished doctoral dissertation, University of Texas.

Escobar, A. 1978. *Variaciones Sociolingüísticas del Castellano en el Perú*. Lima: Instituto de Estudios Peruanos.

Ferguson, C. A. 1959. Diglossia. *Word* 15: 325–40.

Fishman, J. A. 1964. Language maintenance and language shift as fields of inquiry. *Linguistics* 9: 32–70.

Fishman, J. A. 1968. Sociolinguistic perspective on the study of bilingualism. *Linguistics* 39: 21–49.

Gingràs, R. C. 1972. An analysis of the linguistic characteristics of the English found in a set of Mexican American child data. Los Alamitos, CA: Southwest Regional Laboratory for Educational Research and Development. ED 111 002.

Gingràs, R. C. 1974. Problems in the description of Spanish/English intrasentential code switching. In G. Bills ed., *Southwest Area Linguistics*. San Diego, CA: Institute for Cultural Pluralism.

McCarthy, K. F. and R. B. Valdez 1985. *Current and Future Effects of Mexican Immigration in California*. Santa Monica. CA: The Rand Corporation.

Metcalf, A. A. 1979. Chicano English. *Language in Education: Theory and Practice* 21.

Navarro Tomás, T. 1971. *Pronunciacion Española*. Madrid: Consejo Superior de Investigaciones Cientificas.

Oroz, R. 1966. *La Lengua Castellana en Chile*. Santiago: Universidad de Chile.

Peñalosa, F. 1980. *Chicano Sociolinguistics*. Rowley, MA: Newbury House.

Pfaff, C. W. 1979. Constraints on language mixing. *Language* 55: 291–318.

Poplack, S. 1980. Sometimes I'll start a sentence in Spanish y termino en español: toward a typology of code–switching. *Linguistics* 18 (7,8): 581–618.

Rosenblat, A. 1962. *El Castellano de España y el Castellano de América: Unidad y Diferenciación*. Caracas: Universidad Central de Venezuela, Instituto de Filología Andres Bello.

Sawyer, J. B. 1975. Spanish English bilingualism in San Antonio, Texas. In E. Hernández-Chavez et al., eds., *El Lenguaje de los Chicanos: Regional and Social Characteristics of Language Used by Mexican Americans*. Arlington, VA: Center for Applied Linguistics.

Teschner, R. V., G. D. Bills and J. A. Craddock, 1975. *Spanish and English of United States Hispanos: A Critical, Annotated, Linguistic Bibliography*. Arlington, VA: Center for Applied Linguistics.

Timm, L. A. 1975. Spanish/English code switching; el porque y how-not to. *Romance Philology* 28: 473–82.

U.S. Bureau of the Census. 1985. Current Population Reports, *Population Characteristics,* Semes P-20, No. 403, "Persons of Spanish Origin in the United States: March, 1985 (Advanced Report)." December.

Valdés-Fallis, G. 1978. Code switching and the classroom teacher. *Language in Education: Theory and Practice* 4.

Wentz, J. and E. McClure 1975. Aspects of the syntax of the code-switching discourse of children. Presented at the Mid-American Linguistics Conference, 1975. ED 121 068.

Zamora Vicente, A. 1970. *Dialectologia Española*. Madrid: Editorial Gredos.

CHAPTER

5

The Language Situation of Puerto Ricans

Ana Celia Zentella

When the first groups of Puerto Rican emigrants left that Caribbean island for the United States at the end of the nineteenth century, even before the U.S. occupation of the island in 1898, the trip by boat could take up to 9 days. In 1910 the first U.S. Census recorded the presence of over 1,000 Puerto Ricans on the mainland. After Puerto Ricans were made American citizens, a few weeks before the United States entered World War I, the emigration flow increased, particularly during the bleak 1930s. But it reached its culmination during the era after World War II (1945–1955), when over 50,000 Puerto Ricans left each year in search of some relief from the dire economic conditions on the island, which were ironically the result of a more pervasive U.S. control of the economy. The plane service established between the island and New York City in 1946 to provide cheap workers for that city's booming businesses, particularly the garment industry, made the trip in 9 hours. Over 90 percent of the immigrants during the first half of the twentieth century ended up in New York City. During the second half, the trend was away from New York City to other parts of the Northeast and even as far west as Ohio, Illinois, and California, particularly among the second generation, although 60 percent of the Puerto Rican population in the United States continued to live in New York City. By the 1970s, there was a reverse pattern in the migration flow because major budget cuts and lay-offs in New York pushed the poor out of that city while the hope of a second chance pulled them back to the homeland. This push–pull, between hardship conditions that push Puerto Ricans out of either the United States or Puerto Rico on the one hand and the promise of better opportunities, which pull them toward the other shore, is shaped by the economic forces set in motion in Washington, D.C., which create favorable or unfavorable working and living conditions in the metropolis and the colony. The circular migration pattern begun at the beginning of the twentieth century continues to shape the destiny of the majority of Puerto Ricans; accordingly, it is one of the most significant determinants of Puerto Rican educational, social, political, and economic incorporation into the mainstream (Bonilla 1983).

Those who journeyed for 9 days via ship in the first decades of this century left a different Puerto Rico and came to a different New York than those who hop a jet for 3½ hours today: the earlier groups left small pueblos and rural areas, and significant numbers of them had trades and/or strong literacy skills. More of the later groups came out of the poor barrios and shantytowns of the capital area without much work experience, and showed the ravages of an inferior educational experience and an English-only policy imposed by the United States. Yet they shared other more important characteristics: both groups left the warmth of the tropics and of shared patterns of behavior for the cold of New York City's ghettoes and conflicting lifestyles, and both became "racial minorities" immediately upon stepping onto the mainland, after having been part of a culturally defined Puerto Rican majority all of their lives. Most important, both brought the same dreams of success for themselves and their children, and both have failed in being able to realize them. Today, the second generation (which, as of the 1980 Census, accounts for over 50 percent of the total number of Puerto Ricans in the United States) and the uncounted third generation do not know much about the island or its history, nor do most yearn to return, but their situation here is not significantly different from that of their parents or grandparents.

An overview of migration patterns is important because an adequate analysis of the language and education nexus in the U.S. Puerto Rican community must take into account the formative experiences of the community. Since language both reflects and transmits the collective experiences and ways of being of its speakers, we expect the migration to affect what and how Puerto Ricans speak, read, and write. Similarly, even a cursory review of Puerto Rican history reveals other significant experiences that contribute to the group's cultural and linguistic identity, that is, the Taino, Spanish, African, and U.S. colonial legacies. The original inhabitants of the island were the unwarlike Taino natives who welcomed the Spanish colonizers and were largely exterminated within 60 years of the latter's arrival. During the 400 years (1493–1898) of Spanish rule, the Spanish language, religion, and way of life were adopted, and were in turn influenced by the languages, religions, and way of life of the African slaves (seventeenth to nineteenth centuries). In the twentieth century, Puerto Rico has undergone extensive economic and cultural North Americanization as a Commonwealth of the United States, which has created the conditions that trigger the migration cycles.

We find indications of each of these influences in the linguistic codes or language varieties that Puerto Ricans in the United States speak, in their language socialization process at home and in the community, and in the ways of speaking that they bring into the classrooms, which I shall address in turn. Language issues affect policy design and implementation in every field, but perhaps nowhere more so than in education, where it has become popular to view "the education problem" as synonymous with "the language problem". This chapter will question the validity of that approach and suggest another. But I will begin by addressing specifically those areas of the linguistic and cultural reality of Puerto Ricans in the United States that must be understood by those who want to make the great promise of education a reality for Puerto Ricans.

Although it is obvious that a child who speaks another language will have difficulty with instruction in English simply because it is a foreign language, the work of Hymes (1974) and Heath (1983) among others has alerted us to the fact that many of the problems encountered by language minority and non-standard-English-speaking children in mainstream classrooms stem not from the differences in languages alone, but from the conflict between the community's ways of speaking—where, when, how, why, to whom one speaks—and those required by the school. Therefore, the language component of an effective educational program must be based not only on a knowledge of the structural rules of the linguistic codes that children bring into the classroom, but also on the community's language norms. The focus of this chapter is the language varieties and community language norms of Puerto Ricans in the United States; it is based on ethnolinguistic research conducted on *el bloque,* "the block," in East Harlem, New York City, from 1979 to 1981 (Zentella 1981c and partly summarized in Zentella 1983, 1985). *El bloque* is one street of tenements in New York's best-known Puerto Rican ghetto, *el Barrio,* "the neighborhood"; 19 families with 34 children who lived on the block were studied. I begin by categorizing the major communication patterns in Puerto Rican homes and then go on to summarize the varieties of Spanish and English that are part of everyday life in *el Barrio,* and in all lower working class Puerto Rican barrios in the United States. The importance of individual differences and the inappropriateness of applying other communities' norms are stressed. Finally, I will comment on the educational implications of the community's language varieties and language norms.

LANGUAGE PATTERNS AT HOME

There are four distinct communication patterns in Puerto Rican homes; they differ in terms of the language(s) that the parents speak to each other, the language(s) that the parents speak to the children and vice versa, and the language(s) that the children speak among themselves (Zentella 1985). The major patterns are diagrammed in Figure 5.1, and correspond to the following:

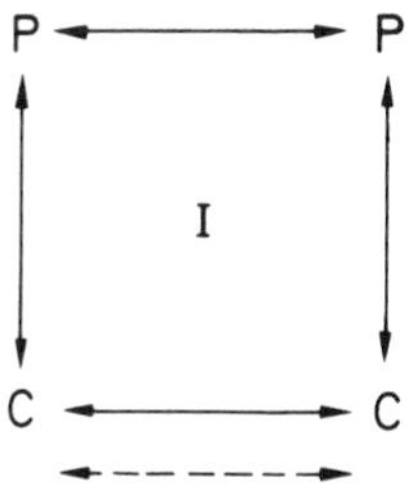

I.

The parents speak only Spanish to each other and the children, who respond to them in Spanish but speak English and Spanish to each other.

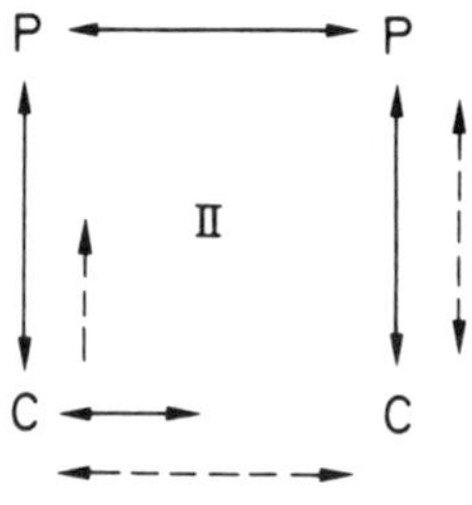

II.

The parents speak Spanish to each other and the children; one of them sometimes speaks English as a second language to them. The children respond in both languages, preferring Spanish for their parents and English for each other.

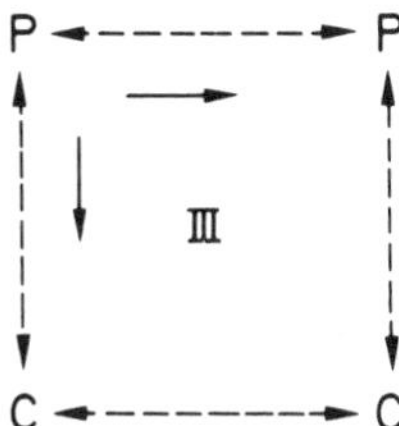

III.

The parents speak English to each other and to the children; one speaks some Spanish to them. The children respond in English and speak it to each other.

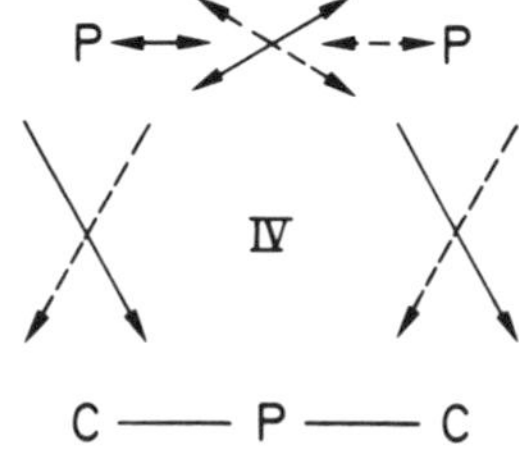

IV.

The parents code switch frequently among themselves and to the children, who are too young to speak yet.

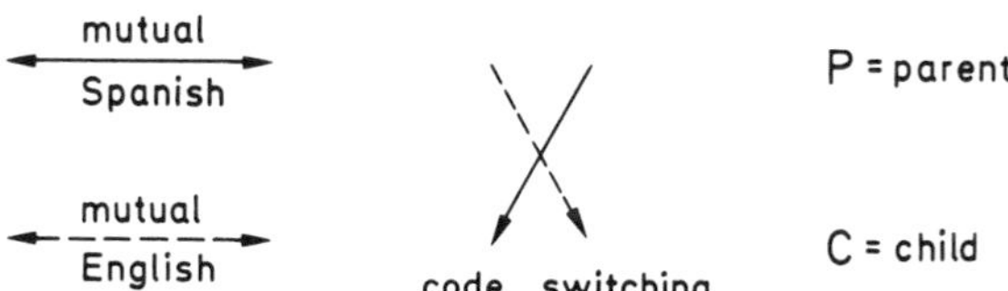

Figure 5.1. Communication patterns in the home. (*Source:* Zentella, A. C. 1985. The fate of Spanish in the U.S.: The Puerto Rican experience. In N. Wolfson and J. Manes (eds.) *Language of Inequality.* Berlin, New York, Amsterdam: Mouton de Gruyter, p. 50.)

I. The parents/caretakers speak only Spanish to each other and to the children; the children respond to their parents in Spanish but they speak Spanish and English to each other. (This accounted for 26 percent of the 19 families in the study.)

II. The parents/caretakers speak Spanish to each other and to the children, but one of them sometimes speaks English as a second language to them. The children respond in both languages, preferring Spanish for the adults and English for their siblings (47 percent of the families studied).

III. The parents usually speak English to each other and to the children; one parent speaks some Spanish to them. The children understand Spanish but respond in English and speak it to each other (16 percent of the families studied).

IV. The parents code-switch frequently among themselves and to their infants, who are just learning to speak (11 percent of the families studied).

In the majority of the families (patterns I and II, 73 percent) children hear their parents speak Spanish at home to each other, and are always spoken to in Spanish by at least one caretaker. The parents in these groups had emigrated to the United States after spending their youth, including early adolescence, in Puerto Rico. These children are the ones who most closely approximate the one language–one environment principle in that they must speak Spanish at home to at least one parent and English outside the home. Among these families we find a greater percentage of fluently bilingual children, but they also include children who are more fluent in English than in Spanish. These differences correspond to a number of factors, which will be addressed below.

Parents who were born and raised in New York City, or who left Puerto Rico before late adolescence, or who married a monolingual English speaker (one mother) speak mainly English to each other and to their children (pattern III). As expected, English-dominant and even English monolingual children are raised in these families, but such families also raise some children who are Spanish dominant, or fluent bilinguals.

The interaction in the homes of two young couples in their early twenties who were born and/or raised in New York City is characterized by frequent code-switching between English and Spanish with each other—more English than Spanish—and with their four young children (pattern IV). The incipient vocabulary of these children consisted of words from both languages.

As should be obvious from even this brief overview of the predominant patterns, it is difficult to make accurate predictions about the level of bilingual fluency of children based on the language patterns of their home. This is because our brief description of the patterns in each group of families is adequate only as a sketch of one of the principal communication patterns in which the children participate every day. It is not correct to assume that children in groups I and II do not speak much English with adults in a home setting, or that group III children do not interact in Spanish with adults while doing chores, eating, and so on. This is because families do not raise their children in nuclear units isolated from the neighbors. The entire block is like a clan, reflecting the dense and multiplex network structures that characterize lower working class communities around the world (Milroy 1980). Everyone knows everyone else, and people relate to each other in a variety of ways: as kin, co-workers, friends, neighbors. On *el bloque,* 9 of the 19 families are members of the same family, related by blood, marriage, or *compadrazgo,* "ritual kinship." Two other family groupings link four more families to each other. Some members work together fixing cars, in the local numbers parlor, in the candy store, and in the *bodega,* and several sell items to each other. There is constant visiting, exchanging, sharing; the children are as likely to be found in one living room as another. Older children from one family babysit for the infants of another, and all children have the run of most apartments. Whenever people out on the street are unsure of the whereabouts of a child in a building, the problem is resolved by calling up the stairwell; the child appears from any one of a number of doors. Once they are out on the block, the children's exposure to language variety increases.

LANGUAGE VARIETIES ON THE BLOCK

Spanish

Life on the block is not only a bilingual experience, it is also a bidialectal experience. References to "English" and "Spanish" here do not do justice to the language variety that characterizes the Puerto Rican community, which reflects the community's diverse regional, class, and ethnic identification with Puerto Rico's past and New York City's present. There are first-generation adults who came from the island's larger towns, from families a little better off than most; they were privileged enough to be able to pursue education beyond the elementary grades. These community members speak the standard Spanish of Puerto Rico, which falls perfectly within the framework of Latin American Spanish, specifically the Spanish of the Antilles (the islands of the Caribbean). The pronunciation of Latin American Spanish differs from the Castilian variety from Spain primarily in intonation and the replacement of two consonants, the palatel *l,* spelled *ll,* and the *th* sound, spelled *c* (before *e* and *i*) or *z*. These two sounds are replaced by sounds similar to the English *y* and *s*, respectively, and are known as *yeismo* and *seseo.* All Spanish speakers will have trouble pronouncing the English phonemes that are not part of the Spanish language's phonological inventory, such as *v,* which will be pronounced like *b;* or *sh,* which will be pronounced like *ch;* or *z,* which will be pronounced like *s;* and the vowel sounds in *bat, bit, but, book, bottle,* which tend to be pronounced as if they were spelled "bot," "beet," "bote," "buuk," and "boatel." As is customary for every speaker learning a new language, the consonants and vowels in the speaker's native language that most closely approximate those of the new language will replace the unknown phonemes. Since this linguistic interference will affect the reading and spelling of learners of English as a second language, it is important to be aware of them, so as not to mislabel normal interference as abnormal speech impediments. Many excellent studies on the differences between Spanish and English exist (e.g., Stockwell, Bowen and Martin 1965; Stockwell and Bowen 1965), and Spanish–English dictionaries offer short summaries of the contrasting pronunciations of these languages (e.g., Castillo and Bond 1981).

In addition to the features shared by all Spanish speakers, Puerto Ricans, as well as other Caribbean Spanish speakers (e.g., Dominicans and Cubans), tend to drop the final *-s* in informal styles of speech. This is not because they are lazy speakers, as some ill-informed people believe, but because these characteristics were inherited from the Andalusian variety of Spanish brought to the New World by the first colonizers. When the *-s* is dropped, as in *gracias* "thank you," it may be replaced by a light aspiration as if it were spelled "graciah," or disappear altogether, as if it were spelled "gracia." The only uniquely distinctive feature of Puerto Rican Spanish phonology, besides its intonation patterns, is the velar version of the trilled *rr* (written in Spanish as double *rr* in the middle of a word but as a single *r* at the beginning). Alongside the widespread apicoalveolar version that is customary in Spanish, Puerto Ricans may produce a French-like *r,* or a devoiced *r* that sounds like the *ch* in the German pronunciation in Bach. Since the trilled *rr* does not exist in English, it causes trouble for English speakers learning Spanish, but not for Spanish speakers learning English.

The majority of any lower working class Puerto Rican community's residents were born and raised in poor families, often in rural areas of Puerto Rico, and they pass on to their second-generation children all of the phonological features just described, as well as a few nonstandard features, particularly the substitution of *l* for syllable-final *r* (e.g., *puerto* "port" pronounced as if it were "puelto," or *vivir* "to live" pronounced as if it were "vivil"). Although this does cause problems for spelling in Spanish, English words with syllable-final *r* are not written as *l,* perhaps because the lower working class of New York tends to delete this *r,* and teachers emphasize it accordingly. Also, it is one of the few features that elicits negative comments in the community.

It is important to underscore the fact that speakers of every language share certain features of pronunciation, grammar, and word formation with others in their community, and these become important symbols of membership in a particular group. This variety is what is meant by the word "dialect''; dialects distinguish each geographical region, class, ethnic group, and race from the others. Everyone in the world speaks a dialect of their language; historical, political, and economic circumstances that favored one group over another led one dialect to be given greater status (e.g., Castilian over Andalusian Spanish) but nothing in the pronunciation or grammar of one code is intrinsically superior to another. A popular definition of ''standard'' as ''the dialect with the army'' reflects the truism that the selection of a standard is a question of political, not linguistic, superiority, since each dialect is rule-governed and meets the communication needs of its speakers. The consistent attacks that Puerto Ricans encounter against their variety are the consequences of a linguistic posture at the service of political goals. It seemed imperative to the United States after its occupation of the island in 1898 to stress the superiority of English and the American way of life in general, and the inferiority of Spanish, and Puerto Rican Spanish and culture in particular, in order to foster the allegiance of the new colony to the U.S. government (Zentella 1981a). Spanish was virtually banished from the schools and courts of Puerto Rico for nearly 50 years, and the negative linguistic and educational effects of this policy are still being suffered by the offspring of the succeeding generations.

In this country, the low status of Spanish, and of Caribbean Spanish in particular, is still being reinforced by the schools in various ways, including outright denunciation of Puerto Rican Spanish as an ''inferior dialect'' that is not ''real Spanish.'' The detractors of Puerto Rican Spanish are unaware of basic notions of dialectal variety and its social correlates, and of the historical processes that produce word borrowing, loan translation, and other examples of language contact in many parts of the world. People from Great Britain, for example, say *flat* for what North Americans call *apartment,* and pronounce *questionnaire* with a *k* (not *kw*) sound at the beginning; both groups have kept the originally French pronunciation in certain words borrowed from French, such as the consonant sound at the end of *rouge*. Except in the minds of some arch-Anglophiles, British English is not considered superior to American English, and no one suggests eliminating hundreds of words borrowed from French and other languages as ''barbarisms.'' Similarly, Puerto Ricans say *china* for *naranja;* pronounce *islas* as if it were spelled ''ihlah''; and have borrowed *bloque* and *lonche* ''lunch'' to reflect their new cultural experiences. If the objective is the expansion of the linguistic repertoires of students to include the prestige standard variety, this can be accomplished best by recognizing and accepting the local dialect, and building upon it.

English

The principles of linguistic diversity and equivalence I have referred to in discussing Puerto Rican Spanish must also be invoked when we turn our attention to English in the community. There is a greater divergence in the varieties of English spoken on the block that we studied than in the varieties of Spanish. Both first and second generations speak Puerto Rican Spanish (PRS), but those who were reared in Puerto Rico speak English marked by Spanish interference phenomena, while the second generation speaks two kinds of non-standard English: Puerto Rican English (PRE) and/or black English vernacular (BEV). Although teens with extensive black contacts may sound indistinguishable from black Americans (Wolfram 1974), PRE is the principal linguistic code shared by those who were born and/or raised on the block. The items of vocabulary, pronunciation, word formation, and grammar that PRE borrows from BEV and from Spanish and others that distinguish it from both, have yet to be studied in depth, but a few differences have already been noted, such as the use of relative pronouns, as in "You know that thing, that it gots points on it" (Urciuoli 1980). Despite the fact that each social network is generally identifiable with one code over the others (e.g., older males with PRS, young "dudes" with BEV, and elementary school children with PRE), residents of the block often speak more than one variety, depending on their interlocutors and speech situations. This is true of all Puerto Ricans in the United States, if they live in predominantly Puerto Rican neighborhoods, as do the majority. Thus, except for the very small middle class that has left the barrios, Puerto Ricans are often bilingual and bidialectal as well. Each network's interactions with the others reinforces this variation.

All the children are exposed to and/or participate in activities that require English, Spanish, or both. Girls as well as boys participate in many physical activities: bicycle riding, roller skating, impromptu races, batting practice, playing with clic-clax and hoola hoops, hide and seek, making castles out of cardboard boxes, getting doused by the fire pump in the summer and having snowball fights in the winter, dressing and feeding dolls, and singing and dancing to the music of the juke box. Most of these activities are engaged in primarily in English, as are watching television, going to the movies, and shopping. Spanish, however, is always in the background: songs and prayers from the Pentecostal Church storefront, salsa records, the comments of the domino players, the conversations of the *bodegueros* (grocery store owners) and their clients, the older mothers' admonitions to children and their personal chats, the hawking of wares by passing street vendors and hustlers, and the thrice-daily lamenting over the *bolita* (illegal lottery number). None of these activities, however, is the impenetrable domain of either English or Spanish: each one is likely to be invaded by the other language, because monolingual speakers interrupt or partake in the activity, or because bilingual speakers switch languages momentarily.

English enjoys a favored position because it is the language of widest applicability outside of the community. As the children grow, so does the number of their activities beyond the confines of the block: education, sports, dancing, and movies. These activities and the English media serve to enhance the status of English: not only is it considered more useful because it enables them to communicate with a greater number and variety of people, it is also considered more successful because almost every affluent person they see or meet speaks English, whereas the emigrants from Spanish-speaking countries are traditionally the poorest families in the neighborhood.

WHO SPEAKS WHAT TO WHOM?

In the face of such variety, how do children decide what to speak to whom? In general, they start out in Spanish to anyone known to be a Spanish monolingual, and to any newcomer who greets them in Spanish. If the child initiates an interaction with someone new to her or him, the usual procedure is to greet *Latino* infants and women of their parents' age and older in Spanish; young people and men are expected to be able to understand English. If the child's initiation in one language is met with a blank stare, he or she quickly switches to the other language. Off the block, children are likely to speak English to people whom they do not know, particularly if those people enjoy some status or have business connections. In the following exchange, for example, Linda (8 years old) began by asking the man at the counter of a candy store on a nearby block the price of a candy, in English:

LINDA: How much this costs? [no response]
How much this costs? [no response]
You 'stand Spanish?
STOREKEEPER: *Si.*
LINDA: *Cuanto vale esto?* (How much does this cost?)
STOREKEEPER: *Veinticinco centavos.* (Twenty-five cents.)

In fact, the storekeeper speaks English; he did not answer Linda right away because he was busy, but Linda and other children often interpreted a lack of response or a questioning look as a request to switch to the other language. Although Linda appears to have inferred that the storekeeper did not know English, her question to him about what language he spoke was posed in English, not Spanish, as might have been expected. One explanation for this apparent inconsistency is that children may assume that such basic queries as "Do you speak or understand X language?" are part of everybody's rudimentary knowledge, since it is one of the first questions a monolingual learns in order to get along.

Given the presence of monolinguals, every child on the block comes to know that they may be called upon to switch language for a change of participants in any speech situation. Even those children who speak no Spanish are sometimes addressed in Spanish by a monolingual adult from the block, or by other adults who do not know the child's limitations in Spanish. These interactions become less frequent as the adults become more fluent in

English and as they accommodate the children by speaking to them in English. The only block members whom the English-dominant children can neither avoid, nor force to accommodate them, are the infant children of recent migrants. Given the close proximity of the families (two tenements within 15 feet of each other house 34 children), and the gathering spots that community members share (three *bodegas,* a video arcade, the stoops, the street, the *banca* "numbers parlor") code-switching for different participants is a predominant characteristic of communication on the block. In our second example, below, 8-year-old Maria switches from English to Spanish to English to Spanish for three different interlocutors:

Context: Maria (M) is in the local *bodega* with Corinne (C), another Puerto Rican 8-year-old, but one who barely speaks and understands Spanish. Jennie (J), the 2-year-old daughter of a recent migrant, follows them into the store. The *bodeguero* (B), a Puerto Rican in his forties, is Spanish-dominant but speaks English well also.

C to M: Buy those.
M to C: No, I buy those better.
M to B: *Toma la cuora.* (Take the quarter.)
M to C: What's she doing here? [referring to Jennie]
M to J: *Vete pa' dentro.* (Go inside.)

Maria's language alternations reflect her awareness of the language abilities of her interlocutors and her respect for the guiding community norm, which requires that people be addressed in their dominant language.

CODE-SWITCHING

Up to now, I have limited my remarks to the norms guiding the selection of one language or another for a different interlocutor. Children attempt to speak the language that the hearer knows best, and this often requires switching from one language to another as the child's addressees change. But frequently children switch languages while speaking to the same person. What accounts for the instances when children choose to start in one language and then switch to their other language even in the middle of a sentence? One factor that can influence this unexpected alternation is the use of language- or code-switching as an organizing discourse strategy, one that highlights a switch in topic, focus, role, or other factor, by switching languages (see 24 discourse strategies accomplished by switching in Zentella 1983, 1985). In these cases, the speaker's decision to signal a discourse strategy with a switch in language sometimes overrides normal consideration for the dominant language of the hearer and the speaker. However, it is most likely to occur among bilinguals who know that the other speaker(s) share(s) both codes. To paint an abbreviated picture of stages in the acquisition of code-switching, switches for different monolingual addressees accustom the child to moving from one phonological and syntactic system to another with ease, and this facility is then extended to intrasentential code-switching for effective discourse management. My research and that of others (LPTF 1980, 1983, 1984; Poplack 1979; Valdés 1976, 1981) demonstrates that the most fluent bilinguals are the most fluent code-switchers, in contrast to the definition of the ideal bilingual proposed by Weinreich (1953), as one who never switches when in the same situation with the same speaker.

The increasing command of code-switching in the community and the tolerance of English in Puerto Rican homes is an indication that the traditional linking of "they" with outsider language (English) is making inroads into the "we" intimate domain, formerly limited to Spanish, and that in some cases it is being reversed. All of the children whom we studied spoke more English than Spanish to their siblings by the end of the study, and almost 50 percent spoke more English than Spanish with at least one caretaker. All of them code-switched within the boundaries of a sentence, but at a rate that did not exceed 25 switches per hour.

ISSUES OF PROFICIENCY AND MAINTENANCE

To sum up the contributions of our ethnographic observations to our understanding of proficiency, we can say that contrasting language patterns at home notwithstanding, these differences may make no difference in the proficiency levels of the children of each group of families. Children from each group may end up with very similar language abilities or not. It is true, as Figure 5.1 indicates, that the children of group I spoke more Spanish to each other than those of group III. That is, it seems that English usage among the children increases in proportion to the amount of English that is understood and spoken by their parents, which usually reflects the parents' length of residence in this country. By the end of the study, however, the school age children in group I were speaking to each other predominantly in English, despite the fact that their caretakers did not demonstrate marked improvement in their knowledge of English. Nor are these isolated cases: communication in English is the norm for school age sisters and brothers among Puerto Ricans in the United States. The principal exceptions are among those siblings who emigrated to the United States during or after their teen years. This holds true even for older sisters and brothers who have lived more years in New York than their early years in Puerto Rico: those who arrived at 16 and 18 still speak Spanish to each other at 42 and 44, or at 62 and 64. They may, however, speak only English to their children. In this way, the Puerto Rican community is similar to European immigrants of the late nineteenth and early twentieth centuries whose fate it has been to lose their mother tongue by the third generation.

More significant, however, are the differences that may interfere with or impede the expected replacement of Spanish. Primary factors involve macro social and economic issues, for example, the rate and residential patterns of the migration flow to and from Puerto Rico, out-marriage rates, female and male employment opportunities, accessibility of public housing and the success of its attempts at desegregation, urban renewal, and others. In the block that is home to our subjects, the prevalent configurations of these factors favored the continued presence of Spanish during the period of the study: a greater number of residents came from Puerto Rico than left, the overwhelming majority of households included Puerto Ricans only (one Anglo spouse was the only exception), female and male unemployment worsened, few families caught up with the 6-year waiting list for public housing, and Spanish monolingual relatives continued to visit and migrate. The presence of one dominant family network intensified the residents' complex and dense relationships, and the high percentage of unemployed residents guaranteed the continuous availability on the block of members of diverse networks. Soon after the completion of our study, the unexpected arrival of Cuban Marielitos (see García and Otheguy, this volume) contributed a new group of Spanish monolinguals and a new variety of Spanish. Each of these factors undoubtedly contributes to the language development of the children; they are in continuous contact with Spanish and English monolinguals who speak different regional and class dialects, with various levels of Spanish and English proficiency, and with various patterns of interaction outside of their homes.

THE CAUSES OF INDIVIDUAL DIFFERENCES

Differences in bilingual proficiency between children of different families are to be expected, but differences within families may be more surprising, particularly to those teachers who teach sisters and brothers in different years. The differences in siblings can be accounted for by many situational, educational, or cultural variables (Zentella 1986a); of particular interest is the socialization of young Puerto Rican children into appropriate male and female roles (Zentella 1987). This process provides girls with more exposure to and participation in Spanish than their brothers: greater restriction to the house and/or mother, to play and friendships with girls, caretaking responsibilities with infants, attendance at Spanish religious services, and inclusion in female discussions and activities, such as cooking, sewing, cleaning, taking clothes to the washing machines, and watching the *novels* (soap opera). The work of Labov (1966, 1972a, b, 1981) and other sociolinguists has consistently indicated that females in western, class-stratified societies are more sensitive to prevalent language norms than males. This is corroborated on the block and becomes more apparent as girls grow older and take up maternal roles, which are increasingly carried out in Spanish.

Despite the immersion of females in Spanish-linked activities, the impact on all female children is not the same: not all sisters speak Spanish equally well, nor do all brothers speak it poorly. Within each family one or more members will be subject to one or more Spanish or English influences and to varying degrees; this affects each child's personal language history and development. One child may visit Puerto Rico more frequently or for longer stays than another, one may be enrolled in a bilingual program and the others may be in a monolingual English class, one may spend more hours out on the block and others may be more confined to the apartment, one may spend more time with African Americans than with Puerto Ricans, one may participate in religious programs that require literacy in English or Spanish. Other major factors include national identity, that is, identification as a Puerto Rican or as an "American," and racial identity, as black, white, *jabao, trigueno,* or one of the other Puerto Rican color categories.

As if this staggering variety of situational variables were not enough, they also interact with cognitive and social variables that help determine who becomes a proficient bilingual. Wong Fillmore's (1983) 2-year study of Chinese- and Spanish-speaking (Mexican American) children in school, from kindergarten to second grade, proved that it is very difficult to gauge the respective weight of cognitive, social, or situational variables; while each contributes to the process of becoming bilingual, we do not know how much each contributes.

The social and cognitive variables that Wong Fillmore identified as helpful in language learning are the same for children in school and in the community. The cognitive abilities that are required to discern the patterns of the units, the structure, and the meanings that make up language include memory, inductive reasoning, mental flexibility, and pattern recognition. The social abilities needed to become bilingual are those that provide language learning practice; this requires sociability, outgoingness, and talkativeness. Wong Fillmore did find that high ratings in the social and cognitive abilities were characteristic of children who picked up their second language easily, as might have been expected, but she also found that this was not always the case: some children who scored high in these areas did not learn English as fast as others who did not. Her most important finding was that variation in language learning ability is widespread and greater than expected, despite cognitive and social ratings: what some children learned in 8 months took others who were even "brighter" 2–3 years to learn.

The most thorough and recent research on the relationship between bilingualism and higher-order cognitive skills in lower working class Puerto Rican students was conducted by Hakuta (NCBE 1985). This large (392 children) longitudinal (3 years, K–6) study is important because it documents the positive influence of bilingualism on cognitive ability in nonbalanced bilingual children who were dominant in one of their languages. Regardless of proficiency level, the cognitive skills demonstrated by metalinguistic ability, nonverbal intelligence, and spatial relations were significantly related to bilingualism. As for language learning, students who were initially more capable in Spanish tended to become more capable in English as they moved up through the grades. Two significant implications of this research for educational practice are (1) "by encouraging strength in two languages, teachers may also be developing students' verbal and non-verbal cognitive abilities" and (2) "strength in a student's first language leads to greater strength in a second language" (NCBE 1985:2).

Situational variables also contribute to success or failure in learning a second language. In the school setting these variables include the organization of the class (whether it is learner- or teacher-centered) and the mix of students (the number of limited-English-proficiency students and monolinguals). In the community, these situational variables correspond to the families' language patterns and to the children's participation in diverse networks on the block. In Wong Fillmore's study, whole classes turned out to be full of predominantly slow or fast learners because the organization of the class and the mix of students proved very influential. She concluded that the most effective classroom in which to learn a new language is one in which there is an open atmosphere: learner-centered, with a mix of language proficiency abilities. This type of classroom allows students maximum interaction with an adult speaker on a one-to-one basis, and it provides exposure to peers with better language ability. This, obviously, is similar to the situation I have described for "*el bloque,*" where the situational variables correspond to the families' language patterns and the children's participation in diverse social networks, but it is not what the children of *el bloque* encounter in their school settings. All of their classes are either teacher-centered English monolingual classes, or teacher-centered bilingual classes, in which over 60 percent of the teachers' talk is in English (Romero 1983). The net effect is that neither type of classroom stimulates language learning to the maximum, except that the bilingual classes do instruct in both languages and allow the children to socialize with a greater mix of language proficiencies. Life on the block is more representative of the situational variables most conducive to second language learning than is the education in the schools.

Although my research did not seek correlations between the types of classrooms in which the children of *el bloque* studied and the children's level of bilingualism, two facts in this regard are worth noting. The best students on the block were also the most fluent bilinguals, and often products of bilingual programs; they represent the strongest evidence against the position held by Rodriguez (1984) and others that the public person can be developed only via the public language, English, and not in bilingual classrooms. The star student on the block was Maria, a popular 8-year-old who was born and raised in *el Barrio;* she had been in bilingual classes for 3 years, read above grade level in both languages, and was generally a good student. There were fluent bilinguals on the block who attended English monolingual classes, but they could not compete in reading and writing Spanish with

Maria and other students from the bilingual classes. The latter were called upon to read signs, advertisements, greeting cards, and other materials aloud in Spanish for older children. This contributed to their linguistic security and their overall self confidence, which may be one of the factors that explain why "participants in bilingual education programs are four times as likely to finish high school, and the number entering college has increased" (Santiago 1983).

EDUCATIONAL IMPLICATIONS

Failure and Its Causes

Lack of knowledge of the variety of the linguistic codes and ways of speaking in Puerto Rican communities we have reviewed above has contributed to the alarming rate of educational failure in the Puerto Rican community, which in turn is linked to its severely depressed socioeconomic condition. Puerto Ricans in the United States are not only a product of exploitative colonialism, revolving door migration, and stigmatized racial mixture, but they recently had the sad distinction of being named "the most disadvantaged group in the U.S." (Puerto Rican Forum 1981:3). They have the lowest income, the largest percentage of families living below the poverty line, and the highest unemployment rate of any ethnic group in the country. Traditionally, education has not offered a way out: the Puerto Rican dropout rate far exceeds the rate of high school graduates (33 percent) in every city with a large Puerto Rican student body, as the following examples indicate:

> In Chicago, "a 1971 study by Dr. Isidro Lucas put the dropout rate for Puerto Rican youth at 71.2 percent". In March 1984 "more than one-half of all Hispanic youth entering Chicago public schools do not graduate nor receive a high school diploma" (Reyes 1984:5).
>
> In Philadelphia, more than one-third (34.7 percent) of the public school youngsters surveyed (505 Puerto Rican boys and girls in the study) who entered the tenth grade left school by their senior year (Reyes 1984:5).
>
> In New York City, where Puerto Ricans constitute over one-fourth of the 1.1 million students in the public schools, Aspira of New York (1983) estimates that the current dropout rate for this group has worsened over the last two decades and is now as high as 80 percent.

Analysts who seek an explanation for these devastating rates of failure necessarily conclude that the failure of the educational system to serve the language needs of these students is at the heart of the problem. In New York, for example, "the 12 percent of the school population that is limited-

English-proficient (LEP) contributes a disproportionate share to the city's 42 percent dropout rate; Hispanics, who represent more than three-quarters of the city's LEP students, drop out at almost twice that rate'' (Willner 1985:3). Recognition of the link between limited English proficiency and school failure led parents and educators to demand bilingual education as a remedy nearly 20 years ago. The United Bronx Parents, led by Evelina Antonetty and other Puerto Rican parents, was in the leadership of that movement. Today inaccurate media coverage has led too many people to believe that bilingual education has been tried but that it has not worked. The truth is that although in 1968 bilingual education was enacted based on the federal Civil Rights Act in response to a strong movement, and a 1974 U.S. Supreme Court decision, *Lau* v. *Nichols,* mandated special educational programs for students whose dominant language is not English (see Wong, ''Educational Rights of Language Minorities,'' this volume), school systems throughout the country continue to fail to provide legally mandated services: ''New York City schools are still not providing any legally-required language instruction to more than 44,000 limited-English proficient students, almost 40 percent of all those entitled to services'' (Willner 1985:1). Another 30 percent receive partial services and only 30 percent receive the full bilingual instructional program mandated by the 1974 Consent Decree between the New York City Board of Education and Aspira. Armed with these facts, the community organizes to defend its rights, but at the very same time that the EPP data were released, the Secretary of Education announced his intention to weaken federal requirements for these programs (Fiske 1985).

In addition, other powerful forces rallying around an English-only cry are delivering the latest blow to the progress of Puerto Ricans and other speakers of other languages in the United States. By passing legislation that limits bilingual education, eliminates bilingual ballots, and makes the delivery of crucial services (e.g., emergency operators) illegal if they are not in English, eight states have already further damaged our hopes for a better education, curtailed our participation in electoral politics, and jeopardized our health and welfare. In New York State, the attempt of Senate Bill #901 to continue this disturbing national trend is being countered by the efforts of the Committee for a Multilingual New York, which affirms the importance of English as the predominant language but points out the divisive and dangerous repercussions of English-only legislation.

Solutions

To ensure educational excellence and equity in the United States, there is a need to inform the public about the importance of these policy issues, the compelling reasons for bilingual education and the research that documents its success (Hakuta and Snow 1986), and the cognitive advantages linked to bilingualism (NCBE 1985). Communities as poor and politically weak as the Puerto Rican communities in the United States need the support of a broad spectrum of enlightened citizenry and legislators who see the fight for language rights as central to basic democratic principles and in the best interests of the future of the entire nation. Recent national demands for improved foreign language competency for all U.S. citizens are directly linked to the need to preserve and expand the language repertoire of those whose native language is not English (Zentella 1986b). The language resources of the United States are sadly deficient: not only are monolingual English speakers not learning other languages, those who are born speaking another language end up losing it. To return to the Puerto Rican experience in New York City—the fabled melting pot of the world—"about half of those who enter the school system deficient in both Spanish and English eventually lose their Spanish skills and gain no skills in English" (Willner 1985:3). Our first responsibility must be to reverse this dismaying process by joining the efforts of those committed to maintaining and improving the native Spanish language skills of Puerto Ricans as well as to achieving excellent oral and literate proficiency in English. These are not antithetical objectives; they are complementary and, as such, require an alliance among foreign language, bilingual, and English as a second language educators to achieve them.

Additionally, and more importantly, ultimate success in reversing the negative situation of Puerto Ricans in the United States will be achieved only when we recognize that language, as important as it is, is not the only or even primary determinant of Puerto Rican success or failure here. Recent studies demonstrate the greater economic success of *Latinos* in the United States who have less English skills than Puerto Ricans. In New York City in 1980, "the ratio of Puerto Rican income to that of 'other Hispanics' was 0.70, about $8,200 and $12,000 respectively," despite the fact that 44 percent of the "other Hispanics" spoke English "not well" (26.5 percent) or "not at all" (17.5 percent), whereas only 30 percent of the adult Puerto Rican population spoke English "not well" (21.3 percent) or "not at all" (8.7 percent) (Mann and Salvo 1985:4). These facts prove that historical, political, racial, and economic forces that favor some communities over others can override a struggling community's efforts to become more proficient in English. This is not to ignore the importance of language, but to place it in perspective. Students should not be told that "their problem" is a language problem, because the problems have not gone away for the large numbers of the second generation who know English. Admittedly, this continued failure may be interpreted as evidence for the proponents of genetic inferiority theories, but experiments that prove that Puerto Rican children can excel when their educational program is solid, well-administered, responsive to parents, and supported by teachers, belie any racist interpretations of the facts.

An Additive Approach

The Puerto Rican community values bilingualism highly; as one Puerto Rican parent in Connecticut put it: "Un hombre que habla dos idiomas vale por dos" ("a man that speaks two languages is worth two men") (Zirkel 1973:24). Parents expect the schools to help develop their children's language skills, but when the children of *el bloque* enter the schools their bilingual skills are not seen as assets. They soon feel attacked because they speak Puerto Rican Spanish, because they speak black English vernacular or Puerto Rican English, because they want to speak Spanish and English too, and because they speak both languages together. This is the case in many bilingual as well as monolingual classes because few of the teachers are aware of the features of Caribbean Spanish, the rule-governed nature of nonstandard dialects, or the process of becoming bilingual that characterizes the community. One linguistic challenge that the schools must meet is the acceptance of the stigmatized varieties of both Spanish and English that the children speak. Acceptance can only be based on knowledge, and this knowledge should be the basis for effective teaching of the standard dialects. The approach must be additive, not subtractive; the expansion of the linguistic repertoires of our children, not their reduction, will contribute to their future success in and out of school.

Educators must also become aware of the factors that determine language choice in the community and of the discourse strategies accomplished by code-switching. Classroom norms may be in conflict with community norms if students are never allowed to code-switch in any part of a lesson or a school day. The feelings of insecurity that negative labels such as "Spanglish" foster serve only to obstruct important educational objectives (Zentella 1978, 1981b). Finally, sensitivity is required in relation to issues of linguistic and cultural change; teachers' searches for prevalent patterns in the communities they serve or among the children they teach must be alert to the conflicting pressures of norms in flux. Almost none of this knowledge is presently part of teacher training. The system continues to function on the premise that its problems would be solved if only Puerto Ricans became English-dominant, and there is increasing public pressure to make this happen. The architects of this policy ignore fundamental linguistic and sociopolitical issues as well as the best of recent research.

It is easy to understand why so little is known about our community, and why its language behavior is so misunderstood. Most studies of bilingualism have usually been case studies of individual middle class children in nuclear families, often the children of researchers who spoke the prestige language and were enriching their lives by adding another, nonessential, language. Most often these children learned their languages in strict adherence to a one language–one environment principle: they usually spoke a different language to each parent, or one language in the home and the other outside the home. This led to Weinreich's 1953 definition of the "ideal bilingual" as one who never switched in the same situation with the same interlocutor. When bilingual communities have been studied, they too seem to emphasize compartmentalization of their languages, either along the lines of classic diglossia, which limits the low (stigmatized) language to informal activities and requires the high (prestige) language for all public and/or formal interactions (Ferguson 1964) or in accordance with topics, locales, or domains (Fishman 1967).

But early studies of communities with stable economic, demographic, and social parameters cannot be adequately compared to the language experiences of *el bloque* (Pedraza, Attinasi and Hoffman 1980). It is precisely the complexity of the *vai–ven* (go–come) migration caused by Puerto Rico's colonial status, the push–pull of economic, educational, and social forces that keep most members locked in poverty, the experiences that alternately reinforce Spanish or English, and the cultural membership in the "dos worlds/two mundos" (Padron 1982) that characterize the process of growing up bilingual in *el barrio*. One definition that attempts to incorporate the diversity that results from this process is the concept of "interpenetrating bilingualism": "the fluid and creative use of all of the environmental language resources at hand without the purist separation of languages and without the wholesale condemnation of the varieties spoken by uneducated Spanish speakers or by English speakers, including BEV" (Attinasi 1983:10).

The question of cultural identification is central in the process of becoming bilingual: children in Puerto Rican *barrios* love people who speak Spanish and people who speak English, they love Puerto Rico and the United States, and they feel like Puerto Ricans and New Yorkers, or New Jerseyites, or Chicagoans. They learn to admire members of the community who are fluent in both languages and for whom code-switching is one of the ways of speaking. Attempts to judge or interpret this process based on principles that work for different communities will suffer the fate that befalls any inadequate theory: such attempts will misinterpret, mislabel, and stigmatize. Even worse, they will fall short of capturing the strength and diversity of the language abilities of Puerto Rican children in order to build upon them, and will condemn the children to continued failure in the schools.

Nearly 50 percent of the Puerto Rican community is under the age of 17; education is our best and last hope for success. The community has always supported teachers and schools who know how to work with them on behalf of the children, if the methods and programs tackle the underlying causes of failure. Language is not the primary problem. Moreover, it is unlikely that the schools will be able to tap into children's language skills in order to expand them by isolating the linguistic issues from the more fundamental problem plaguing the educational system, that is, its disabling approach to minority students. Fundamental change, in the teaching of language and all other areas, requires a commitment to the four basic principles enunciated by Cummins (1986): (1) strengthening of the native language, (2) building upon L1 in the teaching of L2, (3) strong parental inclusion, and (4) an advocacy role for educators and psychologists to challenge discriminatory assessments that locate the cause of the academic problems within the students. Educators who are sincerely committed to carrying out successful educational programs must grapple with the complex web of linguistic, political, economic, and cultural issues we have described without imposing preconceived frameworks and without losing heart at the apparent magnitude of the task. The sensitivity to difference, willingness to learn, and acceptance of change that are the hallmarks of every good educator can lead to great success when they guide an overall educational effort truly meant to empower minority students.

CONCLUSION: WHAT DOES THE FUTURE HOLD?

In sum, if a language policy of the educational system or other macrosocietal institution is to be effective, it must build on observed community language practices, take into account the social, economic, and political structures and needs of the classes and ethnic groups linked to each language in the community, and be part of a larger effort to enable, not disable. As the United States Puerto Rican community raises its third generation, changes in the community affect whether or not code-switching will constitute a permanent part of a bilingual's proficiency, or only represent a stage in the transition to monolingual English, as in the case of previous immigrant groups. The processes that affect the language future of Puerto Ricans are as disparate as the revolutions that challenge the United States' role in world politics (especially in relation to Latin America), English-only efforts that foster harrassment of foreign language speakers, bilingual education programs that exclude Puerto Ricans who speak English, public housing patterns that uproot Puerto Ricans from their dense and multiplex networks, lack of employment opportunities, increased or decreased migration rates, among others. In the last two decades, the particular configuration of these factors in the New York City's Puerto Rican community has contributed to the strengthening of language alternation as a badge of dual cultural membership, and as an effort to maintain both languages.

What will the future hold in New York City and elsewhere with large Puerto Rican communities? Like the immigrant groups before them, Puerto Ricans in the United States live ghettoized lives in areas where they are the poorest newcomers at the bottom of the social and economic ladder. Unlike the previous waves of European immigrants, however, the Puerto Rican first generation arrived as citizens with a history of U.S. control of their national language, and the second generation came of age during a period of social unrest and struggle against class and social stigma in which, together with blacks and *Chicanos,* they participated. Constant migration between the island and mainland contributes to the reaffirmation of Puerto Rican identity, and the language question will continue to be a crucial part of the quest for identity. Throughout the history of Puerto Rico, the battle for the survival of the Puerto Rican nation has often been couched in terms of the battle for the survival of Spanish. In the United States, that battle can now be redefined as the struggle for an excellent and empowering education, one which helps us achieve standard fluency, in verbal as well as literacy skills, in both English and Spanish.

EXPLORING THE IDEAS

1. Puerto Ricans, unlike refugees such as Cuban Americans or Vietnamese Americans, travel freely between their homeland and the United States.

In what ways do you think this fact influences the language retention and language loss of the Puerto Rican community?

2. In Figure 5.1, Zentella depicts four major types of family interaction patterns that were evident in her study of *el bloque*. Zentella points out that it was difficult to make accurate predictions about the level of bilingual fluency of the children in the family based on this information alone since the language pattern of the home was only one of many factors that influenced language use.

What other factors, both social and individual, could influence young Puerto Ricans' level of bilingual fluency?

3. Zentella states that in her study, when a child initiates an interaction with a stranger, the typical procedure is to greet *Latino* infants and older women in Spanish and young people and men in English.

Why do you think children used this strategy in initiating conversations?

4. Zentella found that by the end of her study, the school age children of all the groups, even group I, were speaking to each other predominantly in English. The one exception to this finding was among siblings who emigrated to the United States during or after their teenage years.

Why do you think this particular group continued to use Spanish with each other even after they had lived in the United States for a considerable number of years?

5. Zentella lists the following factors as significant in promoting the continued use of Spanish in *el bloque:* an influx of immigrants from Puerto Rico and Cuba, households composed of only Puerto Ricans, high unemployment, housing shortages, and visits by Spanish-speaking relatives.

Discuss how each of these factors could contribute to the maintenance of Spanish among members of *el bloque*.

6. Zentella lists a variety of factors that can contribute to differences in bilingual proficiency, such as gender, the pattern of home interaction, and personality traits.

List as many individual and social variables as you can that can affect the degree of an individual's bilingual proficiency.

7. Zentella points out that Puerto Ricans have "the lowest income, the largest percentage of families living below the poverty line, and the highest unemployment rate of any ethnic group in the country."

What are some factors about this community, in contrast to other ethnic groups in the United States, that may be contributing to this fact?

APPLYING THE IDEAS

1. Zentella points out that there are several excellent studies on the structural differences between Spanish and English.

Read one of the Spanish–English contrastive studies. (Stockwell, Bowen and Martin, 1965, and Stockwell and Bowen, 1965, are especially thorough.) Then list some of the major syntactic and phonologic features of English that may be especially problematic for native Spanish speakers.

2. Zentella notes that in her study of *el bloque* there was a great divergence in the type of English spoken. Many second-generation speakers used both Puerto Rican English (PRE) and/or black English vernacular (BEV).

The use of BEV within the Puerto Rican community has been extensively studied by Wolfram (1974). Read Wolfram's study and summarize his findings on the use of BEV among the Puerto Rican community in New York City.

3. Zentella points out that in her study one reason for individual differences in bilingual proficiency was the socialization of young Puerto Rican children into appropriate male and female roles. She notes that the work of sociolinguists has consistently indicated that females in western societies are more sensitive to prevalent linguistic norms than males.

Research the area of male/female differences in regards to prevalent linguistic norms. You might begin with the work of Labov (1966, 1972a,b, 1981), cited by Zentella.

4. Zentella cites Hakuta and Snow (1986) and the National Clearinghouse of Bilingual Education (1985) in reference to the cognitive advantages of bilingualism.

Using these sources and others, research the question of the influence of bilingualism on cognitive development.

SUGGESTED READINGS

Readers who are interested in educational issues in the Puerto Rican community should contact Aspira of America in Washington, D.C., for its ongoing national studies and reports from various local chapters.

Important collections of articles devoted to *Latino* language(s) in the United States allow readers to compare studies of two or more of the national groups, particularly Mexicans and Puerto Ricans: J. Amastae and L. Elías-Olivares, (eds.) (1982). *Spanish in the United States: Sociolinguistic Aspects*. London: Cambridge University Press; and R. Durán, ed. (1981). *Latino Language and Communicative Behavior*. Norwood, NJ: Ablex Publishing Corporation.

For more in-depth analysis of language variety and related historical, cultural, and socioeconomic issues in the Puerto Rican community, consult the Centro de Estudios Puertorriqueños (Hunter College, C.U.N.Y.) Working Papers series and the works cited in the bibliography for Zentella (1978, 1981a,b,c, 1983, 1985, 1986a,b, and 1987).

REFERENCES

Aspira of New York. 1983. *Racial and Ethnic High School Dropout Rates in New York City: A Summary Report/1983*. New York: Aspira of New York.

Attinasi, J. 1983. Language attitudes and working class ideology in a Puerto Rican barrio of New York. Unpublished ms.

Bonilla, F. 1983. Manos que sobran: Work, migration and the Puerto Rican in the 1980's. Paper presented at the National Puerto Rican Coalition meeting, December.

Castillo, C. and O. Bond. 1981. *The University of Chicago Spanish-English, English-Spanish Dictionary*. New York: Pocket Books.

Cummins, J. 1986. Empowering minority students. *Harvard Educational Review* February:25–31.

Ferguson, C. 1964. Diglossia. In Hymes, D. (ed.), *Language in Culture and Society*. New York: Harper & Row.

Fishman, J. A. 1967. Bilingualism with and without diglossia: Diglossia with and without bilingualism. *Journal of Social Issues* 23:29–38.

Fiske, E. B. 1985. Education department seeking to alter bilingual efforts. *New York Times,* September 26 A1.

Hakuta, K. and C. Snow. 1986. The role of research in policy decisions about bilingual education. *NABE NEWS IX* (3) Spring: 1, 18–21.

Heath, S. B. 1983. *Ways with Words: Language, Life and Work in Communities and Classrooms*. London: Cambridge University Press.

Hymes, D. 1974. *Foundations in Sociolinguistics: An Ethnographic Approach*. Philadelphia: University of Pennsylvania Press.

Labov, W. 1966. *The Social Stratification of English in New York City*. Washington, D.C.: Center for Applied Linguistics.

Labov, W. 1972a. *Language in the Inner City: Studies in the Black English Vernacular*. Philadelphia: University of Pennsylvania Press.

Labov, W. 1972b. *Sociolinguistic Patterns*. Philadelphia: University of Pennsylvania Press.

Labov, W. 1981, ed. *Locating Language in Time and Space*. New York: Academic Press.

Language Policy Task Force (LPTF). 1980. *Social Dimensions of Language Use in East Harlem*. New York: Centro de Estudios Puertorriqueños.

LPTF. 1983. *Intergenerational Perspectives on Bilingualism*. New York: Centro de Estudios Puertorriqueños.

LPTF. 1984. Speech and ways of speaking in a bilingual Puerto Rican Community. Final Report to the National Institute of Education, G 81-0054. New York: Research Foundation of the City University of New York.

Mann, E. and J. Salvo. 1985. Characteristics of new Hispanic immigrants to New York City: A comparison of Puerto Rican and non-Puerto Rican Hispanics. *Research Bulletin of the Hispanic Research Center* 8 (1&2):1–8.

Milroy, L. 1980. *Language and Social Networks*. Baltimore: University Park Press.

National Clearinghouse for Bilingual Education (NCBE). 1985. The development of bilingualism, cognitive flexibility, and social-cognitive skills in Hispanic elementary school children. Part C Research Agenda. Washington, D.C.: NCBE.

Padron, H. 1982. Dos worlds/two mundos. Unpublished poem.

Pedraza, P., J. Attinasi and G. Hoffman 1980. *Rethinking diglossia*. Language Policy Task Force Working paper #9. New York: Centro de Estudios Puertorriqueños.

Poplack, S. 1979. "Sometimes I'll start a sentence in Spanish y termino en espanol": Towards a typology of code switching. Working Paper #4. New York: Centro de Estudios Puertorriqueños.

Puerto Rican Forum. 1981. *The Next Step Toward Equality*. New York: National Puerto Rican Forum.

Reyes, L. 1984. Minority dropouts: Systemic failure in inner city schools. Paper presented at the Second Seminar on the situation of Black, Chicano, Cuban, Native American, Puerto Rican, Caribbean, and Asian Communities in the United States. Casa de las Americas, Havana, Cuba.

Rodriguez, R. 1984. *Hunger of Memory*. New York: Bantam Books.

Romero, M. 1983. Significant bilingual instructional features research: Teacher/student talk. Paper delivered at the National Association for Bilingual Education annual conference, February 17, Washington, D.C.

Santiago, R. 1983. Teach immigrants in their own language? Interview with Ramon Santiago, Director, Georgetown University Bilingual Service Center. *U.S. News and World Report,* October 3. 61–62.

Stockwell, R. and D. Bowen. 1965. *The Sound Patterns of English and Spanish*. Chicago: University of Chicago Press.

Stockwell, R., D. Bowen and J. Martin. 1965. *The Grammatical Structures of English and Spanish*. Chicago: University of Chicago Press.

Urciuoli, B. 1980. Social parameters of language contact. Paper delivered at conference on Spanish beyond the Southwest, University of Illinois, Chicago Circle, October.

Valdés, G. 1976. Social interaction and code switching patterns: A case study of Spanish/English alternation. In G. D. Ketter, R. V. Teschner and S. Viera (eds.), *Bilingualism in the Bicentennial and Beyond*. Jamaica, NY: Bilingual Press, 53–85.

Valdés, A. 1981. Code switching as a deliberate verbal strategy: A microanalysis of direct and indirect requests among Chicano bilingual speakers. In R. Durán (ed.), *Latino Language and Communicative Behavior*. Norwood, NJ: Ablex Publishing Corporation.

Weinreich, U. 1953. *Languages in Contact*. New York: Linguistic Circle of New York.

Willner, R. 1985. *Ten Years of Neglect: The Failure to Serve the Language Minority Students in the New York City Public Schools*. Report prepared for the Educational Priorities Panel, October. New York: EPP.

Wolfram, W. 1974. *Sociolinguistic Aspects of Assimilation: Puerto Rican English in New York City*. Arlington, VA: Center for Applied Linguistics.

Wong Fillmore, L. 1983. Who needs bilingual education to learn English? Paper delivered at the National Association for Bilingual Education annual conference, February 17, Washington, D.C.

Zentella, A. C. 1978. Code switching and interactions among Puerto Rican children. *Working Papers in Sociolinguistics* No 50. Austin: Southwest Educational Development Lab. Reprinted in J. Amastae and L. Elías-Olivares (eds.), *Spanish in the United States: Sociolinguistic Aspects*. London: Cambridge University Press, 1982.

Zentella, A. C. 1981a. Language variety among Puerto Ricans. In C. Ferguson and S. B. Heath (eds.), *Language in the U.S.A.* London: Cambridge University Press.

Zentella, A. C. 1981b. " 'Tá bien, you could answer me en cualquier idioma": Puerto Rican code switching in bilingual classrooms. In R. Durán (ed.), *Latino Language and Communicative Behavior*. Norwood, NJ: Ablex Publishing Corporation.

Zentella, A. C. 1981c. "Hablamos los dos. We speak both.": Growing up bilingual in el Barrio. Ph.D. dissertation, University of Pennsylvania.

Zentella, A. C. 1983. Spanish and English in contact in the U.S.: The Puerto Rican experience. In E. Chang Rodriguez (ed.), *Spanish in the Western Hemisphere*. Special issue of *Word*, 33 (1&2), April-August: 42–57.

Zentella, A. C. 1985. The fate of Spanish in the United States: The Puerto Rican experience. In N. Wolfson and J. Manes (eds.), *The Language of Inequality*. The Hague: Mouton, pp. 41–59.

Zentella, A. C. 1986a. Individual differences in growing up bilingual. In M. Saravia Shore (ed.), *Cross-Cultural and Communicative Competencies: Ethnographies of Educational Programs for Language Minority Students*, Council on Anthropology and Education Publication. West Cornwall, CT: Horizon Communications.

Zentella, A. C. 1986b. Language minorities and the national commitment to foreign language competency: Resolving the contradiction. *ADFL Bulletin* 17 (3): 32–42.

Zentella, A. C. 1987. Language and female identity in the Puerto Rican community. In J. Penfield (ed.), *Women and Language in Transition*. Albany, NY: S.U.N.Y. Press.

Zirkel, P. 1973. Puerto Rican parents: An educational survey. Paper presented at the annual meeting of the American Orthopsychiatric Association, May.

CHAPTER 6

The Language Situation of Cuban Americans

Ofelia García and Ricardo Otheguy

There are approximately 1 million Cuban Americans in the United States, accounting for approximately 7 percent of the total Hispanic population of the country (Bureau of the Census 1982). Cuban Americans, along with other Hispanics, have contributed to making Spanish a language of widespread use in private and public domains in many parts of the United States. But the unique circumstances of the Cuban migration, their peculiar social and demographic characteristics, and their unusual pattern of geographic concentration have allowed Cubans to play a role in shaping the use of Spanish in this country that goes well beyond what their numbers would warrant. This chapter will focus on the relationship between these sociocultural factors that characterize the Cuban Americans and their use of and attitudes toward both English and Spanish.

HISTORY OF IMMIGRATION

By the latter part of the nineteenth century there were approximately 100,000 people of Cuban origin living in New York, Tampa, and Key West (Dixon 1983). The turn of the century was witness to the boom in the cigar-making industry in Tampa, the Spanish-American War (which was fought largely in Cuba), the first occupation of Cuba by the United States, the first independent Cuban government, and the second North American occupation of the island. These events caused close to 56,000 persons of Cuban origin to be admitted into the United States between 1896 and 1910 (Pérez 1986).

Throughout the first half of the twentieth century, Cuban immigration to the United States was steady but slow, with an increase in the period 1951–1958, when 63,000 Cubans fled Fulgencio Batista's regime (Pérez 1986). A sharp increase in the number of arrivals occurred after the revolution that gave Fidel Castro control of the Cuban government, beginning in January, 1959. Between that time and the end of September, 1983, over 805,000 Cubans arrived in the United States.

But the Cuban exodus to the United States throughout the three decades of Castro's revolution has been highly episodic. Immigration has started and stopped, and then started again, producing some periods when large numbers have arrived in the course of a few weeks and others when immigration has slowed to a trickle for months. The complex sociolinguistic situation created by this pattern of immigration by Cubans—some of whom have been in the United States for over a quarter of a century while others have arrived as recently as 1980; some of whom have come in groups of ten, while others have arrived in the company of tens of thousands—is the subject of this chapter.

Although both Portes and Bach (1985) and Boswell and Curtis (1983) speak of five periods of Cuban migration, we generally follow Llanes (1982), with some modifications, in recognizing three large waves of arrivals from Cuba since 1959, and three intervening periods when immigration was restricted, as described below.

The First Wave: Exiles from the Upper Middle Classes: January 1, 1959, to October 22, 1962

This period involves those Cubans who left the island between the start of the Revolution and up to the missile crisis of October, 1962, when the Cuban government stopped immigration. The first wave was granted refugee status by the United States government and was made up of approximately 215,000 people (Portes and Bach 1985; Boswell 1984). They were mostly white and well-educated, and included a disproportionate number of middle-aged people (Llanes 1982).

The First Interlude: October 22, 1962, to September 18, 1965

Approximately 56,000 persons of Cuban origin entered the United States during this period. Many came through intermediary countries, especially Spain or Mexico. Some 7,000 Cubans arrived clandestinely in small boats. Prisoners of the failed Bay of Pigs invasion and their families made up another 6,000 arrivals during this time (Boswell 1984).

The Second Wave: The Reunification of Families: September 28, 1965, to April 6, 1973

Fradd (1983) has referred to this stage as the family reunification period. In September, 1965, the Cuban government announced that it would allow

Cubans in the United States to pick up relatives from the port of Camarioca. Approximately 5,000 Cubans left in boats. In December, 1965, the United States and Cuba agreed to an orderly airlift. Two daily "Freedom Flights" brought approximately 302,000 Cubans to the United States (Boswell 1984). This second wave of Cubans was racially and socially more heterogeneous than the first. Although 94 percent of the first wave had been white, 24 percent of those who arrived during the second wave were either black or Asian. Although most were educated, there were many more members of the middle and working classes. This second wave included 1,600 teachers, 18,000 lawyers, 2,500 doctors, and 4,600 carpenters and masons (Llanes 1982).

The Second Interlude: April 6, 1973, to April 21, 1980

Approximately 50,000 Cubans arrived during this hiatus, mostly through third countries (Boswell 1984).

The Third Wave: The Mariel Boatlift: April 21 to September, 1980

The pressures to emigrate that led thousands of Cubans to take refuge in the Peruvian Embassy in Havana in April, 1980, forced the Cuban government to open up the port of Mariel. The boatlift brought 125,000 Cubans to the United States in a period of 6 months. Reports that this group contained large numbers of people that the Cuban government regarded as undesirable (criminals, thieves, and homosexuals) were prevalent at first (Michelmore 1982). We now know, however, that this wave is differentiated from the two earlier waves only by the larger number of blacks, younger single males, and unskilled or manual laborers (Dixon 1983). The 1980 Refugee Act, passed by the United States Congress months before the boatlift started, lowered the number of Cubans allowed to enter the United States legally. Therefore, Cubans from this third wave were denied the status of refugees granted to those of the first and second waves. Instead, the Cubans from Mariel were given the status of "entrants."

The Third Interlude: December, 1980, to the Present

From the time the Mariel boatlift ended there has been a continuous trickle of Cubans entering the United States through third countries or in small boats. It is estimated that approximately 20,000 Cubans have arrived in the United States since the end of the Mariel boatlift.

The unique circumstances of immigration by Cuban Americans have facilitated what is usually referred to as "structural incorporation" into the host society, that is, incorporation into the economic system of the United States. The personal, educational, professional, and financial resources of the Cubans of the first wave paved the way for the others. By the beginning of the 1980s, the economic activity of these Cubans had fueled the growth of the economy of Dade County, Florida (made up of Miami and its surrounding communities where, as we shall see, there were by 1983 close to 20,000 Cuban-owned businesses), to the point where the county was able to incorporate the large masses of less skilled Cubans who arrived in subsequent waves.

SOCIODEMOGRAPHIC CHARACTERISTICS

Several sociodemographic characteristics distinguish Cuban Americans from other Hispanics in the United States. Cubans are by far the oldest, the most foreign-born, the most educated, and the most economically successful Hispanic group in the country. In 1985 the median age of Cubans in the United States was 39.1 years, making them much older than Puerto Ricans (median age 24.3) and Mexican Americans (median age 23.2), and even older than the general population of the United States (31.4) (Bureau of the Census 1985). Cuban Americans are also mostly Cuban-born, first-generation immigrants. In the 1970 census, 80 percent of the Cubans surveyed had been born outside the United States. Their educational attainment is again higher (median of 12.0 school years completed) than that of Puerto Ricans (11.2 school years), or Mexicans (10.2 school years) (Bureau of the Census 1985).

Even though the Cuban American community still labors under serious economic difficulties, particularly when compared to the United States population as a whole, Cuban Americans have had more success than other Hispanics in achieving economic incorporation. Whereas 42 percent of Puerto Ricans and 24 percent of Mexican Americans have incomes below the poverty level, only 13 percent of Cuban Americans fit that category (Bureau of the Census 1985). In 1985 the median income of Cuban Americans was estimated to be $22,587, whereas the median income was $19,184 for Mexican Americans and $12,371 for Puerto Ricans.

There seems to be little doubt that the rapid economic integration of Cuban Americans compared to other Hispanic groups is due to the higher level of racial and social congruence, as well as class congruence, between Cubans of the early waves and the power groups in the United States (García and Otheguy 1985).

With regard to race, we have already pointed out that even though many Cuban Americans are black or Asian, there is also a high proportion of what Anglophone North Americans regard as whites. In fact, fewer Cuban Americans than any other Hispanic group are seen by white North Americans as nonwhite.

With regard to social and class factors congruent with those of North American power groups, it must be remembered that unlike other groups made up of immigrants driven here by economic need, Cuban immigration was the direct result of a revolution that, particularly during the years of the early waves, brought many elite, educated Cubans to the United States. These first Cubans should really be regarded as political exiles rather than immigrants. And even though the more heterogeneous subsequent waves—which began to show some of the characteristics of an economic migration—have created a Cuban American population that counts in its ranks many poor and working-class people, the Cuban American community still includes a larger middle class and a more substantial professional and entrepreneurial group than other Hispanic communities in the United States. Not, one might add, because they availed themselves better than other Hispanics of opportunities provided here, but because in most cases they had already attained these social levels in their country of origin. Once settled in the United States, these people came to occupy, after an initial period of adjustment, positions in the social scale similar to the ones they had had in Cuba.

Finally, the greater congruence between the characteristics of Cuban Americans and those of North American power groups is manifested in the fact that the majority of Cubans are politically conservative and belong to the Republican Party, although Cuban Americans under 35 are more likely to be Democrats (Goonen 1984).

In addition to the factors of congruence just discussed, evidence suggests that the economic success of Cuban Americans is also due to the large number of workers per family (Pérez 1986). The percentage of Cuban American women in the labor force is even higher (55.4 percent of Cuban women hold jobs) than that of female workers in the entire population (49.9 percent).

Going beyond the factors of congruence and of numbers of workers per family, Portes and Bach (1985) have focused on the community dimension in explaining the greater economic integration of Cuban Americans. They have presented evidence showing the beneficial effects of what is often called "ghettoization," that is, the concentration of members of a minority in one area where they interact socially and economically mostly with each other. Cuban Americans of the first two waves quickly created their own Cuban-owned and Cuban-run enterprises that provided jobs for other Cuban Americans, who in turn became the customers of these Cuban American businesses. In fact, Dade County, where 60 percent of Cuban Americans live, ranks second to Los Angeles in the number of Hispanic businesses. Dade County is also home to the largest Hispanic business firms to be found in the United States. The number of Cuban-owned enterprises in Dade County increased from 919 in 1967 to 18,000 in 1983 (Boswell and Curtis 1983).

Still, the economic picture is not all positive. It is important to note, for instance, the underutilization of the professional and managerial skills that many Cubans brought to the United States (Rogg and Cooney 1980). Even though the professional levels attained by many here were, as we have noted, a case of returning to an earlier Cuban status rather than the result of progress in this society, the fact remains that on the whole Cuban Americans have experienced downward occupational mobility (Fradd 1983). Even though there is a higher proportion of managerial and professional occupations among Cuban Americans (19 percent of Cuban-held jobs are at those levels) than among Puerto Ricans (13 percent) and Mexican Americans (9 percent), the modal occupational status of Cubans is still that of blue collar workers (Bureau of the Census 1985).

In short, Cuban Americans are a highly successful group compared to other Hispanics, but continue to be, in many ways, a struggling minority that is not completely incorporated structurally into American society. Moreover, Cubans have "made it" in the United States, in part, simply because they trace their origins mostly to a Communist revolution that pushed out onto North American shores a large pool of highly educated, highly skilled professionals who, in the mostly small-town environment of Dade County, were able to use their skills and their status as welcome allies of North American power groups. In addition, the evidence suggests that Cuban Americans owe a large part of their success to their having turned a deaf ear to those who praise the virtues of integration and dispersion as the keys to success.

GEOGRAPHIC CONCENTRATION: DADE COUNTY AND NEW JERSEY

More than 60 percent of Cuban Americans live in Dade County, Florida, and another 20 percent live in areas of New York and New Jersey (Boswell and Curtis 1983). In an effort to disperse the Cuban American population, the Cuban Refugee Program, established in February, 1961, under the United States Secretary of Health, Education and Welfare, mounted a massive resettlement program. By 1978, approximately 470,000 Cubans had been resettled (Portes and Bach 1985).

Despite the efforts made by the government to relocate the Cubans in different parts of the United States, it turned out that Florida, New York, and New Jersey ended up with close to 80 percent of the Cubans who came to the country between 1970 and 1978. The 1980 Census counted 470,250 Cuban Americans in Florida, 80,860 in New Jersey, and 76,942 in New York. Other states with a significant number of Cuban Americans were California with 61,004, Illinois with 19,063, and Texas with 14,124 (Bureau of the Census 1982).

Despite government efforts to disperse them, Cuban Americans appear to have chosen to live in close ethnic enclaves. By 1978, 50 percent of Cuban immigrants intended to reside in Dade County. Of the 125,000 Cubans of the Mariel period, 60 percent settled in Dade County (APWA 1981). Since 1978 there has been a steady decline in the Cuban American populations of New York and New Jersey and corresponding increase in that of Dade County. In fact, a 1978 survey by the *Miami Herald* confirmed that 40 percent of the Cuban Americans in Dade County had lived in other parts of the United States (Boswell 1984).

In Dade County, the Cuban American population grew from 20,000 in 1959 to 600,000 in 1983. In 1976, white North Americans represented 76 percent of Dade County's population. But with the added concentration of Hispanics in the area, by 1984 the white North American population represented only 59 percent of the County's entire population (CAPC 1986). Although approximately 80 percent of the Hispanics in Dade County are Cuban Americans, in the last decade 100,000 other Hispanics have settled in the area, attracted by job opportunities within the Cuban American economy that require little or no knowledge of English (Boswell and Curtis 1983).

In the 1980 Census, four cities in Dade County had Hispanic populations in excess of 50 percent. Sweetwater, the first city in the United States with a Cuban American mayor, Jorge Valdes, had a Hispanic population of 81 percent. In Hialeah, 74 percent of the population was Hispanic, and a Cuban-born mayor, Raul Martinez, was elected in the early 1980s. West Miami's population was 62 percent Hispanic, whereas 56 percent of the population in the city of Miami was Hispanic (Boswell and Curtis 1983).

Even though Cuban Americans have, by and large, attained considerable economic success in Dade County, there is much animosity toward them from both white and black Anglophone North Americans. Cuban Americans have yet to be integrated into the political and social life of Dade County. The results of a Roper Poll conducted in March of 1982 showed that only 9 percent of respondents felt that the presence of Cuban immigrants had been "a good thing for the County," whereas 59 percent felt it had been "a bad thing" (Boswell and Curtis 1983).

At the county level there is only one Hispanic County Commissioner and only one Hispanic school board member (CAPC 1986). Hispanics are likewise underrepresented in academic institutions. For example, at the North Campus of Miami Dade Community College, where 45 percent of the student body is Hispanic, only 4 percent of the faculty is of Hispanic descent. Although an enormous effort has been launched to integrate Hispanics into the political life of the county, in 1976 Hispanics represented only 10 percent of the electorate, although by 1984 this figure had increased to 21 percent (CAPC 1986).

The animosity toward the Spanish-speaking community of Dade County, and in particular toward the Cuban American community, has increased as their numbers have risen and they have become economically successful. Although in 1973 the Dade County Commission officially declared the County to be bilingual, 7 years later xenophobic groups succeeded in rescinding that decree. On November 4, 1980, supported by a 3 : 1 margin in a referendum, an ordinance was passed declaring that Dade County was no longer officially bilingual and forbidding the expenditure of county funds for any activity involving languages other than English.

West New York–Union City, New Jersey, encompasses a large part of the north section of Hudson County, New Jersey. The settlement of Cuban Americans in West New York started in the 1960s. By 1970 over a third of West New York's total population of 40,666 was of Cuban origin. In 1978, almost two-thirds of the population was Hispanic, with Cubans constituting the vast majority (Rogg and Cooney 1980). Most of the Cuban Americans who have settled in West New York are from either the province of Havana or Las Villas. Many came because they had relatives and friends in the city. As in Dade County, Cuban Americans in West New York have created a strong ethnic enclave. Bergenline, the main shopping street, is full of Cuban businesses where most Cuban Americans do their shopping.

The evidence suggests that Cuban Americans have been more economically successful than other Hispanic groups because, as the Norwegian anthropologist Fredrik Barth (1969) has suggested, they have been able to establish ethnic boundaries. The geographic concentration of Cuban Americans distinguishes their settlement pattern from that of other Hispanics in the United States. Cuban Americans numerically dominate neighborhoods much more than do Puerto Ricans and Mexican Americans, who are more residentially integrated with other groups. For example, in Little Havana and Hialeah in Dade County, and in West New York in New Jersey, many census tracts show Cuban American population concentrations of over 70 percent (Boswell 1984).

Cubans have been successful in establishing ethnic boundaries because they arrived in large groups, because they had the appropriate economic and social resources upon arrival, and because they settled in what was then an underdeveloped, predominantly rural and small-town area of the United States (Dade County), or in a suburban area that was then also quite underdeveloped (West New York–Union City). Their concentration in these two geographic areas and their closely knit communities and businesses have protected them to a very large degree against the economic and personal ravages of discrimination that other Hispanics have had to face.

LANGUAGE USE BY CUBAN AMERICANS

Cubans of the first generation speak Spanish natively. Some middle class Cubans of the first wave had some knowledge of English before they came to the United States, since many of them, as is the custom in many

Latin American countries, attended, in Cuba, English–Spanish bilingual schools or schools that stressed the teaching of English. Many more Cubans, however, spoke little or no English upon arrival. Some have acquired some English through classes and contact with English-speaking North Americans, while others have remained totally monolingual Spanish speakers.

Cubans of the second generation, many of whom are by now adolescents or young adults, usually speak English fluently. Their command of Spanish, however, is quite variable. This section will analyze bilingualism among Cuban Americans and explore the nature of the Spanish and English they use to communicate with their immediate community and with the Anglophone community that surrounds them.

The issue of the survival of Spanish in the United States is more relevant for Cuban Americans than for any other Hispanic group. Whereas other Hispanics have access to the Spanish standard of their respective countries of origin through newspapers and radio and television programs, few Cuban Americans ever read *Gramma,* the official Cuban newspaper, or any other Cuban periodical, or listen to *Radio Reloj,* the Cuban all-news station, or to any other Cuban radio program, even though Cuban broadcasts come through clearly on the AM band in many areas of South Florida where Cubans live. The embargo imposed on Cuba by the United States government, and the Cuban Americans' own disdain toward the current Cuban regime, have resulted in their almost complete separation from Cuba, not only from the geographic, social, and political standpoints, but from the linguistic standpoint as well. To make matters worse, the flow of mail between Cuban Americans and their relatives and friends in Cuba is cumbersome and slow, and even telephone calls are restricted and difficult to make.

It is against this unusual background that we should first look at the question of linguistic proficiency in both English and Spanish among Cuban Americans, and then turn to a discussion of Cuban American Spanish.

Language Proficiency

It is well known that the Cuban American community in the United States has the highest percentage of monolingual Spanish speakers. In 1976, 33 percent of Cuban Americans were monolingual speakers of Spanish, and 80 percent were either Spanish monolingual or Spanish-dominant. In contrast, only 18 percent of Puerto Ricans and 13 percent of Mexican Americans were classified as Spanish monolingual (NCEP 1982). It seems clear that this greater incidence of Spanish among Cubans is due to the fact that first-generation people account for a greater proportion of the total ethnic group among Cuban Americans than among other Hispanics. We expect that since the compiling of these figures in 1976 the proportion of Spanish dominance in the Cuban American community will have increased, due to the arrival in

1980 of 125,000 Cubans from Mariel, only 2 percent of whom spoke English upon arrival (Dixon 1983).

In addition to reflecting their mostly first-generation status, the high level of Spanish monolingualism among Cuban Americans is the result of the economically viable ethnic enclaves in which 80 percent of them live and work. As we have stressed, most Cuban Americans of the first generation operate in a social and economic context that allows them to hold jobs, do business, and make money in Spanish. There are many other segregated areas in the United States that are home to other Hispanics, of course, but the Cuban "*barrio,*" due to its unusual beginnings as a beachhead for professional and entrepreneurial refugees, rather than for poor immigrants, has generated the economic and personal resources that other Hispanic settlements have found difficult to produce. Mexican Americans and Puerto Ricans must seek employment for the most part in North American-owned, Anglophone establishments where lack of proficiency in English is a serious handicap. In contrast, many Cuban Americans are able to work in Cuban-owned enterprises where enough business is conducted in Spanish that their poor command of English represents a much smaller disadvantage.

The widespread belief that level of English proficiency among members of United States ethnic minorities correlates with level of economic attainment turns out not to be true, at least for Hispanic Americans. Cuban Americans, who are clearly the least Anglophone of all Hispanic groups, are also clearly the least poor. The job-generating ethnic enclave makes it possible for them to be economically successful regardless of their level of knowledge of English.

Even though the Cuban American group as a whole is the most Spanish-speaking among Hispanics, the second generation of Cubans shows the same pattern of preference for English found in second-generation Mexican Americans and Puerto Ricans. According to the NCEP survey mentioned above, only 6 percent of second-generation Cuban Americans considered themselves Spanish monolingual in 1976, a figure not unlike the 1 percent of second-generation Puerto Ricans and the 5 percent of second-generation Mexican Americans who said they were Spanish monolingual.

Caution must be used, however, in interpreting these 1976 figures for the second generation. The sample surveyed in 1976 was between 22 and 51 years of age. Thus, this second-generation sample was made up of Cubans who came to the United States before the Castro revolution. For the most part, Cuban Americans who came prior to the establishment of the Communist regime in 1959 have not been full participants in the ethnic enclave and do not partake of the experiences of the refugees.

Although there have been no published studies of the language use of postrevolutionary Cuban Americans of the second generation (those born in the United States between 1960 and 1986), we expect their level of Spanish monolingualism to be as low as that of prerevolutionary Cubans. Indeed, preliminary results of a study based on data from West New York (Fernández 1987) confirm the high degree of English proficiency among second-generation Cuban Americans.

Still, for these Cubans who were born in the United States of parents who came here after the revolution, we should expect their degree of Spanish maintenance, if not their degree of Spanish monolingualism, to be higher than that of the prerevolutionary group. Our expectation is partly based, as we have mentioned, on their numerical strength in their neighborhoods. Moreover, and at least for those who live in Dade County, an educational policy of teaching Spanish to Spanish speakers in public schools might also be responsible for a higher degree of language maintenance among this group.

Still, second-generation Cuban Americans, even those living in Dade County and West New York, are for the most part English-dominant. These young people (most second-generation Cubans are still adolescents or young adults) appear to have more contact with, but, ironically, less interest in or attachment to the Spanish language than do young Mexicans and Puerto Ricans in the United States. A 1980 study of high school sophomores shows that only 7 percent of Cubans, as compared to 22 percent of Puerto Ricans and 14 percent of Mexicans, report speaking Spanish usually (NCES 1980). On the other hand, these Cuban American sophomores who seldom use Spanish live in homes that are more Spanish monolingual than is the case with Mexican Americans and Puerto Ricans. Whereas 24 percent of Cuban Americans sophomores live in homes where no other language but Spanish is spoken, only 16 percent of Puerto Ricans and 11 percent of Mexican Americans live in such settings.

Some of the preference for English among Cuban Americans results from their greater degree of intermingling with Anglophone youngsters. The rate of exogamy in the Cuban American population is quite high, no doubt due to their considerable degree of racial and social congruence with North American communities, as mentioned above. In Dade County, 15 percent of all marriages are between Spanish-surnamed whites and non-Spanish-surnamed whites (Dixon 1983). Furthermore, English also seems to be the language usually spoken by young Cuban Americans among themselves.

A basic difference between the situation of Cuban Americans and that of Mexican Americans and Puerto Ricans may account for the young Cubans' higher interest in the English language. Although Mexican Americans and Puerto Ricans can, and in fact do, go back and forth to their countries of origin, Cuban Americans, and especially young ones born in the United States, have only in very few cases ever gone back to Cuba, since their families, and perhaps they themselves, regard the present Cuban government as an illegitimate usurper and Cuba as a place to be avoided, with exceptions being made only for visits to elderly relatives. The Cuban government, in turn, often reciprocates this antagonism by making it difficult, and sometimes impossible, for Cuban Americans to travel to Cuba. Therefore, even though constant waves of new arrivals replenish the ranks of monolingual Spanish speakers, most young Cuban Americans have had contact with Spanish only in the United States. Most have never had the experience of being in a country where Spanish is the language of power and prestige. They have never been in a social setting where Spanish is the only language written, spoken, and heard. They have never been totally immersed in Spanish. Furthermore, to them, Spanish is truly the language of the past, the language of *la Cuba de ayer,* "the Cuba of yesterday," in the familiar plaintive phrase of Dade County exiles. In addition to being the language of their communities, Spanish to Puerto Ricans and Mexicans is the language of a more or less viable country of origin, no matter how unfamiliar.

The schools have played an important role in shaping the language proficiency of young Cuban Americans. Although 80 percent of Cuban American students attend public schools (Solé 1980), over 20 percent go to what in a separate study we have called "ethnic" schools (García and Otheguy 1985, 1987). For the most part, and especially in Dade County, these are privately owned Cuban schools (but not "private schools" in the elite, exclusive, and expensive sense the phrase has come to convey) where instruction takes place in Spanish.

These ethnic schools provide middle and working class Cuban American children with a context where Spanish is to some degree the language of power and prestige, since the principal and most of the teaching staff are Cubans with a commitment to teaching Spanish as a "first language." In most of these schools children are completely bilingual and biliterate. Likewise, Cuban American children in the Dade County public schools participate in a voluntary program of Spanish for Spanish speakers. Although the time devoted to the Spanish language is very short (about a half-hour daily), Spanish is taught by a separate teacher, most often of Cuban origin and in most cases a monolingual speaker of Spanish. Although the rate of success in becoming completely biliterate is smaller for these Cuban American children than for those attending the ethnic schools, it is nevertheless true that more support is given to the development of the Spanish language in Dade County schools than in most public school systems in other parts of the country.

The presence of grandparents living at home is another important factor relating to the Spanish language proficiency of young Cuban Americans, among whom the three generation family is still a common arrangement. In 1980, 31 percent of Cubans over the age of 65 lived in a household headed by a relative other than the spouse, which is a high ratio compared to the 20 percent of the Puerto Rican elderly and the 17 percent of the Mexican American elderly who lived in such an arrangement (Pérez 1986). Cuban American children are forced to interact in Spanish with these monolingual older people on a daily basis. Of those surveyed by Alvarez (1976), 92 percent reported that they used only Spanish to communicate with their grandparents.

The Spanish of Cuban Americans

The Spanish of Cuban Americans, as befits a still mostly first-generation community, resembles that of the country of origin in most of its phonologic and morphosyntactic characteristics. In these two respects, Cuban American Spanish, particularly among the Cuban-born generation, is thus simply Cuban Spanish (for studies on Cuban Spanish, see Guitart 1976 and López Morales 1971).

However, in regard to phraseology and vocabulary, the Spanish of Cuban Americans has started to show the effects of dialect leveling as Cubans come into increasing contact with speakers of other varieties of Spanish. Furthermore, and even among the first generation, the Spanish of Cuban Americans has begun to show the effects of contact with English, both in the importation of English lexical elements and in the loss and alteration of Spanish ones. The Cuban American situation thus reflects the familiar pattern of the lexicon being more susceptible to outside influences than either phonology or morphosyntax (Klein 1985).

Even before the rise of a discipline of sociolinguistics characterized by a sophisticated approach to the description of linguistic variation, the postulation of dialect zones for a language was hedged with disclaimers acknowledging the conceptual problems and limitations of a strictly geographical approach. Nevertheless, Cuban Spanish is usually rightly regarded as part of Caribbean Spanish, a grouping that for Zamora Munné and Guitart (1982) includes the three Antillean islands as well as the coastal areas of Mexico, Panama, Colombia, and Venezuela.

With regard to pronunciation, studies such as those of Terrell (1977) tend to focus on several phenomena associated with syllable-final consonants. Guitart (1978) characterizes Caribbean Spanish in general, and Cuban Spanish in particular, as a radical Spanish dialect whose phonetic output is not as close to the orthography (which he uses as a rough equivalent to the level of phonological representation) as other, more conservative Spanish varieties, such as that spoken in Quito, Ecuador, or La Paz, Bolivia. Guitart distinguishes four phonological phenomena in Cuban Spanish:

1. **Segment deletion.**
   Ex: [ma] for /más/, *más,* "more."
2. **Segment-internal changes.**
   Ex: [sekka] for /serka/, *cerca,* "near".
3. **Epenthesis or the addition of segments.**
   Ex: [fuistes], for /fuiste/, *fuiste,* "you went."

4. Metathesis or the transposition of segments.
Ex: [delen] for /denle/, *denle,* "give him."

Most phonological features of Cuban Spanish have been retained by Cuban Americans, although a more conservative pronunciation often emerges when they interact in Spanish with more conservative speakers.

With regard to morphosyntax, Cuban Spanish shares with all other Latin American varieties, in comparison to Spain, the absence of a fifth person in the verbal paradigm (Cubans, and all Latin Americans, say *tienen* where Spaniards say *teneis* for "you [plural] have"). Furthermore, all forms of Cuban Spanish, like the Spanish in most of Latin America but unlike that in Spain, show an absence of certain stigmatized innovations in indirect object pronominal usage (Cubans go along with the general standard in saying *le dije* for "I told her" where many substandard varieties in Spain commonly say *la dije*). And Cuba, along with the rest of the Caribbean, Spain, Mexico, and sections of the rest of Latin America, uses a *tú* rather than a *vos* second person for the verbal paradigm (Cubans say *tú tienes* for "you [singular] have" whereas many Central and South Americans say *vos tenés*).

With regard to vocabulary, which has been studied by, among others, López Morales (1971), it seems clear that many characteristic lexical features of Cuban Spanish have been retained by Cuban Americans. Yet, as happens in phonology, the constant use of Spanish in interactions with speakers of other varieties of the language has led Cuban Americans to abandon many of the lexical items prevalent in their speech in Cuba. For example, Cuban American college students in New York City regularly use the word *salon* to refer to a classroom, even though in Cuba the word *aula* would have been used. This is no doubt as a response to the exigencies of communication with speakers of Spanish from Puerto Rico and many areas of Latin America where *salon* is the norm.

This leveling of regionalisms occurs particularly in the Spanish of Cuban Americans who have settled in areas with large concentrations of other Spanish speakers. Nowhere is this more prevalent than in the Spanish of Cuban Americans who have settled in Puerto Rico, who, though seeming reluctant to adopt phonological features of Puerto Rican Spanish, such as the velarization of /r/, often take up lexical items that distinguish Puerto Rican Spanish from other varieties of Caribbean Spanish. For example, Cuban Americans in Puerto Rico say *chavos* instead of *dinero* for money, *pantis* instead of the Cuban *blumes* for panties, and *bolsa* instead of *cartucho* for a paper bag.

Although the Spanish of Cuban Americans in Dade County is more insulated from other dialects because of the high concentration of Cubans and the high prestige of Cuban Spanish in the predominantly Cuban area, the recent influx into Dade County of Central and South Americans, especially from Nicaragua and El Salvador, has started to have a leveling effect too.

Like the Cubans of the first wave, some of these Latin American newcomers were members of the elite in their native countries, are more reasonably thought of as exiles than immigrants, and tend to enjoy social and economic prestige in the fiercely anticommunist ambiance of Dade County. Due to the recency of their arrival and their hopes for an early return to their countries, they are often more interested in the retention of Spanish by their children than are Cuban Americans, who are by now more committed to a North American life. For instance, García and Otheguy (1985) noted that a large proportion of the Spanish-speaking population of the elite Loyola School, a private, prestigious bilingual Cuban-owned school in Dade County, is not of Cuban origin. The social prestige of this group of non-Cuban Hispanics is beginning to have an effect on the Spanish spoken by Cuban Americans. Thus the Cuban word for car, *máquina,* appears to be in open retreat in the face of *carro* and others of wider currency, a fate similar to *embullarse,* a term referring to the act of getting excited or enthusiastic about something, which Cubans often find of little communicative value when interacting with many other speakers of Spanish.

Another important factor promoting the influence of Central and South American lexical features on the Spanish of Cuban Americans is the frequent travel of Dade County Cuban businessmen to Latin America, which constitutes their only association with monolingual Spanish-speaking societies.

But the channel for transmission of dialect features is not only at the professional level, since the new Latin Americans of Dade County are not all wealthy or professional. In many Cuban cafeterias and restaurants in Dade County, the waitresses are no longer of Cuban origin. Cuban women, as was previously noted, have been successful in obtaining employment in offices, banks, and factories. Entry level positions for many of the recently arrived poorer Latin American women often exist only in these Cuban cafeterias, where now the Cuban *platanito maduro* has become *maduro* and where the Nicaraguan dessert *las tres leches* competes with the more popular Cuban *flan*.

Although this influence from other forms of Spanish on the language spoken by Cuban Americans cannot be underestimated, the influence of English is most significant (for other studies in this area see Guitart 1987, and Varela de Cueller 1974). Although most Cuban Americans express a purist attitude toward Spanish, the effects of contact with English on their phraseology and vocabulary are easy to find. It needs to be restated that Cuban Americans do not hear or read standard monolingual Cuban Spanish of the type spoken in Cuba. What they hear and read most is precisely the Spanish spoken by themselves and other Hispanics who live in the United States, which shows wholesale importation of lexical elements from North American English.

Perhaps the weak sociolinguistic support of their Spanish language experienced by first-generation Cuban Americans leads them to take on such purist attitudes about their language. For example, the Spanish language daily of Dade County, *El Diario Las Américas,* publishes a daily column by a Cuban journalist, Olympia Rosado, entitled "Cuestiones Gramaticales." Rosado regularly chastises her readers for using English elements in Spanish. In a content analysis of Spanish language dailies in the United States, García and Burunat (in press) found that *El Diario Las Américas* expressed a far more purist attitude than *El Diario La Prensa* of New York and *La Opinión* of Los Angeles. Perhaps for the same reason, although studies of the Spanish spoken by Mexican Americans and Puerto Ricans in the United States abound, there are very few studies of the Spanish spoken by Cuban Americans. Cuban Americans have, for the most part, failed to accept the necessity of English influence if Spanish is to be used successfully in a predominantly English-speaking nation.

In contrast, most young Cuban Americans seem to accept the influence of English as inevitable. For example, although most older Cuban Americans are often critical of what they find to be an inordinate amount of English influence in Puerto Rican Spanish, younger Cuban Americans in Dade County uphold the Spanish of their Puerto Rican classmates as the purer variety of the two. "When I speak in Spanish," a 17-year-old cashier in a Dade County Cuban-owned drug store told us, "I use half-English, half-Spanish. Our Spanish is not like that of Puerto Ricans. They speak real Spanish." When we questioned her, it turned out that she, as well as her other Cuban-American classmates, had either been born in the United States or had come at a very early age. Their Puerto Rican classmates, however, were recent arrivals. It seems to us that the gap between the extreme purist attitude manifested by most older, first-generation Cuban Americans, and the actual sociolinguistic state of the Cuban American community might be harmful to the stabilization, maintenance, and development of Spanish among the younger Cuban American generation.

Using modifications of the familiar typologies of Haugen (1950) and Weinreich (1953), lexical features imported from English into the Spanish of Cuban Americans have been classified by Otheguy and García (in press) with respect to whether what is imported from English or altered in Spanish is a signal with its meaning (loan words), a sequence of signals with their meanings (code-switching), or only the meaning (word and phrasal calques).

Loan Words These are words that use English signals. A loan word is a single or compound word that is imported whole from English, with greater or lesser phonological adaptation. Following the familiar terminology of Saussure (1916), what is imported in loan words is an English signal together with an English meaning.

Ex: Necesito hacer un *part-time* para ganar dinero.
I've got to work part-time to make money.

Code-Switching This is the use of multiword sequences in English unadapted in any way to Spanish.

Ex: Sí, sí, él habla mucho, pero cuando llegó la hora no se atrevió a *bring it up at the meeting.*
Yes, sure, he talks a lot, but when the time came he didn't have the guts to bring it up at the meeting.

Calques These words use Spanish signals with meanings imported from English. In a calque the *form* of the element in question belongs to the borrowing language in its own right, but is being used in a manner that calques the usage of the lending language. *Word calques* include only one signal; *phrasal calques* include more than one signal.

Merged Word Calques. These are words that exist in Spanish but are being used with the meaning of a phonologically similar English word rather than with their own Spanish meaning. The Spanish and the English word show similarities in meaning that lead speakers to establish a complete identity. In addition, they are similar in form, the English and Spanish signals having become merged.

Ex: El martes me *registré* en la universidad.
I registered at the university on Tuesday.

Independent Word Calques. These are the same as merged word calques, except that the Spanish word and the English word whose meaning is being adopted do not have any phonological similarities.

Ex: Creo que *corrió* para alcalde de Hialeah.
I think he ran for mayor of Hialeah.

Phrasal Calques. A phrasal calque uses a series of elements that belong to the Spanish language but are being used as they would be if they were English elements.

Ex: Preguntale si *sabe como hacerlo.*
Ask him if he knows how to do it.

Cuban American Spanish shows these different types of lexical innovations to varying degrees. Otheguy and García (in press) have shown that Cuban Americans in Dade County consider loans totally unacceptable but use them readily. The speech of Cuban Americans also shows a great abundance of calques, perhaps because of the lesser visibility of these innovations, which, so to speak, smuggle English elements into Spanish under the cover of Spanish words. Regardless of their proficiency in English, Cuban Americans use borrowings and calques readily. In fact, we found that monolingual Spanish speakers were even better adopters of these innovations than bilingual Spanish speakers, probably because for them the loans and calques constitute adaptations of the Spanish system within a new speech community, the origin of the adaptations being unknown to them and thus not subject to stigmatization. For bilinguals, however, innovations remain elements from the English language that have found their way into the Spanish the community speaks, being thus stigmatized as part of the purist stance toward Spanish already noted. In contrast, code-switching is more prevalent among Cuban American bilinguals, particularly among the young and those who have either been born in the United States or came when they were young, the reason for this being, quite obviously, that it is necessary to know English in order to switch into it.

The English of Cuban Americans

We have already stated that fewer Cuban Americans are English-proficient than other Hispanics. First-generation Cubans speak English to varying degrees and with more or less of a Spanish accent. Second-generation Cubans, as is usually the case with all second-generation Hispanics, speak English fluently and with a native North American accent. Yet the complex sociolinguistic situation in which young Cuban Americans find themselves—living in homes where mostly Spanish is spoken while they themselves speak English most of the time—has an effect on their English. Although most studies on languages in contact in the United States deal with the influence of English on languages other than English, it is important to point out that, especially in the case of Spanish, and most significantly in the speech of second generation Cuban Americans, influences of Spanish on English are also found.

This is not to say that these native-born young Cuban Americans speak English poorly. On the contrary, and as we have already mentioned, their English is usually indistinguishable from that of other North Americans of comparable geographic and social areas. But these young bilingual speakers often speak English with features that would be puzzling to someone who did not also speak Spanish. First, Spanish loan words creep into their English, and second, their English is often peppered by calques from Spanish, both phenomena occurring mostly when they are speaking, in English, to relatives who understand English but answer them in Spanish.

For example, our 10-year-old son, who understands both languages perfectly but prefers English and speaks Spanish only when he has to (with people who do not speak English), plays cards with us and asks: "Is it my turn to rob?" The word "rob" is a merged word calque from the Spanish *robar,* which is the word used in Spanish to mean "draw a card." Likewise, he will ask: "Where is the picker upper?" or "Are we going to pull bad grass from the garden today?" Only someone familiar with Spanish would recognize "picker-upper" for *recogedor,* the word used in Spanish for "dust pan,'' and ''bad grass'' for *yerba mala,* the term used in Spanish for what in English are usually called ''weeds.''

Bilingual speakers who are constantly surrounded by two different linguistic systems are also exposed to different semiotic systems. The difference between their two worlds is not only the way that these two worlds use different languages, but also that these two languages lexicalize different meanings and convey different types of messages (Culler 1976; Otheguy 1982, 1983). The innovation comes precisely from the fact that messages expressed in one language are not always readily expressible in another unless subjected to some alteration. Thus, one can expect that even in the fluent native English of young Cuban Americans, as is the case of our son cited above, some message features of Spanish, which are lexicalized differently from English, might alter their native English speech.

Teachers in the United States who come into contact with Cuban Americans of the second generation are not likely to encounter any major difficulties with regard to their English. But teachers who come into contact with Cuban-born, and particularly recently arrived Cuban Americans, regardless of their age, are likely to notice difficulties in their English attributable to some degree to the interfering effects of Spanish. Even though there exists now a much more sophisticated understanding of the ways in which first languages affect the acquisition of a second, teachers can still profit from knowing some of the details of Spanish structure that are likely to play a role in the English of their students. Classic comparative studies between Spanish and English will be useful for this purpose (Lado 1957; Stockwell, Bowen and Martin, 1965; Stockwell and Bowen 1965) as will more recent comparative works such as those of Nash (1977) and Whitley (1986).

In particular, teachers will notice that the Caribbean Spanish tendency mentioned above toward weakening of syllable-final segments, particularly syllable-final /s/, can transfer over to English where it will produce both phonological and morphosyntactic effects that, in our experience, can be troubling to teachers. Problems with English plural and third person /s/ can be successfully brought to the attention of Cuban American students by first pointing out similar problems in their writing of Spanish. Likewise, teachers who, in our experience, are puzzled by Cuban American students writing such sentences as ''If that decree becomes in the official law, it will be bad'' can profit from an awareness that ''becoming in'' is simply a straight calque from Spanish, where the verb *convertirse* ''to become'' is typically used in a collocation with the proposition *en.*

LANGUAGE MAINTENANCE OR LANGUAGE SHIFT?

For the most part, Cuban Americans are highly loyal to the Spanish language. In most surveys, they report more positive attitudes towards

Spanish language maintenance than either Puerto Ricans or Mexicans. For example, a 1981 survey conducted by Yankelovich, Skelly and White Inc. found that 95 percent of Cuban Americans, compared to 83 percent of Puerto Ricans and 77 percent of Mexican Americans, reported that preserving the Spanish language was of the utmost importance. Likewise, Otheguy and García (in press) found that 96 percent of Cuban Americans surveyed in Dade County regarded maintaining Spanish alive in the United States as very important, while 95 percent said that it was important for their children to speak Spanish.

Although Cuban Americans tend to show a relatively high degree of loyalty to Spanish, they are also very attached to the English language and to a traditionally conservative notion of North American society and of the United States government. Otheguy and García (in press) found that 96 percent of those surveyed regarded knowing English and being bilingual as very important.

Carlos Solé's classic studies of language attitudes among Cuban American high school students (1980, 1982) also support the highly favorable attitude that even these young Cuban Americans hold toward the Spanish language. For example, 96 percent of those surveyed felt that Spanish was necessary because it is part of their cultural heritage. Solé's study indicates that young Cuban Americans, like their elders, show highly positive attitudes toward the English language and bilingualism. This "dual linguistic loyalty," as Solé has called it, is a result of a young population that is not conflicted about the importance of Spanish in the ethnic enclaves in which they live and work and the importance of English in the wider society.

The stronger loyalty to their ethnic identity coupled with a more positive loyalty to the United States is characteristic of most of the feelings of Cuban Americans. For example, more Cuban Americans feel "Hispanic first" (74 percent) than Puerto Ricans (55 percent) or Mexican Americans (34 percent) (Yankelovich, Skelly and White, Inc. 1981). Yet the present Cuban American emigrants are in the United States to stay. Goonen (1984) reported that 80 percent of Cuban Americans surveyed said that they would remain in the United States even if the Castro regime fell. Only 25 percent said that they have tried to visit their land of origin, compared to 75 percent of Puerto Ricans and 56 percent of Mexican Americans. The return migration rate for Cuban Americans is also less than 5 percent (Boswell 1984).

The question of whether Cuban Americans will become monolingual English speakers in the long run or will continue to be bilingual depends on many factors that may still be unknown. An interesting note on the sociolinguistic situation of Cuban Americans in the United States is that their prospects for language maintenance or shift will result not from the presence of the monolingual country but from the success that their minority language community will continue to experience in this country. Whereas other Hispanic groups can depend on the linguistic continuity and the continued immigration from their home countries for Spanish language maintenance, Cuban

Americans must foster Spanish within a United States context. To date, their continued use of the Spanish language attests to their tenacity in establishing strong ethnic enclaves where Spanish is a necessity. In 1980 in Dade County, over 45 percent of all entry-level jobs advertised in a given month required or encouraged Spanish–English bilingual proficiency (Llanes 1986). There is no question that the position of Spanish among Cuban Americans in Dade County and West New York is, for the time being, quite strong.

What are the prospects for language maintenance or language shift among Cuban Americans in the United States? Fishman (1972) has proposed that only a societal arrangement in which the two languages each have secure compartmentalized functions can succeed in creating a stable and enduring bilingual situation that can extend beyond a three-generation period. Fishman's term for this enduring societal arrangement is "diglossia." Yet it is clear that the Cuban American community in Dade County is not in any way diglossic. Bilingual Cuban Americans do not compartmentalize their use of the two languages and, as has been seen, use English widely among themselves and even in their Spanish-speaking homes. During the 25 years that Dade County has been a Cuban area, much language shift has taken place among the younger Cuban Americans, although this shift has not been replacive (subtractive) but displacive (additive). That is, most second-generation Cuban Americans are English-dominant, but continue to speak Spanish to different degrees. What will happen in another 25 years?

In addition to diglossia, Fishman (1977) has identified five factors that are important in any discussion of the maintenance of minority languages within majority communities: demographic, sociocultural, economic, philosophical/ideological, and political.

It seems to us that in the case of the Cuban American community, only the demographic factor is favorable to continuous language maintenance, whereas the sociocultural, economic, ideological, and political factors are at present creating pressures toward language shift. As we have seen, the presence of a strong ethnic enclave with a large number of older, skilled Spanish speakers is a demographic factor that favors language maintenance. Although originally the ethnic enclave was self-sufficient, the Cuban American business community, especially in Dade County, has now developed an interdependent economic relationship with North American corporations, especially those doing business with Latin America. This more fluid economic relationship between the Anglophone and Cuban American business community, as well as the economic and social mobility of Cuban Americans, might indeed constitute an economic factor that will, in the long run, work against language maintenance. Likewise, Spanish language maintenance is not supported by sociocultural factors. According to Goonen (1984), 85 percent of Cuban Americans are Roman Catholics, and although masses are said in Spanish, there is little religious reinforcement of Spanish language use. Most often priests of Hispanic origin say Spanish masses in

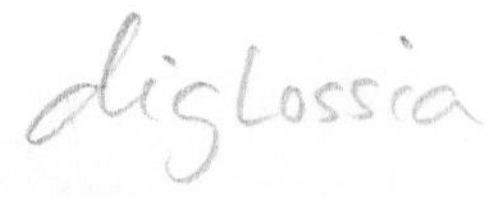

parishes where Anglophone North Americans were once prevalent, and the older members of the congregation resent the Spanish-speaking congregation (Llanes 1986).

Cuban Americans have a stronger network of ethnic schools than other Hispanics in the United States, but still the education of their children is mostly in the hands of an Anglophone public school system. And although Dade County schools have been kinder than others toward Spanish and the role it plays in the development of Cuban American children (García and Otheguy 1985), these schools are still not supportive of Spanish language maintenance.

There is also little political and legal support for Spanish language maintenance at the present time. In fact, U.S. English, an organization that supports making English the official language of the United States, has gained ground in the last few years. Dade County, as we have seen, has rescinded its official support for bilingualism. Florida has started to prepare against the backlash of xenophobic groups by drafting a Florida Language Rights Bill, which was being proposed in 1987. Under the Bill, English would be recognized as the common language of the state, but all individuals will be guaranteed the right to speak, read, write, or in any other way communicate in their mother tongue. Still, there are few Cuban American agencies committed to either civil or language rights. Whereas Mexican Americans have La Raza and Puerto Ricans have Aspira, Cuban Americans have few, if any, civil rights organizations that would be capable of mobilizing them in favor of Spanish language maintenance.

Finally, although Cuban Americans are particularly loyal to Spanish, there is no clear philosophical or ideological support for Spanish language maintenance. In fact, most Cuban Americans have a more incorporative than particularistic view of themselves within the United States society. They do not see themselves in an antagonistic relationship with majority society. Nor do they view themselves as being separate or inferior. They are simply different, for now, although no strong ideological positions would support these differences for their children.

To summarize, there is no question about the strength of Spanish–English bilingualism among Cuban Americans. Like most Hispanic children in the United States, second-generation Cuban American children acquire English easily and they continue speaking Spanish to varying degrees. Although xenophobic groups continue to rally against the use of Spanish, it is clear that unless the Cuban American community develops strong educational, religious, social, and civil institutions that reinforce their language; unless these institutions help shape an ideology of Spanish language maintenance; and unless the political and legal system of the country at large supports the language minority community in maintaining a language other than English, we will, although perhaps not during our lifetimes, see the total shift to English among third-generation Cuban Americans.

EXPLORING THE IDEAS

1. In discussing the sociodemographic characteristics of Cuban Americans, García and Otheguy note that Cuban Americans are the oldest, most foreign-born, most educated, and most economically successful of all Hispanic groups. They also note that fewer Cuban Americans are seen as nonwhites by white North Americans.

How might each of these factors influence Cuban Americans' efforts to maintain the use of Spanish and to acquire English?

2. García and Otheguy point out that the first Cubans to arrive in the United States should actually be considered as political exiles rather than as immigrants.

How might the fact of being a political exile rather than an immigrant affect language retention and language loss?

3. García and Otheguy point out that there may be some benefits for an ethnic group in "ghettoization." Senator H. I. Hayakawa, on the other hand, in an interview in the *New York Times* (October 26th, 1986, p. 6), maintained that "the encouragement of linguistic ghettos of one kind or another" is a threat to social cohesiveness.

What are some social and economic benefits for ethnic group members in "ghettoization"? What are some disadvantages? What are the likely effects of "ghettoization" on language maintenance and loss?

4. García and Otheguy cite the results of a survey conducted by Yankelovich, Skelly and White, which found that Cuban Americans ranked first in their desire to maintain the use of Spanish, Puerto Ricans next, and Mexican Americans last.

What are some factors of the immigration history, settlement patterns, economic and educational level, and political outlook of each group that might be contributing to this difference in attitude toward language maintenance?

5. Spanish speakers make up the largest language minority in the United States. The group has "one of the highest proportions of people who do not speak English at all," according to Waggoner (this volume). Waggoner believes that with the help of appropriate language programs, Spanish speakers will "forge ahead." On the other hand, Zentella (this volume), in her analysis of the Puerto Rican situation, believes that language is often not the main obstacle to the full participation of minorities.

To what extent is the disadvantaged status of Spanish speakers caused by the language barrier? To what extent is the retention of Spanish a matter of historical, social, and economic factors that are not directly related to schooling? (Review the chapters on Hispanics by García and Otheguy, Valdés, and Zentalla before generalizing.)

APPLYING THE IDEAS

1. García and Otheguy point out that in Dade County there is an educational policy of teaching Spanish to Spanish speakers in public schools. Dade County also has programs in which Spanish-speaking students and English-speaking students are placed in the same classroom with the goal of helping each group of students to become bilingual. Such programs are called two-way bilingual programs.

If there is a two-way bilingual program in your community, interview the principal of the school to find out about the history and current program of the school. If your community does not have a two-way bilingual program, review the history and program of the schools in Dade County. An excellent presentation of this information is contained in Mackey, W. M. and V. N. Beebe. 1977. *Bilingual Schools for a Bicultural Community*. Rowley, MA: Newbury House.

2. García and Otheguy give examples of loan words in Cuban Spanish.

Select a language (either English or a second language that you are familiar with) and compile a list of loan words in the language.

3. García and Otheguy point out that languages "lexicalize different meanings and convey different types of messages." Hence, it may be difficult to express in one language an idea that is easily expressed in another.

Interview a bilingual individual and ask this person to provide you with examples of concepts that are easily expressed in his or her first language but are difficult to express in his or her second language. If you are bilingual, compile such examples yourself.

SUGGESTED READING

Boswell and Curtis (1983) offer the most insightful volume on the Cuban American experience. Llanes (1982) provides the reader with a cultural ethnography of Cuban Americans told by the almost 200 Cuban Americans interviewed for the book. For an excellent summary of the sociodemographic factors that affect Cubans in the United States, see Pérez (1986). Portes and Bach (1985) also offer an insightful interpretation of the Cuban American community.

The Spanish of Cubans has been studied by López Morales (1971) and Guitart (1976). Varela de Cuellar (1974) and Otheguy and García (in press) examine English influences on the Spanish of Cuban Americans. The most extensive sociolinguistic studies on Cuban Americans have been done by Solé (1980, 1982). Finally, for a better understanding of the education of Cuban Americans, see García and Otheguy (1985, 1987).

REFERENCES

Alvarez, O. 1976. *Estudio demográfico, social y economico, de la comunidad Latina del Condado Dade*. Miami: Ed. AIP.

American Public Welfare Association (APWA) 1981. Statistical reports. *Refugee Reports* 2(16):8.

Barth, F. 1969 (ed.). *Ethnic Groups and Boundaries, The Social Organization of Culture Difference*. Oslo: Universitetsforlaget.

Boswell, T. 1984. The migration and distribution of Cubans and Puerto Ricans living in the United States. *Journal of Geography* 83(2):65–72.

Boswell, T. and J. Curtis. 1983. *The Cuban-American Experience: Culture, Images and Perspectives*. New Jersey: Rowman and Allanheld.

Bureau of the Census, U.S. Dept. of Commerce. 1982. *1980 Census of Population, Persons of Spanish Origin by State: 1980*. Washington D.C.: Government Printing Office, August.

Bureau of the Census, U.S. Dept. of Commerce. 1985. *Persons of Spanish Origin in the United States: March 1985* (Advance report). Washington D.C.: Government Printing Office, December.

Cuban American Policy Center (CAPC). 1986. Ethnic relations in the Cuban community. A summary of workshop proceedings. The third national conference of the Cuban National Planning Council. Miami, Florida, August.

Culler, J. 1976. *Ferdinand de Saussure*. New York: Penguin Books.

Dixon, H. 1983. An overview of the black Cubans among the Mariel entrants. Paper presented at the Conference on Immigration and the Changing Black Population in the United States, Ann Arbor, MI, May 18–21.

Fernández, M. 1987. Spanish language use among Cuban Americans of the first and second generation in West New York. M.S. thesis, City College of New York, School of Education.

Fishman, J. A. (1972). *Sociology of Language*. Rowley, MA: Newbury House.

Fishman, J. A. (1977). The spread of English as a new perspective for the study of language maintenance and language shift. In J. A. Fishman, R. Cooper and A. Conrad (eds.), *The Spread of English*. Rowley, MA: Newbury House, 108–133.

Fradd, S. 1983. Cubans to Cuban Americans: Assimilation in the United States. *Migration Today* 11(4-5):34–42.

García, O. and S. Burunat. In press. La Prensa Hispana en los Estados Unidos. *Boletín de la Academia Norteamericana de la Lengua Española* 6–7.

García, O. and R. Otheguy. 1985. The masters of survival send their children to school: Bilingual education in the ethnic schools of Miami. *Bilingual Review/Revista Bilingue* 12(1-2):3–43.

García, O. and R. Otheguy. 1987. The bilingual education of Cuban-American children in Dade County's ethnic schools. *Language and Education* 2:in press.

Goonen, N. 1984. Cuban-Americans in the United States. ERIC ED263294.

Guitart, J. 1976. *Markedness and a Cuban Dialect of Spanish*. Washington, D.C.: Georgetown University Press.

Guitart, J. 1978. Conservative versus radical dialects in Spanish: Implications for language instruction. *The Bilingual Review* 5(1):57–64.

Guitart, J. (1987). The future of Cuban Spanish in the United States. Paper presented at the Symposium, 25 years of Cuban Culture in Exile, Florida International University, September 24–26.

Haugen, E. 1950. The analysis of linguistic borrowing. *Language* 26:210–231.

Klein, F. 1985. La cuestión del anglicismo: Apriorismos y métodos. *Thesaurus: Boletín del Instituto Caro y Cuervo*. 60(3):533–548.

Lado, R. 1957. *Linguistics Across Cultures: Applied Linguistics for Language Teachers*. Ann Arbor, MI: The University of Michigan Press.

Llanes, J. 1982. *Cuban-Americans: Masters of Survival*. Cambridge, MA: ABT Books.

Llanes, J. 1986. Bilingualism and Dade County. Paper presented at Community Relations Board Meeting, December.

López Morales, H. 1971. *Estudio sobre el español de Cuba*. New York: Las Américas.

Michelmore, P. 1982. From Cuba with hate: The crime wave Castro sent to America. *Reader's Digest,* December, 223–248.

Nash, R. 1977. *Comparing English and Spanish: Patterns in Phonology and Orthography*. New York: Regents Publishing Company.

National Center for Education Statistics (NCES). 1980. Opening fall enrollment survey, unpublished tabulations. Washington D.C.: Statistical Information Office of NCES.

National Commission for Employment Policy (NCEP). 1982. *Hispanics and Jobs: Barriers to Progress*. Washington, D.C., September.

Otheguy, R. 1982. Una visión comunicativa del calco linguístico como factor explicativo de la influencia del inglés sobre el español de los Estados Unidos. Paper presented at the 7th Symposium on Spanish and Portuguese Bilingualism. Mayaguez, Puerto Rico, November 12.

Otheguy, R. 1983. Linguistic calquing as an innovation in the message, not a mixture of systems. Paper presented at Colloquium on Bilingualism, Bidialectism and Communication Disorders, Lehman College, New York, March 19.

Otheguy, R. and O. García. In Press. Diffusion of lexical innovations in the Spanish of Cuban Americans. In Ornstein-Galicia, J., G. K. Green and D. Bixler-Marquez (eds.), *Research Issues and Problems in United States Spanish*. Brownsville, TX: Pan American University Press.

Pérez, L. 1986. Cubans in the United States. *The Annals of the American Academy of Political and Social Science* 487:126–137.

Portes, A. and R. Bach. 1985. *Latin Journey. Cuban and Mexican Immigrants in the United States*. Berkeley, CA: University of California Press.

Rogg, E. M. and R. S. Cooney. 1980. *Adaptation and Adjustment of Cubans: West New York, New Jersey*. New York: Hispanic Research Center.

Saussure, F. 1916. *Cours de linguistique generale*. Paris: Payot.

Solé, C. A. 1980. Language usage patterns among a young generation of Cuban-Americans. In Blansitt, E. and R. Teschner (eds.), *Festschrift for Jacob Ornstein*. Rowley, MA: Newbury House, 274–281.

Solé, C. A. 1982. Language loyalty and language attitudes among Cuban-Americans. In J. A. Fishman and G. Keller (eds.), *Bilingual Education for Hispanic Students in the United States*. New York: Teachers College Press, 254–268.

Stockwell, R. and J. Bowen. 1965. *The Sounds of English and Spanish*. Chicago: The University of Chicago Press.

Stockwell, R., J. Bowen, and J. Martin. 1965. *The Grammatical Structures of English and Spanish*. Chicago: The University of Chicago Press.

Terrell, T. D. 1977. Constraints on the aspiration and deletion of final /s/ in Cuban and Puerto Rican Spanish. *The Bilingual Review/La Revista Bilingue* 4(1-2):35–51.

Varela de Cuellar, B. 1974. La influencia del inglés en los cubanos de Miami y Nueva Orleans. *El Español Actual* 26: 16–25.

Weinreich, U. 1953. *Languages in Contact,* (1974 rpt.). The Hague: Mouton.

Whitley, M. S. 1986. *Spanish/English Contrasts*. Washington, D.C.: Georgetown University Press.

Yankelovich, Skelly and White, Inc. 1981. Spanish USA. A study of the Hispanic market in the United States. New York: SIN National Spanish Television Network.

Zamora Munné, J. C. and J. M. Guitart. 1982. *Dialectología Hispanoamericana*. Salamanca: Editorial Almar.

CHAPTER

7

The Language Situation of Chinese Americans

Sau-ling Cynthia Wong

In 1977, in a review of Maxine Hong Kingston's best-selling fictionalized autobiography of Chinese American life, *The Woman Warrior: Memoirs of a Girlhood among Ghosts* (1976), *New York Review of Books* critic Diane Johnson wrote: "The Chinese-Americans are a notably unassimilated culture. It is not unusual in San Francisco to find fourth- or fifth-generation American-born Chinese who speak no English" (Johnson 1977). Her description of the group immediately provoked scathing rebuttals from Chinese American critics (Chan 1977; Tong 1977). This minor anecdote in American cultural history, though in one sense merely a result of individual oversight, is in fact an apt encapsulation of the Chinese American sociolinguistic situation. Johnson's statements, if somewhat extreme in their ignorance, actually reflect a fairly common perception of Chinese Americans' relationship to the English language. Such a perception, in turn, embodies a complex set of assumptions about the group's place in American society: a legacy of history. Contrary to popular belief, it is not only what the Chinese "bring with them" (often conceptualized as a mysterious language tied to an alien culture) that shapes Chinese American language use patterns. Rather, the experience of being Chinese in America has a transforming influence that sometimes neutralizes the ethnic heritage itself. Any account of the Chinese American language situation must therefore be guided by an understanding of the sociohistorical context in which the community's main languages, Chinese and English, operate.

IMMIGRATION HISTORY

According to the 1980 Census, the Chinese, numbering over 812,000, make up the largest of the Asian American groups (Gardner, Robey and Smith 1985:5). However, the Chinese have not always been welcome in this country. Over the last 130 years, there have been many fluctuations in the size and composition of the Chinese American community, as a result of changing attitudes and policies toward the Chinese. The following is a brief account of Chinese immigration to the United States, based mainly on works by Lyman (1974); Lai, Huang and Wong (1980); and Chen (1981).

Early Laborers

Although Chinese presence in the United States dates back to the end of the eighteenth century (Lai, Huang and Wong 1980:12; Chen 1981:3–13), the Chinese did not begin emigrating in significant numbers until gold was discovered in California in 1848 and news of the "Gold Mountain" reached China, which at that time was plagued by political corruption under Manchu rulers, civil strife, domination by Western powers, and economic collapse. Guangdong (Kwangtung) Province in southern China, a densely populated, poverty-stricken area with a long seafaring tradition, became the main source of early Chinese immigrants. Surging in 1852, emigration from China subsided to an average of 8,000 annually during the next two decades (Lai, Huang and Wong 1980:20). However, the Chinese were quickly driven out of the mines by an exorbitant, discriminatory tax, and a pattern of concentrating in noncompetitive, service occupations such as restaurants and laundries, which is still observable today, began (King and Locke 1980:17).

In 1865, Chinese laborers began to be hired to build the western section of the transcontinental railroad; eventually, some 12,000–14,000 Chinese worked on the project (Lai, Huang and Wong 1980:23). After the transcontinental line was completed in 1869, most workers made their way back to California (Lai, Huang and Wong 1980:25; Chen 1981:75). There they played a key role in opening up the West, developing agriculture, fishing, and various light industries by providing not only labor but also expertise (Lai, Huang and Wong 1980:26–33; Chen 1981:79–116).

The Anti-Chinese Movement

In 1868, the United States and China signed the Burlingame Treaty, allowing reciprocal free immigration (Chen 1981:128–129). "In the next decade, immigration averaged more than 12,000 a year and the Chinese population steadily rose to over 105,000 by 1880" (Lai, Huang and Wong 1980:25). However, when economic conditions took a turn for the worse in the 1870s (Chen 1981:134–135), Chinese laborers, who had been subject to racism since mining days (Lyman 1974:58–62), easily became the target for public discontent. An anti-Chinese movement swept the nation, resulting in riots and lynchings, restrictive legislation regarding the occupations and lifestyles of the Chinese, and, most importantly, exclusionary immigration laws (Lyman 1974:54–85; Lai, Huang and Wong 1980:38–39; Chen 1981:127–180).

The Exclusion Period: 1882–1943

In 1882, the Chinese Exclusion Act was passed barring the entry of Chinese laborers for 10 years and prohibiting naturalization of Chinese. Only certain exempt classes, such as officials, teachers, students, merchants, and travelers, were allowed entry (Lai, Huang and Wong 1980:39). The Act was renewed in 1902, and then extended indefinitely in 1904. In 1924, the National Origins Law, which favored northwestern European immigration, was passed; among other things, it barred all aliens ineligible for citizenship from entry (Chinese included); redefined the provisions in the 1882 Chinese Exclusion Act even more stringently (Lyman 1974:111); and prohibited the entry of Chinese wives of U.S. citizens (Chen 1981:144–171). In the words of a Chinese American leader, exclusion, in effect, meant extermination (Chen 1981:171). Although a substantial number of Chinese continued to enter by resorting to the fraudulent "paper son" system (Lyman 1974:110–111; Lai, Lim and Yung 1980:20, 22),[1] the community during the Exclusion era was far from a growing one. It became a "bachelor society" with no family life to speak of; in 1890, the male/female ratio among the Chinese in America was as high as almost 27 : 1 (Lyman 1974:88). "Old-timers" from the Exclusionary period are still part of today's Chinatowns (Lyman 1974:86–92; Nee and Nee 1972:13–122). The 1910–1943 period was one of "institutional racism" for the Chinese, who were confined to Chinatowns, the "legitimized ghettos" (Lyman 1974:86–118).

Limited Immigration: 1943–1965

In 1943, because of both China's role in the Second World War and the United States' concern for its credibility as a world leader (Chen 1981:204–207), the Chinese Exclusion Act was repealed. The repeal did not lead to a sudden influx of Chinese immigrants. Rather, an annual quota of 105 came into effect and remained until 1965. However, during the 1943–1965 period, Chinese immigration was augmented by the presence of several groups entering on a nonquota basis. After the War, under the War Brides Act of 1945 and the Act of August 9, 1946, many Chinese women entered as alien wives of veterans and U.S. citizens (Lai, Huang and Wong 1980:70; Yung 1986:80). When the Communists defeated the Nationalists in the Chinese civil war and established the People's Republic of China (PRC) on the mainland in 1949, some 5,000 "stranded students" and other intellectuals remained in the United States (Lee 1960:103–112; Tsai 1986:120–124). Chinese also entered as refugees under the Refugee Relief Acts of 1953, 1957, and 1959 (Chen 1981:212–213); and as "parolees" under President Kennedy's Executive Order of May, 1962 (some 15,000 entered between 1962 and 1965; see Tsai 1986:152). As more women entered the United States (between 1944 and 1953, some 82 percent of immigrants were women; see Yung 1986:80), the male/female ratio became more balanced, climbing from 2.9 : 1 in 1940 to 1.3 : 1 in 1960 (Yung 1986:80). Gradually, the Chinese American community became more of a "family society" (Nee and Nee 1972:141–249).

The 1965 Immigration Reform

As with other Asian American groups, for the Chinese the turning point in their recent immigration history was the 1965 Immigration and Naturalization Amendments, which took effect in 1968. It abolished the discriminatory national origins quota system based on race and established a preference system based on family reunification and occupational skills, permitting up to 20,000 entries per country per year (Chen 1981:216). Thus began an influx of Chinese immigrants of varied backgrounds, mainly from Taiwan and Hong Kong, which is still continuing today. Between 1966 and 1974, an annual average of over 16,000 Chinese "quota" immigrants (i.e., subject to numerical limitations) plus roughly 4,000 "nonquota" immigrants (i.e., immediate relatives, including spouses, minors, unmarried children, and parents of adult citizens) entered the United States. In addition, the immigration reform allowed over 40,000 Chinese who were in the United States on a temporary basis to adjust to permanent residency status (Tsai 1986:152–153).

Immigration from Hong Kong

Immigrants from Hong Kong are not as numerous as those from Taiwan, but they have been no less instrumental in bringing about the transformation of the Chinese American community. On the average, over 4,000 have been admitted annually from Hong Kong (INS 1981:34). Hong Kong is a British colony, ceded to Britain after the Opium War, and will remain under British rule until 1997, when the tiny "city-state" will revert to China. Thus the quota for Hong Kong is charged against that for Great Britain. The allotment is inadequate compared to the number of people in Hong Kong who want to emigrate due to both population pressures and apprehension about the city's future. The recent immigration reform of 1986 increased the quota for Hong Kong from 600 to 5,000 (Public Law 99-603, November 6, 1986). It is expected that the role played by Hong Kong immigrants in the Chinese American community will continue to grow in the next decade.

Immigration from the PRC

Another new and important source of Chinese immigration is the PRC. After the normalization of diplomatic relations between the PRC and the United States in 1979, population movement between the two nations, cut off for decades, resumed. In 1981, "the annual 20,000-per-country quota for immigrants from 'China' was changed to apply separately to the PRC and Taiwan, resulting in an increase in immigrants from the two countries from 25,800 in fiscal year 1981 to 35,800 in fiscal year 1984" (Gardner, Robey and Smith 1985:37). Because of the family reunification provision of the current immigration laws, most new immigrants from the mainland are relatives of former Chinese immigrants; thus some recent PRC immigrants are similar in background to Cantonese "old-timers" while others resemble the "stranded intellectuals" in origin.

Ethnic Chinese from Other Regions

Adding to the Chinese population in the United States are ethnic Chinese from areas of political instability, including Cuba, Burma, and in particular Indo-China (Lai, Huang and Wong 1980:79). The Vietnam–China border conflicts of 1979 led to the exodus of a large number of Chinese Vietnamese. Lopez (1982:6) estimates that as many as 100,000–200,000 of the refugees from Vietnam are "essentially Chinese . . . in race and language." (See also Chung, this volume.) These ethnic Chinese are, of course, not counted under the quotas for China and may sometimes be overlooked when one considers Chinese immigration, but their visibility in the community has been steadily increasing.

Immigration Trends to the Year 2000

By 1985, the numbers of Chinese Americans are estimated to have reached 1,079,400, representing a 32.9 percent increase over a mere 5 years (Gardner, Robey and Smith 1985:5). It is projected that the Chinese American population will reach over 1,250,000 in 1990 and over 1,680,000 in 2000, which will put it behind Filipinos as the second most numerous Asian American group (Gardner, Robey and Smith 1985:37).

CURRENT DEMOGRAPHICS: DIVERSITY IN THE CHINESE AMERICAN COMMUNITY

The "Old" and "New" Chinese American Community

As the above review of Chinese immigration history suggests, it is much easier to generalize about the early Chinese American community than about the contemporary one. The "old-timers" up through the Exclusion era shared a fairly uniform background. Most of them hailed from eight districts (a district is comparable to an American county) in southern Guangdong Province, a small region about the size of the San Francisco Bay area (see Lai, Huang and Wong 1980:16–17). The majority came from rural backgrounds, had little formal schooling, and were predominantly male; the community structure reflected their relative homogeneity and cohesiveness (Lyman 1974:29–53; Tsai 1986:33–55), characteristics that were further reinforced by the fact that so few children were born in the United States (Lyman 1974:112–115).

In contrast, the contemporary Chinese American community defies ready generalization. A definition by negation—that it is no longer predominantly Cantonese, rural, male—is the safest generalization but hardly illuminating. It may be more useful to think of succeeding groups of immigrants as layers of deposit in a geological formation, discernible in any cross-section, whether cut by settlement patterns, nativity, occupation, educational attainment, or, of course, language. (Even the ways surnames are spelled tell stories of dialect origin and adaptation, as pointed out in Louie 1985–6.) In short, we may see the vicissitudes of Chinese immigration and settlement as leaving their mark on the community in many different ways.

Settlement Patterns

According to the 1980 Census, Chinese Americans are concentrated overwhelmingly in the West: 52.7 percent as compared to 26.8 percent in the Northeast, 11.3 percent in the South, and 9.2 percent in the Midwest (Gardner, Robey and Smith 1985:11). The five states with the most numerous Chinese population are, in descending order, California (40.1 percent), New York (18.1 percent), Hawaii (6.9 percent), Illinois (3.6 percent), and Texas (3.3 percent) (Gardner, Robey and Smith 1985:11; a more detailed breakdown is provided by Tsai 1986:152–153). Like other Asian Americans, Chinese Americans tend to be urban dwellers: there are over 50,000 Chinese in four metropolitan areas: San Francisco, Honolulu, New York, and Los

Angeles (Gardner, Robey and Smith 1985:12), with the New York–New Jersey and the San Francisco Bay area topping the list at over 100,000 each (Tsai 1986:153). This settlement pattern reflects, among other things, the historical role of the Chinese in developing the West and the continuing importance for new immigrants of Chinatowns, which served not only as entry points for newcomers but also as refuges from persecution during the era of Exclusion.

The Importance of Nativity

Immigration has played a vital role in the formation of the post-1965 Chinese American community: fully 63.3 percent of the Chinese in America are foreign-born (Gardner, Robey and Smith 1985:5). Given this breakdown, generalizations about the community must be made cautiously. Often, as soon as the native-born/foreign-born distinction is taken into account, the picture of a given demographic characteristic will look quite different.

Economic Situation

A good example of heterogeneity along nativity lines concerns the economic situation of Chinese Americans. Chinese Americans, along with other Asian Americans, are often portrayed in the media as a prosperous "model minority" that has reached parity with whites (e.g., Kasindorf et al. 1982; Raspberry 1984; Ramirez 1986). It is true that 1980 Census figures show the median income for a Chinese American full-time worker to be almost identical to that for a white worker: $15,573 and $15,572, respectively (Gardner, Robey and Smith 1985:34). However, a closer look reveals that the Chinese American community actually has a "bimodal" economic structure, with high concentrations of both affluent and poor (Chang 1986). The native-born/foreign-born distinction proves to be crucial here: the foreign-born Chinese earn substantially less than their native-born counterparts. In fact, "[f]or families headed by immigrants arriving 1975–80 who were born in Taiwan or Hong Kong, the proportion below the poverty level was 23 percent," compared to 7 percent for whites and 27 percent for blacks (Gardner, Robey and Smith 1985:35). Of course, even within the "immigrant" designation, there is great variation; for example, among the Hong-Kong-born are a handful of wealthy investors who are "hedging their bets" over Hong Kong's political future by emigrating and bringing in capital to the United States (King 1985; Itow 1987). Still, on the whole, place of birth is a significant factor in income distribution among Chinese Americans.

Occupational Patterns

A similar picture obtains for occupational distribution, which also shows the effect of nativity. According to the 1980 Census, foreign-born Chinese are heavily concentrated in service occupations (49 percent) while only 12 percent of the native-born are similarly employed (Gardner, Robey and Smith 1985:31). Within Chinatowns, where many of the foreign-born live, there is in fact a "subeconomy" heavily dependent on two industries: tourist–restaurant operation and garment making (King and Locke 1980:32–33). While ownership of small businesses is quite common, the Chinese tend to be underrepresented as "*salaried* managers and administrators" (King and Locke 1980:22). Within the "professional" group, there tends to be a high concentration of engineers (King and Locke 1980:22), a legacy of the employment discrimination against Chinese that abated only when World War II created a demand for technical personnel (Guthrie 1985:35). All in all, the nativity-related differences in occupation today show the cumulative influence of employment restrictions on Chinese Americans in the past (King and Locke 1980).

Educational Attainment

As with occupation, the educational attainment of Chinese Americans shows a pattern, albeit qualified, of success for the native-born contrasting with the disadvantaged status of the foreign-born. Chinese Americans receive frequent publicity for their outstanding achievements in education, especially high school and college students in the science and technical fields (e.g., McGrath 1983; Givens et al. 1984; Tsai 1986:163–164). Taken as a group, Chinese Americans do show a consistently higher rate of enrollment in school and college, from age 3 through age 34, than whites (Tsang and Wing 1985:18). They also surpass whites in the percentage of the population with a college education (Kan and Liu 1986:21). However, several facts must be noted. To begin with, many immigrants completed their schooling *before* immigration, thus inflating the figures for educational attainment for the group (Tsang and Wing 1985:16); the statistics they provide do not prove success within the U.S. educational system. Secondly, Chinese Americans also have a higher proportion of the population with no or minimum education (Kan and Liu 1986:21). Moreover, 15.7 percent of Chinese families with school-age children are below the poverty level, compared to 10 percent of white families (Kan and Liu 1986:23).

The effect of foreign nativity on education is modified by length of residence in the United States, however. The percentage of Chinese American families with school-age children below the poverty level decreases sharply with length of residence (Kan and Liu 1986:23). This accords with a pattern described by Tsang and Wing for Asian Americans as a whole, including Chinese (1985:12): namely, that "those who have lived here for five or fewer years scored substantially lower than white students in both verbal skills and sciences [though not in mathematics]." In contrast, those who were born in the United States or have lived here for at least 6 years equaled or surpassed whites in mathematics, science, as well as verbal skills.

"Some Have Made It, Some Have Not"

At the risk of oversimplification, one might use one of Chen's (1981:219) chapter titles, "Some have made it, some have not," to describe the Chinese American community. On the one hand, there are the native-born of the second and third generation or beyond, as well as the highly adaptive foreign-born elite who are already equipped with education and capital upon immigration. Within the former group are descendents of the early laborers and small merchants who have benefited from their ancestors' struggles, as well as children of the "stranded" intellectuals who had a more or less privileged start. Within the latter group are former Nationalist officials and businessmen from Taiwan, and professionals and capitalists from Hong Kong (Chen 1981:223). The successful Chinese Americans live in suburban areas and on university campuses (Chen 1981:225), and are Americanized in lifestyle. The "have-nots" are comprised of victims of past discrimination and the majority of recent immigrants, who live in crowded Chinatowns, struggling to survive and trying to build a brighter future for their children (Chen 1981:227–228).

LINGUISTIC DIVERSITY IN THE CHINESE AMERICAN COMMUNITY

The historical legacy and current complexity of the Chinese American community are both reflected in linguistic heterogeneity. There is no single language situation shared by all Chinese Americans: an adequate account must focus on each subgroup separately.

Adult Chinese American Immigrants and Their Language Situation

Because adult Chinese American immigrants do not go through the American educational system, they should be examined separately from school-age immigrants. Native language background plays a more important role in their language use patterns than in those of their children.

The Chinese Language. There are seven major dialect families in the Chinese language: Mandarin (spoken by 70 percent of the total population), Wu (8.4 percent), Xiang (5 percent), Gan (2.4 percent), Hakka (4 percent), Min (1.5 percent), and Yue (5 percent) (Li and Thompson 1981:3); within each dialect family are further varieties. (What is loosely called "Cantonese" in the United States is a group of Yue dialects.) The dialects are often mutually unintelligible. The Mandarin of the Beijing (Peking) area is the national language for both the PRC and Taiwan. For transcribing sounds (so-called "romanization"), the former uses the *pinyin* system, which has a Roman alphabet; the latter uses the *zhuyin* system made up of non-Roman phonetic symbols.

While spoken Chinese is varied, written Chinese is uniform, made up of characters each representing a sound. Modern written Chinese is largely based on Beijing Mandarin. Speakers of other dialects, in learning to read and write, not only have to learn the standard pronunciation of characters but also have to contend with differences in vocabulary and sometimes syntax. The PRC uses a simplified script, which the Chinese in Singapore have also adopted. Taiwan adheres to the traditional script, as do Hong Kong and most other overseas Chinese communities, including those in North America.

The PRC has been promoting the use of Mandarin (known there as *Putonghua*, "the common language") since 1955 (Barnes 1983:295); Mandarin is supposed to be the medium of instruction in school. However, it has been difficult to implement the policy fully, especially in rural areas (Barnes 1983). Taiwan, with a much smaller area, has been more successful in promoting Mandarin in both education and other areas of public life (Tse 1982).

Chinese Backgrounds of Chinese Immigrants in America. An immigrant's Chinese background depends on where he or she comes from. Despite the large number of dialects in the Chinese language family, only a handful have played key roles in the Chinese American community.

The term "Cantonese," as used in the American context, is used to refer both to the immigrant's origin (Guangdong province) and the dialect. However, a single term, "Cantonese," is inadequate for describing the nuances in language use among Chinese Americans from Guangdong; in fact, the label "has projected over the course of time an artificial view of the unity of a diverse resident Chinese population" (Chan and Lee 1981:121). (In the following account, the "Cantonese" pronunciations of dialect and place names, which are often more commonly heard in the United States, are supplied in parentheses). As mentioned above, early Chinese immigrants were mostly from a small region in Guangdong made up of eight districts: the "Three Districts," the "Four Districts," plus Zhongshan (Chungshan). The "Three Districts," Sanyi (or Sam Yup), consist of Nanhai (Namhoi), Panyu (Punyu), and Shunde (Shuntak), and include the city of Guangzhou (Canton), the provincial capital (Chen 1981:16). The "Four Districts," Siyi (or Sze Yup), consist of Enping (Yanping), Kaiping (Hoiping), Taishan (Toishan), and Xinhui (Sunwui) (Lai, Huang and Wong 1980:16–17; Chen 1981:16–18; Chan and Lee 1982:129). Depending on the degree of precision desired, an immigrant might identify himself or herself as simply "Cantonese," or as "Sze Yup," or further as "Toishan," and so on.

In early Chinese American society, a dialect served as a strong unifying force among its speakers, representing not only linguistic but also territorial and even ethnographic distinctions (Chan and Lee 1981:122); certain trades were dominated by immigrants and their descendents from certain districts/dialect groups (Chen 1981:19). The American experience also had a transforming effect: over time, the varieties of Cantonese as spoken in the United States have evolved to include terms about American life not heard elsewhere (see, for example, T'sou 1973:134–135), forming what some researchers call "Chinatown Chinese" (Dong and Hom 1980; but see Chan and Lee 1981). Since 1965, however, old dialect loyalties have been undermined by radical changes in the community's structure.

Immigrants from Hong Kong speak the "standard" variety of Cantonese—which is the one spoken in Guangzhou and is therefore a kind of Sanyi—as opposed to the rural varieties of many of the early settlers. Standard Cantonese (alongside English) is the medium of instruction in Hong Kong schools (see below), although some schools have started teaching Mandarin in preparation for the political change in 1977. As a city dialect, standard Cantonese is more prestigious than the rural versions. In addition, Hong Kong Cantonese, having evolved in a modern, cosmopolitan city, has the image of being slangy and "hip"; it is the version used in the widely distributed popular songs and movies of Hong Kong. Standard Cantonese has become the lingua franca of some Chinatowns (Guthrie 1985:42–43), sometimes causing resentment against speakers of dialects such as Taishan, which once dominated the community (Guthrie 1985:43).

The importance of Cantonese speakers is enhanced by the influx of ethnic Chinese from Vietnam, the majority of whom are Cantonese speakers (Bilingual Education Office, California State Department of Education 1984:8–9), the rest being speakers of Chaozhou (Teochew) (Him Mark Lai, personal communication, June 5, 1987). In addition, many recent immigrants from the PRC sponsored by relatives in the United States are Cantonese speakers.

Mandarin is also increasingly being heard in Chinatowns (Guthrie 1985:43–44). As the national language on which writing is based and in which works of literature are composed, it has the advantage of greater prestige and wider currency over Cantonese. It is also used in popular songs and movies from Taiwan and the mainland. As increasing numbers of Mandarin-speaking immigrants of the middle class, residing in suburbs or distant towns with no Chinatowns, come into Chinatowns to dine and shop, Cantonese shopkeepers and waiters have to pick up a functional command of Mandarin, however heavily accented, to deal with their customers (Guthrie 1985:44).

It should be noted that "Mandarin-speaking" is by no means synonymous with "being from Taiwan." The language situation in Taiwan is more complex than many Americans realize. The overwhelming majority of the population in Taiwan are native speakers not of Mandarin but of "Taiwanese" or "Southern Fukienese," a Min dialect (Tse 1982:2; Kaplan and Tse 1982:33–35). The native Mandarin speakers can loosely be identified as the "mainlanders" who took over Taiwan from Japan at the end of World War II and who fled the Communists in 1949. Because of political oppression of the native Taiwanese by the Nationalists (Tsai 1986:180), Mandarin-speaking "mainlanders" are resented by some Taiwanese speakers. Although Mandarin education has been successful in Taiwan, so that over 94 percent of the population can now speak the national language (Tse 1982:34), it is in many ways a language imposed on the population (Tse 1982:37). Taiwanese remains the dialect of private life, in a fairly stable diglossic arrangement (Tse 1982:35–37; see also Van den Berg 1986). For the estimated 100,000 Taiwanese immigrants in America, many of them highly educated (Tsai 1986:179), Taiwanese continues to be important. According to one historian, there is "a big gap between the Cantonese-speaking population of America's Chinatowns and the Taiwanese-speaking population in the suburbs of American metropolitan cities" (Tsai 1986:186).

Among Chinese immigrants in America, "dialect can be viewed as a factor of both division and unity" (Chan and Lee 1981:127). Although dialect loyalties are no longer as strong as they used to be, they continue to play a role in the interactions within the Chinese-speaking segment of the Chinese American community.

English Backgrounds of Chinese Immigrants in America. Depending on the background of an adult Chinese immigrant to America, his or her initial command of English upon entry may vary from no knowledge whatsoever to native proficiency. After immigration, acquisition or improvement of English of course takes place; however, compared to school-age immigrants, adults are probably influenced more strongly and more persistently by the degree of their preimmigration exposure to English. Prior exposure to English is often more a function of social class than of place of origin; still, some generalizations may be made because various Chinese communities have different foreign language policies.

Hong Kong has had a long-standing relationship with English because of its colonial status. English has been and remains the language of the ruling class; Chinese was not recognized as an official language (and then only symbolically) until as late as 1974 (Cheung 1984:273–274). English, as the "language of power" (Cheung 1984:276), is considered much more important than Chinese. English begins to be taught as early as in kindergarten or first grade (Bilingual Education Office, California State Department of Education 1984:18), and is the main medium of instruction at the secondary and tertiary levels (Gibbons 1979:6). As the number of Chinese-only schools declines, enrollment climbs in "Anglo-Chinese" (i.e., bilingual) schools (Cheung 1984:282), where English is the medium of instruction, with Chinese taught as a "second language"—an anomaly considering that the Hong Kong population is almost 99 percent Chinese-speaking (Gibbons 1979:5). Notwithstanding the official importance of English, "on the whole the results [of English language instruction in Hong Kong] have been rather dismal" (Ho 1979:45). The language policy in Hong Kong is avowedly colonial and flies in the face of the natural language use patterns of the populace, with many limited English-proficient Chinese teachers being made to teach in English (Johnson 1983). Mixing of Chinese and English is widespread (Gibbons 1979:6; Johnson 1983; Cheung 1984:274). However, Cantonese is still the "language of solidarity," and "using [English] for intra-ethnic communication is regarded as being in very bad taste and an indication of severance from the Chinese community" (Cheung 1984:279, 274).

Hong Kong immigrants from an elite background, benefiting from "additive bilingualism" (Johnson 1983:282), will enter the United States with near-native or native command of English and will make a relatively smooth transition into American society. At the other extreme, though, are Hong Kong immigrants who remain weak or illiterate in English after going through part or all of a supposedly bilingual school system. As a result of the language barrier, they are confined to menial jobs in Chinatowns (Nee and Nee 1972:278–290). This in turn perpetuates the low proficiency of their English; attempts to learn English in adult school classes often fail because of the stresses of adult immigration life, such as fatigue after work (Tucker 1969:44; Loo 1985:500).

In contrast to Hong Kong schools, schools in Taiwan do not start teaching English as a foreign language until junior middle school; English is required through the first year of the tertiary level (Kaplan and Tse 1982:2; the following account is drawn mostly from this source). Because of American political, economic, and cultural influence, English is the most popular foreign language taught, although no firm statistics on the distribution of English are available. In addition to the public schools, a vast market exists for private, commercial English instruction, as well as for preparation to pass the Test of English as a Foreign Language (TOEFL), a prerequisite for studying in the United States. English teaching in Taiwan is troubled by problems in approach, materials, teacher training, and lack of real opportunities for practice. On the whole, English, though valued by society, is not frequently used; if used, it tends to be confined to the work environment. While many people are favorable toward English "for instrumental and pragmatic purposes," some oppose it "for nationalistic reasons" (Kaplan and Tse 1982:3).

There are no statistics available on the English proficiency of adult immigrants from Taiwan upon their entry into the United States. As far as this writer can determine, they also exhibit a wide spectrum of English proficiency, as in the case of Hong Kong immigrants, although the range may not be as extreme. College-level or postgraduate students who came here to study and subsequently adjusted their status (Tsai 1986:152), as well as those already in the elite class before immigration (Chen 1981:223), can be presumed to be fairly proficient in English. Working-class immigrants from Taiwan are expected to have problems with English similar to those of working-class Cantonese-speaking immigrants from Hong Kong.

The PRC, as a result of ideology, went through a period of emphasizing Russian before turning to English (associated with Western imperialism) as its main foreign language (Scovel 1983:107). Since the mid-1970s, the waning of extreme leftist ideology, normalization of diplomatic relations with the United States, and in general a comparatively more open attitude toward the West have led to nationwide interest in the study of English. There are now an estimated 50 million students studying English in Chinese schools (Hou 1987:25). Students are supposed to begin learning English in junior high school, and in some prestigious urban schools English is introduced in the third grade (Bilingual Education Office, California State Department of Education 1984:18–19). However, caught by this sudden increase in demand after a decade of xenophobia and educational chaos during the Cultural Revolution, the foreign language teaching profession in China is ill-equipped to provide adequate English instruction (Wang 1982). High school English instruction is plagued by lack of trained teachers, poorly designed texts, and weak motivation among students (Wang 1982:6–7). At the college level, although English is required for all students regardless of major, the picture is equally discouraging; some college students in fact have to start from the alphabet (Wang 1982:6). Given the fast pace of policy change in today's China, much may have changed in English instruction from the time of Wang's assessment in 1982; however, a recent account (Hou 1987) shows that many problems remain, especially in methodology.

There has been no large-scale, systematic study of English–Chinese bilingualism among Chinese immigrants in the United States. However, T'sou (1973), based on a modest study of "asymmetric bilingualism" among Cantonese speakers in the United States and elsewhere, suggests that the linguistic behavior of immigrants progresses through stages corresponding to cultural assimilation: "linguistic importation" corresponds to the "sojourner phrase"; "linguistic substitution," to the "congregated phase"; "code switching," to the "transitional phase"; "bilingualism," to the "acculturated phase"; and finally, "residual interference," to the "assimilated phase." Much research is needed before either the scope or dynamics of Chinese–English bilingualism in the United States can be fully understood.

School-Age Chinese American Immigrants and Their Relationship to English

Compared to their adult counterparts, the way school-age Chinese immigrants learn and use English is influenced less by their language background in the home country. A more important, though less commonly examined, influence is the experience of relocation and going through the American educational system as members of a minority. Any account of foreign-born Chinese students that focuses solely on their linguistic and cultural "baggage" will be incomplete, if not misleading.

Of course, depending on when they enter the United States, school-age Chinese immigrants will be affected to varying degrees by their prior exposure to Chinese and English. In this they are no different from adults, and the information in the last section on the Chinese and English backgrounds of adults from different regions also applies to children. What one needs to guard against is generalizing about the immigrant children's English proficiency based on place of origin and length of U.S. residence alone, without taking into account their socioeconomic background and the type of school they attended. A Chinese immigrant of the elite class from Hong Kong who has been in the United States only half a year may have better English skills than a working-class immigrant who has been living in San Francisco's Chinatown for the last 5 years. Such a discrepancy is due to no fault of the latter: it is not laziness or lack of commitment to American life but a vast network of sociolinguistic variables that causes the latter's problems with English.

Teachers often ask whether the Chinese language, which is so different from English, interferes with the immigrant student's learning of English. On the hypothesis that there must be interference, some well-meaning if insufficiently informed teachers and counselors have advised Chinese immigrant parents to stop using Chinese at home. While the question admits of no simple answer (for a detailed analysis, see Wong 1984), several points may be made to clarify the issue. First of all, with regard to phonology and morphology, there is a fair amount of consensus among researchers on contrasting features between the two languages that tend to cause problems with English (e.g., Ho 1973; Lay 1975; Lee 1976-7; Chen 1979). The picture is not so clear at the syntactic and discourse levels. Schachter and Rutherford (1979) and Rutherford (1983) have hypothesized that the topic-prominent nature of Chinese may be transferred to English, a subject-prominent language, but empirical evidence is still sketchy. A Chinese "written discourse accent" may also have been created by unnative-like use of cohesive devices (Hu, Brown and Brown 1982; Johns 1984). Kaplan (1966, 1968, 1976, 1986) has suggested that Chinese learners of English tend to use a deeply ingrained "cultural thought pattern"—one favoring circularity and indirection as opposed to English linearity—and to rely on the traditional "eight-legged essay'' form when they compose. His theory, though well known, is flawed in both reasoning and evidence (Wong 1984; Mohan and Lo 1985). However, it seems to apply in the rhetorical organization of Chinese speakers negotiating face-to-face in English (Young 1982).

Interesting as the question of possible linguistic transfer is, in the case of Chinese immigrant students in the United States, it is much more important to focus on the sociolinguistic context of English learning. Both the immigrant situation and the Chinese ethnicity of the students have a bearing on their relationship to the English language (Wong, forthcoming).

Bouvier and Tong (1968), Leong (1972), Wang (1972), Chao (1977), Sung (1979), and To (1979) have pointed out that Chinese immigrant students, especially newcomers from low-income families, suffer a number of economic and emotional stresses peculiar to or accentuated by the immigrant situation. As Kleinmann (1982) suggests in a related context, such pressures of daily life could affect the ability to concentrate on language learning. More importantly, Chinese immigrant students, being members of not only a visible minority in this country but also one with a long history of denigration and discrimination, are often made to feel their Chinese linguistic and cultural background as a source of shame. A Chinese accent, unlike a European one, is regarded as ugly (Wang 1972:55) and is made fun of by English-speaking peers or even teachers (Wang 1972:54). ''Chinese English'' is traditionally stereotyped as either ludicrously florid, like Fu Manchu's, or primitive and pidgin-like, of the ''no tickee, no washee'' variety (Kim 1976:46-48; 1982:12–14). Thus, unless a Chinese immigrant student comes into an American school with an already native command of English, he or she will most likely feel a tremendous pressure to get rid of the traces of any Chinese background.

The results of the pressure toward linguistic assimilation as a badge of one's cultural assimilation vary according to the individual's coping strategies.[2] Some Chinese immigrant students ''lose their accent'' with astonishing speed and go on to master English fully with little trouble; others may acquire accent-free speech but continue for years to have difficulties with written English; still others may react to the hostility of the target language group by withdrawing and socializing primarily with other speakers of their Chinese dialect (e.g., Nee and Nee 1972:331). In situations of linguistic discrimination that are, in the last analysis, racially motivated, high socioeconomic status does not necessarily afford protection. A recent account of the plight of so-called ''little foreign students'' from Taiwan (Lin 1987)—minors sent to study in U.S. schools while their well-to-do parents continue to make a living in Taiwan, a post-1979 phenomenon caused by uncertainty over Taiwan's future (see Yuan 1987:84)—shows that in both their English classes and the schoolyard, such youngsters endure prejudice from native English speakers very similar to that experienced by low-income Chinese immigrant students. The rapid linguistic and cultural assimilation of young foreign-born Chinese Americans, the subject of many a success story in the media, is often achieved at a high cost to self-esteem.

Monolingual English-Speaking Chinese Americans and Their Language Situation

For the foreign-born bilingual Chinese American, knowledge of Chinese, while often an occasion for ridicule from English speakers, can also be a source of ethnic pride, a kind of psychological cushioning against the shock of relocation and adjustment. For the monolingual English-speaking Chinese American of the second or third generation and beyond, however, the Chinese language and the traditional culture it embodies can be yet another instrument of oppression. At the same time that the environment urges a virtually inevitable shift to English, native-born Chinese Americans are told by their elders that by "losing their Chinese" (which is not really theirs to begin with), they are guilty of a crime of betrayal against their own kind. For the majority of the native-born, who are descended from the Cantonese peasant–immigrants of the past (Lai, Huang, and Wong 1980:16; Tong 1971:4), there is an added irony in the situation: their ancestors were actually outsiders to the class that formed the "repository of thousands of years of sophisticated civilization" in China (Tong 1971:4).

One manifestation of the pressure that the English-monolingual Chinese Americans feel from their ethnic culture is the tension between the so-called "ABCs" (American-born Chinese) and "FOBs" (fresh-off-the-boat, i.e., recent immigrants). The former, growing up English-monolingual, are seen by the latter as having been "white-washed," "stupid fools who know little or nothing of the great Chinese traditions." "Even for those who grew up in Chinatown and learned Chinese as kids [see section below on Chinese language schools], the dialect of Chinese spoken is different from that of Hong Kong immigrants"; further, most of them have "very limited Chinese vocabularies" and are unable to communicate well (Leong 1972:35). Conversely, the ABCs tend to see the FOBs as "stupid and ignorant because they can't speak English" and are "not sophisticated in American ways" (Leong 1972:36). The rivalry between the two groups is vividly portrayed in David Henry Hwang's play, *FOB* (1983).

Native English-speaking whites also impose unreasonable expectations on monolingual-English Chinese Americans, based on a distorted understanding of Chinese American history and of the group's sociolinguistic situation. It is a common experience for native-born Chinese Americans with Enlgish as their mother tongue to be asked where they are from and complimented on their accent-free speech. Frank Chin, a fifth-generation

Chinese American playwright, angrily recalls a humiliating encounter with a white American who assumed he must be "foreign": she refused to accept his American name as his "real" name, insisted on knowing how long he had been in this country, and attempted to improve his English vocabulary (Nee and Nee 1972:379–381). Another Chinese American (Lincoln 1976:48) tells of saleswomen who addressed her blond friends on the assumption that she understood no English; strangers who came up with Chinese calligraphy for her to interpret; and students in Chinese language classes who tried to practice conversation on her. She eventually decided to enroll in Chinese class herself, "to alleviate my lack of authenticity," as she puts it wryly. At an institutional level, the outcome of such expectations from white English speakers is hardly innocuous, however: when native-born Chinese were trying to break into the teaching profession in San Francisco, their "Chinatown accent" was routinely used as an excuse for excluding them—and even candidates raised among whites were alleged to have such an accent (Low 1982:169–171).

The double pressure from both Chinese speakers and white English speakers causes Chin (1976:557) to lament that English-monolingual Chinese Americans are "a people born without a native tongue":

> We have no street tongue to flaunt and strut the way the blacks and Chicanos do. They have a positive, self-defined linguistic identity that can be offended and wronged. We don't. With us, it's dangerous to say anything, dangerous to talk because every time you open your mouth you run the risk of being corrected.

The native-born Chinese American critics' outraged response to Diane Johnson's remark on Chinese "unassimilability," alluded to in the introduction, must be understood in this context. Because of the long history of Chinese settlement in the United States and the overwhelming pressure on Chinese to assimilate, English is in fact the *only* language—not the second language—of the majority of the native-born (see below). The English verbal performance of native-born Chinese Americans is no different from that of whites (Tsang and Wing 1985:12).[3]

In recent years, more and more English-monolingual Chinese Americans are creating works of literature, both fiction and poetry, to give voice to their unique experience (Kim 1982:321–328). The writers are asserting their claim to the English language as rightful heirs. It remains to be seen how long it will take mainstream society to recognize that, in spite of the Chinese influx due to immigration, there are some 270,000 Chinese Americans born and raised here, the majority of whom are native English speakers.

LANGUAGE SHIFT AMONG CHINESE AMERICANS

The overall picture that has emerged from the discussion so far is that the shift to English is taking place at a fast rate in the Chinese American community. Such an impression is borne out by several studies.

Kuo (1974), in an earlier, small-scale study of Mandarin-speaking immigrant families in the Midwest, notes certain patterns of language use within the family that would sound familiar to many Chinese Americans. Although the parents spoke mainly Mandarin in the home, the children of preschool age were already shifting to English: half of them spoke English all or most of the time when talking to their siblings and other Chinese children, and when talking to themselves (Kuo 1974:129). Because of the use of English among siblings, later-born children were losing Chinese faster than first-born ones (Kuo 1974:130). One parent commented: "He [the son] didn't like to speak Chinese as soon as he picked up some English . . . unless he cannot express himself in English. We still speak to him in Chinese; he'll answer in English." Another parent said of his daughter: "[She] probably thinks there is no need for her to speak Chinese since we [the parents] know English too" (Kuo 1974:134–135).

Kuo's subjects were upper-middle class, which suggests that the parents, having better command of English than working-class immigrants, were themselves partly responsible for accelerating language shift. This might lead one to hypothesize that socioeconomic status (SES) and language shift are positively related. Nevertheless, in an analysis of 1970 Census data, Li (1982) shows that the relationship between SES and language shift is in fact quite complex. "There is a negative correlation between SES and language shift . . . although the relation may not be linear" (Li 1982:118). "The lowest SES group has the highest propensity for language shift": "among persons with less than a high-school education, the proportions are about 15 percent in the second generation and 51 percent in the third generation; but among those with more than a high-school education, the proportions are 9 percent in the second generation and 47 percent in the third generation." At the same time, the "more-than-high-school" group shifted to English more than the "high-school" (as opposed to the "less-than-high-school") group (Li 1982:116). Thus middle-class Chinese Americans are most likely to retain Chinese.

Li further points out that over the last 60 years an extensive language shift has been taking place. "Among second-generation Chinese Americans . . . the use of Chinese as the mother tongue was virtually universal 60 years ago, but not today" (Li 1982:114). We recall that the 1920s fell within the Exclusion period, when Chinese were segregated in Chinatowns and when very few children were born in this country; thus shift to English was in fact actively prevented by mainstream society. In the post-1965 era, the picture is different. In the second generation, almost 12 percent had English as their mother tongue: in other words, 12 percent of the immigrants had ceased to raise their children in Chinese. "Moreover, it is doubtful that even half of the 88 percent [who had Chinese as their mother tongue] can communicate intelligibly in Chinese, since mother tongue has only a slight bearing on language proficiency" (Li 1982:113). By the third generation, almost half, or 49 percent, were reared in English.

Li's picture agrees with Fishman's (1985). Fishman finds that in 1970 there were 337,283 claimants of Chinese as their mother tongue, of whom the overwhelming majority, 308,039, were of foreign stock, that is, foreign-born (186,039) or of foreign or mixed parentage (122,000). Only 29,244 Chinese mother-tongue claimants were "native of native parentage" (115), indicating a phenomenal shift to English between the second and third generations.

Finally, Veltman (1983:48), using a different set of data for 1976, gives a similar picture about overall shift to English among Chinese Americans. Among the Chinese foreign-born, 34.1 percent had made English their usual language (made up of 28.1 percent who were bilingual and 6 percent who were English-monolingual). When this number is further analyzed by time of arrival in the United States, it is revealed that of those arriving before 1960, 43.4 percent had made English their usual language; of those arriving in the 1960s and 1970s, somewhat less than 30 percent.[4] For the last subgroup, length of residence in the United States would at most be 6 years. Thus any shift to English as the usual language must be seen as extremely rapid (56).

THE CHINESE LANGUAGE SCHOOL: AN EVOLVING INSTITUTION

Within the context of a rapid shift to English among Chinese Americans, it would be worthwhile to examine in detail a long-standing community institution, the Chinese language school, which, in theory, has the potential to arrest the erosion of the ethnic language. Such an examination would enable us to determine more precisely the dynamics of language change.

Early Chinese Language Schools

Ethnic language schools are by no means unique to Chinese Americans; many language groups throughout American history, such as speakers of German and Yiddish, have had such schools (Fishman 1980). For the Chinese, the ethnic language school can be said to have a history of 100 years, with the first one established in San Francisco in 1886 (Liu 1976:355). Yet it would be misleading to portray Chinese language schools as forming a continuing and monolithic institution, for over the decades, depending on American attitudes and policies toward the Chinese and the changes in the composition of the Chinese American community, the role played by such schools has undergone constant revision.

The earliest Chinese school in San Francisco shared one crucial feature with its modern counterparts: it was supplementary to "regular school" and took place "after hours" (Liu 1976:355–357). (Note, however, that at that time "regular schools" for Chinese were racially segregated; see Low 1982:59–111). In most other respects, the school was very different: the curriculum was highly traditional, involving the Chinese classics. In 1908, an official of the Manchu government toured both the United States and Canada and, with the help of local community leaders, established Chinese schools in San Francisco, Sacramento, New York, Chicago, Portland, Seattle, Vancouver, and Victoria (Liu 1976:361). The arguments given by the official for establishing Chinese schools were to reinforce sentiments of patriotism toward China, to retain trained people for China's benefit, and to ensure a smooth transition when Chinese Americans returned to work in China (Liu 1976:358). After the overthrow of the Manchus and the founding of the Republic of China in 1911, in which Chinese in America played an important role, more Chinese schools were founded, some under the auspices of the Kuomintang or Nationalists, in such places as Oakland, Stockton, Fresno, Boston, and Phoenix (Liu 1976:368). There were also church-sponsored private Chinese schools (Liu 1976:367), and schools operated by district associations (Jung 1972:310; Leung 1975:54).

The functions of the earliest Chinese schools, then, were not linguistic and cultural in the sense of preserving a threatened language and way of life. Rather, at the turn of the century, under Exclusion, the Chinese in America had no chance for integration into American life and were therefore seen as logical candidates for contributing to the development of China. Moreover, with the often arbitrary enforcement of harsh immigration restrictions on the Chinese, the prospects of returning to China someday, by choice or by necessity, were very real. It would therefore be sensible to supplement an American education with a Chinese one.

Chinese Language Schools during Exclusion

A study published shortly before the repeal of the Exclusion Act (Tom 1941) shows the changes that occurred during the Exclusion years. The advantages cited in the schools' favor are that they facilitated parent–child communication in Chinese and helped solve family problems; that they prevented children from forming inferiority complexes due to ill treatment from mainstream society; that they provided social life and recreation; and that they were a kind of vocational preparation. ''Many college-graduate American-born Chinese have no chance to get a satisfactory job in the Chinese community. Therefore, a good knowledge of the Chinese language is a help, and in many cases a necessity, in securing vocational opportunities'' (Tom 1941:561). The Chinese language school had evolved during the first half of the twentieth century into a community resource, functioning to enhance family and social life and to alleviate the effects of discrimination against the Chinese.

Post-1965 Chinese Language Schools

A post-1965 study of Chinese language schools (Leung 1975) judges Chinese language schools to be on the decline because they had ''outlived their usefulness'' (63): after the Communists took power in 1949, preparation for return to China is no longer a good reason to attend Chinese school (8). Moreover, with decreasing discrimination and improved employment opportunities during the 1960s, Chinese Americans are more integrated into mainstream society, making a knowledge of Chinese unnecessary and attendance at Chinatown schools difficult (63–65). The Chinese schools' ostensible raison d'etre—to teach the Chinese language—is no longer seen as important by many parents. In fact, the language-teaching capacity of the schools is undermined by a host of practical problems (58).

Leung may be too pessimistic in his assessment of the Chinese language school's future. After suffering from declining enrollment and community interest in the early and mid-1970s (Jung 1972:311; Leung 1975:72), Chinese language schools seem to have experienced a revival. Fishman and Markman (1979) reported 127 Chinese language schools nationwide; Fishman (1980), 142; and Fishman (1985), 172 (on the basis of a 1982 survey). Lin (1986) received responses from 99 schools, about half of those surveyed. The actual number of such schools is likely to be much higher if one includes the many semiformal Chinese language classes, run by small groups of concerned parents, which would not reach any official list. Most of the current schools were established after 1960 (Lin 1986:7), suggesting a link between increased immigration and the apparent revival of Chinese language schools.

Difficulties in Fulfilling the Language-Teaching Function

Yet if we scrutinize the actual setup of the schools, we might raise serious questions about their effectiveness as language maintenance institutions. Of the schools surveyed by Lin, 55 percent held classes on Saturdays; 36 percent on Sundays; and only 5 percent on weekday afternoons (11). Given the picture of language shift outlined in the previous section of this paper, we might ask how well one could expect to counteract societal influences and instill a functional proficiency in Chinese by holding class 2 or 3 hours a week, out of which a portion was devoted to cultural activities (12). Only the handful of schools meeting after "regular school" on weekday afternoons are likely to succeed in teaching language.

There are, in fact, a formidable number of factors, some already operating decades ago, working *against* the success of Chinese language schools. These include difficult choices necessitated by the inherent complexity of the Chinese language and the Chinese American sociolinguistic situation; pedagogical, administrative, and logistical problems; and, ultimately, the unfeasibility of linguistic maintenance as a goal given the minority status of Chinese in American society.[5]

Lin (1986:14) found that fully 94 percent of the schools surveyed have not done any evaluation studies on the effectiveness of their programs. One wonders what any formal evaluations would have found. Judging from the author's extensive contact with college-level Chinese Americans, most of those who attended Chinese school did so only because their parents made them, learned very little Chinese in school, and forgot most of it after discontinuing.

(It should be added, however, that these graduates or former dropouts of Chinese language school frequently express regret that they did not learn more Chinese and a desire to take Chinese again sometime in the future. This seems to suggest that as Chinese American young adults emerge from adolescence, many begin to shed the internalized negative perceptions of themselves and their language and feel a need to incorporate the ethnic language into their evolving identity.)

Nonlinguistic Functions of the Chinese Language School

If the maintenance of the Chinese language is, as Li (1982:113) describes it, "an uphill, if not an unrealistic, struggle," the interesting question is why Chinese language schools, taken as a group, have enjoyed such longevity in the community. One can only conclude that the schools are in fact not primarily language-teaching institutions; rather, they serve vital, *nonlinguistic* functions.

The most important function of contemporary Chinese language schools seems to be to create a sense of cultural and ethnic pride (see the responses in Lin 1986:7). In fact, this function seems to be the main connecting thread between the schools over the decades, unifying programs that have been highly disparate in subject matter and format. None of the practical purposes served by earlier Chinese schools are cited any more by Lin's respondents, suggesting that parents too see little "use" for the Chinese language but have decided, however implicitly, that the language is associated with many essential but intangible advantages. This view is supported by the fact that many modern Chinese language schools include a heavy cultural component, such as Chinese calligraphy, brush painting, crafts, folk dancing, and martial arts (Lin 1986:12). Apart from the explanation that such activities enhance student motivation and make the language-learning portion more palatable, we may also infer that Chinese Americans are increasingly seeing the Chinese language as only a part, and not necessarily an indispensable part either, of their overall "ethnic heritage." Under the given circumstances, in the face of massive shift to English, parents would be willing to give up insistence on functional proficiency in the Chinese language in order to preserve the children's interest and pride in being Chinese. The existence of summer Chinese language schools (Lin 1986:11), which of course are only nominally language-teaching programs, is further evidence that Chinese language maintenance is taking a new form and serves a new function in today's Chinese American society.

Other nonlinguistic functions of the Chinese language school include, in the case of Chinatown "after-school" schools, providing "daycare" as well as a smoother educational transition for recent immigrant children; in the case of parent-supported weekend programs, providing an occasion for socializing and group involvement among the parents; and in general, providing more opportunities for the children to interact with other Chinese, which may, indeed, prove to enhance ethnic pride as effectively as structured cultural activities.

Besides "after-hours" Chinese language schools, there are other educational settings in which the Chinese language plays a significant role, but they are insufficient to arrest the overall language shift of the Chinese American community. Chinese–English bilingual education programs in the public schools, besides sharing many of the problems (e.g., in materials and teaching training) of private Chinese language schools, also suffer from problems related to the educational bureaucracy; in any case, they are intended to be primarily transitional (Wong 1980; 15–18; Guthrie 1985). Immersion, a potentially promising but as yet experimental type of program for language maintenance, is being tried out in Cantonese and English in a San Francisco public school (Wong 1987:145); the results are still inconclusive. As for private immersion efforts, there is at present one Mandarin–English elementary school in San Francisco, the only one in the United States (Swope 1987). However, given the high tuition and the limitations imposed by demographics, it is unlikely that such schools will form a trend in the nation.

CONCLUSION

If the above assessment of the language-teaching efforts of Chinese language schools and related institutions is well-founded, what is one to make of the promising picture of Chinese maintenance that seems to be suggested by some researchers?

Although Veltman documents a rapid shift to English among Chinese Americans, he also notes repeatedly that the Chinese are the most language-retentive of the non-Spanish groups (1983:49, 53, 55, 58 for the foreign-born; 60 for the native-born). In Fishman et al.'s (1985) national survey of community resources for ethnic language maintenance, in addition to the 172 schools, the researchers have found as many as 375 "local religious units," 36 TV and radio broadcasting stations, and 42 publications, making a total of 625 resources nationwide, by far the highest number among the Asian American groups. On the basis of these and other data and using a criterion combining several factors, Fishman (1985:156–167) places Chinese ninth among 37 ethnic languages listed on a scale of survival potential, which would make Chinese the most likely among Asian American languages to survive. These seem to suggest bright prospects for Chinese language maintenance, one apparently at odds with our previous picture of language shift and apparently agreeing with the popular image of the Chinese American community.

On the other hand, a closer analysis reveals that the strength of the Chinese language group is actually more a function of continued immigration than of intergenerational transmission of the language. Fishman's (1985) data on community ethnic language maintenance resources provide tallies but not an in-depth study of how they function. As we have seen, a large number of Chinese language schools in itself does not mean successful teaching of Chinese to the children. As for "local religious units," so-called Chinese churches often provide separate services in English and Chinese, so that, strictly speaking, they are not maintaining the language between generations. Often Chinese language schools are sponsored by Chinese churches, so that the actual total number of resources may be lower. While the Chinese language press in America has had a long history (Tsai 1986:128–132; Lai 1987), the current flowering of Chinese language publications is due mainly to a rise in immigrant readership (Tsai 1986:132; Lai 1987:37) and the influx of Hong Kong and Taiwan capital (Lai 1987:38–39). The electronic media, such as Chinese TV programs and now videotapes, are perhaps the only truly useful instruments for teaching children Chinese, since they do not involve literacy; however, at present their availability is limited to urban or suburban centers with high concentrations of Chinese.

Moreover, when we examine closely Fishman's criteria for language survival potential, we will find that by the criterion of institutional strength alone, Chinese ranks fifteenth, lower than Korean, Thai/Lao, Cambodian/Vietnamese, and Hindi (Fishman 1985:163); it is because Chinese ranks high (sixth) by the criterion of number of claimants (165) that the group is able to lead other Asian American groups on the combined criterion. Finally, both Veltman and Fishman use parentage, rather than place of birth, in categorizing their data for speakers of Chinese and English. However, because of the practice of entry through the "paper son" system during the Exclusion period, the category "native of native" actually contains an unidentified number of Chinese born and raised abroad. The presence of this group might have inflated the number of Chinese mother-tongue claimants in the "native of native" category, giving a misleading estimate of how many third-generation Chinese Americans continue to be raised in or speak Chinese (Him Mark Lai, personal communication, June 5, 1987).

To the question, then, of "What are the prospects for the maintenance of Chinese in America?" the answer depends very much on how one defines maintenance as well as how the place of Chinese Americans in the United States changes in the future. If retention is taken to mean intergenerational transmission of the language, the evidence points to rapid shift to English between the second and third generations, resulting in loss of Chinese from the third generation on. This trend is expected to continue unless policymakers adopt a language-as-resource orientation and society as a whole ceases to denigrate the Chinese language and its users. However, if the term refers to a large Chinese-speaking population, it is safe to say that barring major changes in public policy toward the Chinese, the presence of the Chinese language will continue to be strong.

EXPLORING THE IDEAS

1. In her introduction, Wong points out that even highly educated white Americans tend to have an inaccurate image of Chinese Americans as linguistically and culturally "unassimilated."

Why do you think that such an image has persisted, even though Chinese Americans have been in the United States for over 130 years?

2. Wong observes that generalizations about the Chinese American community must be made cautiously, since nativity has an important effect on a given demographic characteristic.

Why is the native-born/foreign-born distinction so vital in our understanding of the Chinese American situation in economic, educational, and especially linguistic terms?

3. Wong notes that the various dialects of Chinese spoken by Chinese immigrants have different images and connotations. For example, Hong Kong Cantonese is slangy and "hip," while Mandarin has the prestige of national status backed by a literary tradition.

Think of parallels to this phenomenon in the American English language situation. What are the images and connotations associated with varieties of American English such as the black vernacular or a Brooklyn accent? What gave rise to these images and connotations?

4. According to Wong, immigrant students from denigrated language groups such as the Chinese tend to feel an immense pressure to attain linguistic and cultural assimilation (or at least acquire external signs of such assimilation), often at the expense of their self-esteem.

If you were a teacher with a recent immigrant student speaking a denigrated minority language in your class, what would you do to alleviate his or her potential loss of self-esteem?

5. Chinese-American writer Frank Chin laments that Chinese Americans don't have "a positive, self-defined linguistic identity" like the blacks or Chicanos.

Although the Chinese in America have a long immigration history and, like the blacks, are also a minority of color, they have not developed a distinct "yellow English" comparable to "black English." What differences in the two groups' historical and contemporary experiences have caused this divergence in linguistic development?

6. Wong observes that Chinese American youngsters go through different stages in their relationship to the ethnic language. Those who attend Chinese language school often drop out during adolescence but express a renewed interest in the language in young adulthood.

Why do you think such age-related attitude changes occur?

APPLYING THE IDEAS

1. Wong's account of the English background of Chinese immigrants from various regions show that foreign language education policy (in this case, English-teaching policy) is often determined by politics—in particular, by a government's relationship to English-speaking Western powers and the sense of political identity it wishes to establish in its citizens.

Investigate the English-teaching policy of a third-world nation to see how it is related to politics.

2. Contact your local school district to see if it has a significant number of Chinese American students. Find out as much as you can about them: how many are foreign-born and how many native-born, how many are limited-English-proficient (LEP) students and whether they are given language assistance, what dialects are spoken by the LEP students, etc. Analyze the information in terms of the historical and demographic background provided by Wong.

3. Read the last chapter, "A Song for a Barbarian Reed Pipe," in Maxine Hong Kingston's *The Woman Warrior,* which is cited by Wong. Analyze

the protagonist's relationship to the English language portrayed in the chapter, using some of the concepts in Wong's paper.

4. The essay below was written by a "Chinese school drop-out"; although the author lived in Canada, the Chinese school he described is typical of Chinese schools in the United States as well.

Study the ways in which the essay illustrates some of the issues raised by Wong regarding the difficulties of teaching Chinese in "after-hours" programs.

If an "after-hours" Chinese language school exists in your community, visit the school or interview the principal or the teachers to determine if Wong's analysis applies. In particular, pay attention to whether nonlinguistic functions are served by the school.

MEMOIRS OF A CHINESE SCHOOL DROP-OUT

By ?? . . . alias Kevin Wan

(Author's note: All the names in this autobiographical work have been changed to protect the embarrassed.)

Every Monday, Wednesday, and Friday, from four to six o'clock, I would go to Chinese School, which was held in the basement of St. Matthew's Church. I hated and resented it. I hated going there to see the people and the depressing surroundings and to breathe the air which had a smell reminiscent of pickled socks. But I went—for three whole years (which shows you how much of a juvenile dissident I was.)

It's not that I didn't enjoy school. I loved elementary school and some of my greatest achievements included being editor of the class newspaper, "Head Boy" of my class—and captain of the safety patrol (all very prestigious positions). Here I was, this quiet and slight kid, bespectacled with thick, black frames; but in Chinese School, I was an insurgent rebelling against my parents and anything too Chinafied for me to take in.

On my first day of Chinese School, I was placed in the beginners' class for small children and older kids who could not cough up anything Chinese in their speech. I was one of the latter. Being put in a class comprised mainly of cute, talkative six year-olds is no fun for a brash twelve year-old who thinks he is mature for his age. Unfortunately, my other friends were in different classes, either because they started Chinese school at an earlier age or were immediately placed in more advanced classes upon enrolling.

The only kid in my class who was close to my age was Eddie, a mentally bankrupt but otherwise nice kid. We would skip out together by going to a nearby shopping centre or hiding out in the "forest", an undeveloped lot next to the church. There we traded hockey cards and read comic books. I skipped out a lot, a practice which later prepared me for high school and university.

Our teacher, Mrs. Tsang, was a stern Chinese woman who had compelling features—dark, stained teeth; black, crumbling fingernails (which I had concluded were burnt regularly by matches)—and breath that was beyond description. Rice breath, I think we called it. We always wondered if she had a bowl of rice every recess period before she breathed all over us kids.

Recess was formerly announced by the ringing of a brass bell. The biggest honour for any teacher's pet is be given the bell. The rest of us would be playing floor hockey, flipping cards against the wall, or what was even more fun, terrorizing little kids. Spitballs, rubber bands and red bean trajectories were the order of the day and we got one teacher's pet by yanking on her tightly secured ponytail any chance we could get. I remember, though, being afraid that one more time and her eyes would bug out like goldfish.

Cheating is a word synonymous with Chinese School—and most of my time was spent chiselling the characters from the to-be-memorized passages into the wooden board which served as desks and great sources of information. Other cheating schemes included retracing characters with ink over your lightly pencilled marks made the night before, or scribbling in your test-book during the exam and later handing in another book with your lesson already nicely printed out! Eddie, who was so original, wrote his lesson out in invisible ink. But when the time came to write the passage out by memory, he discovered that the developing part of his pen had dried out. "Life is tough on Eddie," I sighed with all the wisdom of a 12 year-old, "especially if he's stupid."

The worst part of Chinese School was the end of class, when we lined up in pairs in front of the door. Just before leaving we were coerced into singing some ditty extolling the virtues of studying hard and being good to your parents, teachers and classmates. When the rest of the class, who were faithfully chirping out the song, came to the ending, Eddie and I would shout out the last line (which was the only one I could remember), "Joy geen Seen Saang, joy geen TEUNG HOK!!!" (*"Good-bye, teacher; good-bye, fellow classmates."*) Then we'd all run out as if we were being freed from the Gulag Archipelago. But many times we tried to sneak out to avoid this great social embarrassment. After all, the other classes didn't have to sing it. They would head out the door smirking at us. It was worse, though, if you were caught leaving without singing your good-byes to the teacher and classmates. Being pulled back in by your ear is simply not good form, especially if you happen to be twice the age of your classmates.

My illustrious career came to an end after a mutual decision made by my parents: "We spent all that money on you and you still can't speak or write a word of Chinese, Nyah, nyah, nyah . . . "

They said I'd grow up regretting not learning the language—and it's true, I do.

Source: THE ASIANADIAN Vol. 4, No. 1

Acknowledgment. I am indebted to Mr. Him Mark Lai, Chinese American historian and Archivist in the Asian American Studies Library, University of California, Berkeley, for referring me to many useful sources.

SUGGESTED READINGS

Lai et al. (1980) and Chen (1980) both give highly readable historical overviews of the Chinese experience in America, accompanied by a wealth of illustrations. Nee and Nee's (1972) work, which is not a history but an ethnographic study with many oral histories, is also a good introduction but is somewhat dated. More recent data are provided by Tsai (1986).

A journal jointly published by the PRC, Hong Kong, and Britain, *Language Learning and Communication* (now unfortunately defunct), is a good source on the language situation of many Chinese language communities (except Taiwan) outside the United States.

As for the language situation of Chinese Americans, most available sources are articles scattered in such journals as *Amerasia* and *International Migration Review*. Lopez (1982) gives a concise overview of demographic and language shift patterns among Chinese Americans but is based on 1976 data. Guthrie (1985), who has written one of the few book-length studies, provides an in-depth ethnographic account of how a bilingual education program functions in a Chinese American community. Leung's (1975) dissertation remains the only detailed account of Chinese language schools.

Veltman (1983) and Fishman (1985) have written large-scale and rather technical studies of language shift and maintenance, which help to place the Chinese American language situation in a national context.

NOTES

1. Under the "paper son" system, a Chinese man with American citizenship, after visiting his wife in China, would later claim the birth of a child in China, thus creating a "slot" for a new U.S. citizen eligible for future entry into the United States. This "slot" could then be sold, usually to someone who wanted to join his or her family in the United States but was barred by law from doing so. During the Exclusion period, Chinese immigrants were subjected to detention and interrogation on a "guilty until proven innocent" basis (see Chen 1981:189–190; Lai, Lim and Yung 1980:8–29).

2. There has been no in-depth study of the process specifically focusing on Chinese immigrant students; the account given here is based on the author's observations and on the theoretical and research literature; see Wong (forthcoming).

3. Hsia (1988:70–78) does note that Asian Americans in higher education show differential performance in English and mathematics; however, the population studied includes a large proportion of nonnative English speakers. Asian Americans having English as their best language (presumably mostly American-born) "had the highest average self-reported class rank and English grades" of all groups. No separate figures are given for Chinese Americans.

4. There is apparently an error in Veltman's tables, as identical figures are given for arrivals during the 1960s (55) and during the 1970s (57). From the text, it seems that

the percentage of Chinese immigrants making English their usual language is below 30 percent in both cases.

5. The following is a complete list of problems cited in Tom (1941), Jung (1972), Leung (1975), and Lin (1986), and observed by the author: (1) dialect diversity: difficulty of having enough students of a single dialect group to form a class or school; (2) age diversity and lack of correspondence between age and Chinese proficiency: need to mix students, causing teaching difficulties and shame and resistance among older but less proficient students; (3) divergence in pronunciation, syntax, and vocabulary between Mandarin and vernaculars: dilemma of choosing between students' home language and the national standard; need to decide whether to emphasize speaking/understanding or reading/writing; (4) choice of script: The traditional script is more difficult but is the one used in North America; the simplified script is easier to learn but will not give students access to Chinese materials available in the United States and will be resisted by anti-PRC parents; (5) decision about whether to use romanization as an aid and, if so, whether to use *pinyin* (easier for students in an English environment but associated with the PRC) or *zhuyin* (requires learning an additional system but familiar to and favored by many parents from Taiwan); (6) difficulty of obtaining consensus among parents concerning program goals, approach, etc., especially if they are from different places of origin, generations, and socioeconomic backgrounds; (7) lack of appropriate materials: For propagandistic purposes, the Nationalist government's "Overseas Chinese Affairs Commission" prepares and disseminates language-teaching materials, which are quite widely used (Leung 1975:51; Overseas Chinese Affairs Commission 1982:519–528; Lin 1986:12). These, however, reflect the values considered by the Taiwan regime to be worth encouraging among "overseas Chinese." Chinese language arts texts specially produced in the United States for Chinese Americans in bilingual programs (see ARC 1987) are few in number. Overall, parents and teachers have very limited choices in materials. (6) lack of teachers trained in language teaching and high turnover among teachers: many teachers are volunteers; others work part-time at a salary; most are not language teachers by profession (Lin 1986:9). The fact that many of them are highly educated in other fields does not mean that they will be familiar with the language learning process or language teaching methodology. (7) use of outdated methods such as rote learning and excessive homework; (8) overemphasis on discipline; (9) lack of student motivation due to the above three problems plus fatigue after "regular school"; reluctance to attend school on weekends; competition from other extracurricular activities; perception of Chinese as irrelevant; unwillingness to be "different" from mainstream peers. High dropout by secondary school students is reported by all of the researchers cited; (10) lack of parental support: In the case of English-monolingual parents sending their children to get what they themselves missed, they will not be able to help the children with the Chinese schoolwork. In the case of parents who fail to maintain Chinese at home but expect the school to do the job, the home environment will undo the school's efforts; (11) lack of support from the English-speaking environment: For many students, especially those from the suburbs, Chinese is seldom seen or heard outside school. Mainstream society's denigration of Chinese causes students to dislike Chinese and to look down upon Chinese language teachers whose English is less native-like than theirs (Leung 1975:60); (12) other practical difficulties such as securing facilities, transportation to and from school, finances, and so on.

REFERENCES

Asian Resource Center (ARC). 1987. *Catalog of Curriculum Materials*. Oakland, CA: ARC Associates, Inc.

Barnes, D. 1983. The implementation of language planning in China. In J. Cobarrubias and J. A. Fishman (eds.), *Progress in Language Planning: International Perspectives*. Berlin: Mouton, 291–308.

Bilingual Education Office, California State Department of Education. 1984. *A Handbook for Teaching Cantonese-Speaking Students*. Sacramento, CA: California State Department of Education.

Bouvier, P. and T. Tong. 1968. *Education in San Francisco Chinatown*. San Francisco: Intercollegiate Chinese for Social Action, San Francisco State College.

Chan, J. 1977. Jeff Chan, chairman of SF State Asian American Studies, attacks review. *The San Francisco Journal*. May 4.

Chan, M. K. M. and D. W. Lee. 1981. Chinatown Chinese: A linguistic and historical re-evaluation. *Amerasia Journal* 8:1, 111–131.

Chang, M. 1986. Immigration, education, and occupational bimodality: The social development of Chinese Americans, 1940–1980. Paper presented at the National Association for Asian and Pacific American Education Conference. Los Angeles, April 24–26.

Chao, R. 1977. *Chinese immigrant children*. Preliminary report, Monograph No. 5. New York: Department of Asian Studies, The City College, City University of New York.

Chen, C.-C. 1979. An error analysis of English compositions written by Chinese college students in Taiwan, Ph.D. dissertation. University of Texas at Austin.

Chen, J. 1981. *The Chinese of America*. San Francisco: Harper & Row.

Cheung, Y. 1984. The uses of English and Chinese languages in Hong Kong. *Language Learning and Communication* 3:3, 273–287.

Chin, F. 1976. Backtalk. In E. Gee (ed.), *Counterpoint: Perspectives on Asian America*. Los Angeles, CA: Asian American Studies Center, University of California, Los Angeles. 556–557.

Dong, L. and M. Hom. 1980. Chinatown Chinese: The San Francisco dialect. *Amerasia Journal* 7:1.

Fishman, J. A. 1980. Ethnic community mother tongue schools in the U.S.A.: Dynamics and distributions. *International Migration Review* 14:2, 235–247.

Fishman, J. A. 1985. The community resources of ethnic languages in the USA. In J. A. Fishman (ed.), *The Rise and Fall of the Ethnic Revival: Perspectives on Language and Ethnicity*. Berlin: Mouton.

Fishman, J. A., M. H. Gertner, E. G. Lowy and W. G. Milan. 1985. Ethnicity in action. The community resources of ethnic languages in the United States. In J. A. Fishman (ed), *The Rise and Fall of the Ethnic Revival: Perspectives on Language and Ethnicity*. Berlin: Mouton.

Fishman, J. A. and B. Markman. 1979. *The Ethnic Mother Tongue School in the United States: Assumptions, Findings and Directory*. New York: Yeshiva University.

Gardner, R. W., B. Robey and P. C. Smith. 1985. *Asian Americans: Growth, Change, and Diversity. Population Bulletin* 40:4.

Gibbons, J. 1979. U-gay-wa: A linguistic study of the campus language of students at the University of Hong Kong. In R. Lord (ed.), *Hong Kong Language Papers*. Hong Kong: Hong Kong University Press.

Givens, R. M. Mittelbach, L. Goldberg, K. Christopher, J. Genachowski, J. Reed, M. Cook and D. Butler. 1984. The drive to excel. *Newsweek on Campus*. April.

Guthrie, G. P. 1985. *A School Divided: An Ethnography of Bilingual Education in a Chinese Community*. Hillsdale, NJ: Lawrence Erlbaum.

Ho, D. Y. F. 1979. English language skills and academic performance. In R. Lord (ed.), *Hong Kong Language Papers*. Hong Kong: Hong Kong University Press.

Ho, W. 1973. An investigation of errors in English composition of some pre-university students in Singapore, with suggestions for the teaching of written English. *RELC Journal* 4:1, 48–65.

Hou, Z. 1987. English teaching in China: Problems and perspectives. *TESOL Newsletter* 21:3, 25–27.

Hsia, J. 1988. *Asian Americans in Higher Education and at Work*. Hillsdale, NJ: Lawrence Erlbaum.

Hu, Z. D. F. Brown and L. B. Brown. 1982. Some linguistic differences in the written English of Chinese and Australian students. *Language Learning and Communication* 1:1, 39–49.

Hwang, D. H. 1983. *FOB*. In *Broken Promises: Four Plays*. New York: Avon Books. 1–57.

Immigration and Naturalization Service, U.S. Department of Justice (INS). 1981. Immigrants admitted by country or region of birth, fiscal years 1972–1981. *1981 Statistical Yearbook of the Immigration and Naturalization Service*. 34–37.

Itow, L. 1987. Hong Kong's quiet Bay Area presence. *San Francisco Examiner* June 7.

Johns, A. M. 1984. Textual cohesion and the Chinese speaker of English. *Language Learning and Communication* 3:1, 69–74.

Johnson, D. 1977. Review of *The Woman Warrior*. *New York Review of Books* February 3.

Johnson, R. K. 1983. Bilingual switching strategies: A study of the modes of teacher-talk in bilingual secondary school classrooms in Hong Kong. *Language Learning and Communication* 2:3, 267–285.

Jung, R. K. 1972. The Chinese language school in the U.S. *School and Society* 100, 309–312.

Kan, S. H. and W. T. Liu. 1986. The educational status of Asian Americans: An update from the 1980 census. *Pacific/Asian American Mental Health Research Center Research Review* 5:3/4, 21–24.

Kaplan, R. B. 1966. Cultural thought patterns in intercultural education. *Language Learning* 16, 1–20.

Kaplan, R. B. 1968. Contrastive grammar: Teaching composition to the Chinese student. *Journal of ESL* 3:1, 1–13.

Kaplan, R. B. 1976. A further note on contrastive rhetoric. *Communication Quarterly* 24:2, 12–19.

Kaplan, R. B. 1986. Culture and the written language. In J. M. Valdes (ed.), *Culture Bound: Bridging the Cultural Gap in Language Teaching*. Cambridge: Cambridge University Press. 8–19.

Kaplan, R. B. and J. K. Tse. 1982. The Language situation in Taiwan (The Republic of China). *The Linguistic Reporter* 25:2, 1–5.

Kasindorf, M., P. Chin, D. Weathers, K. Feltz, D. Shapiro and D. Junkin. 1982. Asian Americans: A "model minority." *Newsweek* December 6.

Kim, E. 1976. Yellow English. *Asian American Review*. Berkeley: Asian American Studies Program, University of California, Berkeley.

Kim, E. 1982. *Asian American Literature: An Introduction to the Writings and Their Social Context*. Philadelphia: Temple University Press.

King, H. and F. B. Locke. 1980. Chinese in the U.S.: A century of occupational transition. *International Migration Review* 14, 15–41.

King, Jr, R. 1985. Room at the top. *San Francisco Focus Magazine* March.

Kingston, M. H. 1976. *The Woman Warrior: Memoirs of a Girlhood among Ghosts*. New York: Alfred A. Knopf.

Kleinmann, H. H. 1982. External influences and their neutralization in second language acquisition: A look at adult Indochinese refugees. *TESOL Quarterly* 16:2. 239–244.

Kuo, E. C. Y. 1974. Bilingual pattern of a Chinese immigrant group in the United States. *Anthropological Linguistics* 16:3, 128–140.

Lai, H. M. 1987. The Chinese-American press. In S. M. Miller (ed.), *The Ethnic Press in the U.S*. New York: Greenwood Press.

Lai, H. M., J. Huang and D. Wong. 1980. *The Chinese of America: 1785–1980*. San Francisco: Chinese Culture Foundation.

Lai, H. M., G. Lim and J. Yung. 1980. *Island: Poetry and History of Chinese Immigrants on Angel Island, 1910–1940*. San Francisco: HOC DOI Project.

Lay, N. D. S. 1975. Chinese language interference in written English. *Journal of Basic Writing* 1:1, 50–61.

Lee, M. 1976-7. Some common grammatical errors made in written English by Chinese students, *CATESOL Occasional Papers* 3, 115–119.

Lee, R. H. 1960. *The Chinese in the United States of America*. Hong Kong: Hong Kong University Press.

Leong, J. 1972. Hong Kong immigrants and the public schools. *Asian American Review*. Berkeley: Asian American Studies Program, University of California, Berkeley.

Leung, E. C. 1975. A sociological study of the Chinese language schools in the San Francisco Bay area. Ph.D. dissertation, University of Missouri.

Li, C. N. and S. A. Thompson. 1981. *Mandarin Chinese: A Functional Reference Grammar*. Berkeley: University of California Press.

Li, W. L. 1982. The language shift of Chinese-Americans. *International Journal of the Sociology of Language* 38, 109–124.

Lin, J. 1987. [In Chinese] Diary of a teacher of "little foreign students." *Jiushi Niandai* April, 86–96.

Lin, Y. J. 1986. Survey of Chinese language schools. Unpublished paper.

Lincoln, M. W. 1976. I'm very sorry, but I don't know Charlie Chan. *Bridge* July, 48.

Liu, P. C. 1976 [In Chinese] *A History of the Chinese in the United States of America*. Taipei: Liming.

Loo, C. M. 1985. The "biliterate" ballot controversy: Language acquisition and cultural shift among immigrants. *International Migration Review* 19:3, 493–515.

Lopez, D. E. 1982. *Language Maintenance and Shift in the United States Today: The Basic Patterns and Their Social Implications*. Volume IV: *Asian Languages*. Los Alamitos CA: National Center for Bilingual Research. 1–28.

Louie, E. W. 1985–6. A new perspective on surnames among Chinese Americans. *Amerasia Journal* 12:1, 1–22.

Low, V. 1982. *The Unimpressible Race: A Century of Educational Struggle by the Chinese in San Francisco*. San Francisco: East/West Publishing Co.

Lyman, S. M. 1974. *Chinese Americans*. New York: Random House.

McGrath, E. 1983. Confucian work ethic. *Time* March 28.

Mohan, B. and W. A. Lo. 1985. Academic writing and Chinese students: Transfer and development factors. *TESOL Quarterly* 19:3, 515–543.

Nee, V. G. and B. D. Nee. 1972. *Longtime Californ': A Documentary Study of an American Chinatown*. New York: Pantheon Books.

Overseas Chinese Affairs Commission. 1982. [In Chinese] *Fifty Years of Overseas Chinese Affairs*.

Ramirez, A. 1986. America's super minority. *Fortune* November 24.

Raspberry, W. 1984. Beyond racism. *Washington Post* November 19.

Rutherford, W. E. 1983. Language typology and language transfer. In S. Gass and L. Selinker (eds.), *Language Transfer in Language Learning*. Rowley, MA: Newbury House.

Schachter, J. and W. E. Rutherford. 1979. Discourse function and language transfer. *Working Papers in Bilingualism* 19, 3–12.

Scovel, J. 1983. English teaching in China: A historical perspective. *Language Learning and Communication* 2:1, 105–109.

Swope, S. 1987. Survey of Chinese bilingual education in independent schools. *East/West News* June 18, 8.

Sung, B. L. 1979. *Transplanted Chinese Children*. New York: City College of New York.

To, C.-Y. 1979. The educational and psychological adjustment problems of Asian immigrant youth and how bilingual–bicultural education can help. Paper presented at the National Association of Asian and Pacific American Education Conference.

Tom, K. 1941. Functions of the Chinese language schools. *Sociology and Social Research* 25, 557–561.

Tong, B. R. 1971. The ghetto of the mind: Notes on the historical psychology of Chinese America. *Amerasia Journal* 1:3, 1–31.

Tong, B. R. 1977. Critic of admirer sees dumb racist. *The San Francisco Journal* May 11.

Tsai, S. H. 1986. *The Chinese Experience in America*. Bloomington: Indiana University Press.

Tsang, S. and L. C. Wing. 1985. *Beyond Angel Island: The Education of Asian Americans*. New York: Clearinghouse on Urban Education.

Tse, J. K. 1982. Language policy in the Republic of China. In R. B. Kaplan (ed.), *Annual Review of Applied Linguistics*. Rowley, MA: Newbury House. 33–47.

T'sou, B. K. 1973. Asymmetric bilingualism: A sociolinguistic study of Cantonese emigrants. *Journal of the Chinese Language Teachers Association* 8:3 134–144.

Tucker, G. A. 1969. The Chinese immigrant's language handicap: Its extent and its effects. *The Florida FL Reporter*, 44–45.

Van den Berg, M. E. 1986. Language planning and language use in Taiwan: Social identity, language accommodation, and language choice behavior. *International Journal of the Sociology of Language* 59, 97–115.

Veltman, C. 1983. *Language Shift in the United States*. Berlin: Mouton.

Wang, L. C. 1972. The Chinese-American student in San Francisco. In *Chinese Americans: School and Community Problems*. Chicago: Integrated Education Associates.

Wang, Z. 1982. English teaching and English studies in China. *Language Learning and Communication* 1:1, 5–20.

Wong, A. 1980. Chinese bilingual education: Current status and issues. Paper presented at the National Conference on Chinese American Studies, San Francisco, October.

Wong, S. C. 1984. Understanding Asian immigrant students in the ESL classroom. Paper presented at CATESOL Annual State Conference. San Jose, CA., April 13–15.

Wong, S. C. Forthcoming. The language learning situation of Asian immigrant students in the U.S.: A socio- and psycholinguistic perspective. *NABE Journal*.

Wong, S. C. 1987. The language needs of school-age Asian immigrants and refugees in the United States. In W. A. Van Horne, and T. V. Tonnesen (eds.), *Ethnicity and Language*. Milwaukee, WI: University of Wisconsin System Institute on Race and Ethnicity. 124–159.

Young, L. W. 1982. Inscrutability revisited. In J. J. Gumperz (ed.), *Language and Social Identity*. Cambridge: Cambridge University Press. 72–84.

Yuan, J. 1987. [In Chinese] Taiwan's "little foreign students" in the U.S. *Jiushi Niandai* April, 84–85.

Yung, J. 1986. *Chinese Women of America: A Pictorial History*. Seattle: University of Washington Press.

CHAPTER

8

The Language Situation of Filipino Americans

Rosita Galang

Filipino Americans, numbering 774,640 at the 1980 Census, are the second largest Asian American group; with a rate of increase of 125.8 percent from 1970 to 1980, they also make up one of the fastest-growing minorities in the United States (Suzuki 1983). Yet they lack the visibility and distinctiveness of some of the other Asian immigrant groups, such as the Chinese or the Koreans. Largely because of the former colonial relationship between the Philippines and the United States, Filipino Americans have become probably "the most Westernized among the Southeast Asians" (Cabezas, Shinagawa and Kawaguchi 1986–7). In terms of the Filipino Americans' language heritage, the group shares a unique experience with a non-Asian immigrant group, Puerto Ricans, in having had U.S. English language policies implemented in their land of origin (Beebe and Beebe 1981). An account of the current language situation of Filipino Americans will reveal some basic similarities but also many striking differences between them and other Asian language minorities.

IMMIGRATION HISTORY

Filipino presence in North America was recorded as early as the mid-eighteenth century, when slaves, sailors, and shipbuilders from the Spanish imperial galleons of the Philippine–Mexico trade jumped ship and settled in Louisiana, Baja California, and other coastal regions frequented by the fleet (studies of these early Filipinos by Espina are reviewed in Posadas 1986–7:97). These early settlers intermarried with other ethnic groups (Morales 1976). By the turn of the twentieth century, there were some 2,000 Filipinos in the New Orleans area (Macaranas 1983).

Since the ceding of the Philippines to the United States by defeated Spain in 1898, at the end of the Spanish–American War, there have been several waves of Filipino immigration to the United States (Naming of the waves varies from author to author, but the characteristics of each distinctive group of immigrants, whether called a "wave" or not, are well agreed upon. The following is a composite account from several sources.)

The first wave—a group termed "potential immigrants" by Macaranas (1983), since many eventually did not settle permanently in the United States—began with Filipino students enrolled in American universities who planned to return to the Philippines (Melendy 1977). Following the passage of the "Pensionado Act," a program was launched in 1903 to send promising young people to obtain professional training in the United States on government scholarships. Upon their return, the "pensionados" gained leadership positions in the Philippines. Their success prompted other students to come to the United States on their own. Between the 1920s and 1930s, over 80 percent of the Filipino students enrolled in American universities and colleges were completely self-supporting (Obando 1936). Between 1910 and 1936, as many as 14,000 were enrolled in U.S. institutions of higher education. However, the high cost of living, language problems, inadequate academic preparation, and other factors prevented many of them from succeeding in their academic pursuits and forced them to drift into unskilled work (Melendy 1977).

The second wave of Filipino immigration consisted of farm laborers, both in Hawaii and on the mainland, who emigrated between 1907 and 1934. After the Chinese, Japanese, and other groups providing cheap labor for the United States were excluded by law at the end of the nineteenth century and the early decades of the twentieth, the Philippines became a replacement source for unskilled workers. Unlike the other immigrants, Filipinos, being under U.S. rule, were considered "nationals": not U.S. citizens but not "aliens" either, and traveling on American passports, exempt from immigration restrictions (Posadas 1986-7).

Recruiters went to the Philippines, offering jobs and free transportation, and brought a small number of Filipino workers to the Hawaiian sugar plantations in 1907 (Vallangca 1977). This began a trend of growing immigration to Hawaii. Poverty, inadequacy of arable land, and increasing farm tenancy encouraged Filipinos to leave their homeland in search of a better livelihood in the United States. The movement was abetted by misleading advertisements and unscrupulous employers (Catapusan 1940). The 1930 Census counted some 65,000 Filipinos in Hawaii (Posadas 1986–7). Some of the plantation workers returned to the Philippines after accumulating enough savings; others stayed on. Still others sought work on the mainland; between 1909 and 1931, over 18,000 moved to the Pacific Coast (Clifford 1954). A small number hoped eventually to obtain an education on the mainland (Vallangca 1977).

Parallel to the Hawaiian immigration was an influx of Filipino agricultural workers to the Pacific coast states. In 1923, close to 2,500 Filipinos arrived in California; nearly 2,000 per year continued to come to the United States for the next few years (Beebe and Beebe 1981). The 1930 Census showed, together with remigrated laborers from Hawaii, over 31,000 Filipinos in California: 67 percent of the total of 47,000 on the mainland (Posadas 1986–7).

The 1920s were a period of economic development on the West coast. The majority of Filipinos engaged in menial, low-paying work: as farm laborers such as migrant fruit and vegetable harvesters; as domestic and service workers such as houseboys, bellboys, dishwashers, and janitors; and as seasonal cannery workers in Alaska (Beebe and Beebe 1981; Macaranas 1983). In addition, following recruitment for World War I, a significant percentage of Filipino Americans were in the U.S. Navy as messboys and other low-status workers (Rabaya 1971).

Filipino immigrants of the second wave, while similar to Mexican Americans in their work experience, resembled early Chinese immigrants in composition. They were overwhelmingly male, young (in their 20s and 30s), of rural origin, uneducated, with limited English, and single. Due to labor recruitment practices, the male/female ratio in the Filipino American community during the second-wave period was severely imbalanced, estimated at somewhere between 12:1 (Macaranas 1983) and 14:1 (Beebe and Beebe 1981). These characteristics not only had a noticeable impact on the U.S. job market but also created negative stereotypes of the Filipino American community. One can still get a vivid sense of the persecution and humiliation suffered by Filipino laborers in Carlos Bulosan's well-known *America Is in the Heart* (1943), one of the first Asian American works of literature. As economic conditions worsened into the Depression, discrimination against Filipino Americans increased, and race riots broke out (Bogardus 1976, cited in Macaranas 1983).

The Tydings–McDuffie Act of 1934 marked a turning point in the history of Filipino immigration to the United States. Under the provisions of the Act, which paved the way for Philippine independence, the Philippines was considered a separate country and immigration was limited to an annual quota of 50 persons (Coloma 1939). (Section 8 of the Act did allow "limited Filipino immigration to the islands [of Hawaii] if a need could be demonstrated"; this was invoked only in 1946, when 7,300 Filipinos migrated to Hawaii to meet an unexpected postwar labor shortage in sugar plantations [Melendy 1976].) Further efforts at curtailment of Filipino immigration resulted in the 1935 Repatriation Act, which offered Filipino Americans free transportation to the Philippines on condition that they would not reenter the United States. However, only 2,000 repatriated, since economic conditions at home were even worse (Beebe and Beebe 1981). When the Philippines became independent in 1946, the immigration quota was fixed at 100 a year. This remained in effect until the immigration reform of 1965 (passed that year but taking effect in 1968). Thus between 1934 and 1965, Filipino immigration to the United States came to a virtual halt. (It should be added, however, that even during this period Filipinos continued to enter the United States: those who joined the U.S. Navy, mostly as messboys and stewards, could obtain U.S. citizenship after 3 years of service and could then bring their families into the United States outside quota restrictions; see Cabezas, Shinagawa and Kawaguchi 1986-7.) In the current Filipino American community, this segment of immigration history is reflected in the presence of a distinct group of "old-timers" (Posadas 1986–7).

In 1965, the immigration law was liberalized to allow 20,000 immigrants per country per year, and massive immigration from the Philippines resumed, continuing up to today. Whereas in 1967 Filipino immigrants did not even rank among the top five groups to which U.S. immigration visas were issued, "they jumped to third place in 1969 and have remained second to Mexico since 1971" (Beebe and Beebe 1981:329). "Once again, the Philippines became an exporter of labor to the United States, and a direct contributor to America's economic and social well-being" (Beebe and Beebe 1981:329)—but in new ways. The new immigrants of the third wave are very different in characteristics from their predecessors. In response to the occupation-based preference category in the 1965 law, many of them are well-educated professionals from urban backgrounds, including medical doctors, nurses, social scientists, teachers, engineers, dentists, accountants, pharmacists, and lawyers (Morales 1976); their emigration from the Philippines has caused a "brain drain." In addition, instead of just single, young men, families with large numbers of school-age children, as well as senior citizens have been emigrating to the United States (Melendy 1977). (The family reunification provision of the 1965 law allows direct relatives of citizens to enter on a "nonquota" basis, so that the annual number of entering Filipinos actually exceeds 20,000.) Within the post-1965 influx, Morales (1986–7:123), using a somewhat different system of classification, distinguishes another wave (called "the fourth wave") of "political exiles and refugees of the martial law era." Overall, the Filipino American community has become much more diverse in composition than ever before.

CURRENT DEMOGRAPHICS

The Filipino American population has increased 125.8 percent from 1970 to 1980 (Suzuki 1983). Its annual growth rate of 8.7 percent is eight times that for the national population. About three-fourths of the 1970–1980 *growth* (as opposed to the population total) has been due to immigration rather than births within the United States, which means that composition of the Filipino American population has become predominantly foreign-born (Lopez 1982:60–62). In 1970, 53 percent of Filipino Americans were foreign-born (based on figures supplied in Beebe and Beebe 1981:330); the percentage has reached 65 percent by the 1980 Census (Tsang and Wing 1985:4). If we assume that the high rate of Filipino emigration as well as the national population increase continue on their present courses, it is projected that there will be 1,240,000 Filipinos in the United States in 1990, 70–75 percent of whom will be immigrants (Lopez 1982:62).

As far as geographical distribution is concerned, according to the 1980 Census, nearly half (46 percent) of the Filipino American population are in California, 17 percent in Hawaii, 6 percent in Illinois, 5 percent in New York, and the rest in Washington, New Jersey, and Texas (Cabezas, Shinagawa and Kawaguchi 1986–7). In the past, Filipinos have been relatively "invisible" due to "weakly nucleated settlement patterns," but this pattern is changing as communities with large Filipino concentrations grow in number (Macaranas 1983).

Despite the middle class background of many of the post-1965 Filipino immigrants, the problem of underemployment is serious. On the basis of 1980 Census data, it has been estimated that in the 25–44 years age bracket, American-born Filipino men earn only 70.6 percent of what white men earn; foreign-born Filipino men earn 62.6 percent. The picture is even bleaker for women: American-born Filipino women earn 47.6 percent of what white men earn; foreign-born Filipino women, as little as 43.4 percent (Cabezas and Kawaguchi 1987). Even highly trained immigrant professionals often encounter discrimination: "their foreign credentials [are] not recognized, their foreign accents unacceptable" (Beebe and Beebe 1981:329); as a result, they are often forced to take low-skill, low-paying jobs.

LANGUAGE BACKGROUND

While it is customary in studies of the language situation of immigrant groups in America to examine the linguistic features of the ethnic language as a factor in immigrants' English acquisition, the approach may not be entirely appropriate for Filipino Americans. Because of their unique colonial past and the resulting language policies involving varying roles for English, sociolinguistic rather than purely linguistic factors may be more relevant. The information in this section will thus be confined to the larger picture of language policy in the Philippines. Readers interested in the specific linguistic features of Philippine languages (primarily Tagalog) are referred to Ramos (1971), the summary in Beebe and Beebe (1981), and Li (1983:15–17), who outlines salient common grammatical features of Philippine languages with respect to the structure of English.

The Philippines has a complex language history. On top of the indigenous languages of the islands, Spanish colonizers imposed Spanish as the language of government. Subsequently, under American rule, English joined Spanish as an official language. Then a national language, Pilipino, was developed as a new official language, based on one of the indigenous languages, Tagalog. According to the 1986 Philippine constitution, Filipino and English are the official languages in the country (Republika ng Pilipinas 1986). Today, "[m]ost Filipinos are, in fact, multilingual" (Kaplan 1982).

Indigenous Languages

The Philippines, comprised of some 7,100 islands (with a total land area comparable to Nevada) spread over a huge area of the Pacific Ocean, is populated by speakers of numerous languages. Depending on exactly how one defines a language, estimates range from 70 (Kaplan 1982) to 80 (Beebe and Beebe 1981) or more languages. These languages belong to the Malayo-Polynesian (also known as Austronesian) language family, which extends from parts of Taiwan in the north to parts of New Zealand in the south, and from Easter Island in the east to Madagascar in the west (Beebe and Beebe 1981).

Eight of the indigenous languages were designated major languages because they were spoken natively by the eight largest ethnic groups in the Philippines (Constantino 1971). The 1975 census indicated the figures given in Table 8.1 for the major languages (National Census and Statistics Office 1978).

According to the 1980 census of population and housing, the eight major languages are generally spoken in an aggregate of 87.48 percent of private households (National Census and Statistics Office 1983) (Table 8.2).

Thus, while Cebuano was spoken natively by a greater number of Filipinos in 1975, it was outranked by Tagalog in the number of private households where it was generally spoken in 1980.

Each of the major languages is further broken up into several dialects (Llamzon 1978).

Table 8.1. NATIVE SPEAKERS OF THE EIGHT MAJOR LANGUAGES OF THE PHILIPPINES

Language	No. of native speakers	% of Population
Cebuano	10,262,735	24.4
Tagalog	10,019,214	23.8
Ilocano	4,685,896	11.1
Hiligaynon	4,204,825	10.0
Bicol	2,928,245	7.0
Samar-Leyte (Waray)	1,945,005	4.6
Pampango (Kapampangan)	1,442,607	3.4
Pangasinan	948,820	2.3

Table 8.2. PRIVATE HOUSEHOLDS WHERE THE MAJOR LANGUAGES ARE GENERALLY SPOKEN

Language	% of Households
Tagalog	29.66
Cebuano	24.20
Ilocano	10.30
Hilgaynon	9.16
Bicol	5.57
Samar-Leyte (Waray)	3.98
Pampango (Kapampangan)	2.77
Pangasinan	1.84

(In addition to the indigenous languages, there are substantial numbers of speakers of Chinese and Arabic; see Kaplan 1982.)

Spanish

Colonizers typically either impose their language on the indigenous population or limit access to it to native elites; both policies are calculated to strengthen the colonizers' rule. The Spanish colonizers of the Philippines chose the latter "divide and rule" course as a means of controlling "the natives"; thus in a 1870 census, only 2.4 percent of the population of the Philippines were found to speak Spanish. For evangelistic purposes, the mother tongues of the native population were used (Gonzalez 1980). However, Spanish was the official language even through the American period, up to 1935 (Gonzalez 1980). Today about 3 percent of the total population are Spanish speakers.

English

After the United States took over the Philippines from Spain in 1898, it adopted an opposite course in language policy, making English the common means of communication and the medium of instruction (Beebe and Beebe 1981). In 1919, English was made the official language for use in local government and the legal system, gradually edging out Spanish in influence.

Pilipino

In the mid-1930s, Filipinos began a movement to develop a national language as a symbol of new independence and unity. Although at the time there were fewer people living in Tagalog-speaking areas than in Visayan-speaking areas (Gonzalez 1980), Tagalog was the language of the greater Manila area and was considered by many to be more highly developed. Visayan is commonly used to refer to (1) the islands between Luzon and Mindanao, (2) the cultural group from the Visayan islands, or (3) one of the languages or cluster of languages spoken in the Visayan islands (Llamzon 1978; McFarland 1980). In 1937, Tagalog was declared to be the basis of the new national language. In 1940, the teaching of this national language began. In 1959, the official name *Pilipino* was given to the national language (Beebe and Beebe 1981).

A few words should be said about the terms *Pilipino, Filipino,* and *Tagalog,* which sometimes cause confusion among Americans unfamiliar with Filipino language history. Tagalog is the regional language on which the national language is based. Many Filipinos surveyed by Sibayan (1975) did not consider that there were any differences between Tagalog and Pilipino, but in fact conscious efforts have been made by language planners to adapt the regional language (by, for example, borrowing), so that it could fulfill all the functions needed by a modern, national language, such as transfer of scientific and technological information (Laygo 1977; Gonzalez 1980; Beebe and Beebe 1981). Since its gaining of official status, the spread of Pilipino has been encouraged by its use in the educational system and the mass media (Kaplan 1982). Regional varieties of it have developed (Beebe and Beebe 1981), so that the national language can no longer be identified completely with the language of the greater Manila area. In general, the term *Pilipino* is officially preferred because *Tagalog* tends to be associated with regionalism. (Even now, Tagalog speakers are but a bare majority of the population.) As for the term *Filipino,* among language planners it refers to a linguistically "pure" lingua franca, serving as an even more appropriate symbol of national identity than Pilipino, to be developed sometime in the future (Gonzalez 1980; Kaplan 1982); this dream is as yet unrealized. All these fine nuances notwithstanding, in the United States the terms *Tagalog, Pilipino,* and *Filipino* tend to be used loosely.

The Educational Roles of Various Languages in the Philippines

From 1901 to 1956, as noted above, English was the medium of instruction in the Philippines. In 1957, following the Iloilo I Study of 1948–1954 in which the superiority of initial vernacular education was demonstrated, the vernacular was made the medium of instruction for the first two elementary grades, with English and Pilipino as subjects; from third grade on English was to be the medium of instruction, with Pilipino the auxiliary medium up to high school (Board of National Education 1958:18). This "vernacular policy" was strictly enforced only in public schools. Many elite private schools were able to continue using English as a teaching medium from the first grade (Otanes 1974).

In 1974, the policy on educational language was again changed, following the Rizal and Iloilo II experiments in 1960–1966 (some of whose results, however, were ignored by policymakers) (Ramos 1979). Under this new "bilingual policy," Pilipino was to be the medium of instruction in social studies/social science, character education, work education, health education, and physical education. English was to be used to teach science, math, and related areas (Department of Education and Culture 1974). This policy is still in effect today.

The degree of implementation of official bilingualism in the Philippines is summarized in Table 8.3, adapted from Beebe and Beebe (1981):

Table 8.3. PERCENTAGE OF POPULATION ABLE TO SPEAK PILIPINO AND ENGLISH:

Year	Pilipino	English
1939	23.4	26.6
1948	37.1	37.2
1960	44.4	39.5
1970	55.2	44.7

Recently, however, the Philippine government has expressed concern over a probable decrease in the English proficiency of younger Filipinos as well as a slow decline in written Pilipino (Kaplan 1982). This rather disturbing phenomenon raises questions about the Philippines' unique bilingual educational policy.

Current Multilingualism in the Philippines

As the above brief review makes clear, depending on what ethnolinguistic group and what type of environment (rural or urban; high or low socioeconomic status; with access or without access to the mass media, etc.) a Filipino comes from, he or she may command at least two, if not more, languages. Ramos (1979:1) notes that "[l]earning a second, third, fourth and even a fifth language is a way of life among the majority of Filipinos." Gonzalez (1980:149) describes the multilingualism in Filipino society as follows:

> The Filipino is, in reality, multilingual, using a vernacular in his intimate familial interaction; a lingua franca (a regional vernacular and increas-

> ingly Tagalog-based Pilipino akin to the language of the Greater Manila area) in his urban communities and in his transactions with other ethnic groups; English in business, industry, academia, for negotiations in international circles and as a language of wider communication.

These languages are, however, in complementary distribution, so that their pattern of coexistence is likely to be stable (Gonzalez 1980).

In this context of multilingualism, as Gonzalez (1982:218) points out, "English now has a life of its own." Switching between English and another language is common, with language choice depending on participants, settings, topics, purposes of communication, and other factors (Beebe and Beebe 1981; Pascasio 1983–4). In fact, the English language itself has been modified in a process of indigenization. Some scholars suggest that there is now "a Standard Filipino English which educated Filipinos speak and which is acceptable in educated Filipino circles" (Beebe and Beebe 1981:326; Llamzon 1986). Moreover, educated Filipinos often use a mixed form of English, both spoken and written, called variously Taglish (if Tagalog predominates), Engalog (if English predominates), Halo-Halo, or Mix-Mix (a Pilipino term with pejorative connotations) (Gonzalez 1982). This variety is used to establish rapport and an atmosphere with the audience, "perhaps unconsciously excluding a native speaker of English who is familiar with only one code and likewise perhaps unconsciously establishing one's credentials as a nationalist, albeit Westernized" (Gonzalez 1982:217). Gonzalez prefers the term "code-switching variety of English" (which underscores the fact that the speaker must have competence in both languages) and differentiates it carefully from Pilipino–English mixtures due to inadequate knowledge of both languages (which are actually unstable "interlanguages" characteristic of children and other learners). In addition, one might distinguish an even more rudimentary variety of pidgin English, called "carabao ("water buffalo") English" (Beebe and Beebe 1981).

In the course of a typical Filipino's schooling and work experience, exposure to different registers of English in different settings can show a complex pattern (Gonzalez 1982:222):

> The variety or dialect of English that he learns in school is the formal variety, which is used in class (when the teacher is not code-switching between a language that the student understands and the one he is learning in the early stages of schooling), in textbooks, and science and mathematics class. Outside of the classroom, even in the schoolyard and the corridors, he switches to the local language, either the vernacular or Pilipino, depending on the area. The only contact that the Filipino has with a different variety of English would be in literature classes . . . , on TV, and in the movies, if other "accents" of English are used. . . .
>
> Beyond schooling, the uses of English continue to be important but are limited to certain domains. Most every day business and commercial

> transactions in the Philippines . . . are done in the local language (if not Pilipino). Even in offices, the local language prevails. Only in reading technical materials, in journals, in newsletters, etc. does one begin to use English again, and this, once more, in its formal style.

FILIPINO AMERICAN EDUCATIONAL ATTAINMENT: DOES LANGUAGE PLAY A ROLE?

From the above review, it can be seen that Filipino Americans have a language legacy in their homeland very different from that of other Asian nations. Since language plays such an important role in schooling, a natural question to ask regarding Filipino Americans is whether their unique language background is a factor in their performance in the American educational system.

Filipino American youth are dropping out of school at a higher rate than other Asian American groups (Tsang and Wing 1985). Census data from 1960 to 1980 show that "on a national level, college-aged Filipinos were enrolled in school at a much lower rate than either Chinese or Japanese, and closer to the enrollment rate of Black and Hispanic populations" (Azores 1986–7:40). In the case of a minority student population with a large percentage of second-language or second-dialect speakers, underachievement in school is often attributed to language differences. Does this explanation apply to Filipino Americans?

The answer seems to be "no," or a highly qualified "yes" emphasizing factors other than the usual "ESL problems." With regard to the question of possible interference from the native language among Filipino immigrant children or native-born children growing up in bilingual households, Ramos (1979), reviewing a number of (admittedly superficial) morpheme studies on Filipino second language acquisition, finds little relationship between Filipino language background and English acquisition. Tatlonghari (1984) finds no differences in reading strategies between limited English-speaking Filipino children and native English speakers. A few studies contrasting Tagalog and English and suggesting problem areas (Schwab 1955; Pascasio 1961; Castelo 1963) use a dated contrastive, structuralist approach and offer little insight into actual difficulties encountered by Filipino Americans learning English in a social context.

In addition, from examining the language situation in the Philippines, one might deduce several reasons why Filipino Americans are unlikely to encounter typical ESL problems comparable to what other East Asian immigrant groups experience. The Philippines is "unlike most Asian nations . . . in having an indigenous national language written in the roman alphabet" (Beebe and Beebe 1981:325). Thus a Filipino immigrant child in America need not learn a new script, as many other Asian children do. Prior exposure to English in the schools, even among the nonelite, would also mean an easier transition to English.

If an indigenized or "Filipinized" variety of English is the one in which a Filipino immigrant has been the most comfortable, upon emigration to the United States, his or her adaptation to the all-English environment may be more similar to that of speakers of nonstandard American dialects than to that of ESL learners. Difficulty with registers may be a problem. The English used in schools in the Philippines may be "bookish," and teaching may have been by nonnative speakers of English, causing the new immigrant to use a more formal, outdated, and sometimes heavily accentuated variety of English than native speakers of standard American English (interview with Dr. Jose Icasiano, Counselor, San Francisco City College; Charlesworth 1987). However, compared to the confrontation with a totally unfamiliar script and language that many Asian immigrant children experience, the transition of Filipino immigrants must be said to be relatively smooth.

One might then rule out ethnic language background as an important cause of the educational difficulties of Filipino Americans. Various other theories have been offered in explanation, including cultural deficit—lack of "support and mechanism for educational advancement in family and community" (Lott 1980), or unrealistic expectations by students (Azores 1986–7)—and economic inequities (examined in Macaranas 1983). Not to be dismissed, also, is the possibility that the humiliating historical stereotyping of Filipinos as a "primitive" dark race suited for colonial domination (Melendy 1976:431) may have influenced teacher and community expectations of the educational potential of Filipino Americans. None of the theories is entirely satisfactory; most likely, a combination of factors has brought about the disadvantaged status of Filipino American youths in the educational system.

Still, Azores (1986–7) does find some not-so-obvious connections between language and education:

> Language use affected educational aspirations indirectly through its influence on occupational expectations. The analysis found that bilingual students had higher occupational expectations than the monolingual English speakers. . . . [T]wo possible explanations may be explored for future research:
>
> 1. Bilingual students are influenced by the high value that Philippine society places on college education as a status symbol both for one's self and one's family.
> 2. Bilingual students, who are generally recent immigrants, are aware that a Filipino accent in speaking English, along with different nonverbal communication patterns, can serve as barriers to social acceptance and upward mobility. However, they believe that the difficulties can be minimized with high educational attainment.

STUDIES OF FILIPINO AMERICAN LANGUAGE USE PATTERNS

Filipino Americans originate from several major Filipino language groups. "Ilokanos were among the first Filipinos to immigrate to the United States"; "even though they comprise only about 11 percent of the Philippine population," their presence in the Filipino American community is still strong (Beebe and Beebe 1981:331). In contrast, post-1965 immigrants are predominantly native speakers of Tagalog.

Depending on prior experience with English, entering immigrants may exhibit a wide range of control in one or more registers of English, ranging from the "carabao English" of the uneducated, to the fluent if accented English of many middle-class professionals, to the native command of the elite.

The multilingualism that Filipino immigrants bring with them will continue in the United States; an immigrant may continue to function in several languages, but the distribution of functions will most likely differ. This will in turn affect the language situation of the native-born generation. The following review covers some studies of language use patterns among Filipino Americans. However, a word of caution should be offered: some of the studies do not distinguish between Philippine languages, using an umbrella term "Filipino," and some data are compiled for Tagalog only, making extrapolation from and comparison between studies difficult.

According to 1970 Census data, Filipino Americans appear less language retentive than the Chinese or Japanese, even though the proportion of foreign-born was higher. Note, however, that only information on Tagalog was obtained, so the data must be interpreted cautiously (Lopez 1982:63).

According to Veltman (1983), in 1976, although Filipino Americans had a much higher percentage of foreign-born (94.3 percent) than Chinese Americans (87.3 percent), they also had a much higher percentage of monolingual English speakers (15.3 percent compared to 6.0 percent) as well as English-dominant bilinguals (46.4 percent compared to 28.1 percent). In fact, the percentage of claimants of English as the usual language was the highest among the Asian groups listed: 61.7 percent compared to 34.1 percent for Chinese, 53.4 percent for Japanese, 46.6 percent for Koreans, and 33.2 percent for Vietnamese. This is an indication of rapid language shift to English. It is not clear just which languages are included in "Filipino" in a 1975 U.S. Bureau of the Census survey (U.S. Bureau of the Census 1976). However, this survey provides important information. Among Filipinos aged 14 and or older, 82 percent have Filipino as their mother tongue; in 28–30 percent of the households it is the usual language or is spoken by them. When children are included, 20–25 percent use Filipino as their usual language or are in homes where it is the usual language. However, another 40–50 percent use Filipino as a supplementary language.

Table 8.4. LANGUAGE PROFILE OF FILIPINOS IN MOUNTAIN VIEW, CALIFORNIA (%)

	English	Tagalog	Ilocano
Grew up speaking	27	24	33
Use at home	42	24	25
Can speak	95	64	40

A census-type socioeconomic survey for the Filipino Association of Mountain View, California, analyzed in Beebe and Beebe (1981), provided, among other things, a language profile of Filipinos, which the authors assert is not atypical among Filipino Americans (Table 8.4).

Note that while 33 percent of the respondents grew up speaking Ilocano, at the time of the survey only 25 percent used it at home, suggesting a shift to English. Further evidence for the shift to English is seen in the fact that while only 27 percent grew up speaking English, 42 percent now used it at home. This is a striking phenomenon, considering that the home is usually the intimate domain where an ethnic language is preserved, even when shift to a public language has occurred for other functions. Respondents who stated they could speak English made up fully 95 percent, which is an extremely high percentage. Compared to Ilocano, Tagalog has not suffered any loss (constant at 24 percent). This may be due to the differential status of Tagalog, the basis of the Philippine lingua franca, and Ilocano, a minority, regional language.

In October 1981, the *Philippine News* conducted a survey of a select group of students from San Francisco State University, University of California at Davis, San Joaquin Delta College, San Jose State University, University of California at Berkeley, and California State University at Hayward (*Philippine News* 1983). It was found that 77.2 percent of the respondents had parents who spoke a language other than English at home: 57 percent of the students spoke a Philippine language; 46 percent of those who claimed they could speak a Philippine language spoke Tagalog, and 16.5 percent spoke Ilocano.

The different proportions of speakers of a non-English language among parents and the students may suggest that, first, the parents were primarily Filipino immigrants; and second, the children, living in an English environment, felt a diminishing link to the ethnic language. The findings might also imply that the parents themselves did not feel a compelling need for retention of the Filipino language.

In a study of normative language usage of 34 multilingual Filipino high school students in San Jose, California (Dar 1981), the following language use patterns are found:

I. In intimacy-related speech situations involving family and friendship
  A. There is an aggregate tendency toward equal use of English and Philippine languages. There are, however, finer differences if language use within each domain is examined separately. The Philippine languages tend to be more frequently used with parents; with friends, however, there is a tendency to use either English and the ethnic language equally, or to use more English.
  B. There is an aggregate tendency toward equal use of Tagalog and one's vernacular (if it is not Tagalog). Again, the vernacular is favored with parents, while equal use is favored among friends.

II. In status-related situations involving religion, education, and employment
  A. There is a tendency toward the use of more English than Philippine languages.
  B. There is a tendency toward equal use of Tagalog and the vernacular.

Given the above picture of language use patterns among Filipino Americans, what are the prospects for shift to English and for maintenance of the ethnic languages?

FACTORS FAVORING SHIFT TO ENGLISH

A number of factors encourage the shift to English. As mentioned before, the Philippines' former colonial status as well as its official bilingual policy could be significant determinants of Filipino Americans' relationship with English. The American presence—political, military (naval bases), economic, as well as cultural—continues to be strong in the islands. Thus a Filipino emigrant to the United States typically would have had more exposure to American culture as well as the English language than many other Asian immigrants.

This is reflected not only in the Filipino immigrant's somewhat faster and smoother transition into American life (Min 1986–7), but also in the fact that toward the second (i.e., American-born) generation, Filipino immigrant parents are less likely to have a negative attitude regarding their children's assimilation, of which the shift to English is a major component and probably the most potent visible symbol. It has been pointed out that the Filipino American community does not attach as much stigma to Americanization as many other Asian groups; "the greatest source of pride among many Filipino parents is to have their children speak English without an accent," notes one instructor of Tagalog at a community college (interview with Tony Guinan, San Francisco City College; Charlesworth 1987).

Interracial marriage to native English speakers, which is another measure of assimilation according to many sociologists, may also be a contributing factor in the Filipino American community's shift to English. The predominance of male immigrants during the earlier period and female ones later has made mixed marriages more common among Filipino Americans than other Asian groups in the United States (U.S. Bureau of the Census 1982). The high status of female Filipino immigrants in contrast to native men, again making interracial marriages more likely, may be another factor in language shift. (It should not be forgotten, however, that in California, antimiscegenation laws forbidding marriage between Filipinos and whites were not abolished until 1948; see Melendy 1976.)

Some writers note weak community cohesion among Filipinos in the United States; this may lead to further shift to English. Rabaya (1971) suggests that "lack of unity began in the first half of the century"; unlike other Asians, Filipinos were not excluded by law, and they did not develop "the solidarity that racial identity can bring in such a situation." Min (1986–7), comparing Filipino Americans with Korean Americans, states that "Filipino immigrants do not maintain the same level of non-kin solidarity. There is a general consensus among researchers that Filipino community organizations suffer from conflicts, disunity, and regionalism." Of course, standards of cohesion are relative. There are many social and political organizations among Filipino Americans, some 400 in California alone by one count (interview with Ms. Belen, instructor of Pilipino, San Francisco City College; Charlesworth 1987). Still, English remains a lingua franca (the other being Pilipino) in these groups if members do not speak a uniform ethnic language.

If the above observations on the community are true, one would expect the Filipino American community to show fewer institutional efforts to maintain their ethnic languages than other Asian groups. This speculation is borne out in a nationwide survey of community resources for ethnic language maintenance (Fishman 1985). The researchers list six items for Tagalog and two for Ilocano under "broadcasting (radio and TV)"; three items for Tagalog and one for Ilocano under "local religious units"; and no publication or language school for either language. While the researchers caution that all the numbers given are probably serious undercounts, one cannot help noticing the sharp contrast between Filipinos and other Asian American groups: not only the older, more established groups like the Chinese or Japanese, but also newcomers like the Vietnamese or Laotians.

As for "formal" resources, the difficulty of implementing bilingual education in the public schools accelerates the shift to English. Depending on an immigrant child's language background in the Philippines, Pilipino may or may not be his or her mother tongue.

> If bilingual education is a transitional step [to English dominance or even monolingualism], there is some justification for the use of Philippine languages other than Tagalog. However, it should be noted that this approach failed to succeed [sic] in the Philippines, because of the lack of curriculum materials in the various languages, a problem in the United States also (Beebe and Beebe 1981:333).

Pilipino/Tagalog is the only Philippine language in which curriculum materials of a reasonable quantity and quality are available, but these are primarily designed for children in the home country, which creates problems with their cultural content, pacing, and so on. Even if the materials are suitable, problems such as staffing and opposition from the mainstream community still exist. Finally, of course, transitional bilingual education in the United States is almost synonymous with eventual loss of the ethnic language. Yet the Filipino American community does not seem to support maintenance bilingual education very strongly. One observer notes: "Filipinos want a transitional bilingual education, unlike Chinese or Spanish who want education in the mother tongue and to learn English later" (interview with Ross A. Quema, Principal, Filipino Education Center, San Francisco; Charlesworth 1987).

On the whole, one can safely say that shift to English among Filipino Americans is strongly favored by various sociolinguistic factors. A projection of survival potential for 37 ethnic languages in the United States (both Asian and non-Asian), based on three different sets of criteria, ranks Tagalog as 12th, 37th, and 37th, respectively (Fishman 1985:161–166).

FACTORS FAVORING MAINTENANCE OF PHILIPPINE LANGUAGES

On the other hand, the trend toward shift to English is counteracted to a certain extent by a number of factors favoring ethnic language maintenance.

The picture for the survival of Philippine languages seems brighter in Hawaii than on some parts of the mainland. In the earlier period of Filipino immigration to Hawaii, the predominantly Ilocano-speaking community was relatively retentive of its ethnic language because of its large size, prevailing attitude of transiency, and isolation from the rest of the population (Reinecke 1969). So far, one ethnic periodical, *Hawaii Filipino News,* has survived; it occasionally uses one of the Philippine languages. The University of Hawaii Philippine Language and Culture Club publishes *Ani,* which prints articles in Ilocano and Tagalog. Ilocano and Tagalog, with English, are most frequently heard on radio station KISA (Teodoro 1981). The same languages are also heard on the radio station KPOI and regular and special television programs. Pinoy TV, which is aired on weekends, features interviews with guests on special topics and replays of television programs in the Philippines.

Leaving the discussion of Hawaii now, we might examine a number of general factors encouraging retention.

First, the language legacy from the Philippines could cut both ways: while it contributes to ethnic language loss, the Filipinos' long-standing and close relationship with English also means that code-switching is widely accepted. Pilipino's openness to borrowing means flexibility in its new setting, which in turn spares Filipino Americans the necessity of giving up their native language completely while they acquire English.

While regionalism is a fact of the Filipino American community, various community organizations based on province or region of origin do provide a chance for Filipino Americans to continue to speak their ethnic languages by sponsoring cultural activities, such as celebration of Philippine Independence Day, picnics, and folk festivals. Even for families who have lost the ethnic language, such social interactions maintain ethnic pride and cultural interest. In the future, some members of the younger generation may decide to reconnect to their heritage by studying their ethnic language as a second language.

In this context, we might note that Pilipino, compared to the other Philippine vernaculars, has the best chance for survival in the United States because of its status as lingua franca. In community organizations where several Filipino language groups mix, communication typically takes place in both English and Pilipino.

Retention of Pilipino, which is the main language of the mass media (Kaplan 1982), may also be reinforced by technological advances: an increasing number of videotape rental establishments import movies using Pilipino. Thus even if the local Filipino population cannot support a theater to show movies, Filipino Americans can still enjoy exposure to both the language and culture of their homelands by watching videotapes at home.

Continued immigration from the Philippines, of course, replenishes the pool of speakers of Philippine languages. While individuals may confirm the trend of attrition, the community taken as a whole may still retain the ethnic languages to a certain extent. As immigration increases, the geographic concentration of Filipino Americans will also increase, providing an environment that slows the shift to English. In addition, the ease and affordability of modern air travel means that immigration is no longer the often one-way process it used to be for the "old-timers." Immigrants can maintain contact with the home country by visiting the islands more frequently, which aids in language retention.

Finally, the recent turn of political events may well have repercussions for Filipino American language maintenance. The overthrow of the Marcos dictatorship and the "bloodless revolution" of Corazon Aquino have created a greater sense of Filipino pride; this in turn enhances the prestige of Pilipino, which may gradually enter domains formerly reserved for English. If future Filipino immigrants arrive in America with less dependence on English, it is possible that the picture for language maintenance may change (interview with Dr. Jose Icasiano, Counselor, San Francisco City College; Charlesworth 1987).

EXPLORING THE IDEAS

1. Galang points out that while the early Filipino immigrants were predominantly young males of rural origin with limited English-speaking ability, recent immigrants are much more diverse in age as well as in economic and educational background, with some familiarity with English. Also, the current Filipino population is predominantly foreign-born, with nearly half of the ethnic group residing in California.

In what ways do you think each of the characteristics listed above is likely to affect the language retention and language loss of the contemporary Filipino community?

2. Galang points out that the use of English in the Philippines is restricted to certain domains such as international negotiations, academia, and journals.

How might the fact that an immigrant arrives with this type of exposure to English affect his or her language use in the United States?

3. Galang notes that Filipino Americans share a unique experience with Puerto Ricans in having experienced the United States' English language policies in their homeland.

After reading Zentella's article on the language situation of Puerto Ricans, discuss other similarities that you see between Filipino Americans and Puerto Ricans.

APPLYING THE IDEAS

1. Galang cites several references on features of the Filipino languages. Among them is Li (1983), who emphasizes how markedly different the major Filipino languages are from English, in that they are verb-initial with the topic of the sentence not necessarily corresponding to the subject of an English sentence.

Research the linguistic features of the Filipino languages. You might begin with the sources cited in the article: Ramos (1971), Li (1983), and Beebe and Beebe (1981).

2. Galang points out that the Philippines has a complex language history that has contributed to changes in the language policies of the country.

Research the language policies of two nations of your choice. It might be instructive to choose one recently established Third World nation and one Western industrialized nation with a significant population of linguistic minorities (either indigenous or immigrant). The following questions might be useful when contrasting the language policies of these countries:

Is there a designated official language? (Or are there designated official languages?) What kind of protection or promotion is accorded the official language(s)? How much tolerance is granted to the ethnic languages of the minorities? Is there a centralized government agency that deals with language issues?

3. Galang cites Min's (1986–7) conclusion that "there is a general consensus among researchers that Filipino community organizations suffer from conflict, disunity, and regionalism."

If a Filipino American community group exists in your area, visit their center to determine whether or not there are conflicts and regionalism within the organization and, if so, why they exist. Pay particular attention to how English and the various Filipino languages are used in the organization.

4. Galang refers to the Rizal and Iloilo II experiments on the use of English and vernacular languages in the schools.

Research the methods and findings of these two studies and the way in which they have influenced bilingual educational policies in the Philippines.

SUGGESTED READINGS

Gonzalez (1980) recounts the Philippines' continuing search for a national language, which is one of the factors that complicate the language situation in the country.

LLamzon (1978) presents summaries of the basic structures of 25 indigenous languages of the Philippines as well as their ethnographic contexts.

Beebe and Beebe (1981) describe the ways in which Filipino Americans are similar to and different from other Asian minorities in the United States in terms of their background and current status.

Lopez (1982) cites census data on the language and demographic characteristics of the growing number of Filipinos in the United States in order to indicate patterns in the group's language shift and maintenance.

Kim (1978) presents demographic and socioeconomic characteristics of two Filipino samples in different settings.

REFERENCES

Azores, T. 1986–7. Educational attainment and upward mobility: Prospects for Filipino Americans. *Amerasia Journal* 13:1, 39–52.

Beebe, J. and M. Beebe 1981. The Filipinos: A special case. In C. A. Ferguson and S. B. Heath, (eds.), *Language in the U.S.* Cambridge: Cambridge University Press. 322–338.

Board of National Education. 1958. *General Education Policies*. Quezon City: Phoenix Press.

Bogardus, E. S. 1976. Anti-Filipino race riots. In J. Quinsaat (ed.), *Letters in Exile: An Introductory Reader on the History of Pilipinos in America*. Los Angeles: Asian American Studies Center, University of California, Los Angeles, 51–62.

Bulosan, C. 1943. *America Is in the Heart*. Seattle: University of Washington Press.

Cabezas, A., L. H. Shinagawa, and G. Kawaguchi. 1986–7. New inquiries into the socioeconomic status of Pilipino Americans in California. *Amerasia Journal* 13:1, 1–21.

Cabezas, A. and G. Kawaguchi. 1987. Continuing explorations of Asian American income inequality: Labor market segmentation vs. The human capital model. Paper presented at the Fourth Asian American Studies Conference of the Association of Asian American Studies, San Francisco State University, San Francisco, CA. March 19–21.

Castelo, L. M. 1963. Tense sequence—A problem for advanced Tagalog students in English. *Language Learning* 13:3–4, 211–216.

Catapusan, B. T. 1940. The social adjustment of Filipinos in the United States. Thesis, University of Southern California.

Charlesworth, J. 1987. The Filipino American community: Language maintenance or shift. Unpublished paper, San Francisco State University.

Clifford, M. D. 1954. Filipino immigration to Hawaii. Thesis, University of Hawaii.

Coloma, C. P. 1939. A study of the Filipino repatriation movement. Thesis, University of Southern California.

Constantino, E. 1971. Tagalog and other major languages of the Philippines. In T. A. Sebeok (ed.), *Current Trends in Linguistics* Vol. 8. The Hague: Mouton.

Dar, R. 1981. Language usage among multilingual Filipino high school students in San Jose, California. Ph.D. dissertation, University of San Francisco.

Department of Education and Culture. 1974. *Implementing Guidelines for the Policy in Bilingual Education*. Department Order No. 25. [The Philippines]

Fishman, J. A. 1985. Mother-tongue claiming in the United States since 1960: Trends and correlates. In J. A. Fishman (ed.), *The Rise and Fall of the Ethnic Revival: Perspectives on Language and Ethnicity*. Berlin: Mouton. 107–176.

Gonzalez, A. B. 1980. *Language Nationalism: The Philippine Experience Thus Far*. Quezon City: Ateneo de Manila University Press.

Gonzalez, A. B. 1982. Three styles of written Philippine English of the mass media. In J. Pride (ed.), *New Englishes*. Rowley, MA: Newbury House, 212–226.

Kaplan, R. B. 1982. The language situation in the Philippines. The *Linguistic Reporter* 24:5, 1–4.

Kim, B. C. 1978. *The Asian Americans: Changing Patterns, Changing Needs*. Montclair, NJ: Association of Korean Christian Scholars in North America, Inc.

Laygo, T. M. 1977. *What is Filipino?* Berkeley, CA: Asian American Bilingual Center.

Li, C. 1983. The basic grammatical structures of selected Asian languages and English. In M. Chu-Chang and V. Rodriguez (eds.), *Asian- and Pacific-American Perspectives in Bilingual Education: Comparative Research*. New York: Teachers College Press, 3–30.

Llamzon, T. A. 1978. *Handbook of Philippine Language Groups*. Quezon City: Ataneo de Manila University Press.

Llamzon, T. A. 1986. Life cycle of new Englishes: Restriction phase of Filipino English. *English World-Wide* 7:1, 101–125.

Lopez, D. 1982. *Language Maintenance and Shift in the United States: The Basic Patterns and Their Social Implications*, Vol. IV: *Asian Languages*. Los Alamitos, CA: National Center for Bilingual Research.

Lott, J. T. 1980. Migration of a mentality: The Pilipino community. In R. Endo, S.

Sue and N. Wagner (eds.), *Asian Americans: Social and Psychological Perspectives*. [Ben Lomond, CA:] Science and Behavior Books. 132–140.

McFarland, C. 1980. *A Linguistic Atlas of the Philippines*. Tokyo, Japan: Institute for the Study of Languages and Cultures of Asia and Africa.

Macaranas, F. M. 1983. Socioeconomic issues affecting the education of minority groups: The case of Filipino Americans. In D. T. Nakanishi and M. Hirano-Nakanishi (eds.), *The Education of Asian and Pacific Americans: Historical Perspectives and Prescriptions for the Future*. Phoenix, AZ: Oryx Press, 65–102.

Melendy, H. B. 1976. Filipinos in the United States. In E. Gee (ed.), *Counterpoint: Perspectives on Asian America*. Los Angeles, CA: Asian American Studies Center. University of California, Los Angeles.

Melendy, H. 1977. *Asians in America: Filipinos, Koreans and East Indians*. Boston, MA: Twayne.

Min, P. G. 1986–7. Filipino and Korean immigrants in small business: A comparative analysis. *Amerasia Journal* 13:1, 53–71.

Morales, R. F. 1976. Pilipino Americans. *Civil Rights Digest*. 9:1, 30–32.

Morales, R. E. 1986–7. Pilipino American studies: A promise and an unfinished agenda. *Amerasia Journal* 13:1, 119–124.

National Census and Statistics Office. 1978. *1975 Integrated Census of the Population and its Economic Activities: Population: Philippines*. Manila: National Census and Statistics Office.

National Census and Statistics Office 1983. *1980 Census of Population and Housing: Philippines*. Manila: National Census and Statistics Office.

Obando, A. B. 1936. A Study of the problems of Filipino students in the United States. Thesis, University of Southern California.

Otanes, F. T. 1974. Some notes on the educational backgrounds of immigrant Filipino children. Talk given to Operation Manong Volunteers, Honolulu, Hawaii. Unpublished.

Pascasio, E. M. 1961. A comparative study: Predicting interference and facilitation for Tagalog speakers in learning English noun-head modification patterns. *Language Learning* 11:1–2, 77–84.

Pascasio, E. M. 1983–4. Philippine bilingualism and code switching. *Philippine Journal of Linguistics* 14–15, 122–134.

Philippine News. 1983. Attitudes of Filipino-American college students. March 22:12.

Posadas, B. M. 1986-7. At a crossroad: Filipino American history and the old-timers' generation. *Amerasia Journal* 13:1, 85–97.

Rabaya, V. 1971. Filipino immigration: The creation of a new social problem. In A. Tachiki, E. Wong, F. Odo and B. Wong (eds.), *Roots: An Asian American Reader* Los Angeles, CA: Asian American Studies Center: University of California, Los Angeles.

Ramos, T. V. 1971 *Tagalog Structure*. Honolulu, HI: University of Hawaii Press.

Ramos, T. V. 1979. Studies in Filipino second language acquisition. Paper presented at the First Summer Institute for Educational Research on Asian Americans sponsored by the Asian American Bilingual Center at the University of California, Berkeley. July 5–20.

Reinecke, J. E. 1969. *Language and Dialect in Hawaii: A Sociolinguistic History to 1935*. Honolulu, HI: University of Hawaii Press.

Republika ng Pilipinas. 1986. Ang konstitusyon ng Republika ng Pilipinas. Manila: Merriam and Webster, Inc.

Schwab, W. 1955. Some structural problems for Tagalog students in English. *Language Learning* 6:1–2, 68–72.

Sibayan, B. P. 1975. Survey of language use and attitudes towards language in the Philippines. In S. Ohannessian, C. A. Ferguson and E. C. Polome (eds.), *Language Surveys in Developing Nations: Papers and Reports on Sociolinguistic Surveys*. Arlington, VA: Center for Applied Linguistics. 115–135.

Suzuki, B. H. 1983. The education of Asian and Pacific Americans: An introductory overview. In D. T. Nakanishi and M. Hirano-Nakanishi (eds.), *The Education of Asian and Pacific Americans: Historical Perspectives and Prescriptions for the Future*. Phoenix, AZ: Oryx, 1–13.

Tatlonghari, M. A. 1984. Miscue analysis in an ESL context. *RELC Journal* 15:2, 44–60.

Teodoro, L. V., Jr. (ed.). 1981. *Out of This Struggle: The Filipinos in Hawaii*. Honolulu, HI: University of Hawaii Press.

Tsang, S. and L. C. Wing. 1985. *Beyond Angel Island: The Education of Asian Americans*. New York: Clearinghouse on Urban Education.

U. S. Bureau of the Census. 1976. Language usage in the U.S.: July 1975. In *Current Population Reports, series P-23 (60)*. Washington, D.C.: U.S. Bureau of the Census.

U.S. Bureau of the Census. 1982. Ancestry and language in the United States: November 1979. In *Current Population Reports,* Series P-23 (116). Washington, D.C.: U.S. Bureau of the Census.

Vallangca, R. V. 1977. *Pinoy: The First Wave*. San Francisco: Strawberry Hill Press.

Veltman, C. 1983. *Language Shift in the United States*. Berlin: Mouton.

CHAPTER

9

The Language Situation of Korean Americans

Bok-Lim Kim

AN OVERVIEW OF KOREANS IN AMERICA

As visible minorities go in America, Korean Americans are not a particularly large group, although their growth in the past decade and a half has forced many politicians, government policy makers, and the public media to take notice. Recognition of Korean Americans as a distinct and important Asian American group in the United States is quite recent. Until the mid-1970s, public awareness and interest in Korean Americans were minimal; in fact, it was not until the 1970 census that they were tallied separately from "other Asians."

This changed as Koreans began to emigrate in large numbers following the enactment of the 1965 Immigration and Naturalization Act. In 1980, the Census showed 354,593 Korean Americans in the United States, a 417 percent increase over the 1970 Census figure (Gardner, Robey and Smith 1985). However, this numerical increase alone is not the only reason for increased interest in Korean Americans in the United States. During this same period, Korea has undergone rapid economic growth, accompanied by a rise in its technological level and an increase in its industrial capacity. Today, Korea is no longer a small, war-ravaged country but a major economic and political force in the Far East that is important to U.S. interests, including playing a major role in U.S. military strategy in the region.

Connected with this growth, Korea has entered the American consciousness in a number of ways. The American media regularly report happenings in Korea, and the American public hears ads for Hyundai cars and buys other Korean products daily. In the past decade, increasing numbers of U.S. firms have gone to Korea to pursue business opportunities.

Closer to home, media coverage of Korean Americans and their communities is also noteworthy.[1] Items commonly reported include the thriving ethnic businesses in Los Angeles' Koreatown, the academic success of Korean American students (along with other Asian Americans), and vignettes of hardworking fruit vendors on the streets of New York. On a more somber note, the media also report growing tension between Korean immigrant merchants and the residents of inner city ghettos.

On a more personal level, many Americans have contact with Korean Americans as classmates at all levels of school, including colleges and universities. Likewise, the adult population have face-to-face contacts with Korean Americans as co-workers, and in customer–client relationships. A rapidly growing number of Korean restaurants and food stores have acquainted Americans in major cities with Korean cuisine and food products.

However, in spite of this increased exposure and greater contact with Korean Americans and with the products of Korean culture, there are important information gaps. Because the growth of the Korean population is so recent, it can be very difficult to find out who the Korean Americans are, where they live, how long they have been in the United States, why they emigrated, and what their language and culture are like. This is basic contextual information that most American teachers would be able to supply for older immigrant groups (for example, the Irish, Italians, or Germans), and it is information essential for the classroom teacher who is teaching Korean American children, or who will be called upon to do so in the near future because of the rapid expansion of this group.

This chapter is divided into three sections. First, it provides an overview of the social, political, and economic context of Korean immigration to the United States, reviews immigration patterns, and summarizes the demographic characteristics of Korean Americans today. Second, it provides a brief summary of features of the Korean language that could affect Korean students' acquisition of English. Finally, it discusses social and cultural factors in the Korean American community that may support or undermine their acquisition and use of English.

The Socioeconomic and Political Context of Korean Immigration

Korea has nearly 2,000 years of written history, but until nearly the turn of the twentieth century it was known as the "Hermit Kingdom of Asia."[2] To emigrate from such a nation, the first wave of Koreans must have had compelling reasons; indeed, severe famine, political instability, and social unrest left much of the population in dire poverty and desperation. During a brief period of early emigration between 1903 and 1905, some 65 shiploads of Koreans arrived in Hawaii to work in the sugar-cane fields as contract laborers. Altogether, 7,226 Koreans, mostly young bachelors (but including 637 women and 541 children) arrived during this period (Choi 1979).

This early emigration came to a halt abruptly, in part because of the

Korean government's alarm over the harsh working conditions to which its people were subjected in Hawaii and Mexico, but also because of the annexation of Korea by Japan in 1910 (Yun 1977). The Japanese government did not want Korean immigrants to be in competition with Japanese workers already in Hawaii, and also wanted to have as much cheap Korean labor available as possible to carry out its expansionist programs in Korea (Yun 1977).

Between 1910 and 1924, about 1,100 "picture brides" came to the United States to marry Korean men (Chai 1987). (Under the "picture bride" system, marriages were arranged on the basis of an exchange of pictures and other information between the man and the woman.) But after 1906 almost the only other Korean immigrants were a small number of students and political exiles (Lyu 1977). Noteworthy among these students and exiles were those who led the Korean independence movement activities in Hawaii and on the west coast of the United States (Lyu 1977). Many Korean immigrants who were not otherwise political became involved in this movement and contributed substantially through fundraising and other activities until Korean independence was achieved in 1945. Sung-Man Rhee, who became the first president of the Republic of South Korea, was one of the leaders of this movement.

During and after the Korean War, which began in 1950, two special groups of immigrants began to arrive in the United States. These were the "war orphans," who were adopted transracially by parents who were U.S. citizens, and "war brides," who married American soldiers in Korea (Kim 1977). According to Immigration and Naturalization Service Annual Reports, between 1951 and 1964 there were about 14,000 Korean immigrants, most of whom belonged to one of these groups.

In this same period, a small number of Korean students came to study in U.S. colleges and universities, and a number of Korean doctors also came for further medical training in U.S. hospitals. Although their total number was small (about 2,000), this group came to play an important leadership role in Korea. Many of them returned to Korea, where they have contributed significantly to such areas as economic planning, scientific and technological research and development, university teaching, and educational policy making. The merit of study abroad for advanced training is well recognized in Korea; therefore, the government, industry, and private citizens continue to send their young people to the United States and to European countries.

The passage of the Immigration and Naturalization Act of 1965 ushered in a new era of racial and ethnic equality in American immigration policy.[3] For the first time, Koreans and other Asians were placed on an equal footing with northern Europeans for immigration purposes. A floodgate was opened, and there has been a 10–12-fold increase in the number of Korean and other Asian immigrants since 1965.

One may ask why, given the relatively prosperous recent history of Korea, so many from the Hermit Kingdom still want to emigrate to America. The answer can be found by studying national and international events since the end of World War II. The end of the war brought the long-awaited liberation of Korea from the yoke of Japanese colonialism; however, it also brought the division of the country into North and South Korea along the 38th parallel, at the hands of the United States and the Soviet Union. The original purpose on the part of the United States may have been political expediency: to divide with the Soviet Union the task of demilitarizing the defeated Japanese troops remaining in Korea. But for Korea, the tragic consequences of this division, in human, economic, and political terms, continue down to the present day. A small, homogeneous nation was divided into two warring camps: a democratic, capitalistic system in the south and a communist system in the north.

In 1948, the new Republic of South Korea was founded and free elections were held; in that same year, communist North Korea established the People's Republic of Korea. Two years after the founding of South Korea, it was invaded by North Korea. The resulting war destroyed cities and ravaged the countrysides of both North and South Korea, killing and maining millions of combatants and civilians, and producing millions of refugees. American military involvement was heavy and resulted in nearly 158,000 U.S. casualties (World Almanac and Book of Facts 1985). This tragic war ended in an uneasy truce in 1953, with Korea still divided. Along the demilitarized zone of the 38th parallel, both sides continue a vigilant watch while preparing for another war.

The war and the division have touched every segment of Korean society and have left indelible lessons for all Koreans. They have learned that Korea can no longer remain a "hermit kingdom." It must modernize and educate its citizens. The government and its citizens must be informed and participate actively in world events and international affairs, whether in the political, economic, or scientific arenas. Korea learned that as a small nation, it must develop and use its national resources (including human resources) wisely and shrewdly, if it is to survive and enjoy self-determination of its destiny.

This long answer helps to explain why Koreans in the 1980s are so eager to study abroad, to travel, and to emigrate to the United States and other Western countries.

The extensive exposure to and contacts with the United States through the Korean conflict and subsequent U.S. aid and exchange programs have meant that many South Koreans view the United States in a positive light. Thus, when the 1965 Immigration and Naturalization Act went into effect, Koreans were ready to take advantage of the increased immigration opportunities to the United States.

Demographic Characteristics of Korean Americans

The 1980 U.S. Census reported a total of 354,593 Korean Americans, which represented an increase of 417 percent over the 1970 Census figure of 70,510. Since that time, an additional, 220,000 Korean immigrants have entered the United States.[4] Gardner, Robey and Smith (1985) estimate that in 1985 there were 542,400 Korean Americans in the United States.

Given that this population has nearly doubled between 1980 and 1987, using the 1980 Census data to describe Korean Americans today is likely to be subject to many inaccuracies. Nevertheless, since the 1980 Census is the only reliable source of information available, it will be used here to describe the demographic and socioeconomic status of Korean Americans.

Nativity, Sex, and Age Distribution. Of the Korean Americans enumerated in 1980, 82 percent were foreign-born, reflecting the relatively recent arrival of the group and the small population base of native-born Korean Americans. The 1980 Census also found Korean Americans to be a young group: the median age was 26 years for men and 27 for women. The age distribution, which is of particular interest in this chapter, was as follows:

Under 5 years: 10.5 percent

5–19 years: 29 percent

20–44 years: 47 percent

45–64 years: 10 percent

65 years and older: 2.5 percent

This age distribution is in marked contrast to that of the white majority population, which is much more even. For example, among the white majority, 11 percent are 65 years of age or older.

There are more women than men (58 percent versus 42 percent) among Korean Americans, in marked contrast to the situation among the early Korean immigrants. Over the last three decades, the sex ratio of Korean Americans has favored females, primarily due to the immigration of young female children adopted by American parents and young, interracially married Korean women. While a trend toward a more balanced sex ratio is evident among the most recent immigrants, the effect of the past imbalance continues to be reflected in the present figures.

Geographic Distribution. The 1980 Census indicated that Korean Americans were urban dwellers: 93 percent lived in cities, while only 7 percent lived in rural areas. They were more widely dispersed among all regions of the United States than any other Asian group. The largest number, 43.4 percent, lived in western states such as California and Hawaii; of the remainder, 19.2 percent lived in the Northeast, 17.5 percent in the north central region, and 19.9 percent in the southern region.

The annual reports of the Immigration and Naturalization Service through 1977 indicate that this pattern of scattered settlement has long been characteristic of Korean immigrants. However, the reports also show secondary migration into such large metropolitan areas as Los Angeles, Chicago, New York City, the District of Columbia, San Francisco, and Honolulu.

Educational Attainment. In 1980, 37.2 percent of Korean Americans had completed 4 or more years of college education; this compares with 17.3 percent of the white population. When men and women are disaggregated, we find that fully 52.4 percent of Korean American men, but only 22 percent of Korean American women, have completed 4 or more years of college. Overall, the Korean Americans are well educated: fully 90 percent of men and 70 percent of women have at least a high school education. The vast majority of 16–19-year-olds are in school, as are over half of the 20 and 21-year-olds and a third of those aged 22–24 (reflecting college enrollments).

Such high educational achievement, however, does not readily translate into high-status and high-paying occupations for Korean Americans. For one thing, most Korean Americans received their college education before they emigrated. Only one third of them received any of their education in the United States. Since they are relatively recent immigrants, their English proficiency level is low, while their unfamiliarity with American social structures and their discomfort in functioning in American society are high. Finally, the different job market and job requirements in the United States make the transfer of Korean education and work experience to the American situation difficult and uncertain.

Employment, Income, and Household Size. In 1980, there were 236,653 Korean Americans 16 years of age and older, of whom 64 percent were employed in the labor force. In this age group, most of the young people are attending school (95 percent of 16 and 17-year-olds, 78 percent of 18 and 19-year-olds, 55 percent of 20 and 21-year-olds, and 30.5 percent of 22 to 24-year-olds) and are therefore out of the labor force. This means that the overall figure represents a very high labor force participation by Korean American adults. There were 140,748 employed Korean Americans, distributed in a number of fields:

Managerial, professional, specialty occupations: 25 percent

Technical and sales occupations: 27.5 percent

Service occupations: 16.6 percent

Semiskilled occupations and common laborers: 20.5 percent

Precision and skilled occupations: 9.9 percent

Farming and fisheries: 0.9 percent

Detailed studies of Korean American communities in Chicago and Los Angeles also indicated high labor force participation (87–95 percent for men and 69–74 percent for women).[5]

In spite of their high educational achievements, a majority of Korean immigrants are employed at middle-level positions such as proprietors and skilled and semiskilled labor. In the Korean American community there is a consensus that many immigrants suffer from underemployment. It is not uncommon to find college-educated Korean immigrants working as filling station attendants or as seamstresses in garment factories.

According to the 1980 Census, median household income for Korean Americans was $18,145 and mean income was $22,537. Thirteen percent of Korean American households were living below the poverty level. When one considers the large proportion of two-wage-earner families among Korean Americans, it becomes clear that these income figures often represent the combined low earnings of two relatively well-educated Korean Americans. In this respect, Korean Americans are not alone. Kan and Liu, who used 1980 Census data to compare the educational status of major Asian American groups with that of the majority white population and with the two largest minority groups (blacks and Hispanics), found that "for many Asian Americans, the economic rewards of education are more limited than they are for majority individuals and non-Asian minority groups" (Kan and Liu 1986:1).

The median household size for Korean Americans in 1980 was 3.8 persons, suggesting that most are nuclear families.

Religious Preferences. Korean immigrants are predominantly Christian: 60 percent are Protestant, 10 percent are Catholic, and about 8 percent are Buddhist (Kim, Sawdey and Meihoefer, 1980:60). This contrasts markedly with the population of South Korea, where only 12 percent are Christians (Korean Overseas Information Service 1982). It has been noted by many community leaders and in many studies that religious institutions in Korean American communities have many roles beyond the usual spiritual ones.[6] These institutions provide social and emotional support and informal help, and they serve, both directly and indirectly, as acculturation agents, at the same time that they help preserve traditional values and the Korean heritage.

In summary, the Korean immigrants came to the United States in several waves. The first group came as contract laborers betwen 1903 and 1905; between 1905 and 1950 a small number of Koreans came as students, exiles, or "picture brides." The third period, which started in 1950, shows a sizable number of "war orphans" and "war brides" entering the United States as dependents of U.S. citizens. This group is still present in the Korean American population, but is overshadowed by the large influx of Koreans who are entering the United States as professional or skilled workers or as relatives of Korean Americans. This fourth wave of Korean immigrants began with the reforms brought about by the 1965 Immigration and Naturalization Act.

Even with the recent, rapid increases, Korean Americans are not a particularly large group and, until quite recently, were largely invisible. In general, Korean Americans are well-educated, tend to be underemployed, have arrived in the United States in the last decade and a half, and are culturally still predominantly Korean. This is especially true with regard to language use and attachment to their ethnic values. As a group, Korean Americans display qualities of hard work, rugged individualism, adaptability, self-confidence, and strong faith in the American dream of unlimited opportunity for all (Kim 1983). A skeptic need only take a stroll through one of the vigorous and thriving commercial districts that have grown up in the Koreatowns of several large American cities to gain a forceful impression of these characteristics.

LINGUISTIC AND USAGE FEATURES OF KOREAN

The linguistic features of Korean are of interest to English speakers who have been puzzled by the idiosyncratic English usage of Korean speakers. Classroom teachers in particular have often witnessed certain problems that Korean immigrant students in the upper grades encounter in learning and using English. This section will present a short account of the history and linguistic features of the Korean language, with particular reference to the effect these have on the way in which Korean American immigrants acquire and use English.

The Korean Language

There are over 61 million Korean speakers in the world, the majority of them living in Korea (Bureau of Public Affairs 1983, 1986). Outside of Korea, there are about 3.1 million persons of Korean ancestry, some of whom still retain and use the Korean language (Kim 1980:134). In both North and South Korea, there are a number of regional dialects, which, in spite of unique phonological and grammatical features, are still mutually intelligible. The use of standard Korean in the mass media and in the schools has contributed to a gradual decline in the use of dialects among South Koreans. The traditionally high regard in which Koreans hold education, and compulsory public education through sixth grade, have resulted in a literacy rate of 90 percent in South Korea and 99 percent in North Korea (Bureau of Public Affairs 1983, 1986).

The History of the Language. Korean is classified as a member of the Altaic language family, which also includes Turkish, Mongolian, Japanese, and Manchu.[7] The languages in this family share certain common features, such as vowel harmony and agglutination processes. The former is a phonological feature that requires an agreement between various classes of vowels and the classes of words in which they are used. Agglutination processes result in compound words or linguistic elements composed of simpler elements. The Altaic languages are also characterized by having no grammatical gender, articles, inflections, or relative pronouns. Some of these features are also found in English and many other languages.

Chinese has had a special kind of influence on Korean: although the two belong to different language families, Korean has borrowed extensively from the Chinese vocabulary. Of the more than 160,000 entries in the *Kun Sajeon* (The Grand Korean Dictionary), more than 50 percent are words of Chinese origin. Most of these words deal with abstract or intellectual subjects, whereas native Korean words express mostly concrete or affective meanings. It should be noted that the words of Chinese origin, whether written in the Korean alphabet or in Chinese characters, are an integral part of the Korean language with unique Korean pronunciations. These words were incorporated into Korean in about the same form in which the Chinese used them at the time they were borrowed, although in many instances the pronunciations and meanings of these words have subsequently evolved so that they are now different from the Chinese.

The invention of *Han-gul* (the Korean alphabet) by King Sejong in the fifteenth century must be ranked as the most significant event in the history of the Korean language; for the first time, Korean-speaking people could use their own alphabet to write their language. Before this, Chinese characters were used to write Korean, using a process known as *Idu*.[8] When it was first promulgated, *Han-gul* consisted of 17 consonantal and 11 vowel symbols. Today, after several stages of evolution, *Han-gul* has 19 consonants, 10 simple vowels, and 11 compound vowels.

A Korean syllable consists of three elements: an initial consonant, a middle vowel, and a closing consonant. A syllable cannot be written without a vowel, and thus the middle vowel is indispensable in a syllable. Although *Han-gul* is an alphabet, it is not used in the same way as the English alphabet. *Han-gul* is used to construct syllables, while the English alphabet is used to make up words. Thus, *Han-gul* may be considered as a special type of alphabet. This special use of *Han-gul* can be seen on the printed page, even by a non-Korean speaker: the consonants and vowels of each syllable are "stacked" together in an array, rather than being strung out linearly, as with western alphabets.

A final important element in the history of the Korean language is the impact of the period of Japanese colonization. From 1905 to 1945, Korea was ruled by Japan. All public use of Korean was suppressed, and the media and the educational system used Japanese exclusively. As a result, one finds many Koreans educated during this period who are fluent in written Japanese, but whose written Korean is much less polished, being based solely on their knowledge of Korean as it was spoken in the home during the period of Japanese rule. Following the liberation of Korea in 1945, the reinstitution and promulgation of the Korean language became matters of intense nationalistic pride among Koreans. Thus, although the use of one's native language is almost always an important symbol of ethnic identity, historical circumstances make this particularly true for Koreans today.

The Morphology of Korean.[9] As mentioned earlier, Korean words do not have gender, number, or case. Gender is expressed by a character prefix denoting sex. Number is expressed by adding a particle denoting plurality. Both gender prefixes and number particles are omitted unless they are indispensable to convey a particular meaning. Case is shown by particles know as postpositions. In common, everyday speech, possessive and objective particles tend to be omitted. In careless speech, subjective propositions are also omitted.

Korean Grammar. There are a number of major differences between Korean and English grammar, including word order, subject–verb agreement, the use of honorifics, article use, and noun deletion.

Some examples can help show some of the many differences in word order between Korean and English:

Korean Word Order	*English Word Order*
1. Subject–object–verb I PIANO PLAY	Subject–verb–object I PLAY PIANO
2. Clause–object YOU LEAVE IF	Conjunction–clause IF YOU LEAVE
3. Noun–locative marker HOUSE IN	Preposition (locative marker)–noun IN THE HOUSE
4. Adjective clause–noun I BOUGHT PENCIL	Noun–adjective clause THE PENCIL THAT I BOUGHT
5. Subject–verb . . . question? FROG JUMP?	Auxiliary–subject–verb-? DID THE FROG JUMP?
6. Adverb phrase–verb IN THE MORNING LEFT	Verb–adverb phrase LEFT IN THE MORNING

In Korean, no grammatical agreement is necessary between a third person singular subject and its verb in the present tense, nor is any gender agreement necessary in pronouns. It is easy to see how these differences lead to many difficulties for Koreans learning English, since these forms of agreement are almost the hallmark of correct English. Likewise, learning the usage rules for English articles (e.g., *a* and *the*) is very difficult for Koreans, because Korean has no comparable articles. Another difference between the languages that presents a stumbling block to Koreans learning English is that while Korean often omits subject or object nouns in a sentence, English tends to repeat them to the point of appearing to create extreme redundancy by Korean standards. For example, compare these two sentences:

> ENGLISH: Although I told Sookja not to hit the dog, she hit it.
> KOREAN: I Sookja the dog hit not told although hit.

Major grammatical differences such as these present difficulties for the Korean speaker attempting to master English, since almost any analogies drawn between usage in the two languages will turn out to be "wrong" in English, usually with results that strike an English-speaking listener as "ungrammatical."

Honorifics. There is no stronger expression of the intricate and hierarchical nature of Korean society than in the honorific structure built into the Korean language: it is impossible to speak Korean without denoting the relationships between the speaker and the listener. Korean verbs have different forms, and entirely different words are used, to denote the gradations of respect between the speaker and the addressee, or a third person. For example, the imperative, "Go," can be expressed in several different ways:

Ka!	Beat it! (with contempt)
Kara (Kagoura)	Go! (to an inferior)
Kage	Please go (to an adult inferior)
Kao or Kasio	Please go (to an equal or a stranger)
Kaseyo	Please go (to a superior)
Kasipio	Please go (to someone much superior)

The lack of such explicit and carefully tuned gradations of respect in English is a source of great discomfort to Korean speakers: English always seems to be too familiar or too formal. There are, of course, many subtle ways for an English speaker to express her or his relationship with an addressee, but these are hidden in the complexities of usage, sentence structure, and spoken intonation, rather than being a part of the surface structure of the language. This discomfort over the lack of English honorifics is one reason why Korean immigrants are reluctant to make much use of English in everyday conversation with one another, even though they may have a good command of the language.

Differential Use of Yes and No.[10] Another area of confusion for Korean speakers learning English (and for English speakers listening to them) is in the use of the response words, "Yes" and "No." In English, these response words are used congruently with the status of the fact: yes for affirmative facts, and no for negative facts. In Korean, they are used on the basis of the relationships between the fact and the form of the preceding stimulus sentence (question, command, or statement). In other words, yes is used to denote an affirmative *relationship,* that is, for agreement between the status of the two elements (stimulus and response), while no is used to indicate a negative *relationship* (disagreement) between the two elements.

For example, when the stimulus sentence is affirmative, "Did you eat?" the response word is "Yes, I ate," or "No, I did not eat." But when the stimulus sentence is negative, "Didn't you eat?" the response word would be "No, I did," or "Yes, I didn't." The status of the response words and the supplementary response sentences are independent of each other. When the form of the stimulus sentence is affirmative, there is a formal agreement between the status of the three elements—fact, response word, and supplementary response—and therefore there is no surface difference in response words between Korean and English. On the other hand, when the form of the stimulus sentence is negative, the status of the response word is always in contradiction to that of the fact and the supplementary response sentence. Since response words are such a basic element of everyday conversation, this difference between Korean and English gives rise to many confusions and misunderstandings in cross-cultural communication between speakers of the two languages.

Challenges Facing Korean in the Contemporary World

As we approach the end of the twentieth century, Korean is facing some new challenges in Korea itself. As we have noted, the Korean language is characterized by a blending of Chinese and native vocabulary, and by many structural features that reflect the intricate social relationships of traditional Korean culture. In many ways, this language has become inadequate to deal with the new scientific and technological terms and concepts of the modern era. This calls for new vocabulary, and one finds authorities in every field hurriedly translating or transliterating words from various Western languages for use in technical fields and in the physical and social sciences. There are concerted efforts to establish uniform technical vocabularies in each field; however, it is not unusual to see the same technical term rendered in Korean in several different ways, depending on who translated it.

In summary, it is safe to say that Korean has long since ceased to be the language of a "hermit kingdom." Its traditional native vocabulary and extensive, borrowed Chinese vocabulary are today being enriched and extended through adaptations from Western languages. At the same time, it is facing many challenges as the language of a sizable minority in the United States. For many of these persons, there are compelling reasons to continue to use Korean in many contexts, while there are equally compelling reasons to become more fluent in English, since this is often the key to success in the larger society.

SOCIAL AND CULTURAL FACTORS AFFECTING ENGLISH ACQUISITION

Acquiring a new language in addition to one's native tongue is never simply an exercise in pure learning; many factors determine whether one will find the process exhilarating, mystifying, or disquieting. In this section, we will discuss some of the major factors that seem to affect English acquisition by Korean American immigrants, including individual attitude and behavior toward acculturation, ethnic community involvement, and the work environment. Often one cannot measure people's attitudes and feelings toward so complex a phenomenon as language use by direct means. However, it is possible to observe what people do and say. The degree of ethnic and English language use, participation in various social networks, such as Korean ethnic churches, and frequency of social contacts within these networks can be a useful measure of acculturation and ethnic attachment. In addition, expressed attitudes and opinions about Korean and American cultural traits can serve as indirect measures.

Korean Language Use

One of the most important factors affecting the acculturation of Korean immigrants in the United States is English proficiency. In various surveys conducted among this group, English acquisition was ranked as the highest priority, but also as the most difficult acculturation task, facing Korean Americans.[11] Because of its obvious utility and advantage in the workplace and in American society generally, high English proficiency commands respect and evokes envy among Korean Americans. In the view of many Korean immigrants, high English proficiency is equated with the prestige of high academic achievement and with economic and social success.

Although there is a strong desire among Korean Americans to achieve high English proficiency, this does not easily translate into actual achievement. For one thing, as noted in the preceding section, the drastically different language structures of English and Korean do not lead to easy learning. Second, the immigrants' exposure to English in their home country has mostly been limited to book learning in high school and college; opportunities to use and practice English in Korea are infrequent. Finally, most Korean immigrants work long hours and then often work a second job after commuting home. This hard work, combined with the general stress of adjusting to a new society, leaves little time and energy to attend English classes.

Considering all these factors, it is not suprising that Korean language use among Korean Americans remains high. Adult communication among Korean Americans is almost exclusively in Korean. Several studies have indicated that over three-fourths of spousal communication and a slightly smaller proportion (72 percent) of parent–child communication is in Korean (Kim, Sawdey and Meihoefer 1980; Hurh and Kim 1984). Kim, Sawdey and Meihoefer (1980) reported a low level of English proficiency among the respondents. Over one-third of the men and nearly half of the women indicated that their ability to speak English was "poor" or "not at all." Only one-fifth of the women and one-quarter of the men thought their spoken English was "good" or "fluent."

Those who rated their English speaking ability to be high thought their reading and writing abilities were even higher. These findings confirm the common observation that Korean American's levels of spoken English proficiency are low, in spite of their relatively high educational levels. This means, of course, that their occupational opportunities will tend to be limited to low-status, low-paying jobs that require limited English proficiency. Kim's 1978 study confirms this observation, finding that low English proficiency was positively correlated with low socioeconomic status among Korean immigrants.

The Social Networks of Korean Americans

The majority of Korean Americans are involved in social networks participated in primarily by other Korean Americans; this is true regardless of their socioeconomic status, geographic location, or the size or concentration of the local Korean population. In this discussion, "social network" is defined as the network of relationships in which affective and social exchange takes place in time of crisis and help and mutual support are available. In this sense, an individual's social network may or may not include relationships in the workplace.

The focal point of network contacts for many Korean Americans is the Korean American church. Several studies have highlighted that close to 80 percent of Korean Americans in Chicago and Los Angeles attend weekly services, and over 25 percent of them hold staff (nonpaid) positions in their churches (Kim, Sawdey and Meihoefer 1980; Hurh and Kim 1984). About 60 percent of Korean Americans in these cities report that they attend Protestant churches, while 10 percent are Catholic and 8 percent are Buddhists. As we have noted earlier, this is in contrast to the population in South Korea, which is only about 12 percent Christian.

Korean ethnic churches serve several unique functions in the lives of Korean Americans, most of whom manifest strong ethnic attachment, regardless of the length of their U.S. residence or of their educational or socioeconomic status (Kim, Sawdey and Meihoefer 1980; Hurh and Kim 1984). The Korean church satisfies the specifically religious and spiritual needs of its members through worship and fellowship; however, it also speaks to their psychological needs by providing peace of mind and relief from the anxiety of living in an unfamiliar (and sometimes hostile) culture, and it addresses their social needs by providing a place where friends can always be found.

Most Korean ethnic churches also serve as a means of exchanging information and practical help. Information about opportunities in employment, housing, schooling, and vocational training is exchanged between old-timers and newcomers. Concrete, practical help—such as assistance in filling out complicated English forms, translation and interpretation, and transportation—are provided by ministers and church members. Thus, the church is a mutual aid society as well as a facilitating agent for the acculturation of its members to the host society.

At the same time that it is fulfilling this acculturation function, however, the Korean church also helps to preserve the ethnic culture: the Korean language is used in services and fellowship, and social etiquette and customs are observed through the preservation of hierarchical social relationships and the celebration of ethnic holidays.

In addition to the churches, there are many other voluntary associations in Korean communities. One finds alumni groups composed of graduates from the various Korean schools and universities; student clubs; purely social clubs; and senior citizens' clubs composed exclusively of Korean members. The latter are particularly important in the Korean American community because elderly Korean Americans often cannot depend on the extended families of which they would have been valued members in the home country.

Aside from their affiliations with formal organizations, most Korean Americans living in the larger Korean American metropolitan areas (Los Angeles, New York City, Chicago, Washington, D.C., San Francisco) tend to socialize primarily with other Korean Americans. Hurh and Kim's 1984 study indicated that high proportions of Koreans (75–90 percent) had close kin, neighbors, and friends who were also Korean. More than half of the kin and a third of the neighbors were persons with whom they had daily contact; only a third had white friends, and these were mostly people they had met through the workplace.

Korean American children also have most of their social contacts with other Korean American children. The 1980 study by Kim, Sawdey, and Meihoefer found that 27 percent of Korean American elementary school children in Los Angeles had American best friends at school, and only ten percent had American playmates at home. By contrast, two-thirds of the group had Korean playmates and best friends.[12] This is, of course, in part a reflection of the concentration of Korean Americans in an urban Koreatown area, and it shows that in such areas even the American public school system may not provide much cross-cultural experience for Korean American children.

From all of these discussions, it is clear that the social networks of Korean Americans are largely ethnic in nature. Within these networks, they continue to use the Korean language and maintain Korean cultural characteristics. Rarely do these networks have any integral connections with non-Korean society.

The Work Environment

Examining the occupational status of Korean Americans can help shed some light on their exposure to English in the workplace. As we have mentioned earlier, the vast majority of Korean Americans are part of the full-time workforce. While no direct studies have been done of English use by Korean American workers, some strong inferences can be drawn from what we know about their occupations: most are employed in small shops owned and operated by Koreans or in unskilled or semiskilled service jobs and hence have little opportunity to acquire or improve their English skills on the job. Over half of the men and nearly three-quarters of the women surveyed in the Kim, Sawdey and Meihoefer study (1980) were engaged in such occupations. We observed that wig shops, fast food shops, and 24-hour convenience stores that require only limited English are operated by Korean immigrants. Likewise, Gardner, Robey and Smith (1985) observed that many new Korean immigrants in New York City opted for "commercial occupations" such as greengrocer, also because of the limited English proficiency that such occupations require.

Employment in these low-paying jobs results in a vicious circle for Korean immigrants: because of their limited English, these are the only jobs the immigrants can get, but once the immigrants are so employed, they are locked into a work environment that hinders acquisition and improvement of English. With over half of the Korean American population working in these occupations, we cannot expect the workplace to be a "natural" setting for these immigrants to learn English.

Cultural Ambivalence: Acculturation versus Ethnic Attachment

Aside from direct evidence of cultural attachment (e.g., membership in predominantly Korean social networks, and dominance of Korean language use), one can also gauge the direction of acculturation indirectly by exploring the attitudes and opinions of Korean Americans about Korean and American cultural traits.

In the Kim, Sawdey and Meihoefer study (1980), Korean American parents showed a strong desire that their children retain Korean cultural traits, while at the same time wanting them to adopt seemingly opposite American cultural traits. For example, the overwhelming majority of the parents (99 percent) wanted their children to speak only Korean at home, and a large majority (over 90 percent) wanted their children to learn about Korean history and culture for their own self-identity, as well as to demonstrate such Korean cultural traits as "respecting parents," "being modest," "saving face," and "placing family needs and duties above individual interests." On the other hand, these same parents wanted their children to adopt American cultural traits such as "social assertiveness," "openness and self-disclosure," and "developing greater individuality." An even more contradictory response was that 18.7 percent of the Chicago and 57 percent of the Los Angeles parents wanted their children to use only English at home. Obviously, this is not only a cultural, but a logical, impossibility; it clearly reflects the ambivalence that these parents feel about the acculturation of their children in America. At the same time, 90 percent of the parents approved of their children visiting American friends at home, which suggests a high degree of openness toward the acculturation process.

On a more personal level, two-thirds of the respondents in the Hurh and Kim study (1984) disapproved of intermarriage between Koreans and non-Koreans, citing cultural differences as the main objection. Only one-fifth approved of intermarriage on the grounds that mutual love and understanding could override cultural differences.

We can speculate that the respondents in these studies may simultaneously feel a strong utilitarian pressure to adopt various traits that are important for success and survival in American society and strong social pressures within the ethnic community to retain various cultural traits closely tied to Korean identity.

This ambivalence, manifested in the seemingly contradictory responses in the studies, seems to be fairly representative of the attitudes of the Korean American community in general. One explanation of this ambivalence can be developed by applying the theoretical paradigm advanced by Hurh and Kim (1984). They state that the acculturation of Korean immigrants as a visibly different racial minority is an "adhesive" or additive adaptation:

> . . . adhesive adaptation is one of the major types of ethnic adaptation in which certain aspects of the new culture and social relations with members of the host society are added on to the immigrants' traditional culture and social networks, without replacing or modifying any significant part of the old. . . . For example, Korean immigrants' progressive

adhesive or additive adaptation

> Americanization and their strong ethnic attachment are not mutually exclusive. (Hurh and Kim 1984:162).

They consider this adhesive adaptation to be inevitable for Korean immigrants in the United States, since ethnic segregation is inherent in the American social structure.

Indeed, several factors come together to produce an environment favorable to this adhesive adaptation: the limited adaptive capacities of Korean immigrants (they have a radically different cultural heritage and speak a non-Indo-European language); the fact that the American social structure resists structural assimilation of racial minority groups; the concentration of Koreans in ethnic enclaves, with a continuing, large influx of new immigrants; the nature of political and economic relations between the United States and Korea; and, finally, an unfavorable labor market in the United States that tends to isolate Korean immigrants in low-status, non-English-using jobs.

THE ACCULTURATION OF KOREAN AMERICANS: LANGUAGE AS FOCUS

A number of factors emerge when we consider the situation of Korean Americans, a surprising number of which are related to questions of language use, retention, and acquisition. These factors are of importance both for those studying the Korean American community and its culture, and for those working with Korean American students at any level in the educational system.

It is essential to recognize, first of all, that the cycle of ethnic language retention and English acquisition is different for Korean Americans than it was for earlier immigrant groups. Korean immigrants are faced with learning a language (English) that is completely outside their native language group. There is no overlap of vocabulary between English and Korean, and few analogies of morphology or grammar are of any use to a speaker of one trying to learn the other. By comparison, English shares relatively large amounts of vocabulary, and much common structure, with the Romance and Germanic (and even, to a lesser extent, the Slavic) languages spoken by most earlier immigrant groups.

Additionally, the Korean language reflects, in very specific ways, much of the cultural history of the nation. Its elaborate honorific structure, its unique melded vocabulary of Chinese and native words, and even the memory (living, for many Koreans) of the language as a symbol of resurgent nationalism following the period of Japanese rule all make the Korean language a powerful force in the cultural lives of Korean Americans. The use and retention of Korean may thus have meaning and significance for Korean Americans even more salient than that usually associated with ethnic languages in America. All of these factors point to a different paradigm for acculturation among Korean Americans than has been observed among previous immigrant groups. As Hurh and Kim (1984) have noted, this may be a paradigm of adhesion, in which elements from both cultures are added together and retained, rather than having one set replace the other. In the case of language, this may mean that many Korean Americans will learn English only for functional purposes (to get a better job, to be able to negotiate the government bureaucracy), while retaining Korean for all or nearly all social purposes.

We must also note that language use and English acquisition among Korean Americans are tied into a paradoxical cycle related to education and employment. A number of factors in recent Korean history have resulted in a wave of emigration to the United States composed largely of relatively highly educated persons. This relatively advanced education does not, however, usually include proficiency in spoken English. Thus, a disproportionately large number of these well educated persons are underemployed in the United States, usually in jobs that do not require much English proficiency, or in employment within the (Korean-speaking) ethnic enclaves in the large cities. In either case, the new immigrant will have few opportunities to improve his or her English proficiency, and will thus likely have to remain in this unsuitable employment situation. The end result is that language use and English acquisition, or the lack of it, are closely tied to the economic situation of many Korean Americans, which, while usually not desperate, certainly does not truly reflect their skills and educational attainment.

Within the Korean American household, language retention and acquisition may be significant issues between parent and child. It is clear that, on the one hand, Korean American parents very much want their children to excel in school, and to go on to college and, if at all possible, graduate or professional school. At one level, the parents are quite aware that their children must have strong English skills to achieve this sort of success in America. On the other hand, the parents very much want their children to retain full use of Korean as their language of social intercourse in the Korean American home and community. For many children, this may be an unrealistic expectation, and there is at least some evidence in the Korean American community that it leads to antagonism and frustration between parents and children.

At this stage in the evolution of the Korean Americans as a distinct subculture, it would be difficult to prescribe a complete set of responses to the problems we have identified related to language, ethnicity, socioeconomic status, and identity. However, it is possible to define some of the areas that need to be addressed. Within the Korean American community itself there needs to be greater effort to address the paradox of retaining full use of Korean while acquiring the English proficiency necessary for full employment and social success in the larger society. Likewise, educational and social welfare establishments must make concerted efforts to work with community leaders to develop appropriate interventions to allow Korean Americans to participate in American society in ways that fully reflect their education and skills, while also addressing their need to develop bicultural identities incorporating their language and cultural heritage. This will require acceptance of a different paradigm for acculturation, one in which major Korean and American cultural elements may continue to be held, accepted, and practiced together by Korean Americans for some time to come.

EXPLORING THE IDEAS

1. Kim maintains that for a long time public awareness of Korean Americans in the United States was minimal; however, recently there has been a growing interest in Korean Americans.

First, why do you think Korean Americans have for so long been an invisible minority? Do you agree with Kim that this outlook is changing? What evidence can you cite to support your opinion?

2. Kim points out that Korean products are common today on the American market.

In what ways do you think the increased demand for Korean products as an indication of growing Korean economic competition might affect language maintenance efforts within the Korean American community?

3. Kim notes the following characteristics of the Korean American community: (1) As of 1980, 82 percent of Korean Americans were foreign-born; (2) In general, Korean Americans tend to be a young group; (3) Koreans are mainly urban dwellers who are dispersed in cities throughout the United States, although recently there appears to be secondary migration to several cities; (4) Overall, Korean Americans are a well educated group; however, most received their college education before emigrating to the United States; (5) Although most Korean Americans are employed, they are mainly employed in middle-level positions; (6) Most Korean Americans live in nuclear households; (7) Korean Americans tend to be active members of religious communities.

Discuss how each of the factors listed above might affect language retention and language loss within the Korean American community.

4. Kim lists three factors that she believes have played an important role in the general tendency of Korean Americans to have poor skills in English: (1) the very different linguistic structure of the two languages; (2) the recent immigrants' minimal exposure to English in their home country; and (3) demanding jobs that leave little time to learn English.

Based on the chapters in this volume, discuss what other language minority groups share any or all of the characteristics listed above.

5. According to Kim, most Koreans are employed as workers in small shops operated by Koreans or in unskilled or semiskilled service jobs. Thus, they have little opportunity to improve their English on the job.

Based on the chapters in this volume, discuss what other language minority groups share a similar occupational profile.

APPLYING THE IDEAS

1. Kim notes that mass media coverage of Korean Americans is on the rise.

Compile a list of recent articles on Korean Americans in the popular press. Then examine several of these articles to determine what insights they provide on language maintenance efforts within the Korean American community.

2. Kim points out that Korean ethnic churches fill a variety of spiritual, psychological, practical, and social needs for the Korean American community.

If there is a Korean church in your area, visit it; otherwise, visit any ethnic church in your area and interview some of its leaders and/or members to determine what functions the church serves in the community. Pay particular attention to the ways in which the church supports the maintenance of the native language as well as the acquisition of English.

NOTES

1. Since the mid-1970s, media coverage of Korean American communities in the United States, their success stories and problems have appeared as lead stories in major newspapers such as *The New York Times, Wall Street Journal,* and *Washington Post*. Weekly magazines such as *Time* and *Newsweek* have also featured Korean American communities. Some examples are: "Korean Americans: Pursuing Economic Success," *Washington Post* (July 13, 1978); "Koreans Find New York a Place of Opportunity," *The New York Times* (October 2, 1979); "The New Ellis Island: Immigrants from All Over Change the Beat, Bop and Character of Los Angeles," *Time* (June 13, 1983); "A Superminority Top Out," *Newsweek* (May 11, 1987); "A Formula for Success," *Newsweek* (April 23, 1984).

2. For an authoritative summary of Korean history with an extensive annotated bibliography, see Choe (1980).

3. This Act abolished the discriminatory national origin quota system for people from Asian countries and adopted a new preference system based on family relation-

ships and occupational skills. It places a ceiling of 20,000 people from any one country per year. Exempted from this numerical limitation are spouses, parents, and unmarried children under age 21 of U.S. citizens and refugees.

4. The U.S. Immigration and Naturalization Service Annual Report indicates that since 1975 there have been over 30,000 Korean immigrants entering the United States as permanent residents per year.

5. This percentage is arrived at by averaging the data from two studies: one in Chicago by Kim (1978) and another one in Chicago and Los Angeles by Kim, Sawdey and Meihoefer (1980).

6. Two studies, Kim (1978) and Hurh and Chung (1979), identify multiple factors involved in church membership and the regular participation of Korean immigrants in Korean ethnic churches. For a fuller discussion beyond statistics, read Chapter 8 of Hurh and Kim (1984).

7. For an extensive and scholarly discussion of the Korean language and its use, read the Korean National Commission for UNESCO (ed.) (1983) and Kim (1980).

8. Before *Han-gul* was invented, Korean used Chinese characters to write Korean even though Chinese ideographs are unsuited phonetically to represent the richly inflective Korean language. During the Three Kingdoms and Silla period (57B.C.–A.D. 935), Koreans found a way to put their spoken language into writing by using Chinese characters. It was called *Idu* or *Hyangch'al*. It was used until the invention and promulgation of *Han-gul*.

9. The author relied heavily on California State Department of Education (1983), 28–50, to write the sections on morphology and grammar.

10. The author relied heavily on Kim (1962) to write this section.

11. Eighty-nine percent of the subjects in the Kim study (1978) in Chicago rated this to be their number one problem.

12. The Korean American Child study (1978–1979) whose findings were published in the Kim, Sawdey and Meihoefer (1980) report, had two research sites: one in Chicago and another in Los Angeles. The total sample size was 417 families and 417 classroom teachers. Ninety-eight families and 98 teachers in Chicago and 309 families and 309 teachers in Los Angeles were involved. The parents, child, and child's teacher were interviewed separately with separate interview schedules, yielding 1,251 interviews.

Considerable differences were noted between the Chicago and Los Angeles samples. Noteworthy for this chapter is the ethnic attachment behavior. For example, the Los Angeles families tended to speak more Korean, associate more with Koreans, read Korean newspapers and watch Korean television more than the Chicago families, after age, educational level, and length of residence in the United States were controlled for. This leads to the conclusion that when there are high ethnic concentrations, the acculturation rate becomes slower. Thus, it is not surprising that the Korean children in Los Angeles played more with Korean children.

SUGGESTED READING

California State Department of Education, Office of Bilingual and Bicultural Education. 1983. *A Handbook for Teaching Korean-Speaking Students*. Los Angeles: Evaluation, Dissemination and Assessment Center, California State University, Los Angeles. (This handbook contains basic and useful information about Korean immigrant students in American classrooms. A succinct discussion of Korean history, immigration patterns, language and culture as they affect the students' learning in the classroom.)

Hurh, W. M., and Kim, K. C. 1984. *Korean Immigrants in America: A Structural Analysis of Ethnic Confinement and Adhesive Adaptation*. London and Toronto: Associated University Presses. (A scholarly book that uses research data to formulate a theoretical paradigm of acculturation of Korean immigrants. For anyone interested in minority group acculturation, this is a valuable reference book.)

Kim, H. K. (ed.) 1980. *Studies on Korea: A Scholar's Guide,* Honolulu: University Press of Hawaii. (As the title suggests, this is an extremely valuable reference book that covers all aspect of Korea. Each chapter is covered by well-known authorities in each field with a valuable annotated bibliography section. A must for any serious researchers of Korea.)

Kim, B. L., Sawdey, and M. Meihoefer, B. 1980. *The Korean–American Child at School and at Home: An Analysis of Interaction and Intervention Through Groups,* Project Report (9-30-1978 through 6-30-1980) Project funded by ACYF, U.S. Dept. of HEW Grant #90-C-1335 (01). (A research-based monograph that contains useful research data on Korean immigrant parents and their children. A good resource book for research students in Asian American studies.)

REFERENCES

Bureau of Public Affairs. 1983. *Background Notes, (South)*. Washington D.C.: U.S. Department of State.

Bureau of Public Affairs. 1986. *Background Notes, (North)*. Washington D.C.: U.S. Department of State.

California State Department of Education, Office of Bilingual and Bicultural Education. 1983. *A Handbook for Teaching Korean-Speaking Students*. Los Angeles: Evaluation, Dissemination and Assessment Center, California State University, Los Angeles.

Chai, A. 1987. Feminist analysis of life histories of early immigrant women from Japan, Okinawa, and Korea. Unpublished paper.

Choe, Y. H. 1980. History. In *Studies on Korea: A Scholar's Guide*. Han-Kyo Kim (ed.). Honolulu: University Press of Hawaii, 27–47.

Choi, B. Y. 1979. *Koreans in America*. Chicago: Nelson Hall.

Gardner, R. W., B. Robey and P. C. Smith. 1985. *Asian Americans: Growth, Change, and Diversity*. 40: 4. Washington D.C.: Population Reference Bureau, Inc.

Hurh, W. M. and K. K. Chung. 1979. *Korean Immigrants in the Los Angeles Areas:*

A Sociological Study, Interim Report. Submitted to NIMH, U.S. Department of Health, Education and Welfare (Grant No. 1 RO1 MH 30475-01), October.

Hurh, W. M. and K. C. Kim. 1984. *Korean Immigrants in America: A Structural Analysis of Ethnic Confinement and Adhesive Adaptation*. London, Toronto: Associated University Presses.

Kan, S. H. and W. T. Liu. 1986. The educational status of Asian Americans: An update from the 1980 census. *P/AAMHRC Research Review* 5:3/4.

Kim, B. L. 1977. Asian wives of U.S. servicemen: Women in shadows. *Amerasia Journal* 4:2, 91–115.

Kim, B. L. 1978. *The Asian Americans: Changing Patterns, Changing Needs*. Montclair, NJ: AKCS Publications.

Kim, B. L. 1983. The future of Korean American children and youth: Marginality, biculturality, and the role of the American public school. In D. T. Nakanishi and M. H. Nakanishi (eds.), *The Education of Asian and Pacific Americans: Historical Perspectives and Prescriptions for the Future*. Phoenix, AZ: Oryx Press.

Kim, B. L., B. Sawdey and B. Meihoefer. 1980. *The Korean-American Child at School and at Home: An Analysis of Interaction and Intervention Through Groups*. Project Report (9-30-1978 through 6-30-1980) Project funded by administration for child, youth and families, U.S. Department of Health, Education and Welfare, Grant #90-C-1335 (01).

Kim, C. W. 1980. Language and linguistics. In Han-Kyo Kim (ed.), *Studies on Korea: A Scholar's Guide*. Honolulu: University Press of Hawaii.

Kim, S. P. 1962. The meaning of yes and no in English and Korean. *Language Learning* 12:1, 27–46.

Korea Overseas Information Service. 1982. *A Handbook of Korea (4th edition)*. Seoul, Korea: Ministry of Culture and Information.

Korean National Commission for UNESCO (ed.). 1983. *The Korean Language*. Seoul, Korea: Si-sa-yong-o-sa, Inc.

Lyu, I. Y. 1977. Korean nationalist activities in Hawaii and the Continental U.S. 1900–1975, Part 1 1900–1919. *Amerasia Journal* 4:1, 23–90.

World Almanac and Book of Facts. 1985. New York: Newspaper Enterprise Association, Inc.

Yun, Y. J. 1977. Early history of Korean immigration to America. In H. C. Kim (ed.), *The Korean Diaspora*. Santa Barbara, CA: ABC-Clio Press.

CHAPTER
10

The Language Situation of Vietnamese Americans

Chuong Hoang Chung

For the Vietnamese, who are among the newest immigrants in the United States, the issues of language acquisition and language maintenance occupy a very important place in their adjustment to a new society, as well as in the protection of their identity now and in the future. The impact of this fastest growing group has been felt in many states where there are large concentrations, and particularly in California where almost 40 percent of the entire Vietnamese refugee population have permanently resettled. To achieve integration, this community has to go through a multiphase process in which acquiring a new language is the first major undertaking. As the community establishes itself, the question of preserving the cultural heritage could be thought of in terms of maintaining not only cherished traditions but also the native language.

To understand these issues, it is necessary to look at the background of the Southeast Asian migration, the demographic characteristics of the different refugee waves, some educational issues concerning language training programs, as well as the problems encountered in community efforts to promote the Vietnamese language. Thus, this chapter will document chronologically the Southeast Asian exodus, the major refugee influxes, their characteristics, and finally the issues involved in the learning of English and the maintenance of Vietnamese. Although the Indochinese refugees are composed of a variety of ethnic groups, due to space limitations this chapter will deal exclusively with the Vietnamese community.

BACKGROUND OF THE SOUTHEAST ASIAN MIGRATION

In April, 1975, several governments in Southeast Asia collapsed under the advance of Communist troops. The long Vietnam War finally came to an end after the last U.S. fighting units disengaged and left the region. With the takeover by new political forces, a massive exodus of the refugees took place; the first and largest wave came out of Vietnam. To date, a total of more than 800,000 Southeast Asians have been admitted to the United States, of whom more than 500,000 are from Vietnam (Refugee Reports, December 13, 1986). Three distinct waves of refugees can be identified from the beginning of the refugee movements. These respective waves show diversity in characteristics reflective of ethnic variation and experiences.

The first refugee wave started in 1975, the second wave in 1978, and the third wave in 1982 (see Chung 1986). While the first wave of refugees was composed mainly of Vietnamese (125,000 of a total of 131,000 Southeast Asians during 1975), the subsequent refugee waves showed large influxes of other Southeast Asians such as Cambodians, Laotians and other tribal groups from Laos, of whom the two major groups are the Lao Hmong and Lao Iu Mien. According to the data gathered by a group of researchers led by Dr. William Liu at Camp Pendleton, a staging facility in Southern California during the early days of refugee resettlement (in 1975), the Vietnamese refugees of the first wave were a young, relatively well-educated and skilled segment of the population (Liu 1979).

The second refugee wave started in 1978 due to the intensified conflict between Vietnam and China (Duiker 1985). Subsequent to the border war that erupted in 1979, the Vietnamese government put in practice a discriminatory harassment policy that sought overtly to encourage emigration of Chinese Vietnamese residents from different localities in Vietnam. Special programs and organized networks were created to facilitate the exit of ethnic Chinese Vietnamese with the unofficial approval of government representatives. An exit permit for ethnic Chinese Vietnamese could be obtained according to different rates or fees, which were paid in gold or currency (Wain 1981; Strand and Jones 1985). It is estimated that of the total 380,000 refugees who were admitted from Vietnam during the period 1978–1981, about 40 percent were ethnic Chinese Vietnamese. The percentage cited is not absolute because it is difficult to determine the criteria for distinguishing between an ethnic Chinese immigrant who is a naturalized citizen of Vietnam and a third-generation Chinese Vietnamese who is considered a full Vietnamese.

The reasons behind the unofficial expulsion of ethnic Chinese Vietnamese are twofold: first, in 1979, hostilities resumed on the border between Vietnam and China, which had its roots in the historical domination and occupation of Vietnam by China; second, Vietnamese feared economic sabotage and control by ethnic Chinese Vietnamese. Ethnic Chinese Vietnamese have long occupied the middleman class, which controls different types of markets in the Vietnamese economy (Duiker 1985). This status has triggered both envy and resentment toward the ethnic Chinese.

During the period 1980–1981, a total of 237,000 Vietnamese and ethnic

Chinese Vietnamese were admitted to the United States (Refugee Reports, December 15, 1985). This massive exodus was encouraged by Vietnamese officials who allowed small vessels to depart from the coastal region of South Vietnam. However, not all made it to the neighboring countries in Southeast Asia. Numerous boatloads of refugees were unaccounted for, and it is safe to speculate that they were the easy targets of pirates as well as stormy conditions.

The year 1982 marked the third wave of the Southeast Asian refugee movement, and it is so called for the following reasons. First, in 1980, Congress amended the Refugee Act of 1975 and replaced it with the Refugee Act of 1980 in which, for the first time, the word "refugee" was defined and clear objectives were established for refugee programs. Since the new act emphasized the immigrants' need to become self-sufficient as quickly as possible, refugees now had to enroll in language training programs, vocational programs, or employment development programs in order to make use of the refugee assistance program. To meet this objective, the Office of Refugee Resettlement was set up to provide funds and to monitor the different programs across the United States. Before entering the United States, refugees were given orientation sessions and information about what to expect in the new environment; also they were taught survival English language skills by voluntary agencies working in Southeast Asian refugee camps. Second, with the setting up and functioning of a new program called the Orderly Departure Program (ODP), many resettled refugees and naturalized Vietnamese Americans were able to petition for family reunification.

Under the new immigration procedure established by the Orderly Departure Program, 80,000 Vietnamese refugees have been allowed to join their relatives in the United States since 1982. Presently, however, the flow of refugees has subsided. Since now the Orderly Departure Program is processing applications according to the criteria set by the refugee authorities and the Immigration and Naturalization Service, a much smaller number of entries are allowed per month. According to the Office of Refugee Resettlement, the quota set for 1984–1985 is 32,000 allowed entries from Southeast Asia, a far smaller number than the 156,000 per year of the 1980–1981 period (Refugee Reports, December 15, 1985).

With the total number of refugees now reaching 813,000 (Report to Congress 1986), California still leads all other states, with more than 300,000 Southeast Asians. In fact, according to the 1986 California State Department of Education, Office of Bilingual Education Report, the total number of limited-English-proficient (LEP) Vietnamese students in the State of California was 30,592 (Le 1986). This was an increase of almost 50 percent from 1981. These numbers, however, do not include many Chinese Vietnamese students from Vietnam who are often identified as nonrefugee Cantonese-speaking students. Indeed, it has been suggested that approximately 75 percent of the LEP and 25 percent of the fluent-English-proficient Cantonese-speaking students are actually Indochinese in origin (Le 1986).

Table 10.1. VIETNAMESE REFUGEE ARRIVALS, FISCAL YEARS 1975–1985

Fiscal year	Refugee arrivals
1975	125,000
1976	3,200
1977	1,900
1978	11,100
1979	44,500
1980	95,200
1981	86,100
1982	42,600
1983	23,030
1984	24,927
1985	25,383

Source: Linda Gordon, Chief Statistician, Office of Refugee Resettlement, U.S. Department of Health and Human Services.

Table 10.2. RANKING OF STATES WITH LARGEST ESTIMATED SOUTHEAST ASIAN REFUGEE POPULATIONS, ENTRIES FROM 1975 THROUGH NOVEMBER 1985

State	Number	Percentage
California	305,400	39.8
Texas	57,900	7.5
Washington	34,700	4.3
New York	29,000	3.8
Pennsylvania	25,700	3.3
Illinois	25,500	3.3
Minnesota	24,400	3.2
Massachusetts	22,900	3.0
Virginia	20,900	2.7
Oregon	17,500	2.3
Subtotal	563,900	73.4
Other States	204,300	26.0
Total	768,200	100.0

Source: U.S. Department of Health and Human Services, Social Security Administration, Office of Refugee Resettlement, Monthly Data Report for November 1985.

SOME INITIAL ADJUSTMENT CONCERNS

In 1975, when the first group of refugee students started to show up at different school districts across the United States, school personnel were caught unprepared for this sudden shift in student population. However, since the majority of the first wave had a fairly strong educational background, they were able to deal with the bureaucracy and lack of compassion they often encountered (Madrid 1980). Many of the success stories shown in the print and electronic media are individuals from this first Vietnamese refugee wave of 1975.

Other reasons contribute to the smooth occupational and educational adjustment of the first wave. Most of the youngsters did not undergo extended school interruption since they left at the end of April, 1975, and after a short period of time in the refugee camp they were put back in the schools at their resettlement location in September. Another reason is that most of these children came with their entire families intact, with little exposure to the harrowing experiences of the subsequent refugee waves. Coming from a high socioeconomic background together with extensive exposure to the French educational system and other forms of Western culture, they only had to overcome the language barrier to catch up with their American counterparts.

Referring to his adjustment to the new American school, a Vietnamese student of the first wave related his experience:

> During my first year in high school, it was an entirely different situation. Here the shock of learning a new language and living in a new environment has eased. In its place was the eagerness to be accepted by my peers. Through my experience with discrimination, which came primarily in the form of cruel jokes, I soon discovered that to eliminate these irresponsible acts, I must be accepted and respected by my peers. To win their respect, I tried to excel both academically and athletically. [At the time of this writing, Thanh Nguyen is working as an engineer for a well-known high tech company in the Los Angeles metropolitan area.]

The refugees of the second wave showed a wide range of backgrounds ranging from the well-educated to peasants with very little experience in schooling, from sophisticated urban dwellers to farmers of the remote countryside. The children of this group reflected the same type of characteristics: from grade level performance to 3 or 4 years below the expected norm. Educators and refugee workers faced a totally new challenge. With little knowledge about the new refugees, educators and social workers used a wide range of strategies in coping with the demands: some were successful, some were not. This difficult situation was further complicated by the poor living conditions in the refugee camps and the long waiting time in those camps.

Suspecting that their children might not be able to cope with the demands of the new American classroom, Vietnamese and other Southeast Asian parents thought it would be best for their youngsters to change their age to match the classroom level they thought appropriate. This strategy was meant to alleviate the educational shock children might suffer if they had been out of school for an extended period of time and if their English was poor. By lowering their children's age by 2–3 years, they thought their children could certainly cope with the new academic setting.

As a direct consequence of this strategy, many students found that their parents, by playing it too safe, had moved too far in regressing their age. Being placed with a much younger group of students, many Vietnamese students encountered not only social and psychological problems, but also academic setbacks that affected their schooling. Many students complained that they did not fit in the class; others said that the materials were boring or childish. To remedy this situation, many parents attempted to change their children's age back, only to be faced with a myriad of tiresome paperwork.

Superficially, the refugee children of the third wave are in some ways very similar to those of the second wave, with some coming from highly motivated middle class families but the majority coming from farming communities in Southeast Asia where their parents had worked in the rice fields most of their life. However, the refugee children of the third wave are unique in two ways. First, in Vietnam many experienced a switch from one educational system to a new one set up by the Communist government, which required nonacademic activities such as street maintenance, political meetings, and political education sessions. Second, the interruption of the schooling of the third-wave children was much longer than that experienced by both the first and the second waves, since waiting time for resettlement could be anywhere from 1 to 2 years.

As early as 1980, refugee resettlement workers started to see, among incoming immigrants, young adolescents arriving from Southeast Asia without their parents or accompanying relatives. Classified as unaccompanied minors, these young adolescents came with little preparation, little education, and many adjustment problems. They came from both urban and rural areas and shared similar experiences such as constant displacement during the war, interruption in schooling, and, for those who lived far away from urban areas, little preparation for living in a technological society. Without family support and supervision, they ran into trouble with schools and sometimes law enforcement agencies due to their "survival"-type behavior (see Chung 1986).

The overall picture of the successive waves of refugees shows that the majority of the Vietnamese students who come to the United States have little English language ability. Only the Vietnamese newcomers from urban areas have been exposed to either English or French as their second language from grades 6 to 12 (Kelly 1978). Since those who lived in the countryside have not received their schooling in a continuous manner due to the war, they have had no exposure to English or French. What kind of problems do these refugees have to face when they get to the United States?

ISSUES IN LANGUAGE ACQUISITION

For a significant number of the Vietnamese refugees, it is not a simple task to learn a new language when most of their life has been spent outside a formal classroom. Even for those with many years of training, achieving English fluency for the workplace and/or the classroom is not something that can be done in a few days. Considering this fact, all efforts during the initial resettlement phase should be devoted to aiding the student in their acquisition of English. However, to become proficient in English, Vietnamese students in English classes face three major hurdles. They can be identified as (1) special social factors related to language learning; (2) differences in teaching methods and classroom expectations; and (3) linguistic interference.

Special Social Factors Related to Language Learning

Schumann (1978) lists a variety of social factors that affect second language acquisition, such as the size of the ethnic group, its cohesiveness, and its desire to preserve its own institutions. For Schumann, social factors such as these are paramount in language learning. In fact, he asserts that language learning is "just one aspect of acculturation and the degree to which a learner acculturates to the TL [target language] group will control the degree to which he acquires the second language" (1978:34).

One important social factor that affects language learning, not mentioned by Schumann, is the ethnic group's reason for migrating. While many immigrant groups migrated to the United States out of choice to achieve such things as economic mobility or religious freedom, the Vietnamese migration was not a matter of choice. There is no question that migration under any circumstance is stressful, but forced migration can be particularly so. As Kleinmann puts it (1982:240), during immigration "the individual's role system and social identity are disturbed, known concepts become unfamiliar notions, and expectancies are transformed into misunderstandings. When migration is forced upon the individual, as in the case of the Indochinese refugees, resettlement is an even more stressful process."

The special adjustment problems brought on by forced migration inevitably affect the language learning process of the Vietnamese student. The fact that students cannot return to their homeland, coupled with painful memories of their homeland and their forced migration, may make it difficult for students to concentrate on learning English. Thus, for any language program to be successful, the special needs of the Vietnamese need to be recognized. Kleinmann (1982:240) is right when he asserts that some means of integrating social services with the language programs for the Vietnamese community "is essential for smooth program operation."

Unfortunately, many public school programs for the Vietnamese are not following Kleinmann's suggestion. As Rubin (1981:29) points out, the most general trend today in public education is to mainstream children as quickly and as much as possible. And as she concludes, this pressure to mainstream is "due in part to a lack of real awareness of the problems which these children may have in adjusting to a new language, a new set of expected behaviors and a completely different school system (or even to *a* school system)." Thus, without the social support services that are needed because of their special migration pattern, Vietnamese students face a special hurdle in acquiring the language, which is compounded by the students' unfamiliarity with prevalent language teaching methods and classroom expectations.

Differences in Teaching Methods and Classroom Expectations

In Vietnam, teaching a foreign language has traditionally been grammar-based, with translation and reading. As a result, the Vietnamese student usually ends up knowing more about English grammar rules or English spelling than about understanding and speaking conversational English. Newer methods such as Total Physical Response (Asher 1982) and the Natural approach (Krashen and Terrell 1982), which are commonly practiced in Western European countries, have never been introduced. Thus, many students have difficulties adjusting to new English as a second language (ESL) methods that emphasize listening skills and verbal interaction.

Differences in classroom expectations also contribute to the Vietnamese students' difficulties in learning English. While the typical American classroom often involves dynamic interaction and exchanges between students and teachers, the typical Vietnamese classroom promotes receptive or passive learning. In Vietnamese classrooms, the teacher is viewed as the giver of knowledge and the student as the receiver of this knowledge. Vietnamese students are generally not used to engaging in extended questions and answers but are more ready to repeat drills and copy down the new vocabulary to memorize. Hence, many students may find it difficult to meet the expectations of their teachers, particularly when these expectations involve a good deal of active participation.

Vietnamese adults also share some unique expectations about the educational system. While Vietnamese parents generally fully support public education, they often believe that educational matters should be dealt with by teachers and administrators. This view, coupled with their often minimal

English skills, makes it appear that the parents have a passive attitude toward their children's education (California State Department of Education 1982:5). Given this fact, school administrators need to pursue parental involvement actively in the educational decision making process.

Linguistic Interference

Vietnamese uses a Roman alphabet with the addition of diacritical marks to account for the different tonal values; thus, Vietnamese students do not have to learn a new writing system as do Cambodian, Lao, or Chinese students. In addition, the system is highly phonetic, more so than either English or French. However, Vietnamese students still experience problems in learning English, particularly in the area of pronunciation and grammar, due to linguistic interference.

Vietnamese words are monosyllabic for the most part and are pronounced without final sounds and consonant clusters. Hence, it is not surprising that the Vietnamese students have a tendency to drop entirely the final sounds in English (i.e., third person singular of the present tense, the plural form, and sometimes the possessive case). Vietnamese being a tonal language with most words pronounced with different tones to express different meanings, it is not uncommon to hear Vietnamese students adding extra tones to English words. Unlike the polysyllabic words of most European languages, stress in Vietnamese words does not have any phonemic value. Thus, Vietnamese students have a difficult time using the correct stress pattern in English.

The following is a compilation of all the "difficult" sounds for the Vietnamese students:

Sounds	*Confused with*
th as in *this*	*d* as in *dog;* or *s* as in *see*
p as in *pin*	*b* as in *boy*
g as in *gum*	*k* as in *king*
zh as in *pleasure*	*z* as in *zebra*
i as in *pin*	*ee* as in *beet*
e as in *bet*	*a* as in *bat* (or vice versa)
oo as in *book*	*oo* as in *boot*
Final consonants	*Pronounced as*
b ending as in *dab*	*p*
d ending as in *bad*	*t*
f ending as in *laugh*	*p*
v ending as in *love*	*b*
ch ending as in *much*	*t* or *sh*
r ending as in *car*	postvocalic *r* dropped

In terms of morphology and syntax, Vietnamese is an uninflected language, so that Vietnamese words do not change form to express grammatical categories such as gender or number. Thus, for example, no distinction is made between the singular and plural form of words, nor is there any marking on the verb for tense. Instead, the time of an action is inferred by the context or expressed by function words (California State Department of Education 1982:16). Word order in Vietnamese is invariable, so that a change in word order will completely change the meaning of the sentence. Unlike English, Vietnamese never inverts the subject in interrogative sentences. Given these differences, Vietnamese students may have difficulty in making plural and tense distinctions in English and in forming questions. (For a complete discussion of Vietnamese linguistic characteristics, see California State Department of Education 1982.)

LANGUAGE MAINTENANCE

Concentrated mostly in several counties in California, the Vietnamese have formed a number of "ideal" language maintenance communities where factors such as public education, language teaching programs, ethnic reading materials, and extensive language use within the boundaries of the speech community are contributing to maintenance efforts. Indeed, in the counties of Los Angeles, Orange, San Francisco, and Santa Clara, the Vietnamese can take advantage of these language maintenance support factors. The question is: Are these factors strong enough to ensure the retention of Vietnamese within the community?

In large refugee concentrations such as Westminster in Orange County, California, a walk down the main Bolsa Avenue can testify to the extensive use and importance of Vietnamese. Another look at directories (Thang Mo, Trieu Thanh) published in Vietnamese and distributed free to Vietnamese shoppers shows that any Vietnamese resident of Orange County can obtain all necessary services without ever having to use English. From social services to health care and other basic needs, Vietnamese speakers are at home. They can also find work within the boundaries of this speech community and, for their work, can use their native language.

The printed media are, of course, an important factor in language maintenance efforts. Currently there is a fairly wide range of printed materials available in Vietnamese. For example, after compiling the advertising brochures from major publishers, I found 1,090 different titles published in Vietnamese with the following breakdown in subjects: 150 on teaching and learning English; 200 nonfiction titles on religion, philosophy, self-improvement, and the Vietnam War; the remaining 740 titles covered a wide range of subjects from Vietnamese novels to translations of Chinese classic novels.

In general, however, these titles appeal to adult readers rather than young Vietnamese who are in the process of learning to read in Vietnamese.

The electronic media are another factor that can support language maintenance efforts. In the San Francisco Bay Area region of San Jose/Santa Clara, three television projects (Channel 48) offer broadcasts in Vietnamese. These programs typically include Vietnamese songs, advertising, news, and interviews. Like the printed material, the topics and the language used in these broadcasts are not for the younger learners of Vietnamese but for fluent Vietnamese speakers. Some areas also offer weekly radio broadcasts (e.g., FM 107 in Los Angeles), which present both community information and language development programs (California State Department of Education 1982:9).

Unlike most other ethnic groups in the United States that span several generations, the Vietnamese community is almost all first-generation, with the influx of immigrants subsiding. Hence, the maintenance of the Vietnamese language rests largely in the acquisition of Vietnamese by young members of the community. The question is: Can the public educational system provide the needed language training for these youngsters? For an answer to this question, I look at two institutions that can provide the necessary training for second language acquisition and for first language maintenance: the public school system and community language programs.

Language Programs in Public Schools

Working as an educational consultant for many school districts in California, I have had many opportunities to observe language training programs, bilingual education programs, and other alternatives for language minority students. I have visited classrooms, talked to teachers, and discussed with fellow Vietnamese teachers the effectiveness of the educational programs in which many newcomer Vietnamese students are placed. What I have seen and found was far from ideal.

Most of the Vietnamese students I have seen are enrolled either in English-only classrooms or in transitional bilingual education programs with an ESL component. One of my students at Berkeley recalls that during his first encounter with the American school system, he was put in a Spanish bilingual program. After 2 months of frustration, he was shifted to an all-English program. This incident unfortunately is not uncommon. Frequently students are placed in inappropriate programs. For example, during my service as a resource teacher for the San Francisco Unified School District, Vietnamese living in the downtown area of San Francisco were bussed to an elementary school inside a nearby Navy base. There, they were put in a Filipino bilingual program. For some reason, the school identified the Nguyens, the Trans, and the Phams as Filipino LEP students and thus bussed them to this school.

My visits to many school sites in the Bay Area reveal that a typical "bilingual" classroom is composed of many different ethnic groups with different linguistic backgrounds and skills. Thus, it is not uncommon to see Chinese, Vietnamese, Laotian, and Samoan students all in the same "bilingual" classroom. Naturally, the only instruction mode possible is English; however, if the students are lucky, they will be "pulled out" and tutored by an instructional aide who can speak their language.

The problems that I encountered in the schools have been experienced by many Vietnamese. As Rubin (1981) points out, the mass migration of almost half a million refugees from Indochina precipitated many problems in the school districts. Among these were difficulty in predicting the number of children in need and the rate of growth of this population, a lack of funding and adequately trained staff, and a lack of appropriate teaching materials.

Vietnamese parents, who think that bilingual education will provide their children with literacy skills in Vietnamese, will be disappointed with the programs of many school districts. Perhaps knowing that they cannot count on public education, many Vietnamese organizations have set up language training programs with volunteer teachers to meet this particular need. Thus, areas with large concentrations of Vietnamese such as Orange County, Los Angeles, and San Jose have organized special Vietnamese language classes.

Vietnamese Language Training Programs

At present there are about a dozen volunteer language programs for Vietnamese children in the San Francisco Bay Area alone. From classes held in religious facilities in San Leandro to more structured programs in San Francisco and San Jose, Vietnamese community members donate time and/or money to help convert meeting halls and public facilities into classrooms.

In San Francisco, for example, the Vietnamese Elderly Association started a language program in 1982. With the assistance of the Center for Southeast Asian Refugee Resettlement (CSEARR), the organization bought a van for student transportation and rented four classrooms to meet the needs of 187 students. The project began with four volunteers who had been teachers in Vietnam.

The instructional program of the school includes Vietnamese reading and writing, civics, folklore and poetry, as well as the history and geography of Vietnam. Aside from these subjects, students are also taught Vietnamese songs and riddles. According to the teaching staff, after 3 months of regular attendance, the students are generally able to read and write basic Vietnamese. A large number of these children start out not being able to read and write in Vietnamese although they possess developed oral Vietnamese skills.

From a high of 180–190 students in 1983, the school, like other language training programs, is experiencing a drop in enrollment to only 60–70 students in 1985. The organization attributes this decline in enrollment to a drop in funding, transportation problems, and population movement caused by secondary migration among the Vietnamese community for better job opportunities, climate, and welfare. In addition, many students find the additional 2 hours a day and 4 hours on Saturday to be too demanding to continue.

Most of the teaching staff at the school were content area teachers in Vietnam rather than language teachers. Lacking background in language teaching methodologies, many devote the majority of class time to correcting pronunciation since they have found the children reading Vietnamese words with English pronunciation. A classic example given was the Vietnamese imperative *xe ra!* (move over!) was pronounced as *She-ra* (a popular character in comics and cartoon programs). Volunteer teachers also complain about the lack of discipline among the students and blame this behavior on the permissiveness of American classrooms during the day.

Religious organizations also participate in this volunteer task of language maintenance. For example, in San Leandro, California, the language program at St. Felicitas Church started in 1979. Sponsored by Father Tran Dinh, classes run from January to July. Students do not have to pay tuition, but they have to contribute a small amount to pay for school supplies. Instructional materials are prepared by the instructors, with a special focus on making them fit into the context of the new society and culture. The reactions of students to the program are mixed. Some say they like it very much since they hope that some day they will be able to communicate with their grandparents who are still in Vietnam. Some students, however, face conflicts at home regarding language use; for example, one Vietnamese girl confided in me that although her father wanted her to learn Vietnamese, her mother felt it was unnecessary.

In order for these language training programs to succeed, there must be appropriate training for Vietnamese teachers, methods of language teaching must be updated, and adequate instructional materials must be developed. Yet, to this date, little of this has been done. Most teachers in Vietnamese classes still use the lecture method and phonic drills with poor instructional materials. There is much emphasis on spelling and grammar but very little on sociolinguistic skills for competence in discourse. At the economic level, language programs must be self-sustaining rather than dependent on community donations and volunteer work, since only with a permanent paid staff can quality language programs be implemented.

CONCLUSION

How likely is it that the Vietnamese community will be able to retain its language in the coming years? Since the majority of Vietnamese are all first-generation, at this point there is no historical evidence for language shift or maintenance among Vietnamese. There are, however, a variety of factors that will undoubtedly affect the community's ability to maintain its language in the United States.

One factor that is working to promote Vietnamese language maintenance is the existence of large language islands. The fact that there are large communities of Vietnamese in Los Angeles, Orange, San Francisco, and Santa Clara counties certainly is contributing to a slowing of language shift. A second factor that is operative in maintaining the use of Vietnamese arises from the fact that the Vietnamese people are primarily refugees who see no possibility of returning to their homeland. One way to maintain a link to the homeland is by maintaining the language and traditions of Vietnam. Thus, realizing that they cannot return to their native soil, many Vietnamese are actively working to promote traditional cultural activities in the native language.

A final important factor that may strengthen language maintenance efforts is the attitude of the host society toward the Vietnamese community. During World War I, when there were strong antiforeign feelings toward the Germans, this hostility solidified the German community, slowing the process of language shift. Weimer (1980:43) contends that in some ways the Vietnamese are experiencing hostility similiar to what the Germans encountered during World War I. As she puts it,

> The United States was humiliated in defeat in Southeast Asia; the American economy is in a downward spiral, a situation often attributed in part to the war economy; and now the Vietnamese alien refugees are streaming into America at a rate of 14,000 per month. No wonder the reception for the Vietnamese is often lukewarm.

To the extent that such hostility exists, this may solidify the Vietnamese community, making the language a symbol of cohesiveness.

However, several factors are contributing to a shift to English. First, the influx of Vietnamese has subsided. Thus, unlike Mexican Americans or Korean Americans, presently there is little growth in the number of new immigrants who speak the language. Second, as was pointed out earlier, both public and private language training programs appear to be largely unsuccessful in maintaining the language. Third, there are differences in education level and ideologies within the Vietnamese community that minimize the cohesiveness of the community and thus undermine language maintenance efforts (Weimer 1980). Finally, and perhaps most importantly, as with many other immigrant groups, the lure of partaking in the American dream with its promise of economic and social mobility may well provide the incentive for Vietnamese to acquire English rapidly and give little attention to language maintenance efforts. Given that the history of the Vietnamese community is so recent, time is needed before any definitive statements about language use in the Vietnamese community can be made.

In the meantime, Vietnamese language maintenance should be researched from a number of perspectives. Psychologists should attempt to identify the attitudes of the majority culture toward Vietnamese. Anthropologists and linguists should examine the reasons for the choice and use of the Vietnamese language in different social contexts. And educators should plan language training programs according to the needs of the Vietnamese community (see Fasold 1984). This is the only way for the Vietnamese to ensure long-term success for their language maintenance programs.

EXPLORING THE IDEAS

1. As Chung points out, the Vietnamese, unlike many other immigrants, did not migrate out of choice.

What other immigrant groups to the United States have shared a similar experience? How do you think this factor has an impact on language maintenance or language loss within the ethnic community?

2. Chung cites Weimer's assertion that the Vietnamese are experiencing hostility similar to what the Germans encountered during World War I brought about by the U.S. defeat in southeast Asia.

Do you think Weimer's assertion is accurate? Do you believe there has been any shift in public attitudes toward Vietnamese? What evidence from media coverage can you cite to support your opinion?

3. Chung points out that one factor that may affect language shift within the Vietnamese community is the lure of the American dream, with its promise of economic and social mobility.

How might the fact that the Vietnamese community is composed primarily of refugees rather than immigrants influence their desire to partake in the American ideal of increased economic and social status?

APPLYING THE IDEAS

1. Chung supports Kleinmann's notion (1982) that language programs for Vietnamese must be integrated with social services.

First, discuss what types of social and support services you believe are important to help refugees make the transition to life in the United States and how these might be integrated into language training programs. Then visit a language program that serves Indochinese refugee students. Notice what type of support is offered in the native language. Also pay particular attention to whether or not social services are part of the program.

2. Chung's chapter deals with the Vietnamese community. The Indochinese refugees, however, also include Cambodians, Laotians, and the Hmong and Mien (tribal people from the mountains of northern Laos).

Select one of the ethnic groups listed above and investigate their immigration and settlement history, the linguistic features of their language, and language retention and language loss within the community.

3. Chung refers to the fact that the Refugee Act of 1980 set clear objectives for refugee programs.

Research the 1980 Refugee Act in terms of the policies set forth in it for refugee admission and resettlement assistance. Pay special attention to the special education services that the Act authorized.

SUGGESTED READINGS

California State Department of Education. 1982. *A Handbook for Teaching Vietnamese Speaking Students*. Los Angeles, CA: Evaluation and Dissemination Center, California State University, Los Angeles. (This book provides an overview of the history of Vietnamese immigration, as well as an overview of the educational situation in Vietnam. It also has an excellent contrastive analysis of English and Vietnamese. The final section has recommendations for curricular strategies for Vietnamese language development.)

Kleinmann, H. H. 1982. External influences and their neutralization in second language acquisition: A look at adult Indochinese refugees. *TESOL Quarterly* 16:2, 239–244. (In this provocative article, Kleinmann argues that because of the severe stress that the Vietnamese in general have experienced in immigration, English training programs for Vietnamese must be joined with social services if they are to be successful.)

Rubin, J. 1981. Meeting the educational needs of Indochinese refugee children. Washington D.C.: National Institute of Education. ED 212 699. (In this report, Rubin examines the issues involved in the planning and implementation of educational programs for Indochinese refugees. She discusses both the cultural and linguistic characteristics of Indochinese ethnic groups in order to arrive at several recommendations for educational programs for the Indochinese.)

Weimer, W. 1980. Factors affecting native language maintenance. In *Ethnoperspectives in Bilingual Research, Volume II: Theory in Bilingual Education*. R. Padilla (ed.), Ypsilanti, MI: East Michigan State University, Bilingual/Bicultural Education Program. (This paper applies various typologies of language shift and language maintenance to the Vietnamese community. Weimer discusses factors that inhibit and encourage language shift within the Indochinese community of the Minneapolis–St. Paul area.)

REFERENCES

Asher, J. 1982. *Learning Another Language Through Action*. Los Gatos, CA: Sky Oaks Productions, Inc.

California State Department of Education. 1982. *A Handbook for Teaching Vietnamese Speaking Students*. Los Angeles, CA: Evaluation and Dissemination Center, California State University, Los Angeles.

Chung, H. C. 1986. Working with Vietnamese high school students. Unpublished paper presented at the National Association for Asian and Pacific American Education Conference.

Duiker, W. 1985. *Vietnam Since the Fall of Saigon*. Ohio University, Center for International Studies, Southeast Asia Series No. 56.

Fasold, R. 1984. *Sociolinguistics of Society*. Oxford, England: Basil Blackwell Publisher.

Kelly, G. P. 1978. *From Vietnam to America*. Denver, CO: Westview Press.

Kleinmann, H. H. 1982. External influences and their neutralization in second language acquisition: A look at adult Indochinese refugees. *TESOL Quarterly* 16:2, 239–244.

Krashen, S. D. and T. D. Terrell. 1983. *The Natural Approach*. Hayward, CA: The Alemany Press.

Le, V. 1986. *Enrollment of Minority Language Children of Indochinese Origin in California*. Los Angeles, CA: California State Department of Education.

Liu, W. T. 1979. *Transition to Nowhere*. Nashville, TN: Charter House Publishers Inc.

Madrid, M. 1980. Indochinese in America—a new minority. *Bilingual Journal,* 5:2.

Refugee Reports, 1985 and 1986. Washington D.C.: American Council for Nationality Services.

Report to Congress, 1986. Washington D.C.: Office of Refugee Resettlement.

Rubin, J. 1981. Meeting the educational needs of Indochinese refugee children. Washington D.C.: National Institute of Education. ED 212 699.

Schumann, J. H. 1978. The acculturation model for second language acquisition. In *Second Language Acquisition and Foreign Language Teaching*. R. Gingras (ed.). Arlington, VA: Center for Applied Linguistics, 27–50.

Strand, P. J. and W. Jones, Jr. 1985. *Indochinese Refugees in America*. Durham, NC: Duke University Press.

Wain, B. 1981. *The Refused*. New York: Simon and Schuster.

Weimer, W. 1980. Factors affecting native language maintenance. In *Ethnoperspectives in Bilingual Research, Volume II: Theory in Bilingual Education*. R. Padilla (ed.). Ypsilanti, MI: East Michigan State University, Bilingual/Bicultural Education Program, 35–46.

Part IV

EDUCATIONAL IMPLICATIONS OF LANGUAGE DIVERSITY

In the United States, because public education has traditionally been considered the major vehicle for linguistic and cultural assimilation, even for language policy implementation, the presence of large numbers of linguistically heterogeneous students in the schools raises many theoretical and practical questions. In the first chapter in this section, Mary McGroarty examines theoretical questions about how language minority children learn languages and how language education programs may take psycholinguistic insights into account. Explaining and assessing the second language acquisition models of James Cummins, Stephen Krashen, and John Schumann, she suggests ways of conceptualizing the interaction between the language learner and surrounding social forces. Sandra McKay approaches the educational implications of language diversity from a pedagogical and administrative perspective. She evaluates a number of educational alternatives—submersion, pull-out ESL, bilingual education, immersion, and two-way bilingual education—using criteria such as feasibility, theoretical assumptions, research evidence, and impact on students. In the final chapter, Sau-ling Cynthia Wong deals with the legal aspects of providing language education services for minority children. She focuses on two central issues in educational language rights—whether submersion is justified by law, and whether there exists a legal mandate for bilingual education—as a way of determining the degree of entitlement enjoyed by language minorities. Her chapter complements McGroarty's and McKay's by grounding the discussion of the educational implications of language diversity in a political context.

CHAPTER

11

Second Language Acquisition Theory Relevant to Language Minorities: Cummins, Krashen, and Schumann[1]

Mary McGroarty

Theoretical frameworks for second language acquisition have been developed in a variety of fields, among them linguistics, psychology, anthropology, and sociology, as well as more recent academic hybrids such as information processing and cognitive modeling (see Hatch 1983a for a detailed discussion of current psycholinguistic questions). All of these disciplines offer insights into the processes and conditions that govern the acquisition of language in general. In this chapter, I will concentrate on the theories of three North American scholars whose work has been widely linked with second language acquisition in a minority language context in order to identify the parameters viewed as pertinent, define the processes that constitute second language acquisition in the views of each, and note the gaps in the theories proposed. The goal here is to be able to identify the factors seen as (in the strong formulations) causing, or at least (in the weaker formulations) co-occuring with the learning of a second language in a minority language context and evaluate the adequacy of each as a possible source of pedagogical information.

Most of the chapters in this book have been devoted to the social factors that influence second language learning and first language retention. Although social influences on language learning and use are critically important, they alone do not completely determine the outcomes of either language learning or education for language minority students. A great range of individual differences also affect second language learning; children representing the same immigrant generation, even children within the same family, often show disparate profiles of first and second language preference and mastery. Individual differences in the areas of, for example, personality, attitude, preferred learning style, and prior language experiences, in addition to differing familial roles and the social conditions of community language use, help to explain why children from similar backgrounds attain different degrees of second language proficiency.

The models of second language acquisition set out by the first two scholars discussed here, psychologist Jim Cummins and linguist Stephen Krashen, address some of the issues related to individual differences in second language learning and thus suggest possible reasons for wide variation in second language attainment, even for students who come from the same minority language community. The affective variables identified in linguist John Schumann's model also describe possible reasons for individual differences in second language learning. Thus these models suggest hypotheses that might explain in part why individual language minority students from the same first language group demonstrate such a great range of second language skills. These hypotheses complement the social considerations raised elsewhere in this volume and described in more detail in Schumann's acculturation model and in Cummins' proposal for educational reform, discussed in the last sections of this chapter. Each of these theories, set out in schematic form in Figure 11.1, identifies some of the individual characteristics that affect second language learning in concert with pertinent social conditions and thus may establish, even for similar students, different personal language histories.

While such theories cannot offer detailed instructional guidance in any given situation, they provide models that stimulate close examination of the learning process, more comprehensive definition of the variables that affect second language acquisition, and a point of departure for defining the goals of informal and formal instruction. The frameworks examined here are suggestive rather than definitive; each emphasizes a different aspect of second language learning and is not exhaustive in its approach. Nonetheless, taken together, the concepts explored here address most of the essential questions in second language acquisition for those concerned with effective education for students from minority language backgrounds.

Three superordinate categories organize the theories presented here: (1) Cummins' descriptions of the learner's cognitive and linguistic abilities; (2) Krashen's hypotheses regarding specific linguistic processes which produce second language acquisition; and (3) Schumann's model of, and Cummins' proposal for changing, the social conditions that shape language learning opportunities. In analyzing the theories proposed by these scholars, we shall note areas of common concern, potential problems with the supporting arguments and evidence, and, finally, their relevance for language instruction and research in a minority situation.

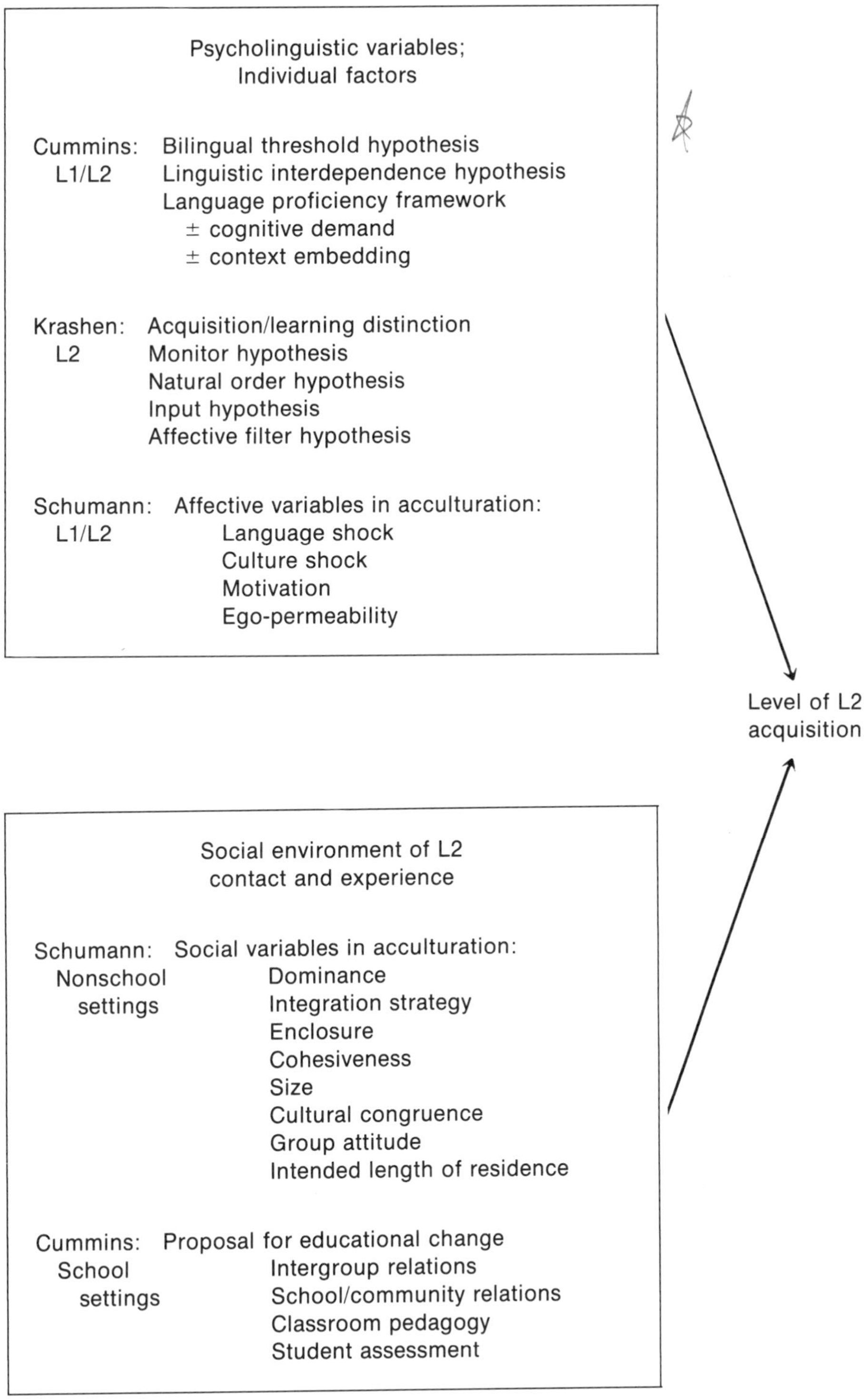

Psycholinguistic variables;
Individual factors

Cummins: L1/L2
- Bilingual threshold hypothesis
- Linguistic interdependence hypothesis
- Language proficiency framework
  - ± cognitive demand
  - ± context embedding

Krashen: L2
- Acquisition/learning distinction
- Monitor hypothesis
- Natural order hypothesis
- Input hypothesis
- Affective filter hypothesis

Schumann: L1/L2
- Affective variables in acculturation:
  - Language shock
  - Culture shock
  - Motivation
  - Ego-permeability

→ Level of L2 acquisition ←

Social environment of L2
contact and experience

Schumann: Nonschool settings
- Social variables in acculturation:
  - Dominance
  - Integration strategy
  - Enclosure
  - Cohesiveness
  - Size
  - Cultural congruence
  - Group attitude
  - Intended length of residence

Cummins: School settings
- Proposal for educational change
  - Intergroup relations
  - School/community relations
  - Classroom pedagogy
  - Student assessment

Figure 11.1. Theoretical considerations in L2 acquisition for language minority students

THE LEARNER'S COGNITIVE AND LINGUISTIC ABILITIES: CUMMINS' MODELS

Let us begin with an explication of the way each language learner's cognitive processes have been represented in the work of Jim Cummins. While not initially disregarding the social factors that affect language acquisition, Cummins' early work emphasizes the interrelationships that may exist between the two languages of a bilingual. In this formulation, the efficiency of second language acquisition is predicated on the level of first language development. To understand how second language acquisition occurs, we must first understand the connection between the first and the second language.

The rationale for examining the nature of first language skill as a predictor of second language potential is most fully presented in Cummins' article, "Linguistic Interdependence and the Educational Development of Bilingual Children" (1979b). In this paper, Cummins begins by addressing the apparent paradox that puzzles those concerned with second language education, namely, why a home–school language switch can result in high levels of bilingualism and academic achievement for middle class language majority children but may lead to inadequate language skills as well as depressed achievement for language minority students (1979b:222). To resolve the question of why one educational approach could have such differing effects—advantageous for majority group children in immersion programs and deleterious for minority language children "submerged" into other language settings—he proposes two hypotheses. Each of these hypotheses addresses issues critical in understanding the realizations of bilingualism in school-age groups and ultimately in designing suitable educational programs. While both of these models remain hypothetical, they have been borne out in the research of Cummins and other investigators consistently enough to warrant thoughtful attention and serious consideration as possible guidelines for educational planning for language minority students.

Some attention to previous scholarly work on bilingualism is necessary to grasp the implications of Cummins' formulations. As he notes, much of the research done with bilingual students prior to the 1960s demonstrated "lack of concern for the interrelationships of language and thought in the bilingual child" (1979b:227). When bilingual students were tested with IQ or achievement measures, there was frequently no concurrent assessment of level of first or second language skill. Thus researchers and educators could not assess cognition or achievement accurately and often blamed low levels of both on a child's bilingualism, without understanding that bilingualism in itself could in fact influence cognition in three different ways: it could enhance cognitive function, have no notable effect, or hinder intellectual development depending on the skill levels in each language and the relationship between the two languages as the child moved through school.

The Threshold Hypothesis

The first model proposed, the "Threshold Hypothesis" (1979b:227), integrates past research on both the positive and negative effects of bilingualism on cognitive development by showing that such effects are a function of the level of skill development in both languages. Although, as Cummins remarks, much early research was marred by lack of control of important factors such as students' levels of language proficiency or socioeconomic class background, even more recent and better designed research did not always show uniformly positive results. In one study, for example, bilingual children were lower in fluency but higher on originality and elaboration than a unilingual group (1979b:228); the cognitive effects of bilingualism appeared not to be clear-cut, and could vary according to the abilities assessed. Additionally troubling in explaining the effect of child bilingualism on intellectual function was the construct of "semilingualism," first proposed by Finnish researchers (Skutnabb-Kangas and Toukomaa 1976, cited in Cummins 1979b), who had noted that some minority language and migrant children seemed to have less than native level skills in both the home language and the second language and consequently experienced many difficulties in school. The semilingualism construct is controversial (Martin-Jones and Romaine 1986; Baral 1980) and is not solely a linguistic one, but includes aspects of social and psychological development. Moreover, it is not reflected in every minority language setting (for example, Hayes 1981 shows that it is not typical of most Mexican American children in northern California). Nevertheless, there is enough evidence to consider the possibility that in some environments, effects of bilingualism on cognitive function may be problematic.

At the same time, abundant evidence for positive effects of high levels of bilingualism on academic achievement also exists, according to the hypothesis. Long a feature of educational programs for elites the world over (see, among others, Grosjean 1982, Chs. 1 and 3, and Lewis 1976), bilingual school programs have also been shown to have favorably influenced the skills of many majority language children who participated in second language immersion programs. Most of this information has come from the Canadian programs in which Anglophone children received all school instruction initially in French and showed appropriate academic development, no loss of English skills, functional competence in French (the second language), and, for students with high levels of proficiency in both languages, improved flexibility of thought (see Genesee 1987 for a thorough review and more detailed presentation of these programs, and Genesee 1986 for a discussion of their relevance to language minority education). Hence there appeared to be a contradiction: in some situations bilingualism seemed to depress cognitive and academic attainment, but in other situations bilingualism was neutral, and in yet others it proved beneficial. Hakuta, Ferdman and Diaz (1986) present some additional historical and methodological reasons for differences observed. To explain these divergent results, Cummins proposed, it was necessary to create a more robust model of the relationship between a bilingual's two languages (Fig. 11.2).

Again expanding on results of his own research with various bilingual populations in Canada as well as other studies done around the world, Cummins posited the existence of two different "thresholds" of relationship, a lower and a higher, between a bilingual's languages as the solution to these apparent contradictions: ". . . there may be threshold levels of linguistic competence which bilingual children must attain both in order to avoid cognitive deficits and to allow the potentially beneficial aspects of becoming bilingual to influence their cognitive growth" (1979b:229; see other references cited there). To avoid difficulties in linguistic development and sustain normal cognitive growth, potentially bilingual children had to reach a native level of language skill in at least one of the two relevant languages. Failure to do so could result in such inadequate development of language that negative cognitive effects might ensue; if the child did not possess age-appropriate skills in at least one of the two languages, neither language could then serve

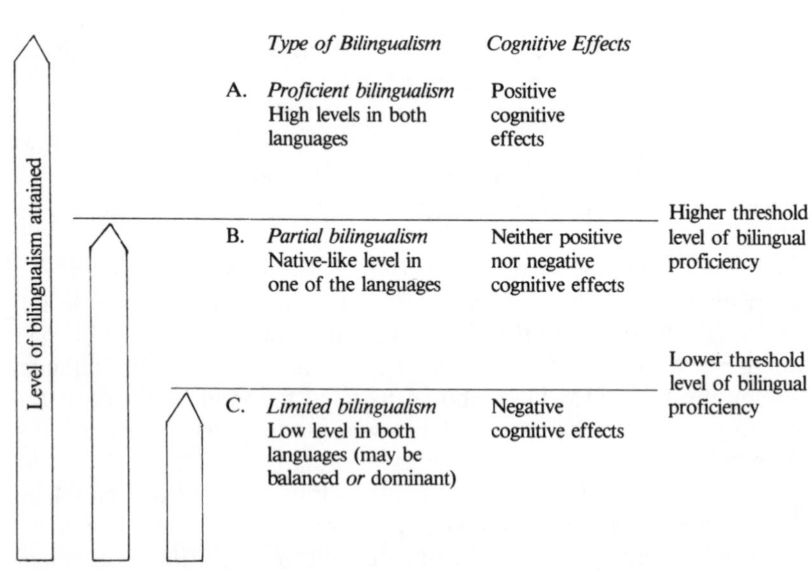

Figure 11.2. Cognitive effects of different types of bilingualism*. (*Source:* Cummins, J. 1981. The role of primary language development in promoting education success for language minority students. In California State Department of Education, *Schooling and Language Minority Students: A Theoretical Framework.* Los Angeles, CA: Dissemination and Assessment Center, California State University, p. 39. Adapted by Cummins from Toukamaa, P. and Skutnabb-Kangas, T. 1977. The intensive teaching of the mother tongue to migrant children of preschool age and children in the lower level of comprehensive school. *Research Reports* 26. Tampere, Finland: Department of Sociology and Social Psychology, University of Tampere, p. 29.)

as a foundation for cognitive growth. This represents the lower threshold of bilingualism. Deprived of a strong linguistic and conceptual knowledge base in at least one language, bilingual children with this linguistic profile could be in jeopardy of lower intellectual and educational progress than unilingual peers. With inadequate levels of skill in both languages, such children might suffer the negative effects of semilingualism; they might experience "subtractive" bilingualism, in which loss of the first language retards mastery of the second (Lambert 1981).

Thus strong skills in at least one of a bilingual child's two languages, Cummins reasons, are essential to avoid deficits. Reaching a native-like level in one of the languages, though, would not necessarily guarantee that a child would enjoy the potential benefits of bilingualism. Once beyond the lower threshold, the student's skills might be those of the "dominant" bilingual who can use two languages in many situations but is clearly stronger in one. Having age-appropriate skills in one language is enough to safeguard against deficits, but it is not enough to enhance intellectual function, according to this hypothesis. Consequently, dominant bilinguals could be expected to show neither positive nor negative effects in terms of cognitive and academic development; academically, we might expect them to be comparable to similar unilingual students in school achievement. In terms of intellectual skills, they would show no deficit, since one language was strong; if only one of the two languages was fully developed in domains relevant to formal education, however, they would show no particular intellectual advantage. For such dominant bilinguals, the effect of bilingualism on cognitive function would be neutral, although they would also possess functional second language skills that might be valuable in many situations.

What levels of skill in each language would ensure that a student could reap the benefits of bilingualism? Enhancement of cognitive function can occur when students reach and surpass the higher threshold, the levels of first and second language proficiency associated with intensive study and experience using the languages for a variety of purposes. Many students who pursue full immersion programs in a second language show these advantages, as do many students who maintain literacy in a language different from that used in school through participating in ethnic or religious programs on an extracurricular basis; they exemplify "additive" bilingualism (Lambert 1981). The advantages enjoyed by those who reach this higher threshold would include an increased awareness of the nature of language, greater flexibility in understanding the arbitrary associations of words and referents, and increased sensitivity to the interpersonal cues of language use (Dolson 1985:10–15). Evidence for these comes from a number of studies carried out in school settings using traditional psychometric instruments (Cummins 1979b:227–229), which show that high levels of bilingual skill are correlated with positive outcomes.

It is important to note that although the threshold model does not directly state this, the hypothesis seems to imply a causal relationship between the degree of bilingualism and other cognitive outcomes. Furthermore, many related discussions and practical prescriptions take the causality as a given. However, because the supporting data are drawn mainly from correlational studies, causality ought not be inferred. It may be that both advanced degrees of bilingualism and superior cognitive skills as measured by available tests are both cumulative results of other factors, such as development of a particular kind of linguistically oriented intelligence (Gardner 1983). The existence of a higher threshold in particular remains speculative, as Cummins admits; the evidence adduced in its favor shows mainly that more language skills are better, not that there is a specific cut-off point that triggers other cognitive outcomes.

To look at language skills as the prior cause of intellectual advantages without considering the influence of social context raises additional questions. Cummins' more recent work, as well as that of other psychologists and linguists concerned with the growth of intellectual, linguistic, and social skills (Tharp and Gallimore 1987; Hatch, Flashner and Hunt 1986; Weisner and Gallimore, 1985), argues for an ongoing reciprocal relationship between language skills, cognition, and social and situational constraints such that they continually condition each other (as the following hypothesis regarding the interdependence of a bilingual's two languages also suggests). Thus unidirectional causality is not an appropriate conceptualization of the relationship between degree of bilingualism and cognitive abilities. Cummins states simply that "the level of linguistic competence attained by bilingual children *may act* as an *intervening* variable in mediating the effects of bilingualism on their cognitive and academic development" (1979b:232; italics added). The nature and extent of intrinsic, necessary, and possible connections between language skills, social factors, and intellectual attainment are still not fully known.

This hypothesis provides at most a provocative model for predicting (in a descriptive sense) the possible cognitive outcomes that co-occur with various levels of bilingualism. It does not directly formulate the developmental relationships between the two languages or the nature of school programs aimed at preventing deficits or enhancing intellectual function. To examine these matters, we turn to Cummins' ensuing proposition, the "Developmental Interdependence Hypothesis."

The Developmental Interdependence Hypothesis

This hypothesis states that "the level of L2 competence which a bilingual child attains is partially a function of the type of competence the child has developed in L1 at the time when intensive exposure to L2 begins" (1979b:233). Research evidence comes from several settings: studies of reading ability that show first and second language reading skills are highly correlated, and studies of minority language children with stronger L1 skills who surpass less proficient L1 peers in L2 schooling (Cummins 1979b:234–235). While, as Cummins notes, motivational factors and features of the educational environment also make a difference in mediating the relationship between the two languages, there is ample reason to assume that the level of first language skills is one of the critical determinants of success in acquiring the second language. This is true for both majority and minority students. However, the social conditions surrounding the languages in question affect the degree to which the two languages should figure in educational programs. Cummins points out that in middle class majority language situations, such as most of the Canadian French immersion programs, the home language, English, "seems to be impervious to 'neglect' by the school" (1979b:233). In many minority language settings, among them the Finnish children mentioned earlier who were schooled in Swedish, and in vernacular language situations exemplified in Modiano's study of Indian children with L1 literacy training whose Spanish (L2) reading skills proved superior to similiar children taught only in Spanish, there is special reason for schools to concentrate efforts on L1 development. If the L1 is a minority language (one that is not used outside the home in a wider community and one that may not be supported by literacy activities in home, church, or community activities), the child may not have experience with the uses of language that facilitate ready acquisition of a second language and, consequently, normal educational progress through the L2, according to the hypothesis. While the social factors that impinge on language learning clearly play a role here, this formulation emphasizes the first language skills the student commands as one of the keys to second language success.

Related to the issue of linguistic interdependence is that of the nature of bilingual proficiency. The critical question here is whether a bilingual's two language systems represent manifestations of a separate underlying proficiency (SUP) or a common underlying proficiency (CUP) model (Cummins 1981:22–34). The SUP model assumes that proficiency in L1 is entirely separate from L2, and that content and skills learned in one language will not transfer to the other. Despite its common sense level of intuitive appeal, Cummins finds no evidence for the validity of the SUP construct. Basing support for the CUP model on evaluations of successful bilingual programs, studies relating age on arrival to second language acquisition, and research linking continued use of a primary language at home with improved school achievement in L2, Cummins concludes that children who experience extensive, natural first language development at home or in school tend to make better progress in school than comparable students whose L1 is not maintained. The inference is that skills learned in the first language transfer into the second, thus establishing the commonality of the underlying language proficiency.

The vital matter of determining which first language skills transfer into the second language suggests the need to specify the nature of language skill more precisely. Accordingly, Cummins proposes a descriptive framework for language skill to elucidate types of language used in developmentally relevant contexts.

A Framework for Language Proficiency

An important corollary of the hypotheses describing the interrelationships between a bilingual's two languages and the developmental aspects of bilingualism is Cummins' conceptualization of a framework for defining types of proficiency in any language. These were first proposed as a distinction between the surface-level skills evident in everyday communicative exchanges (basic interpersonal communication skills: BICS), among them pronunciation and oral fluency; and the abilities to deal with decontextualized language functions (cognitive academic language proficiency: CALP) such as assessment of semantic meaning and analysis of information from texts (Cummins 1979a). This formulation helped to explain why many oral language tests used to assess bilingual students did not predict a student's ability to receive instruction entirely via a second language. According to this hypothetical account of language proficiency, students with apparent oral fluency in the second language could still be developing the skills in comprehension and manipulation of language that were not directly mirrored in the physical context of interpersonal interaction, in other words, according to this construct, in the kind of abstract, text-dependent language found particularly in schools depending on verbal instruction.

Although attractive because of its simplicity, the BICS/CALP dichotomy remained difficult to define in terms of actual, observable language behaviors; even in its later expanded form, it has proven problematic to operationalize for purposes of validation and substantiation of real differences in kind between the two hypothetical poles of language use. Rather than analyzing language proficiencies according to distinguishable aspects of competence, as do typologies such as Canale and Swain's model of communicative competence (1980), the BICS/CALP distinction to some extent confounds different proficiencies with different settings, modes, and purposes for communication. It draws heavily on previous descriptions of oral versus literate language, a distinction that, Cummins states, is involved in the BICS/CALP construct but is not, he implies, synonymous with it. Hence one problem with this framework is the lack of empirical research exemplifying the different skills that constitute these two larger categories. Furthermore, Cummins' ensuing argument that minority children's school failure stems in part from insufficient experience with CALP-related skills in the home environment prior to school entry has been seen as an attempt to rationalize another cognitive deficit hypothesis, reminiscent of 1960s discussions of disadvantaged students, which placed responsibility for minority student failure on the student's own background (Edelsky et al. 1983). To counter such criticism and improve explanatory power, Cummins has expanded the original dichotomy by elaborating the dimensions involved (Figure 11.3).

The expanded framework (see Cummins 1984:136–141) consists of two dimensions, each on a continuum: one axis moves from cognitively demanding to cognitively undemanding activities (the difference between, for example, writing a summary of a text or presentation and writing a shopping list), and the other extends from context-embedded to context-reduced activities (e.g., those where language users can actively negotiate meanings through interactions with other persons and draw on many situational cues versus those where they depend more exclusively on linguistic cues only in texts or talk that does not refer to the immediate surroundings). The intersection of these two axes divides language use into four quadrants that reflect differing demands made on users of language. Of principal relevance to language minority students is Cummins' contention that normal progress in school rests on age-appropriate mastery of skills in each quadrant in at least one language. Basing his claim on the Developmental Interdependence Hypothesis, Cummins states that for language minority students, the language in which mastery is developed should, initially, be the language of the home, since it is in that language that parents and community members can often provide the best support for children's developing language skills. Strong first language skills will then facilitate second language acquisition. Once children have observed and participated in a variety of contextualized and decontextualized language uses in the home and outside of it, they are better

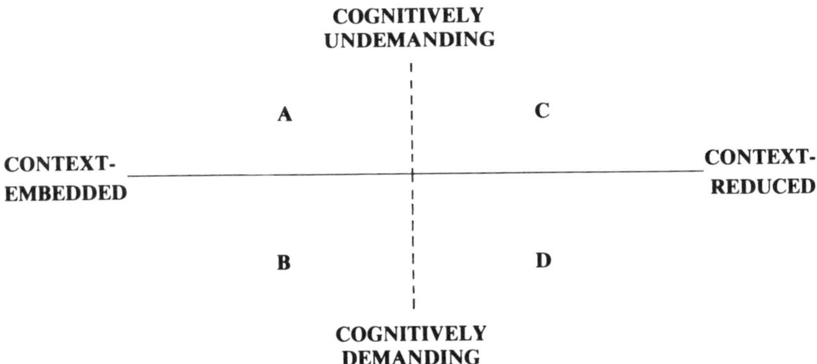

Figure 11.3. Range of contextual support and degree of cognitive involvement in communicative activities. (Source: Cummins, J. 1981. The role of primary language development in promoting education success for language minority students. In California State Department of Education, *Schooling and Language Minority Students: A Theoretical Framework.* Los Angeles, CA: Dissemination and Assessment Center, California State University, p. 12.)

able to deal with the variety of language uses they will encounter in school (see Heath 1986b for related discussions based on ethnographic studies of communication).

Even the expanded framework, which Cummins calls "not a precise model of language proficiency but rather a series of parallel distinctions that are generally consistent with research evidence" that have "important heuristic value" (1984:137), has yet to be completely substantiated in school-based research. Indeed, an initial investigation describing varieties of classroom language (Flashner 1987a,b) shows that most school activities rarely show sharply defined linguistic differences across activities in the degree of cognitive demand and context embedding; the main differences that existed were between oral and written uses of language. The framework is best viewed not as a detailed portrait of the realities of language use but as a stimulus for diversification of the language opportunities available in different activity settings, including but not limited to classrooms. In education, then, the framework can suggest new approaches to offering students a wider range of experiences with different degrees of verbal and nonverbal embedding and contextualization, although its conceptualization of language skill may be nebulous and overly simplified.[2]

In spite of these difficulties, the potential educational implications of these hypotheses are powerful for language minority students. Cummins' framework, along with the two hypotheses already discussed, provides a strong rationale for using a minority language student's home language as the language of initial school and literacy experience wherever feasible; this is the language of the years of experience a child brings to school and the language in which parents and other caretakers can support a child's growing exploration of the uses of languages. It is thus in this language that a comprehensive linguistic foundation for cognitive development can best be built. Students need, minimally, to move beyond the lower threshold of bilingualism, and, optimally, to reach the higher threshold that accompanies academic enhancement. An essential first step in this process is development of strong first language skills. Such primary language skills are additionally crucial for minority language students, the model states, because they mediate a student's ability to master a second language: the stronger the basis of first language skill, the more efficient and accurate the acquisition of a second language, according to the developmental interdependence hypothesis. The strong basis of language skill demands age-relevant mastery of a variety of language uses that comprise cognitively demanding and less demanding and context-embedded and reduced forms of language (whatever these may turn out to be in practice); students need experience with all of these in the first language in order to be able to transfer the skills readily into the second. An additional important consideration, though not one addressed in the models, is the nature of the instruction needed to help students actively transfer their skills; the actual process of transfer may not be automatic in all areas.

Although there are gaps in these models, Cummins' work provides the most thoroughly articulated body of theory and research with specific relevance to language minority students in terms of the nature of the linguistic skills and cognitive processes that contribute to academic success or failure. In his earlier formulations, social factors, while acknowledged as additional determinants of educational outcomes (e.g. 1979b:241–246), are not outlined in detail. In Cummins' recent writings (1984, 1986), there is more explicit attention to the social relationships that shape the educational reality of language minority students. Presently we will consider these together with other models of second language acquisition that address social and psychological relationships as the causal factors in second language acquisition.

First, however, having examined the rationale for first language development in the education of language minority students, we turn to the processes of second language acquisition relevant to all who must learn a second language as defined in the work of Stephen Krashen. Although much of Krashen's theoretical model was developed to explain the general situation of all second language learners, not specifically speakers of minority languages, it offers a provocative account of language learning processes that raises questions and suggests some possible guidelines for second language pedagogy.

PROCESSES GOVERNING SECOND LANGUAGE ACQUISITION: KRASHEN'S HYPOTHESES

Drawing on a variety of research carried out principally with adult learners of second languages, Krashen has proposed five hypotheses that, in his view, account fully for second language acquisition. Four of these describe specifically linguistic processes and one deals with the learner's psychological openness to the new language. The relevant linguistic processes are conceptualized in terms of the nature of the learner's processing of the new language, the order of structural accuracy with which a new language is acquired, and the nature of the language available to the learner. A more detailed critical review of these theories can be found in McLaughlin (1987).

The Acquisition/Learning Distinction

Two hypotheses pertain directly to the kind of processing learners engage in as they encounter a new language. The first, the "Acquisition–Learning Hypothesis," holds that "adults have two distinct and independent ways of developing competence in a native language" (Krashen 1982:10). The first is "language *acquisition,* a process similar, if not identical, to the way children develop ability in their first language"

(1982:10;1981b). Those who acquire a language do so by using it for communication, not by focusing on the correct forms; language acquisition in this sense is thus a subconscious process. While those who acquire a language in this way internalize the systematicity of the language—the rules of competence—they do so by developing a feeling for correctness, not be invoking prescriptive statements about how the language works. In contrast, those who engage in language *learning* attempt to master a language through conscious knowledge, "knowing the rules, being aware of them, and being able to talk about them" (1982:10). Although acquisition may be more typical of children's second language learning, Krashen proposes that all learners can achieve automaticity in second language use by using this facility. However, relying solely on acquisition becomes more difficult as learners mature; both their own attempts to work out the language inductively and the experience of participating in formal instructional settings may lead them to request and rely on explicit rules, particularly in managing the grammar of the new language. For Krashen, such *learning* is relevant mainly for grammatical and syntactic patterns and orthographic conventions, all of which may also be *acquired* under certain conditions. Here features of the learning environment come into play. As defined in Krashen's writings, learning processes are typically found in classrooms where production of correct forms is the major goal of instruction, while acquisition can take place in any environment, classrooms included, where the goal is intelligible communication between the parties involved.

The subconscious/conscious distinction suggests a differential applicability for overt error correction in this scheme: "Error correction has little or no effect on subconscious acquisition, but is thought to be useful for conscious learning" (1982:11). Krashen notes that examination of child language acquisition by many psycholinguists has shown that in the course of natural language development parents and caretakers overwhelmingly correct the meaning rather than the form of an utterance; furthermore, if they try to correct formal structures, the young language learners usually disregard the correction and reply using the grammatical form typical of their stage of development rather than the adult model. In this area, it is problematic to base a theory of second language acquisition entirely on a template of first language acquisition, as Schachter (1986) and Rivers (1980) have pointed out. Second language learners, given their already developed first language awareness and other skills, may well profit from "metalinguistic information" regarding the adequacy and correctness of their utterances. Although there is as yet little solid second language evidence to substantiate the claim of this hypothesis regarding correction, there is also insufficient evidence to refute it. The only suitable correction strategy for acquirers, Krashen implies, is that which addresses semantic meaning rather than grammatical or phonological form. Second language learners, on the other hand, may seek correction, although the extent to which they benefit from it is, according to this hypothesis, negligible. (It should be noted that some classroom studies examining, among other things, error correction, such as Ramirez and Stromquist 1979, have shown that some types of overt grammatical correction directed at accuracy of statements, though infrequent, do indeed improve students' ability to produce language that is not only meaningful but formally acccurate.) Major instructional questions suggested by the Acquisition-Learning Hypothesis are, thus, the optimal conditions for acquisition and learning and the role of explicit attention to form, either by means of overt or indirect correction or other kinds of feedback, in assisting learners to master a second language.

The Monitor Hypothesis

Long a feature of many traditional second language classrooms, focus on form may assist the learner but in a very limited fashion. Krashen's "Monitor Hypothesis" states that "acquisition and learning are used in very specific ways" (1982:15); acquisition triggers utterances and maintains fluency, while conscious learning serves as a "monitor, or editor" that allows a speaker to check on accuracy only when three conditions are met. To use the Monitor, a learner needs (1) to know the relevant rule; (2) to be, at that moment, attending to form rather than meaning; and (3) to have time to apply the rule in performance. Some language tasks, such as writing, are thus far more amenable to application of the Monitor than others, such as conversation, where continued use of the Monitor in every exchange can hinder the exchange of information and exhaust the patience of interlocutors. According to this theory, conscious use of rules has a place in mastering a new language, albeit a limited one: it can help learners improve their accuracy and thus, at minimum, continue the interaction that will enable them to acquire language and, at maximum, move towards automatic control of new second language forms.

Particularly unclear in minority bilingual situations is the relevance of the Monitor Hypothesis for defining the role of first language influence. Krashen holds that use of a conscious, monitored approach to second language production is particularly conducive to intrusion of the first language into second production (1978:13–14). It is important to note that such influence may not hinder communication, particularly where there are structural similarities or lexical cognates between the two languages. Indeed, as Krashen mentions, there is some evidence that those second language structures acquired "earliest and easiest may also be those which show first language influence" (1978:13). He further asserts that interference is most apparent in acquisition-poor environments where learners have little access to peers who speak the second language. With few natural models available, learners must fall back on their still-incomplete knowledge of the second language. When pressed to produce the new language, they attempt to remedy the gaps in performance by using what second-language rules they know and supplementing these with relevant structures or items from the first language. They can thus handle some communication difficulties by means of strategies that include first language use.

Intuitively attractive for explaining aspects of individual student performance in identifying those who over- or undermonitor their production, leading to either extreme concern for correctness at the expense of fluency or to production of fluent speech without regard for accuracy, the Monitor Hypothesis nevertheless does not address some issues of central concern to language minority communities. One is the degree to which language mixing or switching is an acceptable communicative style in the community, rather than evidence of the first language acting as a "substitute utterance initiator" (1978:13). If code-switching is an established mode, first language items that emerge in second language performance may not be a product of a controlled or monitored attempt to fill a performance gap but a naturally acquired and developed communicative channel. Indeed, both historically (see Haugen 1953) and currently (Attinasi et al. 1982:400–422; Poplack 1979), code-switching is a common communicative strategy that may reveal advanced levels of proficiency in both languages.

Another unanswered question is the degree to which first language structures can provide a basis for positive transfer in the new language; for a person in a bilingual community, recognizing and exploiting such points of positive transfer might contribute to a different kind of monitoring—rather like a bilingual editor—that would assess appropriateness according to the co-occurrence of rules from the two language systems and thus suggest a distinctive psycholinguistic process. In such situations, it is possible that the monitor is not language-specific but comprised differentially of L1 and L2 rules. The completeness of conscious rule-learning in each language would then determine how effectively a person could monitor his or her speech (see Krashen 1982:89–98). Here we face intriguing questions of the mental representation of a bilingual's two languages: to what extent, if any, does formal grammatical knowledge in one language interact with formal knowledge of the second? Are these systems separately stored and accessed? Hatch (personal communication 1987) notes that the existence of four separate systems—L1 learning, L1 acquisition, L2 learning, and L2 acquisition—is implausible in terms of the neurolinguistics of language processing. While perhaps not central to the educational practice regarding bilingualism, such matters are important in devising accurate theoretical representations of second language skills in minority language settings.

The Natural Order Hypothesis

Krashen's third proposition, the "Natural Order Hypothesis," states simply that "the acquisition of grammatical structures proceeds in a predictable order'' (1982:12–14) usually little influenced by the first language. Most of the evidence for this comes from cross-sectional comparisons of student responses on discrete-point grammar tests, although samples based on natural language production have also shown similar orders, except for some language tasks such as writing, where conscious monitoring may intervene. Thus Krashen sees all who acquire a second language as following a similar sequence, although the ultimate order may not reflect all of the ''overgeneralizations and intermediate forms'' (1978:8) that learners go through. Furthermore, to the extent that learners rely on formal instruction rather than informal acquisition for exposure to the target language, as they do in any situation where access to native speakers is scarce, the ''natural'' order may be disrupted by instructional effects brought about by use of conscious learning. Because the Natural Order Hypothesis is based on the comparisons of morpheme acquisition between children acquiring a first language and adults and children acquiring a second, obvious questions arise in terms of the differences in the situations of these learners. Moreover, the measures used may restrict the real variation in order of acquisition. Although Krashen states that acquirers (at least, acquirers of English; there is as yet little evidence from other languages; see 1982:14) show the same or highly correlated orders, the tests used are generally aimed at assessing production of the rather small set of obligatory bound morphemes. The observed order may, then, be as much an artifact of the structure of the target language as it is a product of regularities in the learning process itself. This question is important for psycholinguistics but not critical to educational considerations of the needs of bilingual students. Neither Krashen nor other commentators have suggested that such orders, even if they exist, be used as the basis for syllabus design or other input to learners (1982:14, 68–70).

The hypothesis does suggest, however, that second language teachers not be surprised by the systematic approximations of the target language that students produce and, moreover, not strive to correct such errors if students are in a situation where acquisition can take place: as students acquire the language, the hypothesis implies, such errors will be resolved. While the Monitor can be of some limited use in refining second language production according to easily learned rules in certain circumstances (see Krashen 1982:92–104), the Natural Order Hypothesis argues against expecting extensive grammatical instruction to produce learners who can communicate naturally and spontaneously. Appropriateness of Monitor use and degree of tolerance of student errors (by the teacher and the students themselves) depend on the language task involved and the goal of instruction, as Celce-Murcia (1985) points out.

The acquisition-learning distinction, the use of the Monitor, and the Natural Order Hypothesis all address aspects of the learner's own processing and production of the new language; they are internally motivated formulations of second language mastery. We turn now to Krashen's descriptions of the external conditions that affect language acquisition and language learning. Here we find his most ambitious claim in the "Input Hypothesis."

The Input Hypothesis

The Input Hypothesis deals with language *acquisition* as defined in the Acquisition-Learning Hypothesis. Because this is the process responsible for mastery of language use, with conscious learning serving a peripheral role in refining a limited number of skills, this is the process for which Krashen feels any theory of second language development must account. In his view, second language acquisition can be fully explained on the basis of comprehensible input, "the only causative variable in second language acquisition" (1981a:62; 1985). The Input Hypothesis is comprised of four related propositions. First, as noted, the relevant process is acquisition, not learning. Second, acquisition takes place when learners understand a structure a bit beyond their current stage of competence (that is, when the input, "i," is slightly more advanced than their own level of development and thus could be called "i + 1"). Third, when communication is successful and sufficient in quantity, "i + 1 will be provided automatically"; and, fourth, "Production ability emerges. It is not taught directly" (1982:20–22). This hypothesis thus challenges the assumption that grammatically sequenced approaches to language acquisition requiring initial mastery of forms will lead to fluency (see Hatch 1978); it is primarily focused on transmission of meanings that lead to the practice that could eventually bring about structural accuracy (Krashen 1982:21).

Evidence supporting the Input Hypothesis is drawn from two areas of research on simplified codes: the work done by Hatch (summarized in 1983b, 1983a, Ch. 9) and Snow (overviewed in 1977) and their colleagues on caretaker language with young children, and the work inspired by Ferguson (1975) on the modified language of native to nonnative speakers ("foreigner talk"). Caretaker speech is not carried out to teach language explicitly but to comment on the "here and now" situation which the child and the caretaker experience together (Krashen 1982:23). Caretaker speech is also an example of optimal input because it is "roughly tuned" to the child's level of linguistic competence, according to Krashen, rather than "finely tuned" to the exact level of the child. In schematic terms, it includes not just i + 1 but, at times, i + 2, i + 3, etc. Because the immediate context provides so many of the topics for talk, he observes that there is ample extralinguistic support to help the child understand what is going on, and the child's growing understanding makes some of the input interpretable and alerts him or her to aspects of language beyond his or her own competence. Furthermore, "roughly tuned" input provides a built-in review, Krashen says, since with enough natural communication, the critical i + 1 "will occur and reoccur"

(1982:24). Children acquiring a first language thus do so through appropriately adapted input, which leads them to successively more advanced stages.

Because second language acquirers also go through definable stages in production of the new language and are also the targets of simplified input, Krashen sees their experience equally well explained by the Input Hypothesis. Although the simplified codes used to speak to children and to second language learners are not identical, they are comparable in that modifications are made to assist communication, not to teach language directly. According to this hypothesis, the modifications are roughly tuned rather than finely tuned to the learner's level in terms of rate, lexical variety, structural complexity, and, often, length of utterance. In both situations, interlocutors use contextual support such as gestures, objects, or knowledge of the world to help convey meaning if they perceive that verbal means alone are not sufficient (Krashen 1982:24–25; 1981a:128–132). For second as well as first language learners, the model asserts that all learners need is sufficient comprehensible input.

Such a strong claim invites careful scrutiny to assess its acceptability on theoretical and practical grounds, particularly in light of potential pedagogical applications. The Input Hypothesis can be challenged on three major counts that affect its relevance for the second language education of language minority students: (1) the lack of attention to learner production and interaction in the new language; (2) the still unclear theoretical distinction between stages of input and between input (what the learner hears) and intake (what the learner actually processes); and (3) the culturally bound nature of the first language learning model, the analogy on which the Input Hypothesis is based. Theoretical and empirical research in each of these areas qualifies the hypothesis in ways especially pertinent to language education.

Evidence for the insufficiency of comprehensible input comes from longitudinal studies of Canadian immersion programs where, after nearly 7 years of predominantly French medium instruction, students show receptive skills comparable to native speaker peers but productive skills that are clearly nonnative and lack the grammatical and sociolinguistic refinement needed to convey information appropriately (Swain 1985:238, 244). As Swain notes, these students enjoyed maximal second language input that was clearly comprehensible, since they had mastered school subjects taught in French and on achievement measures scored no differently from the English speakers who had received comparable academic instruction in English. Nonetheless, their French did not reach native speaker levels, in part because they had none of the interaction with native speaker peers that would create a press for "comprehensible output," the need to negotiate meaning with fluent speakers of the language. The importance for learner output may vary by proficiency level (see Van Patten 1987), but it must come into play for successful acquisition.

Additional theoretical questions related to the adequacy of input for productive language ability come from the growing body of research demonstrating that even the first language develops through interaction rather than mere exposure (see, for example, John-Steiner and Tatter 1983 and Wells 1985). Linguists concerned with second language acquisition (Hatch et al. 1987; Hatch 1983b; Long 1981) have shown that for these learners too, it is the adaptive quality of interaction—the degree to which responses are contingent on what the learners need to continue communication—that develops productive competence. This position is consistent with findings from ecological psychology showing that many forms of competence, including literacy skills, develop through personal interaction in which more skilled individuals guide the less skilled, who also assist each other, through words or actions (Tharp and Gallimore 1987, Ch. 5; Hawkins 1987; Rogoff 1986). The presence and nature of interaction adapted to the learner's level, not only the availability of an appropriate model, brings about skill acquisition. Both research and more broadly based learning theory argue against Krashen's position that output has only an indirect role in language acquisition (1982:60–62). Current literature from psycholinguistics and from other areas of the epistemology of knowledge acquisition thus suggests that input in itself is not enough to produce mastery.

Even if the commonalities of input outweigh the differences across settings, we must face the question of the boundaries of the stages of input if we are to specify i + 1, i + 2, etc., with any precision. First language research shows that input is modified along various dimensions simultaneously. Except for length of utterance, in which there is a clear trend towards gradual increase, other structural features such as syntactic complexity and propositional density have no easily quantifiable relationship to learner level (Cross 1977). While the discourse pattern as a whole facilitates development through interaction and negotiation, it is not yet possible to break input into distinct stages that correspond closely to learner development. Krashen's discussion suggests that input is not grammatically sequenced; if so, it would be useful to specify the alternative principles of construction of meaning that guide those who produce the language to which learners respond.

Besides needing more information more about the nature of input, we would profit by a better ability to distinguish it from intake; otherwise we cannot assess intake except in a circular fashion (i.e., intake is the input the learner understands). Schachter's (1986) discussion suggests the main areas of investigation, among them validation of the existence of distinct stages of input by means of linguistic description of the gradually more complex structures and more precise statements of the relationship between input and intake in various settings (e.g., Chaudron 1985), needed to demonstrate the full extent of applicability of the Input Hypothesis to second language acquisition and instruction.

Furthermore, the first language analogies used as the basis for defining comprehensible input also need to be analyzed with some circumspection. Much of the research supporting the hypothesis comes from the psycholinguistic literature on first-born children in Western middle class societies. As more detailed accounts of child language acquisition in other settings, both American subcultures (see Heath 1983, 1986b) and other cultures (see Ochs and Schieffelin 1984), become available, it is clear that the highly focused caretaker speech typical of the earlier literature is simply one of many ways children are socialized to language. These more recent accounts show that in some cultural settings children receive rather little personalized input and are expected to learn language through observation of the interactions of others, while in some other settings, children are, in fact, explicitly "taught" to speak by caretakers who model utterances and explicitly correct forms. In spite of all these behaviors, which to some extent counter the Input Hypothesis, all children learn to speak quite adequately and naturally according to community standards. The nature of appropriate input and interaction, then, may be to some extent culture-specific, as may the learner's propensity to use input from different sources. Observational work in classrooms serving Chinese and Hispanic children has shown that in the initial stages of exposure to English, they have somewhat different preferences for and predisposition to profit from teacher- versus peer-generated input (Wong Fillmore et al. 1985:220–232).

One additional consideration is that the development of skills related to manipulation of literate language may follow a somewhat different course from those that reflect oral language use. In emphasizing the exclusive causative role of comprehensible input and the relatively weak contribution of the press for and negotiation of comprehensible output in written as well as oral/aural modes, the Input Hypothesis does not sufficiently account for aspects of language development that include ability to comprehend and produce written texts. Although exposure to written language input is essential to development of text-related skill, as argued by Krashen (1984) it is not sufficient to guarantee mastery. Again, the need for initial oral negotation of the meaning of text and active learner participation, now widely noted in developmental research on the literacy acquisition of native speakers (Wells 1985, Ch. 8; 1981:263; Heath 1986a), suggests that interaction and individual effort to create and modify texts must also take place. Because literacy skills are crucial contributors to educational success for all students, it is particularly important to articulate the nature of the receptive and the active language—the input, negotiation, and output—required for their acquisition. Krashen's Input Hypothesis, while useful in stimulating discussion and research, remains in need of additional elaboration to address this area before it can offer a fuller account of second language acquisition across skill domains and learning in written and oral modes and serve as thence a better guide for educational practice.

The Affective Filter Hypothesis

First proposed by Dulay and Burt (1977, cited in Krashen 1982:31), the "Affective Filter Hypothesis" as formulated by Krashen connects the processes of language acquisition with the variables of anxiety, motivation, and self-confidence (1981a:61–62). It states that learners have an affective filter that determines their orientation to language learning and their predilection to take advantage of acquisition opportunities (Figure 11.4). Those with "high or strong" filters will be unable to use all available input because psychological factors intervene; those with "lower or weaker" affective filters, shaped by stronger motivation, better self-confidence, and lower anxiety, will be more likely to seek input and more open to using it (1982:30–31). The lower the affective filter, the more the learner can exploit the possibilities for acquisition available in the environment; the filter must be "low enough to allow the input in" (1981a:62).

In Krashen's model of second language acquisition, the affective filter plays a critical mediating role: it determines whether or not the learner will seek and be able to take advantage of all the available input. If the learner is anxious, lacks interest in and motivation to acquire the language, or lacks confidence in his or her own ability to learn, acquisition will be hindered and may be almost precluded if the filter is high. It should again be emphasized that these factors are hypothesized to be related to acquisition, not learning, on the grounds that they appear more closely associated with communicative tests and results from students in "acquisition-rich" environments (1982:31). According to this hypothesis, the metaphorical filter apparently serves a neurological function such that in learners with a strong affective filter "even if they understand the message, the input will not reach that part of the brain responsible for language acquisition" (1982:31). Moreover, the affective filter is the sole reason that learners who obtain "a great deal of comprehensible input" still "stop short . . . of the native speaker level" (1982:32); it is hence the cause of fossilization, or reaching a plateau at a level below native-speaker competence.

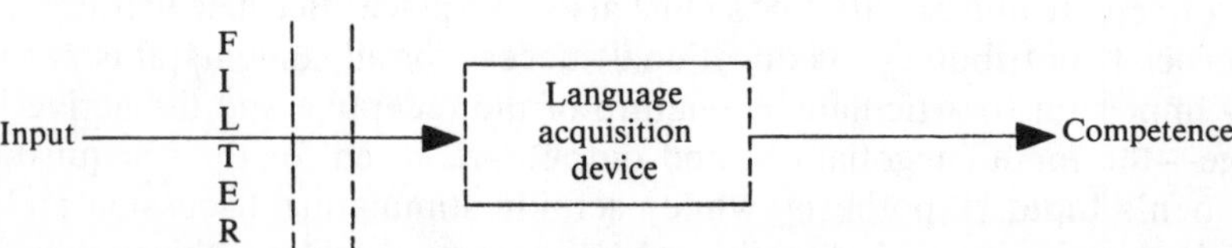

Figure 11.4. The affective filter. (*Source:* Krashen, S. D. 1981a. Bilingual education and second language acquisition theory. In California State Department of Education, *Schooling and Language Minority Students: A Theoretical Framework.* Los Angeles, CA: Dissemination and Assessment Center, California State University, p. 62.)

critique

Although no one would argue that affective variables are unimportant in language learning (or in any other kind of learning), the factors included in the affective filter must be defined in more detail to be more than general indications that a negative attitude makes language acquisition less likely. Certainly extreme anxiety can be disabling, but some slight degree of anxiety or active anticipation can facilitate the acquisition of knowledge and skill in some circumstances. Motivation, too, can take various forms within the overall "positive" or "negative" dimensions suggested here, as we will see in Schumann's discussion of the issue. The proposition that the filter stops input from reaching a particular brain area demands empirical verification; so does the assertion that the presence of a strong affective filter accounts for incomplete mastery of a language when sufficient comprehensible input is available. As we have noted in the discussion of the Input Hypothesis, incomplete mastery may well be a result of inadequate output opportunities unrelated to the learner's filter. Thus the Affective Filter Hypothesis should be seen as a global and metaphorical statement about the learner's predisposition to use available input rather than an exact formulation of the psycholinguistic processes involved in second language acquisition.

These five hypotheses have been used to explain the success of some current nontraditional methods such as Total Physical Response, the Silent Way, and Counseling–Learning. They also provide the basis for Krashen and Terrell's Natural Approach (1983), a methodology aimed at oral skill development for beginning and intermediate students that emphasizes making the classroom a place rich in acquisition possibilities, full of comprehensible input, and low in anxiety. Krashen has, in addition, assessed educational programs for language minority students in light of these hypotheses to derive guidelines for instruction. According to his theoretical view of second language mastery, three conditions must be met to promote full second language acquisition: (1) students must have available to them comprehensible input in the weaker language through classroom instruction or interaction with peers (preferably both); (2) they must maintain and develop their first language skills in order to sustain both age-appropriate cognitive growth and the pride in the home language and culture that will build the confidence needed to deal with the learning of a second language; and (3) students should continue the subject matter instruction necessary to avoid the slowing of normal school progress; instruction in subjects other than language is important to provide the intellectual stimulation that can assist second language acquisition by providing the context for understanding academic input (1981a:66–70).

Overall, in terms of principal theoretical emphasis, it could be said that Cummins' models are mainly concerned with text- and literacy-based dimensions of language proficiency (McLaughlin 1982:14–15), while Krashen's theories and the methodologies they have informed are more relevant to oral skills. Both, of course, are essential.

global

We shall return shortly to the matter of the skills minority language students need for academic and personal success and appropriate pedagogical approaches. First, however, there is one body of theory not yet examined which deals with the social factors affecting the opportunity for second language acquisition. These factors are strikingly absent from Krashen's model, which focuses on individual learner variables and the linguistic properties of the language used to and by the learner. The third model to be considered here combines individual orientations to the second language with an analysis of intergroup relationships to account for second language acquisition.

SOCIAL AND AFFECTIVE CONDITIONS SHAPING LANGUAGE ACQUISITION: SCHUMANN'S ACCULTURATION MODEL

John Schumann's "Acculturation Model" posits "two groups of variables—social factors and affective factors—[that] cluster into the single variable which is the major causal variable in second language acquisition" (1978a:29). This variable is *acculturation,* which Schumann defines as "the social and psychological integration of the learner with the target language group" (p. 29). The Acculturation Model was proposed to explain second language learning in adults "under conditions of immigration or an extended sojourn in the target language area" (1978a) in which "learning takes place without instruction" (1986:385). The model assumes that the nature of the contact and the social–psychological distance between the groups involved is the underlying cause of the interaction opportunities that then shape second language learning. Developed to explain the situation of uninstructed adults, it does not directly address the developmental questions that arise in the course of consideration of children's language acquisition of one or two languages, as do Cummins' hypotheses, nor does it lend itself to direct application in program design or classroom methodology, as do some of Cummins' and Krashen's proposals. Nevertheless, because it brings to center stage the social factors that have heretofore been mentioned only peripherally, the Acculturation Model merits attention from those concerned with education for language minority students, since these factors affect children (though perhaps in different ways and with different degrees of intensity) as they do adults. Furthermore, the social and psychological contexts of second language acquisition have come to be viewed as increasingly important both in understanding why some minority students succeed and others fail (see, for example, Ogbu and Matute-Bianchi 1986) and why certain kinds of contextually sensitive educational interventions hold promise (Diaz 1987; Diaz, Moll and Mehan 1986; Schneider, Hyland and Gallimore 1985). While the Acculturation Model does not deal directly with a language minority situation, it includes several powerful concepts related to aspects of second language acquisition. Particularly important are the social and affective variables that we shall now briefly describe.

Social Variables Influencing Acculturation

In Schumann's model, the social factors that determine the nature of acculturation and thus the nature and extent of second language acquisition are the "variables which involve the relationship between two social groups who are in a contact situation, but who speak different languages" and so "promote or inhibit contact between the two groups" (1978a:29). These factors operate on a group level to mediate contact between the target language and second language communities; they are expressions of collective relationships and affect individual learners only insofar as individuals are influenced or constrained by the social parameters of the model.

Social Dominance. The first social factor that affects second language acquisition is that of *social dominance patterns:* the degree to which one of the groups is "politically, culturally, technically or economically superior" (1978a:30; 1986:380–381) to the other. If the second language group is dominant to the target language group, as were, for example, French colonists in Tunisia, they will tend not to learn the target language, in this case Arabic; the social distance between the groups does not encourage intergroup contact in a variety of domains. Similarly, if the second language group is subordinate in power to the target language group, there will also be considerable social distance and thus less favorable conditions for second language acquisition. Schumann sees this situation as typical of minority groups such as Native Americans in the Southwest who have resisted the learning of English because of this and other social factors (1978a:30). If the two groups are approximately equal in political and social status and power, more extensive intergroup contact and hence more possibilities for second language acquisition will occur. Hence the power relationships reflected in the contacts between the two groups provide the starting place for identification of the social factors influencing second language acquisition.

Integration Strategy. The second social factor in the model is that dealing with the degree of integration between the groups. The three integration strategies pertinent to this factor are *assimilation, preservation,* and *adaptation;* each denotes a different kind of intergroup relationship and thus distinct possibilities for language acquisition. If the second language group abandons its own way of life and adopts that of the target language group, there is maximal contact between the groups and hence much opportunity for second language learning (1978a:30; 1986:381). Additionally, the abandonment of the second language community's own way of life suggests little incentive for maintenance of traditional cultural patterns or a home language that would compete with the target language in any domain; this suggests that minority groups following the assimilation pattern would lose the first language rapidly. If, however, the second language group chooses the option of preservation, maintaining its own life styles, customs, and values and rejecting those of the target group, the social distance that remains between the two groups makes second language acquisition less probable. In minority communities such as the Amish in parts of the United States, who have chosen preservation, the home language is retained for most or all intragroup communication, and English is used little if at all, and then only when contact with the outside world demands it. If the second language group adapts to the life-style and values of the target language community in intergroup contacts but retains its own life-style and values for intragroup use—the adaptation option—there are varying possibilities for contact between the groups, and thus different types and levels of first language maintenance and second language acquisition would be possible.

Here we must point out that for second language acquisition to take place, the model points to *either* assimilation or adaptation as the enabling condition; evidence indicates that adult learners need not assimilate into a culture in order to acquire the language (Haskell 1987). For language minority individuals wishing to learn English, complete assimilation is not essential; all that is required is some degree of adaptation in situations of intergroup contact that will create contexts for second language acquisition. It is notable that neither this theoretical framework nor the other two posits the necessary loss of the first language when the second is acquired; as we have seen, in Cummins' model, the degree to which the first language is mastered will influence the ease of second language acquisition, while second language acquisition is not assumed to diminish first language abilities in any way. In Schumann's model as well, the acquisition of a second language does not imply loss of the first unless the group has chosen (or been forced into) the assimilation option that involves giving up the group's original ways of life and communication in favor of the target group modes (see Paulston 1976, 1980 on these considerations in analyzing the contexts of bilingual education; these considerations motivated the development of the Acculturation Model; Schumann 1978a:27). Consequently the type of integration strategy followed by the group is a critical determinant of second language acquisition; the strategy may well include continued scope for use of the first language as well as the contact that promotes acquisition of the second.

Enclosure. The choice of integration strategies is linked to the third social variable in the model, *enclosure,* or the degree to which secondary social institutions such as "churches, schools, clubs, recreational facilities, crafts, professions, and trades" (1978a:30) are shared by the two groups. If they share many of these institutions, a situation of low enclosure exists; the shared institutions permit many kinds of contact, and second language acquisition is enhanced. In contrast, if few or no institutions are common to both groups so that religious, recreation, and occupational experiences are not shared—a situation historically characteristic of many first-generation immigrant communities in the United States (see, for example, Jones and Holli 1981 on Chicago's ethnic communities; Rippley 1976 on German groups in the Midwest; and Romo 1983 on the Mexican community in East Los Angeles, as well as other chapters in this book for more contemporary accounts of additional immigrant groups)—there is high enclosure and consequently far fewer possibilities for intergroup contact. In such situations, again, the community language remains the major vehicle of communication, since the limited contact provides little incentive or opportunity for comprehensive second language acquisition across domains.

Size, Cohesiveness, Congruence, Attitude, and Intended Length of Residence. The additional social factors that influence second language acquisition at the group level are *group size, cohesiveness, cultural congruence, attitude,* and *intended length of residence.* If the potential second language group is both large and cohesive, tending to look to its own members for all survival needs and able, because of substantial numbers, to satisfy these needs within the ethnic community, there will be less intergroup contact and thus less second language acquisition. If the cultures of the two groups are congruent, similar, or identical on important dimensions of behavior and values, this too will facilitate contact and hence second language learning, as will positive intergroup attitudes on the part of each group toward the other. Finally, the length of time a group intends to reside in the target language community (regardless of the actual length of residence; intention and actual duration can be quite different) can serve to promote or inhibit second language acquisition. A longer intended length of residence usually leads to greater contact with the target language group, which in turn facilitates second language learning (1978a:31; 1986:381–382).

These social variables identify the collective conditions that set the scene for each individual's potential retention of the first language and acquisition of the second. In outlining the individual variables particularly relevant to second language learning, Schumann emphasizes a set of affective variables that, in effect, amplify the constructs that form Krashen's Affective Filter Hypothesis. Having examined the group factors affecting acculturation, we turn now to the individual psychological variables involved.

Affective Variables in Acculturation

Understanding the affective variables that shape second language acquisition is particularly important for those involved in education for language minority students, because these factors illuminate the individual second language experience. Even if the social conditions discussed above appear favorable for second language acquisition, Schumann notes that it may not occur if the individual variables militate against it. Conversely, unfavorable social circumstances for second language acquisition may be superseded by learners whose individual predispositions and attitudes are strongly positive and thus motivate them to make special efforts (Schumann 1978a:31; 1986:382). In the Acculturation Model, the pertinent affective factors are language shock, culture shock, motivation, and ego-permeability.

Language Shock. The matter of *language shock,* or fear of appearing comical when trying to use another language (Stengal 1939, cited in Schumann 1978a, 1986), is one that at first glance seems particularly relevant to adults, who are assumed to have relatively greater social inhibitions and fear of criticism than children, who are more inclined to see language as a form of play, according to the psychoanalyst who first proposed this construct. Additionally, speakers enjoy the "narcissistic gratification" of speaking a language well and temporarily lose this important source of rewards when they try to express themselves in another language. While originally proposed to explain adult–child differences in second language learning, this factor may nevertheless be relevant for language minority children as well. Observational research on Spanish-speaking kindergarteners learning English has shown great individual variation in the willingness to tolerate the frustration of trying to make oneself understood in a new language in a variety of school activities (Wong Fillmore 1979:223–224). The "shock" and frustration of attempting to use a new language to convey concepts already known may in itself inhibit second language acquisition.

Culture Shock. The more familiar construct of *culture shock,* or "the anxiety resulting from the disorientation encountered upon entering a new culture" (Schumann 1978a:32) is one that is also seen as particularly relevant to adults, who may initially become dependent and childlike upon entry into a new environment where their usual coping mechanisms do not apply. Everyday survival and previously appropriate problem-solving strategies do not work, and individuals may become exhausted and discouraged from the effort to continue routine activities. As a result, they may fall back on the original culture to whatever extent possible and isolate themselves from the new culture; reject the original culture and attempt to assimilate completely into the new culture; become marginal persons uninvolved in either culture; or strive for some synthesis of the two (Berry 1983). This construct was developed to describe the situation of adult immigrants but relates to the situation of language minority students in two ways. First, because students may have internalized their original culture before they enter the new culture, they may experience greater culture shock. This would be particularly true of older learners who come into the new culture during or after adolescence, when individual cultural identity has been more firmly established through life experiences. Other things being equal, then, older second language learners would be expected to experience more culture shock. However, even much younger second language learners may very well be affected by the degrees of culture shock affecting their parents and other members of the primary social group. A role model who is enthusiastic or disaffected regarding the new culture can set a powerful example for the young learner to emulate in terms of second language learning as well as other culturally sensitive behaviors.

Motivation. Such influences can be particularly strong in the area of individual *motivation* to learn a second language, which is the third affective factor in Schumann's model. The concept of motivation in second language learning was first presented as a dichotomy between learners drawn to a second language for either "integrative" or "instrumental" reasons (Gardner and Lambert 1972, cited in Schumann 1978a, 1986); the former refers to a desire to associate with or become like speakers of the new language, the latter to a desire to accomplish other goals such as occupational advancement through language. Since then, the area of motivation has been further differentiated to include other aspects of the drive to acquire or learn a second language that may operate in different situations (Ely 1986). Current views suggest that motivation and learning influence each other reciprocally, so it would be inaccurate to see motivation as occurring prior to language skill. It was originally proposed that integratively oriented learners would be motivated to seek out more opportunities to use the new language and, because they wished to become more like those who speak the language, learn it better. Instrumentally oriented learners, on the other hand, would learn the second language only to the point needed to satisfy instrumental goals (Schumann 1978a, 1986). However, research using these constructs as predictors of language learning has shown that in some situations such as occupational or professional advancement, instrumental goals may be more important than integrative orientation in determining the success of second language acquisition. This seems particularly true for adult populations who require second language skills for specific occupational purposes, as Schumann notes (1978a:46). The integrative aspect of motivation may be most applicable to learners who could conceivably have some access to the second language community outside their formal instructional program. The degree to which they see such contact as desirable would then be evidence of integrative motivation, which could enhance second language acquisition. Thus the nature and expected influence of the learner's motivation are conditioned by the social factors posited in the first portion of the model.

Ego-Permeability. The final affective variable to be addressed in the Acculturation Model is that of *ego-permeability,* a concept related to the idea that each person has a "language ego" (akin to the Freudian concept of "body ego") that establishes for him or her a sense of the limits and boundaries of his or her language; such boundaries are flexible in the early stages of development and later become more rigid (Guiora 1972, cited in Schumann 1978a:33; 1978b:94–95; 1986:384). Assuming that rigid definitions of one's language ego make a person less amenable to the new influences that come with exposure to the second language (a condition comparable to having a high affective filter in Krashen's thoery), the model suggests that those whose language egos are more permeable will have more success in second language acquisition. Some evidence favoring this proposition is drawn from research with adult subjects in whom temporary states of lowered inhibition were induced through hypnosis or consumption of alcohol and who then showed somewhat improved pronunciation in a second language (Schumann 1978a:33–34). Schumann then relates this relatively less inhibited state to a learner's hypothetical degree of opennness to target language input (1986:384), thus equating permeability of language ego with specific receptivity to new target language stimuli. This is an intriguing though still speculative connection that could explain some individual differences in second language acquisition.

The constellations of social and psychological variables affecting second language acquisition work in tandem to determine the extent of the social and psychological distance between the learner and the target language community, which are the fundamental constructs of the Acculturation Model (Schumann 1978a:36–37; 1978b:77–91). The social factors show the collective distance between the two language communities that affects the number and nature of contacts between them, which then facilitate or inhibit second language acquisition. The affective factors determine how close or far from speakers of the target language potential learners perceive themselves to be and, thus, how much effort they are likely to expend in acquiring the second language well. Of the two, Schumann suggests that psychological distance may be the more important in determining the degree of acculturation that then promotes or hinders second language acquisition, according to preliminary research on adult Spanish speakers learning English in circumstances of long-term exposure in the United States (Stauble 1978, cited in Schumann 1978a:36–37). A learner who perceives considerable psychological distance between himself or herself and the target language would not be likely either to seek out or be open to using opportunities to develop the second language, and might thus ultimately attain an incomplete mastery of the language likened to a kind of pidgin (Schumann 1978a:40; 1978b). Given sufficient opportunity, input, and motivation to use the target language, a learner could then expand his or her simplified system into eventual conformity with the target language (1978a:44). Lacking these, he or she is unlikely to attain native speaker control of the second language and may reach a plateau at any stage of second language acquisition when the level of linguistic skill reflective of his or her social and psychological integration into and distance from the second language community has been reached. Thus social factors, as well as the psychological variables similar to the affective filter, can account for incomplete mastery in this model.

We have observed that this model was constructed to explain the second language learning of adult immigrants who sojourn in other countries. In these circumstances, Schumann states, the Acculturation Model, with its associated social and affective variables, governs the course of second language learners who learn without formal instruction. In Schumann's formulation, the model does not apply to learners who become bilingual in the course of elite educational programs in their own countries, to the natural interaction of members of families in which two languages are routinely used, or to participants in intensive and specialized courses of second language instruction such as those available at government language schools. Second language acquisition under these circumstances, Schumann holds, is an aspect of *enculturation,* one of the means by which individuals develop their sense of identity within a culture, not a product of the type of contact between two different cultures, which is an essential feature of acculturation (1978a:49). The model is thus relevant to language minority communities insofar as they exemplify the features it assumes. As we have seen in other chapters, the situation of many language minority communities in the United States, and in other large industrialized nations such as Canada and Australia, includes some of these aspects of social and psychological influences on second language learning, although the educational experiences of language minority students in these countries also reflect enculturation as well as acculturation processes (see, for example, Cummins 1983; Gillett 1987; Lo Bianco 1987).

Because the Acculturation Model is so comprehensive in the number of factors posited and in the general nature of the interrelationships proposed, it is best seen as a wide-ranging framework for the study of second language acquisition. It is not a single variable or dimension but rather a whole complex of influences whose multiple interrelationships make the model impossible to dismiss but also difficult to confirm with exactness. Beyond the possibly greater role of psychological rather than social distance (a formulation that is still tentative), it is not yet possible to ascribe differential strengths of contribution to the other sets of variables included. While all of the factors hypothesized certainly play a role, the relative weight of each has not been sufficiently established to allow any but very broad descriptive predictions of second language learning outcomes that result from different social and psychological conditions. Furthermore, as Schumann has emphasized, the model was developed only to account for the untutored second language acquisition of adult immigrants; the factors identified are thus most useful for post hoc analyses of learners in this situation. Not designed to deal with questions of second language study, the model has no direct instructional applications, in Schumann's view (1986:385). Nevertheless, it is reasonable to suggest that the hypothesized factors, to the extent that they affect learners engaged in formal second language learning as well as second language acquisition, may interact with the instructional program offered in ways that influence the outcomes of second language instruction. Like the other relationships mentioned in the model, this possible connection also requires further research to determine its validity.

EMPOWERMENT THROUGH INTERACTION: CUMMINS' RECOMMENDATIONS

Social variables have been directly incorporated into instruction in the last theoretical scheme to be discussed here: Cummins' 1986 formulation of appropriate frameworks for educational intervention for minority students. Although he addresses educational matters not limited to language, the ideas are relevant to our discussion because they incorporate some of the concerns noted in the previous theoretical models. In this article, he presents three hypotheses based on social relationships between majority and minority groups, students, and teachers that assume that "students from 'dominated' societal groups are 'empowered' or 'disabled' as a direct result of their interactions with educators in the schools"(1986:21). In this model, social factors account for the frequent failure of previous attempts at educational reform. Only through a change in role definitions of educators that reflect different orientations to student abilities and contributions can the trend be reversed, which is a theme sounded by other liberal (Goodlad 1984) and radical (Schor 1986) critics of education. Cummins' discussion is directed at minority students in many contexts but is particularly relevant to the case of language minority students who, like many other minority group students in the United States, come from groups dominated in social, economic, political, or cultural relations by a larger community that controls schooling. Thus some political changes, like those proposed for European minority groups (Skutnabb-Kangas 1981:296–327), are implied. Using the concept of dominant/dominated groups (one that reminds us of Schumann's first social variable relevant to second language acquisition for adults), Cummins explains how schools have to date disabled too many minority students and proposes what they must do to empower them instead. Language use is only one of the issues he covers. However, because he places it within a comprehensive prescription for student success, the entire framework merits attention and challenges those concerned with language minority education to take social factors into account and alter them through new definitions of and behaviors in their professional roles.

Balance of Power Between Groups

The first set of relationships relevant to analyzing school failure and promoting success for minority students is that reflecting intergroups power relations. Like many social theorists, Cummins (1986:23) holds that "[m]inority students are disabled or disempowered by schools in very much the same way that their communities are disempowered by interactions with societal institutions." Four elements in the structure of schooling determine the extent to which students will be disabled or empowered. Although only one of them explicitly includes language, all involve linguistic and cultural influences indirectly and are thus relevant to our discussion here. The first critical element is the extent of incorporation of the students' home language and culture into the school program in terms of language of instruction, content of the curriculum, and "adjustment of instructional patterns to take account of culturally conditioned learning styles" (Cummins 1986:25). Where the home language and culture have a legitimate place in school, we have an additive situation likely to benefit students by facilitating cognitive enhancement through attainment of the higher threshold of bilingualism and a stronger self-identity. If the school does not recognize and incorporate the first language and culture, the student may experience the linguistic and psychological deficits associated with subtractive bilingual development. Hence first language, home culture, and associated interaction patterns must be integrated into the educational program, Cummins states, to effect student progress in all areas of education.

School/Community Relations

The three remaining elements of education in need of change reflect linguistic and cultural issues less centrally. Nevertheless, these elements represent the two additional sets of relationships that constitute the model for intervention and consequently merit attention for their practical implications as well as their relevance to second language acquisition. The second structural feature in need of redefinition is that governing school/minority community relations, which can take place in a continuum ranging from exclusionary to collaborative (1986:26–27). A collaborative orientation toward the minority language community would include willingness to work with aides and parents who speak the home language as well as to provide other ways for parents to participate in children's learning, which are suggestions familiar to many second language educators (Ashworth 1985). Educators who do this will empower students and parents and thus help to create a more positive learning environment.

Pedagogy

The central classroom issues of teachers' pedagogy and assessment practices are the final features included in the model. These exemplify the third set of relationships to be redefined: those between educators and minority students. Pedagogical practices that will benefit students are those drawn from the "reciprocal interaction model" (Cummins 1986:28) of education that sees meaningful oral and written interaction between teacher and students and among the students themselves as the matrix of learning. Drawing on Freire's literacy work, Cummins contrasts this with the "transmission" approach to education, predominant in most classrooms, that assumes the teacher's role is to impart known skills and knowledge to students who do not yet know them. In such an approach, minority students are often limited by teachers' preconceived notions of what they can do. Only through interaction in which they are full participants rather than a passive audience do students develop the intellectual and expressive skills that contribute to the "sense of efficacy and inner direction" (1986:29) necessary for academic success. The recommendation for a truly interactive pedagogy is consonant with other current proposals for educational reform (Tharp and Gallimore 1987; Schor 1986; Schneider, Hyland and Gallimore 1985). Such interaction would, of course, be further encouraged if educators knew enough of the home language, culture, and interaction patterns to use them when providing instruction.

Assessment

Related to pedagogy is assessment, which has, according to Cummins, been far too narrowly defined to a "purely psychoeducational" base (1986:29), resting solely on tests given in the first or second language. Because such tests reflect a limited set of classroom experiences that do not in any way take account of "the societal and educational context within which the child has developed" (30), they locate causes of educational failure within the student and thus legitimate "disabling" judgments. Traditional assessment informs external authorities of ranks and norms that legitimate labels of below normal; more constructive assessment would provide individuals with concrete information on their range of strengths.

To counteract these structural tendencies and empower their students, Cummins calls for educators to become advocates for children (as does Cazden 1985), a role they have not been trained or encouraged to assume. Again, the commitment to students that such advocacy implies requires an understanding of all the factors in student background, first language and home culture included, that bear on educational progress. It is not enough simply to know and use the home language or employ culturally congruent patterns in instruction, although these are worthwhile goals. The model suggests that appropriate pedagogy and assessment are developed on the basis of the continued meaningful interaction between students and teacher that allows educators to discover and build on students' strengths instead of labeling their weaknesses. Instruction based on reciprocal interaction between teacher and students or between students themselves, similar to some current models of cooperative learning, (see, for example, Diaz, Moll and Mehan 1986; Kagan 1986; Cohen 1986), can take place in either language or draw on both languages in a bilingual situation to accomplish these ends.

This last framework could be criticized for attributing too much to social factors and too little to individual variation in students. Moreover, it assumes a unitary language minority community, which may not obtain in all circumstances of language minority education: in many schools, there are a variety of language groups to be served. While educators can strive to incorporate all relevant languages, cultures, and community representatives into the educational process, they may have to make principled choices among a variety of alternatives established partly by practical constraints of resources and personnel available. Beyond the many feasibility questions that arise is the fact of internal variation in language minority communities, which may themselves be divided by political, religious, or ethnic loyalties so that they do not provide consistent collective guidance to educators who seek it. Some members of a language community may strongly endorse preservation of the home language and culture, in Schumann's terminology; others may seek to assimilate to the second language, others to adapt and use each language in different domains. Indeed, contemporary historical scholarship (Bodnar 1985) emphasizes the great variety of integration strategies adopted by American immigrant groups regarding retention of cultural patterns and ways of life, including language. While the possible absence of community consensus on this and other issues related to language minority students does not excuse educators from the need to redefine their roles in Cummins' framework, it does suggest that the model oversimplifies the very social conditions that motivate it. The dominance relationships that determine majority/minority interactions in the model may also characterize interactions within language communities; to be an effective guide for action, the model must address intragroup as well as intergroup conflicts.

CONCLUSION

What do all of these models suggest for effective second language learning and educational programs for language minority students? Clearly, a grasp of the social context is important both as a means of understanding students and as a guide to redefinition of educator roles. Specifically relevant to language education are the hypotheses that relate second language learning to level of skill attained in the first and to threshold levels that demonstrate the possible influences of bilingualism on cognition. Second language pedagogy can draw on the concepts of comprehensible input and the affective filter as guides to some of the determinants of an optimal classroom environment for second language learning. Still unanswered are questions of precisely what levels constitute the bilingual thresholds; what types of language tasks demonstrate linguistically identifiable features of cognitive demand and context embedding; what constitutes optimal input at various stages; what the role of conscious monitoring of performance in second language acquisition is; what kind of practice, negotiation, or comprehensible output is necessary to achieve complete mastery of a language; and how to develop appropriate climates for learning and context-sensitive pedagogical methods. These questions need to be posed in various school settings by means of descriptive research to assess the adequacy of the models and their practical implications. Even if not yet proven, the theoretical models discussed here can be useful for educators in identifying the possible factors that influence second language acquisition, suggesting connections between them, and determining their applicability to the many different contexts of language minority education. The theories do not provide blueprints for instruction, but they mark some of the relevant dimensions to be considered in educational planning and pedagogy and signal the many areas still to be investigated.

EXPLORING THE IDEAS

1. Cummins' hypotheses suggest a kind of "double standard" in language education, namely, that language majority children may be safely placed in immersion programs in a second language, while language minority children need to have their first languages reinforced before being introduced to a second language.

What are some of the theoretical and research bases for such a "double standard"? If language programs based on Cummins's hypotheses were to be developed and implemented in the United States, what practical problems might be encountered?

2. Krashen distinguishes between "acquisition" and "learning."

In the life or recent immigrants in the United States, what kinds of environments might be considered "acquisition-rich" and what kinds might be considered "acquisition-poor"?

Do you agree with the emphasis that Krashen places on acquisition and the relatively insignificant role he assigns to language instruction? Why or why not?

3. In addition to psychological variables, Schumann discusses social

variables such as dominance, integration strategy, enclosure, etc. These factors are said to affect the social distance between a learner and the target language group; this distance, in turn, determines the former's success in acquiring the second language.

Choose one of the recent immigrant language minority groups covered in this book and examine it in terms of Schumann's social variables. Does the group's experience confirm Schumann's theoretical framework?

4. Cummins, Krashen, and Schumann have all touched on factors affecting the ways adults and children learn a second language.

Synthesizing the ideas of all three researchers, draw up a list of differences in the second language learning situation of adults and children.

5. Implicitly or explicitly, the concept of a power differential between the language majority and language minorities plays a role in the second language acquisition theories of all three researchers.

Examine how each researcher conceptualizes this power differential and how it fits into his hypothesis.

If the concept that interethnic power relationships affects second language learning is valid, what implications would it have for educational policy?

APPLYING THE IDEAS

1. In her paper, McGroarty mentions the concept of "semilingualism."

If you were a second language acquisition researcher, how would you proceed to investigate semilingualism? What kind of population would you choose to study? How do you think semilingualism would be manifested in everyday life? How would you attempt to measure semilingualism? What difficulties, theoretical or practical, might be encountered if you were to conduct your project?

Working in small groups, draw up a research proposal for a study designed to help you understand semilingualism.

2. Several of the ideas discussed in this paper, particularly Krashen's, relate to the psychological processes involved in second language acquisition.

If you are currently studying a second language, observe yourself carefully over a few days and analyze your language learning experiences, using concepts such as the "monitor," the "affective filter," or "ego permeability."

If you are not studying a language now, obtain permission from a second-language learner to observe him or her for a few days; then interview your subject and write up an analysis using the above-mentioned concepts.

NOTES

1. I am grateful to Evelyn Hatch and John Schumann for critical insights into the issues discussed and to Sandra McKay and Sau-ling Wong for careful attention to matters of substance and presentation in this chapter. The emphases chosen here and any errors of interpretation remain mine.

2. Using Cummins' four quadrants of linguistic proficiency along with related considerations such as differences between planned and unplanned language, researchers and teachers in this project set out to plan activities representative of each one (Hatch et al. 1987). They found that given these opportunities for second language development that were far more varied than those found in the usual curriculum, limited English speaking children proved capable of producing much more, and more complex, language than teachers had initially expected. Findings from this project show the kind of linguistic research needed to validate proficiency frameworks (Flashner 1987a,b) and also demonstrate how collaborative research can provide productive instructional developments (Hawkins 1987).

REFERENCES

Ashworth, M. 1985. *Beyond Methodology*. Cambridge: Cambridge University Press.

Attinasi, J., P. Pedraza, S. Poplack and A. Pousada. 1982. Final report for Intergenerational Perspectives on Bilingualism, National Institute of Education contract #NIE-G-78-0091. New York: Center for Puerto Rican Studies, City University of New York.

Baral, D. P. 1980. The effects of home-school language shifts: The linguistic explanations. In R. V. Padilla (ed.), *Theory in Bilingual Education*. Ypsilanti, MI: Eastern Michigan University, 136–147.

Berry, J. W. 1983. Acculturation: A comparative analysis of alternative forms. In R. J. Samuda and S. L. Woods (eds.), *Perspectives in Immigrant and Minority Education*. Lanham, MD: University Press of America, 65–78.

Bodnar, J. 1985. *The Transplanted: A History of Immigrants in Urban America*. Bloomington, IN: Indiana University Press.

Canale, M. and M. Swain. 1980. Theoretical bases of communicative approaches to second language teaching and testing. *Applied Linguistics* 1:1, 1–47.

Cazden, C. B. 1985. ESL teachers as language advocates for children. Plenary address at 19th Annual TESOL Convention. New York, NY, April 13.

Celce-Murcia, M. 1985. Making informed decisions about the role of grammar in language teaching. *TESOL Newsletter* 19:1, 1, 4–5.

Chaudron, C. 1985. A method for examining the input/intake distinction. In S. M. Gass and C. G. Madden (eds.), *Input in Second Language Acquisition*. Rowley, MA: Newbury House, 285–300.

Cohen, E. G. 1986. *Designing Groupwork*. New York: Teachers College Press.

Cross, T. G. 1977. Mothers' speech adjustments: The contribution of selected child listener variables. In C. E. Snow and C. A. Ferguson (eds.), *Talking to Children: Language Input and Acquisition*. Cambridge: Cambridge University Press, 151–188.

Cummins, J. 1986. Empowering minority students: A framework for intervention. *Harvard Educational Review* 56:1, 18–36.

Cummins, J. 1984. *Bilingualism and Special Education: Issues in Assessment and Pedagogy*. Clevedon, England: Multilingual Matters.

Cummins, J. 1983. Heritage language education: A literature review. Report to Ontario Ministry of Education. Toronto, Ontario, Canada: Ontario Institute for Studies in Education.

Cummins, J. 1981. The role of primary language development in promoting educational success for language minority students. In California State Department of Education, *Schooling and Language Minority Students: A Theoretical Framework*. Los Angeles, CA: Evaluation, Dissemination and Assessment Center, California State University, Los Angeles, 3–49.

Cummins, J. 1979a. Cognitive/academic language proficiency, linguistic interdependence, the optimal age question, and some other matters. *Working Papers on Bilingualism* 19, 197–205.

Cummins, J. 1979b. Linguistic interdependence and the educational development of bilingual children. *Review of Educational Research* 49:2, 222–251.

Diaz, S. 1987. CERRC (Community Educational Resource and Research Center): A model in action. Paper presented at University of California Linguistic Minority Project Conference, University of California, Los Angeles, Los Angeles, April 28.

Diaz, S., L. C. Moll and H. Mehan. 1986. Sociocultural resources in instruction: A context-specific approach. In California State Department of Education, *Beyond Language: Social and Cultural Factors in Schooling Language Minority Students*. Los Angeles, CA: Evaluation, Dissemination, and Assessment Center, California State University, Los Angeles, 187–230.

Dolson, D. P. 1985. Bilingualism and scholastic performance: The literature revisited. *NABE Journal* 10:1, 1–35.

Dulay, H. C., and M. K. Burt. 1977. Remarks on creativity in second language acquisition. In M. K. Burt, H. C. Dulay, and M. Finnochiaro (eds.), *Viewpoints On English as a Second Language*. New York: Regents.

Edelsky, C., S. Hudelson, B. Flores, F. Barkin, B. Altweger and K. Jilbert. 1983. Semilingualism and language deficit. *Applied linguistics* 4: 1–22.

Ely, C. M. 1986. Language learning motivation: A descriptive and causal analysis. *Modern Language Journal* 70:1, 28–35.

Ferguson, C. A. 1975. Towards a characterization of English foreigner talk. *Anthropological linguistics* 17: 1–14.

Flashner, V. E. 1987a. An exploration of linguistic dichotomies in the classroom language of native and non-native English-speaking children. Unpublished Ph.D. dissertation, University of California, Los Angeles.

Flashner, V. 1987b. An exploration of the spoken/written and unplanned/planned dichotomies in the classroom language of Spanish bilingual children. CLEAR Educational Report. Los Angeles, CA: Center for Language Education and Research, University of California, Los Angeles.

Gardner, H. 1983. *Frames of Mind: The Theory of Multiple Intelligences*. New York: Basic Books.

Gardner, R. and W. Lambert. 1972. *Attitudes and Motivation in Second Language Learning*. Rowley, MA: Newbury House.

Genesee, F. 1987. *Learning Through Two Languages*. Cambridge, MA: Newbury House.

Genesee, F. 1986. The baby and the bathwater or what immersion has to say about bilingual education: Teaching and learning in bilingual education—significant immersion instructional features. *NABE Journal* 10:3, 227–254.

Gillett, J. S. 1987. Ethnic bilingual education for Canada's minority groups. *Canadian Modern Language Review* 43:2, 337–356.

Goodlad, J. 1984. *A Place Called School*. New York: McGraw-Hill.

Grosjean, F. 1982. *Life with Two Languages*. Cambridge, MA: Harvard University Press.

Guiora, A. Z. 1972. Construct validity and transpositional research: Toward an empirical study of psychoanalytic concepts. *Comprehensive Psychiatry* 13, 139–150.

Hakuta, K., B. Ferdman and R. M. Diaz. 1986. Bilingualism and cognitive development: Three perspectives and methodological implications. CLEAR Technical Report 2. Los Angeles, CA Center for Language Education and Research, University of California, Los Angeles.

Haskell, D. L. 1987. Predicting acculturation of Americans in the Arab world: An exploratory study. Unpublished MA in TESL thesis, University of California, Los Angeles.

Hatch, E. M. 1983a. *Psycholinguistics: A Second Language Perspective*. Rowley, MA: Newbury House.

Hatch, E. M. 1983b. Simplified input and second language acquisition. In R. W. Anderson (ed.), *Pidginization and Creolization as Language Acquisition*. Rowley, MA: Newbury House, 64–86.

Hatch, E. M. 1978. Discourse analysis and second language acquisition. In E. M. Hatch (ed.), *Second Language Acquisition*. Rowley, MA: Newbury House, 401–435.

Hatch, E., V. Flashner, B. Hawkins, W. Motoike, M. Jacobs and B. Wheeler. 1987. A classroom research project at Encinita Elementary School: A presentation of linguistic/cognitive findings by researchers and observations from a school administrator and teachers. Panel presentation at University of California Linguistic Minority Project Conference, University of California, Los Angeles, Los Angeles, April 28.

Hatch, E. M., V. Flashner and L. Hunt. 1986. The experience model and language teaching. In R. R. Day (ed.), *Talking to Learn: Conversation in Second Language Acquisition*. Rowley, MA: Newbury House, 5–22.

Haugen, E. 1953. *The Norwegian Language in America: A Study in Bilingual Behavior*. Philadelphia, PA: University of Pennsylvania Press.

Hawkins, B. 1987. Scaffolded classroom interaction in a minority language setting. CLEAR Educational Report. Los Angeles, CA: Center for Language Education and Research, University of California, Los Angeles.

Hayes, Z. A. 1981. "Limited" language proficiency: A problem in the definition and measurement of bilingualism. Unpublished Ph.D. dissertation, Stanford University.

Heath, S. B. 1986a. Separating 'things of the imagination' from life: Learning to read and write. In W. Teale and E. Sulzby (eds.), *Emergent Literacy*. Norwood, NJ: Ablex, 156–172.

Heath, S. B. 1986b. Sociocultural contexts of language development. In California State Department of Education, *Beyond Language: Social and Cultural Factors in Schooling Language Minority Students*. Los Angeles, CA: Evaluation, Dissemination and Assessment Center, California State University, Los Angeles, 143–186.

Heath, S. B. 1983. *Ways with Words*. Cambridge: Cambridge University Press.

John-Steiner, V. and P. Tatter. 1983. An interactionist model of language development. In B. Bain (ed.), *The Sociogenesis of Language and Human Conduct*. New York: Plenum Publishing, 79–97.

Jones, P. A. and M. G. Holli. 1981. *Ethnic Chicago*. Grand Rapids, MI: Wm. B. Eerdmans Publishing Co.

Kagan, S. 1986. Cooperative learning and sociocultural factors in schooling. In California State Department of Education, *Beyond Language*. Los Angeles, CA: Evaluation, Dissemination, and Assessment Center, California State University, Los Angeles, 231–298.

Krashen, S. D. 1985. *The Input Hypothesis: Issues and Implications*. London: Longman.

Krashen, S. D. 1984. *Writing: Research, Theory, and Applications*. Oxford: Pergamon Press.

Krashen, S. D. 1982. *Principles and Practice in Second Language Acquisition*. Oxford: Pergamon Press.

Krashen, S. D. 1981a. Bilingual education and second language acquisition theory. In California State Department of Education, *Schooling and Language Minority Students: A Theoretical Framework*. Los Angeles, CA: Evaluation, Dissemination, and Assessment Center, California State University, Los Angeles, 51–79.

Krashen, S. D. 1981b. *Second Language Acquisition and Second Language Learning*. Oxford: Pergamon Press.

Krashen, S. D. 1978. The monitor model for second language acquisition. In R. C. Gingras (ed.), *Second Language Acquisition and Foreign Language Teaching*. Arlington, VA: Center for Applied Linguistics, 7–26.

Krashen, S. D. and T. D. Terrell. 1983. *The Natural Approach*. Hayward, CA: The Alemany Press.

Lambert, W. E. 1981. Bilingualism and second language acquisition. *Annals of the New York Academy of Sciences* 379: 9–22.

Lewis, E. G. 1976. Bilingualism and bilingual education: The ancient world to the Renaissance. In J. A. Fishman (ed.). *Bilingual Education: An International Sociological Perspective*. Rowley, MA: Newbury House, 150–200.

Lo Bianco, J. 1987. *National Policy on Languages*. Report to Commonwealth Department of Education. Canberra, Australia: Australian Government Publishing Service.

Long, M. 1981. Input, interaction, and second language acquisition. *Annals of the New York Academy of Sciences* 379: 259–278.

Martin-Jones, M. and S. Romaine. 1986. Semilingualism: A half-baked theory of communicative competence. *Applied linguistics* 7:1, 26–38.

McLaughlin, B. 1987. *Theories of Second-Language Learning*. London: Edward Arnold.

McLaughlin, B. 1982. Theory in bilingual education: On mis-reading Cummins. In C.

Ward and D. Wren (eds.), *Selected Papers on TESOL,* Vol. 1. Monterey, CA: Monterey Institute of International Studies, 5–18.

Ochs, E. and B. B. Schieffelin. 1984. Language acquisition and socialization: Three developmental stories and their implications. In R. A. Shweder and R. A. Levine (eds.), *Culture Theory*. Cambridge: Cambridge University Press, 276–320.

Ogbu, J. and M. E. Matute-Bianchi. 1986. Understanding sociocultural factors: Knowledge, identity, and school adjustment. In California State Department of Education, *Beyond Language*. Los Angeles, CA: Dissemination, Evaluation, and Assessment Center, California State University, Los Angeles, 73–142.

Paulston, C. B. 1980. *Bilingual Education: Theories and Issues*. Rowley, MA: Newbury House.

Paulston, C. B. 1976. Ethnic relations and bilingual education: Accounting for contradictory data. In J. E. Alatis and K. Twaddell (eds.), *English as a Second Language in Bilingual Education*. Washington, D.C.: Teachers of English to Speakers of Other Languages. 235–262.

Poplack, S. 1979. "Sometimes I'll start a sentence in Spanish y termino en espanol": Toward a typology of code-switching. Language Policy Task Force Report 4, Centro de Estudios Puertorriquéños. New York: City University of New York.

Ramirez, A. G. and Stromquist, N. P. 1979. ESL methodology and student language learning in elementary bilingual classrooms. *TESOL Quarterly* 13:2, 141–158.

Rippley, L. J. 1976. *The German Americans*. Boston, MA: G. K. Hall.

Rivers, W. 1980. Foreign language acquisition: Where the real problems lie. *Applied linguistics* 1: 48–69.

Rogoff, B. 1986. Adult assistance of children's learning. In T. E. Raphael (ed.). *The Contexts of School-Based Literacy,* New York: Random House, 27–40.

Romo, R. 1983. *East Los Angeles: History of a Barrio*. Austin, TX: University of Texas Press.

Schachter, J. 1986. Three approaches to the study of input. *Language Learning* 36:2, 211–225.

Schneider, P., J. T. Hyland and R. Gallimore. 1985. The zone of proximal development in eighth grade social studies. *The Quarterly Newsletter of the Laboratory of Comparative Human Cognition* 7:4, 113–119.

Schor, I. 1986. *Culture Wars: School and Society in the Conservative Restoration 1969–1984*. Boston and London: Routledge and Kegan Paul.

Schumann, J. H. 1986. Research on the acculturation model for second language acquisition. *Journal of Multilingual and Multicultural Development* 7:5, 379–392.

Schumann, J. H. 1978a. The acculturation model for second-language acquisition. In R. C. Gingras (ed.), *Second Language Acquisition and Foreign Language Teaching*. Arlington, VA: Center for Applied Linguistics, 27–50.

Schumann, J. H. 1978b. *The Pidginization Hypothesis*. Rowley, MA: Newbury House.

Skutnabb-Kangas, T. 1981. *Bilingualism or Not: The Education of Minorities*. Translated by L. Malmberg and D. Crane. Clevedon, England: Multilingual Matters.

Snow, C. E. 1977. Mothers' speech research: From input to interaction. In C. E. Snow and C. A. Ferguson (eds.), *Talking to Children*. Cambridge: Cambridge University Press, 31–49.

Stauble, A. M. 1978. Decreolization as a model for second language development. *Language Learning* 28.

Stengal, E. 1939. On learning a new language. *International Journal of Psychoanalysis* 2, 471–479.

Swain, M. 1985. Communicative competence: Some roles of comprehensible input and comprehensible output in its development. In S. M. Gass and C. G. Madden (eds.), *Input and Second Language Acquisition*. Rowley, MA: Newbury House, 235–253.

Tharp, R. G. and R. Gallimore. 1987. *Teaching Mind and Society: Theory and Practice of Teaching, Literacy and Schooling*. Los Angeles, CA: Socio-Behavioral Group, Neuropsychiatric Institute, University of California, Los Angeles.

Van Patten, B. 1987. On babies and bathwater: Input in foreign language learning. *Modern Language Journal* 71:2, 156–164.

Weisner, T. and R. Gallimore. 1985. The convergence of ecocultural and activity theory. Paper presented at American Anthropological Association Meetings, Washington, D.C., December.

Wells, G. 1985. *Language Development in the Pre-School Years*. Cambridge: Cambridge University Press.

Wells, G. 1981. Language, literacy, and education. In G. Wells (ed.). *Learning Through Interaction*. Cambridge: Cambridge University Press, 240–276.

Wong Fillmore, L. 1979. Individual differences in second language acquisition. In C. J. Fillmore, D. Kempler and W. S.-Y. Wang (eds.), *Individual Differences in Language Ability and Language Behavior*. New York: Academic Press, 203–228.

Wong Fillmore, L., P. Ammon, B. McLaughlin and M. S. Ammon. 1985. Final Report for Learning English through Bilingual Instruction, National Institute of Education contract #400-80-0030. University of California, Berkeley and Santa Cruz.

CHAPTER
12

Weighing Educational Alternatives

Sandra McKay

As a nation, we are fortunate to have two avenues available for the development of linguistic resources: we can both encourage foreign language learning and protect the language resources of our minority groups. It is indeed paradoxical that while support is currently growing for the promotion of foreign language learning, support for the preservation of the language resources of recent immigrant groups is waning.[1]

This chapter will explore the educational alternatives that exist to both develop and conserve our language resources. While some attention will be given to educational programs designed to promote foreign language learning, the majority of the chapter will be devoted to examining programs designed to meet the needs of language minority children, a group that includes a large and growing number of school-age children whose special language needs are often ignored.[2] In comparing the educational programs that meet these objectives, I make several assumptions.

First, I assume that schools alone never had and never will have the ability to meet the needs of language minority children in isolation. As Paulston (1981:476) points out, "[e]ducational institutions have limited power in dealing with language acquisition or the lack thereof, a learning process which is primarily the result of social factors." The chapters in this volume have clearly demonstrated that the learning of English and the maintenance of the mother tongue are strongly affected by a variety of social and cultural factors, such as the size and cohesiveness of a language minority group, the dominant culture's attitude toward speakers of a particular language, and the attitude of a language minority group toward its own language and culture as well as toward the host country.

The second assumption I make is that educational services, to be effective, must be designed to meet the particular needs of the students, parents, and community that are being served. Successful language programs have typically demonstrated great flexibility in design so as to meet local educational needs (see Mackey and Beebe 1977). Allowing for local flexibility in design, however, does not mean that there should not be federal involvement. Rather, federal involvement is important both in terms of providing financial support and in implementing policy guidelines that protect the language rights of individuals.

The third assumption I make in this chapter is that multilingualism is an important resource for this nation. As Fishman (1985:7) puts it, "The multilingual civil servant, the multilingual corporate employee or officer, the multilingual professional; they are all stronger, more likely to be effective and successful practitioners in their respective areas of expertise than are their monolingual counterparts." In supporting the value of multilingualism, I certainly do not mean to suggest that the promotion of English literacy skills for language minority children should in any way be neglected. Rather, I fully agree with Hernández-Chavez (1984:171) that

> . . . for language minority children in the United States, strong English proficiency in all domains is essential. English proficiency is indispensable in today's world for advanced academic training. Participating adequately in business, commerce, or the occupational market without a full command of English would be extremely difficult for an individual.

Before I assess various educational alternatives, several terms need to be defined. In this chapter, the term "language minority students" will be used to describe immigrants (i.e., foreign-born children who emigrate with their parents), refugees (i.e., foreign-born children who enter the United States under special conditions), and long-term residents who come from non-English-speaking homes. When it is important to do so, I will make a distinction among these various subgroups. Language minority students who lack proficiency in English will be referred to as "language minority/limited English proficient" (LM/LEP) students." The discussion will focus on educational support services for these students on the K–12 level.

I will examine the following educational alternatives: submersion, pull-out ESL, bilingual education, immersion, and two-way bilingual programs. In order to assess each alternative fully, I believe it is important to consider each option in light of the following questions:

1. Does the alternative place unrealistic demands on school administrators and classroom teachers?
2. Does the alternative meet the personal, educational, and social needs of the LM/LEP student?
3. Is the alternative sound in terms of current research evidence on language learning?
4. What social assumptions underlie the alternative in terms of ethnic diversity and language planning: does the alternative reflect an assimilationist or pluralistic model, and a language-as-problem, lan-

guage-as-right or language-as-resource orientation? (See Ruíz, this volume.)

Table 12.1 summarizes the basic issues that will be addressed in the paper.

SUBMERSION

In submersion programs LM/LEP children are placed in English-speaking classrooms for the entire school day. The school provides no formal program to help the students develop their skills in English, leaving this matter up to the regular classroom teacher. Supporters of this so-called "sink or swim" method argue that children will learn English faster if they are exposed to the language for the entire school day and that, furthermore, children naturally "pick up" a language quite quickly and easily.

Feasibility

The major appeal of submersion lies in the ease with which it can be implemented. Many administrators and taxpayers consider submersion to be the ideal educational program for LM/LEP students because it requires no administrative changes or additional expenses. In addition, this alternative seems to provide a very simple solution to the problem of fairness in educational policy which Oller (1976:68) aptly summarizes in the following manner: "There are many extant native American languages in the United States and there are many other languages represented among the sizeable immigrant populations in all our major cities. How will we decide which one of these languages and cultures to represent in the school?" Submersion appears to offer an easy solution to this problem. The logic is that offering no special services to any student ensures that all students will be treated equally. It was precisely such a stance that the *Lau* v. *Nichols* decision found to be unacceptable (see Wong, "Educational Rights of Language Minorities," this volume).

From the classroom teachers' perspective, submersion creates many problems. Even when teachers and students share the same native language, developing the students' literacy skills and providing content knowledge is a formidable task. Having students who need special help in developing their English proficiency adds another dimension to the teachers' already difficult task, a dimension for which the classroom teacher may have little or no training. In short, while submersion may appear to be the most feasible option, it places a tremendous burden on the individual classroom teacher who is given the charge of developing the language skills of students with very special needs.

Impact on Students

While submersion can be successful in helping individual students acquire English, it may create psychological problems. From the individual LM/LEP students' perspective, a submersion experience can be devastating. As one LM/LEP student wrote in her journal on attending an English-only classroom:

> School was a nightmare. I dreaded going to school and facing my classmates and teacher. Every activity the class engaged in meant another exhibition of my incompetence. Each activity was another incidence for my peers to laugh and ridicule me with and for my teacher to stare hopelessly disappointed at me with [sic]. My self-image was a serious inferiority complex [sic]. I became frustrated at not being able to do anything right. I felt like giving up the entire mess.

Trying to succeed in a new environment without adequate language skills, especially for a young child or newly arrived immigrant, is a frightening experience that may lead to absenteeism and eventual school dropout. In fact, in submersion programs anywhere from 50 to 100 percent of LM/LEP students drop out of school prior to the completion of the twelfth grade (Cardenas 1977:78–79).

Theoretical Assumptions and Research Evidence

Submersion is based on several assumptions about language learning, as well as about the goal of immigrant education. One of the major assumptions about language learning underlying submersion programs is the belief that young children can easily "pick up" a language if they are placed in an environment where it is spoken. Existing research, however, does not support this assumption. Snow and Hoefnagle-Hohle (1978:1122), for example, in investigating subjects of various ages who were learning Dutch by "picking it up" at school or at work with little or no formal instruction, found that 3–5-year olds scored consistently worse than the older groups on all the tests and that the 12–15-year olds showed the most rapid acquisition of all the skills tested. Hakuta and Gould (1987:41), in their review of relevant research, conclude that "the belief that children are fast and effortless second language learners has no basis in fact." The assumption of the effortless language learning of children raises the whole question of what it means to be proficient in a language. While children may gain fluency in face-to-face communicative skills quite quickly, they may have no skills in what Cum-

Table 12.1. COMPARISON OF EDUCATIONAL ALTERNATIVES

	Submersion	Pull-out ESL	Bilingual education	Immersion	Two-way bilingual programs
Administrative feasibility	Requires minimal administrative changes	Requires hiring special ESL staff and scheduling students	Requires hiring teachers with bilingual education credentials	Requires hiring teachers who are bilingual	Requires hiring teachers who are bilingual
			Must have sufficient number of students who share the same language background	Must have sufficient number of interested students	Must have a bilingual community and sufficient number of interested students
Pedagogical feasibility	Classroom teachers need to provide special help for LM/LEP students	Classroom teachers may need to help students catch up with their content subjects	Classroom teachers need to decide how much emphasis to give each language	Classroom teachers need not worry about code switching	Classroom teachers of each language must work close together to integrate the two groups
Impact on LM/LEP students	Students may feel alienated because of a lack of recognition of their language and culture	Students may fall behind in their regular classes and feel stigmatized by being in what is often called a remedial class	Students may gain self-esteem		
			Students can achieve cognitive benefits of bilingualism	Students can achieve the cognitive benefits of bilingualism	Students can achieve the cognitive benefits of bilingualism
			Students may be segregated by ethnic background		Students can be initially segregated by ethnic background

Assumptions about language learning	Students can acquire the language by using it as the medium of instruction	Formal instruction is beneficial to learning a language	Students can acquire the language by using it as the medium of instruction, but formal instruction is also beneficial	Students can acquire the language by using it as the medium of instruction	Formal instruction is beneficial to learning a language
	Initial learning need not take place in the native language	Initial learning need not take place in the native language	Initial learning should take place in the native language	Initial learning need not take place in the native language	Initial learning should take place in the native language
			Skills learned in one language transfer to another	Skills learned in one language transfer to another	Skills learned in one language transfer to another
Social assumptions	Language-as-problem	Language-as-problem	Language-as-right and resource	Language-as-resource	Language-as-resource
			Promotes a bilingual citizenry by preserving minority languages	Promotes a bilingual citizenry by promoting second language learning	Promotes a bilingual citizenry by preserving minority languages and teaching second languages
	Acquiring English is the key to students' academic and social success	Acquiring English is the key to students' academic and social success			
	Adheres to an assimilationist model	Adheres to an assimilationist model	Some adhere to a pluralistic model, others to an assimilationist model	Adheres to a pluralistic model	Adheres to a pluralistic model

mins (1981) calls context-reduced situations, such as formal classrooms. Thus, on the basis of their conversational fluency, teachers may assume children have the necessary English skills to succeed in classroom language tasks when, in fact, they do not.

A second assumption about language learning that is reflected in submersion programs is the idea that children will learn English by interacting with other children and that this interaction will increase if children are placed in the same classroom with native speakers. First of all, it is important to note that young children can play and interact with one another with minimal language skills (Wong-Fillmore 1976; Hakuta and Gould 1987). Moreover, placing children of different language backgrounds in the same classroom does not ensure that they will interact with one another. If nothing is done in the classroom to help children explore cultural differences, majority children could well use ethnic and linguistic differences to exclude minority children from their peer group. In addition, there is no empirical proof to support the notion that more exposure to English necessarily leads to greater proficiency in English (Genesee 1986:230). Submersion programs also assume that any native speaker of English, by the sheer fact that he or she is a native speaker, knows how to teach the language. This naive assumption overlooks the wealth of literature on language teaching and learning suggesting otherwise.

Finally, submersion reflects a language-as-problem perspective. Underlying submersion seems to be the belief that the primary need of LM/LEP children is increased proficiency in English and that once a child has mastered the language, all other needs will be met. As Beck (1975:16) says, "excessive emphasis upon language learning in immigrant education has arisen out of the assumption that once the language has been learned, the rest is fairly straightforward: initiation into the culture of the country." Yet as Beck points out, immigrant education involves much more than developing linguistic proficiency; basically it entails the whole question of whether or not an individual should make a transition to a new culture and, if so, how. In sum, to focus, as submersion does, on language learning as the sole need of LM/LEP children is to ignore important concerns that these children have in terms of their own individual and social identities, concerns that clearly will affect their ability to learn the language. Furthermore, an exclusive focus on language skills as the key to social and economic mobility is misleading to students who may ultimately find that increased language proficiency does not necessarily lead to better jobs. As Spolsky (1972:194) points out in his discussion of the limits of language education, ". . . it is important to distinguish between language as a reason and language as an excuse for prejudice." It may be that minority language individuals do not get hired because of a lack of skill in English, but it may also be that they do not get hired because of discrimination.

PULL-OUT ENGLISH AS A SECOND LANGUAGE

In pull-out ESL programs, LM/LEP children are given separate classes in English language development for part of the day while the remainder of the day is spent in English-only classes with native speakers. The number of children in the pull-out class, as well as the number of hours of instruction per week, can vary greatly. In addition, the instructors of these special classes typically have been trained in English as a second language rather than bilingual education.

Feasibility

From the administrators' point of view, pull-out ESL, unlike submersion, requires additional hiring, training, and scheduling adjustments. In those states that require an ESL or language specialist credential, the administrator must hire teachers with the necessary credentials to teach the ESL pull-out class. Unfortunately, at present, less than half of the states offer a certificate in ESL and, where they are offered, they are not always mandatory for hiring purposes (NCBE *Forum* 1986). What this means is that in many instances the pull-out ESL instructor has had no special training in language teaching.

From the classroom teachers' point of view, one disadvantage of pull-out ESL programs is that such programs may cause their LM/LEP students to fall behind in their content subjects and, thus, the teachers may need to provide additional help to these students in the content areas. However, the advantage for classroom teachers is that the pull-out program will likely lessen the time they need to spend in developing the language skills of their LM/LEP students; this task is now up to the ESL instructor instead.

Historically, some ESL teachers have viewed the primary goal of pull-out classes as developing what Canale and Swain (1980) label grammatical competence: knowledge of formal grammatical rules. To attain this goal, they have selected a traditional audiolingual method, which, as Paulston (1981:481) points out, has contributed to a negative view of the ESL profession. Today, however, a growing number of ESL programs are implementing a task-based syllabus. In this approach, ESL teachers attempt to relate the curriculum of the ESL class to regular classroom content areas and to present students with specific problem tasks they must solve (see Milk 1985). Another approach, which combines language learning with content areas, is what Parker (1985) refers to as "sheltered English." In sheltered classes, English is taught through the content of academic disciplines. The focus of such classes is always on the content of the class rather than on the language per se. (For a discussion of sheltered English programs, see Freeman, Freeman and Gonzales, 1987.)

Impact on Students

For LM/LEP students, pull-out ESL classes, while helping them with their language skills, have several potential drawbacks. First, as noted above, students in these programs, by being away from their primary classes for a certain period of the day, may fall behind in their content areas. Secondly, LM/LEP students may feel stigmatized by being placed in special classes, which, in many instances, are labeled as remedial classes. As a college student wrote in a journal entry reflecting on her ESL class, "the classroom provided a friendly atmosphere, but the fact that I had to leave class every day made me feel abnormal. At age 10, the desire to conform was overwhelming."

There are, however, several important advantages to ESL classes. First of all, students may well benefit from the formal instruction they receive in English, which may help them to understand the structure of the language. Second, students may like the shelter of an ESL class, where they can get special help with their language skills and content classes. Finally, students may gain self-confidence in their ESL classes by being with individuals of other language backgrounds who share a level of English proficiency comparable to their own. In many cases, the ESL class may provide the students with a communicative need to use English with peers who share many of their concerns.

Theoretical Assumptions and Research Evidence

Underlying pull-out ESL programs is the belief that formal instruction is beneficial to developing proficiency in English. While some second-language acquisition theorists, such as Schumann (1978) and Krashen (1981), minimize the role of formal instruction, Long (1983:359), in his review of research findings on second language instruction, concludes that "there is considerable (although not overwhelming) evidence that instruction is beneficial (1) for children as well as adults, (2) for beginning, intermediate, and advanced students, (3) on integrative as well as discrete-point tests, and (4) in acquisition-rich as well as acquisition-poor environments." While Long mentions that further research is needed to examine what kind of instruction (and under what circumstances) is beneficial, ESL programs are based on the premise that formal instruction is essential to achieve full proficiency in English.

Pull-out ESL programs, like submersion, reflect a language-as-problem perspective. Underlying such programs is a view that LM/LEP children are deficient in English and, thus, all they need is special attention to their language skills. The key to academic and vocational success is seen to rest in the acquisition of English. Like submersion, pull-out ESL assumes that if LM/LEP children learn English, they can quickly become initiated into the mainstream culture and function fully in the United States. As Long (1983:380) puts it in the conclusion to his review of research, learning English "is the gateway to education and to economic and social survival."

BILINGUAL EDUCATION

The standard U.S. Department of Education definition of bilingual education is as follows (Paulston 1980:8):

> Bilingual education is the use of two languages, one of which is English, as the medium of instruction for the same pupil population in a well-organized program which encompasses part or all of the curriculum and includes the study of the history and culture associated with the mother tongue. A complete program maintains the children's self-esteem and a legitimate pride in both cultures.

Today bilingual education includes an immense array of programs, some of which include a good deal of instruction in the mother tongue and some of which, ironically, include instruction only in English. In fact, according to a study conducted for the United States Department of Education by Development Associates, Inc. and Research Triangle Institute (1984), 26 percent of the programs for first graders included in the survey provided all instruction in English, which, by the definition listed above, would not even qualify them as a bilingual education program. The great range of programs, which reflects a lack of a coherent philosophy underlying bilingual education, makes it difficult to assess bilingual education as an educational alternative.

One of the main controversies surrounding bilingual education programs has been whether such programs should exist solely to provide a transition to the students' English-only instruction, or whether they should support maintenance of the mother tongue. Those programs that do have a maintenance objective can promote either what Otheguy and Otto (1980:351) term static maintenance (i.e., maintenance of the native language skills the students have upon entering the school system) or developmental maintenance (i.e., development of the students' native language to the point of full proficiency and literacy in the mother tongue). According to Otheguy and Otto (1980:351), the bilingual education movement in the United States "has generated little support for a *developmental* approach to the home language."

For the purpose of this discussion, I will use the U.S. Office of Education's definition even though, in fact, this definition may not cover a good many programs currently receiving Title VII funds. Given this definition, bilingual education programs can still vary in several ways, including the amount of exposure that the students receive in each language and the way each language is used. In some programs, all subject matter can be taught in the mother tongue with only language instruction in English. In other programs, while some classes are taught in the mother tongue, others are in English. Finally, the same content could be taught in both languages with concurrent translation, or some content could be introduced in one language and other content taught in the second language. Presently, most Title VII projects use both English and the native language but place major emphasis on English. The majority of these projects serve Spanish-speaking students in classroom settings that include both language-minority children and children whose native language is English (Rotberg 1984:135).

Feasibility

From the administrator's point of view, bilingual education programs pose several problems. First, some school districts serve students who speak a great variety of languages, some of which are not widely spoken. Thus, administrators may not be able to hire bilingual teachers who are certified and fluent in the students' native language,[3] and it may be difficult to group students with similar language and cultural backgrounds together. The current influx of LM/LEP students from Asia and the Pacific Islands is certainly making this type of problem more widespread.

As Wong (1987) points out, adding to the problem of the students' diverse language backgrounds is the problem of the lack of predictability in the demographic make-up of the student population. Political conditions, such as the Vietnam War, can lead to a sudden and rapid influx of new language groups. Furthermore, the internal migration of established language groups within the United States in a search for better jobs and community support can produce similar demographic fluctuations.

The fact that in many states an arbitrary number of students who share the same language is required to mandate a bilingual education program can create another administrative problem. In some cases, these requirements can result in inequitable situations. Thus, for example, in Massachusetts, where there must be 20 or more students to mandate a program, 11 Vietnamese students in a particular school would not warrant a bilingual classroom. However, in California, where the "triggering" number of students is 10, the same group of students could constitute a bilingual classroom.

One disadvantage of bilingual education programs is the problem of separating children by native language backgrounds. As Epstein (1977:4) puts it,

> Separating students temporarily in basic skill classes in the native language until they learn English . . . can be justified on both compensatory education and civil rights grounds. But keeping students and teachers segregated to maintain the native language cannot be so justified, and the evidence indicates that most maintenance efforts are highly segregated.

In order to avoid segregated classrooms, present federal guidelines specify that up to 40 percent of the students in bilingual classrooms may be fluent English speakers (Ovando and Collier 1985:14).

Teachers in bilingual education programs encounter many special problems. Given the responsibility of developing their students' proficiency in two languages, they are faced with the choice of when and how to use the two languages. Obviously, the decision of when to switch codes has important implications for the students' view of the relative importance of the languages involved, as well as for the students' comprehension of the lesson. In studying the code-switching patterns of bilingual instructors, Tsang (1983:214) found that the teachers' shift in code was a product of their striving to help their students perform well on standardized tests in English. Thus, in order to meet administrative performance objectives, instructors could be under pressure to give major emphasis to developing their students' English proficiency. Another problem that the bilingual teacher may have to cope with is a lack of suitable materials. This is especially true for teachers of Asian and Pacific languages, where the diversity of languages has made it difficult to develop appropriate materials.

Impact on Students

From the LM/LEP students' viewpoint, bilingual education programs can offer several advantages. First, the students will not fall behind in their subjects as may happen in submersion or ESL classes. Second, insofar as the program reaffirms the value of their mother tongue, it can contribute to their own self-esteem, which may have important ramifications for their success in learning a second language. In fact, Paulston, in a survey of several American studies on bilingual education, found that "all of the researchers reported that bilingually taught children showed self-concepts as positive as—and more often, more positive than—monolingually instructed pupils" (cited in Rotberg 1984:141). Second, to the extent that the program leads to the students' full fluency in two languages, the students will benefit from the increased cognitive flexibility that accompanies bilingualism. Although there has been a long tradition of believing that bilingualism is not beneficial and even detrimental to cognitive growth, Diaz (1983:48), in reviewing the research on the impact of bilingualism on cognitive development, concludes that "when compared to monolinguals, balanced bilingual children show definite advantages on measures of metalinguistic abilities, concept formation, field independence, and divergent thinking skills." It is important to note, however, that his conclusion refers to balanced bilinguals, and not individuals who are limited in their second-language proficiency for historical or environmental reasons. This qualification is extremely important for those who would argue that developmental maintenance programs are the most beneficial alternatives for cognitive development.

Another advantage of bilingual education programs is that the students may experience less culture conflict. For example, Philips (1970), in her work on the Warm Spring Indian Reservation, found that one reason for the Indian children's lack of participation in the English-only classroom was that the children's native ways of speaking and learning strategies were very different from those of the Anglo school. While being in a bilingual education classroom may reduce this conflict, the drawback is that the students may not learn the classroom sociolinguistic rules of the dominant culture. For this reason, Paulston (1980:71) reaches the conclusion that LM/LEP students "must have access to Anglo teachers, if they are to learn the rules of mainstream culture." On the same point, McLaughlin (1985:192) rightly recognizes that an effective bicultural program requires exposure to both sets of language-use rules:

> An effective bicultural program is one in which the child's cultural heritage has a central place in instruction and where there is awareness of patterns of language use and interactional style that are customary in the child's culture. At the same time, mainstream values, patterns of language use, and interactional styles need to be gradually introduced so that the child at least has the opportunity to move out and function in the larger society. The point is not that one set of values or behaviors replaces the other, but that the children have access to both sets so that they can form from both their unique bicultural identity.

One possible problem for students in bilingual education programs can arise from a lack of parental support. Parents might not fully support the program's attempt to maintain the native language, believing instead that the key to economic success and assimilation rests in their child acquiring full proficiency in English and, thus, all of their child's instruction should be in English. Indeed, as Hakuta's survey on bilingual education attitudes (1986) demonstrates, many individuals from non-English-language homes oppose bilingual education.

Theoretical Assumptions and Research Evidence

The variety of types of bilingual education programs makes it difficult to conclude whether or not such programs support the notion of formal instruction or acquisition. While some bilingual education programs do include a component of formal language instruction, others use the language only as a medium of instruction. However, all bilingual education programs share the assumption that it is valuable for children to receive instruction in their mother tongue. Research support for this assumption is quite mixed. Indeed, a World Bank review of selected international studies on bilingual education concludes that "There is not one answer to the question of what language to use for primary school, but several answers, depending on the characteristics of the child, of the parent and the local community, and of the wider community" (cited in Rotberg 1984:137).

Rotberg (1984:139–140), based on her review of a number of studies on the effectiveness of bilingual programs, reaches a similar conclusion and contends that initial learning in the native language appears to be more desirable

> . . . for children who come from low-income families and who are not proficient in their mother tongue, in communities where the home language has low status; for students likely to leave school in the early grades; and where teachers are not members of the same ethnic group as the students and may be insensitive to their values and traditions.

Thus, in instances that meet these criteria, which are in fact quite numerous in the United States, initial instruction in the mother tongue is clearly the best alternative.

One argument leveled against bilingual education programs is the idea that training in the mother tongue detracts from the time the students can spend learning English. However, as Hakuta and Gould (1987:41) point out, the idea "that the time spent in the classroom using the native language is wasted or lost" is overwhelmingly rejected by the research. Rather, as Cummins (1981) and others have shown, a strong native language foundation acts as a support for the learning of English and the learning that goes on in the native language transfers to English (Lambert and Tucker 1972). The idea of transfer is vividly described in the following journal entry, in which a Taiwanese student compares his language learning experience with that of his older sister.

> She was nearly 6 years older than me and had developed her language skills in Taiwan by being proficient in Chinese. I only knew a little Chinese and my language skills were undeveloped. My sister had used her knowledge from Chinese as a reference point from which to learn

> English, while I had no reference point from which to start. An analogy can be drawn between language skills and the swimming skills of my sister and me. My sister already knew how to float and she only needed to learn a few new movements to learn a new stroke. On the other hand, I couldn't even float and yet my teachers wanted me to learn a new stroke. I was thrown into the swimming pool and I promptly sank.

Ironically, one of the most cited studies against bilingual education, the Baker and de Kanter study (1983), does, in fact, support the notion of transfer. Based on a review of various studies on bilingual education, Baker and de Kanter concluded that transitional bilingual education programs were ineffective since children in such programs generally did no better in English language art skills than did children who were in traditional programs. This conclusion was based on the fact that of the 46 studies they reviewed, only 11 showed that students in bilingual programs reached higher levels of proficiency in English than did comparable students in nonbilingual programs, while 28 found no difference in proficiency between the two groups. However, as Genesee (1986:231) points out, such results, rather than undermining the value of transitional bilingual education programs, demonstrate the value of such programs since, despite

> . . . the fact that the bilingually-schooled students who were examined in these studies were receiving less English language instruction and exposure than English-taught students, the former actually attained proficiency in English that was at least as good as that of the latter in the majority of cases and was actually higher in a substantial number of cases.

Thus, it appears that students in the bilingual program were transferring the skills they had learned in their native language to English.

Bilingual education programs reflect a perspective of language-as-right, in that they are the result of federal and local mandates. At the same time, in so far as they demonstrate a commitment to preserving and developing minority languages, they reflect a language-as-resource orientation. Underlying the establishment of bilingual education programs are a variety of social assumptions. According to Glazer (1983:145), these social assumptions include the following: the desire to improve the educational achievement of language minority children; the hope of maintaining the culture and language of immigrant groups; and the desire to enhance respect for immigrant cultures. Glazer argues that although these are the major reasons cited for bilingual education, the programs do not, in fact, meet any of the objectives. In terms of educational achievement, he contends that historically such achievement has been due less to bicultural–bilingual education than to the value the subgroup places on it. Glazer also rejects the notion that bilingual education programs are the best or only way to maintain minority languages and increase respect for its speakers, noting that there are mechanisms for achieving these objectives outside the school. In short, he (1983:150) believes it is "a naive argument to say that putting bilingual–bicultural education into the public school curriculum will make a significant difference in affecting the general respect in which a given culture and language are held."

Glazer's conclusions cannot be ignored. His rejection of common beliefs about the value of bilingual education is based on a realistic assessment of the fact that schools alone cannot attain the objectives that are often assigned to bilingual education. This is not to say that bilingual education programs, because they cannot attain their objectives in isolation, should be rejected. Rather, those who support bilingual education programs need to recognize that the family, the community, and the society in general need to support and provide incentives for the maintenance of minority languages before bilingual programs will be successful.

The great variety of programs labeled as bilingual education makes it difficult to state whether this alternative adheres to an assimilationist or pluralistic model. If the programs' primary objective is to mainstream the students into English-only classrooms as quickly as possible, they support an assimilationist view. However, if the programs have a curriculum that strives to maintain the minority groups' language and cultural heritage, they clearly reflect a pluralistic model.

IMMERSION BILINGUAL EDUCATION PROGRAMS

Immersion programs in the United States are based on the Canadian model in which Anglophone students attend schools in French, with French used for all activities and initial reading instruction. In some schools, an English language arts component is added to the curriculum in second or third grade. Participants, for the most part, come from families of middle socioeconomic background. It is important to note that participation in the programs is always voluntary and that the participating youngsters generally speak English, the language of prestige, as their native language. The programs also receive considerably more support from the federal government than do bilingual education programs in the United States (Tucker 1980).

Given the success of immersion programs in Canada, some educators interpret this fact as support for mainstreaming LM/LEP children in English-only classrooms. In fact, in the popular press, "immersion" and "submersion," as defined in this chapter, are often used interchangeably. However, Tucker (1980) notes some important differences in the Canadian and the United States situation. In Canada, the participating students speak the language of higher prestige and widespread use, and since their home language receives significant reinforcement from the larger community, their school experience is likely to result in what Lambert (1984:19) calls additive bilingualism (i.e., the addition of a second language while maintaining and developing the first) rather than subtractive bilingualism (i.e., the replacement of one language with another). In submersion programs, however, since language-minority children often do not have support from the larger community to maintain their native language, their school experience is likely to result in subtractive rather than additive bilingualism. In proposing immersion programs as a means to additive bilingualism, Lambert and Tucker (1972:216) suggest the following general guideline: "In any community where a widespread desire or need for a bilingual or multilingual citizenry exists, priority in early years of schooling should be given to the language (or languages) least likely to be developed otherwise; in other words, the language most likely to be neglected." Thus, according to this principle, it is languages other than English that should be used in the early grades in the United States.

Genesee (1983:31) maintains that for an immersion program to be successful, the following social and educational conditions must be present:

> (1) Respect for and use of the child's native language by administrative and teaching professionals during the daily functioning of the school, (2) use of the child's native language to teach curriculum material, (3) an initial period during which the students are permitted to use their native language with one another and the teacher even though he/she addresses all comments in the child's second language, (4) an emphasis on the child's communicative use of the second language and not on correct grammatical usage, and (5) a desire by the students, their parents and teachers to maintain development of the children's native language.

In submersion programs in the United States, few of these conditions are present. LM/LEP students are not given the opportunity to use their native language initially, nor is any attempt made to maintain their native language. Thus, the idea that the success of immersion programs in Canada is grounds for establishing submersion programs in the United States is simply not an accurate assessment of the situation, since the social and educational variables of the two contexts are quite different.

One recent modification of submersion programs for LM/LEP students involves "structured immersion" programs. In these programs, all of the instruction is in English, using instructional materials that are sequenced according to linguistic difficulty. The programs employ bilingual teachers who will accept students' responses in their native language but will respond only in English. According to Ovando and Collier (1985:44), while such programs have a good deal of support as a new and innovative approach to LM/LEP education, the "reality is that this model is very similar to many transitional bilingual and ESL-only programs that have been implemented throughout the United States."

Immersion programs in the United States, to be consistent with the Canadian model, would entail the placing of English-speaking children in second-language classrooms in which the second language would be the primary language of instruction. In assessing immersion as an educational alternative, this is the model that will be used when the term "immersion" is used. One successful immersion program in the United States for English-speaking children is the Culver City, California, project (see Campbell 1984). One of the first immersion programs for a non-Indo-European language is at West Portal School in San Francisco, which began a program in Cantonese in 1984 (Wong 1987:145).

Feasibility

From the administrators' point of view, immersion programs, like bilingual education programs, require the hiring of teachers who are bilingual in a minority language and in English. However, since in immersion programs students are in the same classroom for the entire day, there are no additional scheduling problems as is the case with some bilingual programs and all pull-out ESL programs. The main problem that the administrator faces is how to attain the necessary community support so that there are a sufficient number of students to warrant the establishment of such a program.

For the classroom teacher, immersion programs are in some ways also less problematic than bilingual or pull-out ESL programs. In immersion programs, teachers need not be concerned with some students lagging behind others in content areas, which may happen with pull-out ESL classes where the students miss some of their content instruction. Nor does the teacher have to consider the problem of when to code-switch, as is the case in bilingual programs. However, the teacher, as in bilingual programs, may be faced with a shortage of adequate teaching materials and thus need to design his or her own materials.

Impact on Students

For the students, who by definition in immersion programs are English-speaking, since the home language is the one of social prestige, there is no potential loss of self-esteem as is likely for LM/LEP students in submersion or pull-out ESL programs. In addition, all of the children in the class share the same native language and begin with no knowledge of the target minority language, which is a very different situation from submersion or pull-out ESL. Finally, since the programs are purely voluntary, the students' parents demonstrate their support for the program in selecting this option, which may not be the case with any of the other programs.

A potential drawback for the students in immersion programs is the issue of adequate development of literacy skills in the target minority language and in English. If the immersion program uses an Indo-European, alphabetic language, and if there is an English language arts component, there may be a good deal of transfer of the literacy skills from one language to the other. However, if the target minority language is non-Indo-European and nonalphabetic, such transfer may be minimal. Unfortunately, little research exists on the transferability of literacy skills between alphabetic and nonalphabetic languages (Wong 1987:145). As Tzeng (1983:92) points out, since reading skills acquired in one orthography may not be the same as those acquired in another orthography, instruction programs that seek to develop literacy in both types of languages need to be carefully designed. (Because the question of the degree transferability of language skills between diverse languages is open to question, the Cantonese immersion program at West Portal School in San Francisco decided to introduce English literacy skills at the kindergarten level rather than in second or third grade.) Until there is more research on the degree of transferability between Indo-European and non-Indo-European languages, adaptations of the immersion model like those at West Portal School are the wisest approach.

Theoretical Assumptions and Research Evidence

From an individual perspective, immersion programs make many of the same assumptions that bilingual education programs do. First, these programs assume that the learning that goes on in one language transfers to the second. Second, these programs assume that there is a cognitive benefit to bilingualism. However, immersion programs differ from bilingual education programs in their view of the importance of developing initial literacy skills in the native language. If immersion programs are designed so that the English-speaking child is first introduced to reading in a second language, this experience is more similar to submersion and pull-out ESL programs, where initial reading is not in the mother tongue, than to bilingual education programs.

In terms of Krashen's (1981) acquisition–learning distinction, immersion programs are based on the assumption that formal instruction in the grammar of the language is not necessary; rather, children will naturally acquire the language when it is used as the medium of instruction. The results of the Culver City project, however, suggest that acquisition alone may not be sufficient since, after 7 years of instruction in Spanish, the students in the program still did not sound like native speakers of Spanish. Rather, their Spanish was accented, with grammatical and pronunciation errors (Campbell 1984:31). Similar results were found in the Lambert and Tucker study (1972).

In terms of language planning, immersion programs demonstrate a language-as-resource perspective. Since at the present time not a great many public immersion programs exist in the United States,[4] it would seem that there is little support for attaining a truly multilingual society. Where there is support for promoting second-language learning for English-speaking students, the support entails the development of separate foreign language classes rather than immersion programs, even though foreign language classes rarely result in balanced bilingualism. While the President's Commission on Foreign Language and International Studies (1979) emphasized the need for foreign language classes on the elementary level, until more people become aware of the economic and social benefits of acquiring a second language, it is doubtful whether there will be a large increase in the number of foreign language programs or immersion schools.

TWO-WAY BILINGUAL EDUCATION PROGRAMS

In two-way bilingual education programs, English-speaking students and LM/LEP students are placed in the same classroom with the goal of making them proficient in both languages. In some cases, the two groups of students have separate instruction through the second or third grade, receiving the development of initial reading skills in their native language. In other instances, while the students are initially separated, they gradually do more and more tasks together until they are integrated into one classroom.

Feasibility

Two-way bilingual programs such as those implemented in Dade County, Florida, and San Diego demonstrate the fact that the feasibility of such programs rests on two important factors: the community itself must be bilingual so that the school district has students who come from both English-speaking and minority language backgrounds; and the parents of both groups of students must be committed to and involved with the program.

From the administrator's point of view, the establishment of two-way bilingual programs often demands a good deal of public relations to gain local support. In Dade County, for example, while most Spanish-speaking parents were convinced of the merits of the program, school administrators needed to work hard to gain the support of the English-speaking community (Mackey and Beebe 1977:97). One of the main arguments given by the administrators in Dade County to persuade English-speaking parents of the benefits of the program was to point to the value of bilingualism in the local job market (Mackey and Beebe 1977:135), which may not be relevant to many communities in the United States. Administrators of two-way bilingual programs may also find it difficult to find qualified bilingual teachers for the programs, as was the case in Dade County (Mackey and Beebe 1977:90). This can be especially problematic at the junior and senior high school level, where the administrator must find a bilingual teacher who is certified in a particular academic subject area.

From the teacher's point of view, two-way bilingual education programs demand close cooperation between teachers so that as both groups of students become more proficient in the other's native language, they can be mixed together for more and more activities to the point that they can function in an integrated classroom. Since the teachers are often from different ethnic backgrounds, there may be underlying tensions among staff members related to socially based conflicts, as was demonstrated in the Cleghorn and Genesee study (1984) of teachers in a French immersion program in Montreal.

Impact on Students

Native English-speaking students involved in two-way bilingual programs may have quite different experiences from the LM/LEP students. If the program separates the English-speaking and LM/LEP students for the first 2 years, the initial learning experience for the English-speaking child is similar to most children in the United States except that they have a foreign language component in the curriculum. However, for LM/LEP children, while they do receive initial learning experiences and literacy in their native language, unlike the English-speaking students, they will not receive reinforcement of their language skills from the larger community. As the program progresses, problems may arise when the two groups are brought together. At this point, both groups may have some established social subgroups and, further, they will have different levels of proficiency in both English and the target minority language that may minimize interaction between the groups and promote a continuation of the initial subgroups.

Theoretical Assumptions and Research Evidence

Two-way bilingual programs, like immersion programs, reflect a social belief that multilingualism is beneficial for both dominant and minority language groups. Both programs clearly demonstrate a perspective of language-as-resource. The programs, however, differ in their pedagogical assumptions. While both programs support the idea that the learning that goes on in one language transfers to the second, in two-way bilingual programs, initial literacy skills typically occur in the native language. Also, two-way bilingual programs provide a mechanism for second-language learners to interact with native speakers of the target language who are their peers. This design allows for the development of possible integrative motivation on the part of the language learner.

CONCLUSION

Clearly there are advantages and disadvantages to each of the options examined here. In terms of language rights, however, submersion programs deprive LM/LEP students of equality in education as established by the *Lau v. Nichols* decision (see Wong, "Educational Rights of Language Minorities," this volume). Thus, even though submersion has administrative advantages, it is, in general, an unacceptable alternative. The choice of the remaining options rests on a variety of considerations including the demographics of the particular school district, the availability of trained staff, community support, and funds. Based on a careful assessment of such variables, school districts need to design programs that are best suited to their particular situation with the interest of the individual LM/LEP student always of primary concern.

One of the central questions raised in the popular press regarding the implementation of educational programs that seek to maintain the native language of LM/LEP students is who should pay for these programs. Epstein (1977:7) phrases the question as follows: "Is it federal responsibility to finance and promote student attachments to their ethnic languages and cultures, jobs long left to families, religious groups, ethnic organizations, private schools, ethnic publications and others?" This question, because it is so widely raised as an objection to any type of bilingual education program, must be addressed if we are ever to obtain the funding needed to promote our language resources. The answer rests, I believe, in an assessment of what social benefits can arise from local and federal funding of educational programs that strive to promote bilingualism.

There are, it seems to me, two major social benefits of special educational programs that strive to maintain minority languages. First, to the extent that such programs result in fewer school dropouts, less grade retention, fewer drug problems, and improved academic performance, the social outcomes of such programs justify the use of public funds. Unfortunately, most assessments of special language service programs have considered only academic achievement and failed to consider any other effects. For example, the Baker and de Kanter study (1983) defined effectiveness solely as the speed with which LM/LEP students acquired English, disregarding other important positive effects of well-designed language programs, such as school retention, positive self-concepts, and lower absentee rates. Yet as Paulston (1980:41) points out, in assessing the effectiveness of a program for LM/LEP students, "It makes a lot more sense to look at employment figures upon leaving school, figures on drug addiction and alcoholism, suicide rates and personality disorders, i.e., indicators which measure the social pathology which accompanies social injustice rather than in terms of language skills." What is needed, then, is more research on the social ramifications of particular educational alternatives for language minority students, rather than an almost exclusive focus on the academic effects of such programs.

The second social benefit that can arise from the public funding of those educational programs that promote bilingualism is the development of this nation's language resources, which can offer advantages to both the public sector and the private sector. What is required to reap the benefits of bilingualism in the workplace is a long-term needs assessment program, along with educational planning, so that foreign and second language learning will be available for those who want it or may eventually need it.

While it may be quite possible, with relevant research, to make a purely economic case for the public funding of educational programs that promote our language resources, the actual implementation of such programs rests in public commitment to these programs. Clearly, until there is widespread acceptance of the notion that there are individual, social, and political benefits to having a multilingual citizenry, the development of educational programs that seek to promote multilingualism is doomed to failure. Unfortunately, current events such as the English-only movement strongly suggest that this type of public support is not forthcoming. Thus, it is the responsibility of those of us committed to the promotion and protection of our language resources to work together to convince the majority that the goal of a multilingual society is worth pursuing.

EXPLORING THE IDEAS

1. McKay suggests that schools working in isolation cannot meet the needs of language minority children.

What are some ways in which the efforts of a language program in school (e.g., one designed to help immigrant children integrate with the English-speaking environment) might be undermined by social factors outside the classroom and outside the school?

2. The Hakuta study cited in McKay's paper finds that many individuals from non-English-speaking homes oppose bilingual education.

Why do you think there is a lack of support for bilingual education among individuals from non-English-speaking homes?

3. Immersion is one way to develop foreign language skills in English-speaking children; conventional foreign language instruction is another.

How are these two types of programs similar? How are they different?

If you were an English-speaking parent, would you enroll your child in an early immersion program, or would you choose foreign language classes in school? Give the reasons for your decision.

APPLYING THE IDEAS

1. McKay's chapter is based on the premise that multilingualism is a resource. However, such a view is apparently not widely accepted in the United States, and advocates of bilingual education or immersion have to work very hard to gain public support.

Investigate the foreign language education policy in another country. Compare and contrast it with that in the United States in terms of effectiveness in preserving and developing language as a resource.

2. McKay points out that in bilingual classes, "the decision of when to switch codes has important implications for the students' view of the relative importance of the languages involved, as well as for the students' comprehension of the lesson."

Observe a bilingual education class, noting how frequently and for what purposes the teacher uses English, and how the students react when each language is being used. Then interview the teacher to determine his or her philosophy on how the two languages should be used in the classroom.

3. McKay cites Spolsky's idea that language can be either a "reason" or an "excuse" for discrimination.

Read the following letter to "Dear Abby"and analyze it in terms of the distinction between "language as reason" and "language as excuse." Write an answer to "No Racist" according to your analysis.

DEAR ABBY/ABIGAIL VAN BUREN

DEAR ABBY: I must take issue with your reply to "Color-Blind"—she wrote about an acquaintance of hers who had taken her son to the emergency hospital and demanded a white, American doctor. You called that woman a bigot and a racist. Abby, I think you were wrong. With the recent influx of foreign doctors, I'm sure all that woman wanted was a doctor she could communicate with. Some have accents so thick, they can't be understood, and other doctors don't understand the questions they are asked. I don't care what color a doctor's skin is, but if I'm paying the doctor bills, I want one I can communicate with.

One smiling doctor even jokingly said to me, "Your 2-year-old speak more better English than me."

This is no joke, Abby. It's a serious problem when a family member is injured or sick and you need to discuss diagnosis, treatment and prognosis with a doctor who just nods and smiles mutely. Did I make my point, Abby?

NO RACIST

(*Source: San Francisco Chronicle,* March 24, 1987)

4. According to McKay, "submersion suggests that any native speaker of English, by the sheer fact that he or she is a native speaker, knows how to teach the language."

Read the following editorial by Guy Wright. List the competencies beneficial to English teaching that any untrained native English speaker might have. Then list the competencies that would require special training.

GUY WRIGHT/LET'S TEACH ENGLISH

ONCE THE HOLIDAYS are out of the way, I plan to spend one evening a week teaching English to immigrants. I hope some of you reading this will decide to do the same thing. Lots of people with strange-sounding names are waiting in line to learn.

I'm not going into this as a sacrifice. Quite the contrary, I expect to meet new friends, have some fun, maybe even get an occasional column out of it.

But beyond that, it just makes sense that those of us who campaigned to make English the official language of California should help new Californians learn it. By volunteering to teach them, perhaps we can dispose of the charge that we were plotting to freeze them out.

If I may dream a little, I would like to see a great statewide grassroots network of English classes for immigrants, staffed by volunteers.

Instead, there is talk of tapping the state treasury to finance more classes through the regular school system. I doubt that's the best way to go. The Legislature will balk when it realizes how much it would cost to hire enough credentialed teachers and professional administrators to cope with the waiting lists for English classes.

Besides, it isn't necessary to take that route. The immigrant doesn't need to learn perfect English, desirable though that would be. He needs survival English. And fortunately there are many of us who can teach him that.

What's missing is an organized recruitment program for volunteers. That's what the state should provide.

For retired people with time on their hands, here is a chance to do something worthwhile. For service clubs hunting new activities, here is a natural.

Why shouldn't Boy Scouts teach English to immigrant kids? And the Junior League to immigrant women? Why shouldn't pastors get their congregations involved?

Most working people can spare one evening a week. If bowling and bridge and Monday night football have become a bore, sign on to teach an English class to immigrants.

Years ago I taught radio for a while. It was technical stuff, and often I had to struggle to get it across. But I'll never forget how gratifying it was to see the light suddenly turn on in a student's eyes. I felt like Steve McQueen in "The Sand Pebbles" when his Chinese helper finally realized how a steam engine worked. I hope to recapture that feeling by teaching English.

If my dream of a grass-roots network of classes should become reality, we'll need a clean, well-lighted place—lots of them. Schools, empty at night, are a logical choice if the red tape can be cut. If not, let's use church basements, lodge halls, union halls, corporate conference rooms, vacant store fronts.

Volunteers will need some guidance from the state. But not too much. A simple briefing and a handbook that set out the lessons should do. I'm not keen on having conventional educators in control. They get hung up on grammar rules and stuff like that.

Better we should draw on the Berlitz method, and the techniques of the Defense Language School at Monterey—and try to find out how European schools teach every kid a second language.

But I'm willing to start with whatever tools are at hand, knowing that each time an immigrant learns a new word his future brightens and the tensions caused by heavy immigration are lowered.

I shall still work for repeal of the bilingual ballot law and for defeat of politicians who peddle ethnic separatism. But I also believe that we who recognize the value of English as a unifying force in our nation should take a more active role in sharing it with those who want to learn.

(*Source:* Guy Wright. 1986. *San Francisco Examiner,* November 23, 1986)

NOTES

1. While the 1980 Report of the President's Commission on Foreign Languages and International Studies emphasizes the need for teaching foreign languages in the nation's elementary schools, federal appropriations for bilingual education are decreasing.

2. According to the 1986 Department of Education *Report on the Condition of Bilingual Education,* there are in the United States between 1.2 and 1.7 million language-minority children. This estimate, however, has been challenged by Waggoner (1986). She maintains that by applying the Department of Education's standards of English proficiency to the language-minority children counted in the 1980 Census and adding to this the number of children born in non-English-speaking countries who have legally emigrated to the United States since 1980, the figure would be closer to between 3.5 and 5.3 million limited-English-speaking children. In addition, Waggoner (1986) disputes the Department of Education's claim that 94 percent of language-minority children are receiving the special service they need. Instead, she contends that at the most only one-third of such children are getting the help they need and have a right to obtain.

3. The difficulty in staffing bilingual programs with fluent speakers is demonstrated by a study conducted in New Mexico, in which only 13 of the 136 randomly selected Spanish bilingual education teachers could read and write Spanish on a third-grade level (as cited in Rotberg 1984:143).

4. As of 1982, there were 27 such programs in the United States (Campbell 1984:140).

REFERENCES

Baker, K. A. and A. de Kanter (eds.). 1983. *Bilingual Education: A Reappraisal of Federal Policy*. Lexington, MA: D.C. Heath.

Beck, C. 1975. Is immigration education only for immigrants? In A. Wolfgang (ed.), *Education of Immigrant Students: Issues and Answers*. Toronto: The Ontario Institute for Studies in Education, 5–18.

Campbell, R. 1984. The immersion education approach to foreign language teaching. In *Studies on Immersion Education*. Los Angeles, CA: California State Department of Education, 114–144.

Canale, M. and H. Swain. 1980. Theoretical bases of communicative approaches to second language teaching and testing. *Applied Linguistics* 1:1–47.

Cardenas, J. 1977. "Response I." In N. Epstein (ed.). *Language, Ethnicity and the Schools*. Washington D.C.: The Institute for Educational Leadership, 71–84.

Cleghorn, A. and F. Genesee. 1984. Languages in contact: An ethnographic study of interaction in an immersion school. *TESOL Quarterly* 18:4, 595–625.

Cummins, J. 1981. The role of primary language development in promoting educational success for language minority students. In California State Department of Education, *Schooling and Language Minority Students: A Theoretical Framework*. Los Angeles, CA: Evaluation, Dissemination and Assessment Center, California State University, Los Angeles. 3–49.

Development Associates, Inc. and Research Triangle Institute. 1984. LEP Students: Characteristics and school services. The descriptive phase report of the national longitudinal evaluation of the effectiveness of services for language-minority limited-English proficient students. U.S. Department of Education, Washington D.C.

Diaz, R. 1983. Thought and two languages: The impact of bilingualism on cognitive development. *Review of Research in Education* 10:23–54.

Epstein, N. 1977. *Language, Ethnicity and the Schools*. Washington D.C.: The Institute for Educational Leadership.

Freeman, D., Y. Freeman and R. Gonzales 1987. Success for LEP students: The Sunnyside sheltered English program. *TESOL Quarterly* 21:2, 361–367.

Fishman, J. A. 1985. Toward multilingualism as an international desideratum in government, business and the professions. *Annual Review of Applied Linguistics* 6:2–9.

Genesee, F. 1983. Bilingual education of majority language children: The immersion experiments in review. *Applied Psycholinguistics* 4:1–46.

Genesee, F. 1986. The baby and the bathwater or what immersion has to say about bilingual education: Teaching and learning bilingual education—significant immersion instructional features. *NABE Journal* 10:3, 227–254.

Glazer, N. 1983. *Ethnic Dilemmas 1964–82*. Cambridge, MA: Harvard University Press.

Hakuta, K. 1986. *Mirror of Language*. New York: Basic Books.

Hakuta, K. and L. J. Gould. 1987. Synthesis of research on bilingual education. *Educational Leadership*. 44:6, 38–46.

Hernández-Chavez, E. 1984. The inadequacy of English immersion education as an educational approach for language minority students in the United States. In

Studies on Immersion Education. Los Angeles, CA: California State Department of Education, 144–183.

Krashen, S. D. 1981. Bilingual education and second language acquisition theory. In *Schooling and Language Minority Students: A Theoretical Framework*. Los Angeles, CA: Evaluation, Dissemination and Assessment Center, California State University, Los Angeles. 51–79.

Lambert, W. E. and G. R. Tucker. 1972. *Bilingual Education of Children: The St. Lambert Experiment*. Rowley, MA: Newbury House.

Lambert, W. E. 1984. An overview of issues in immersion education. In *Studies on Immersion Education*. Los Angeles, CA: California State Department of Education, 8–30.

Long, M. 1983. Does second language instruction make a difference? A review of research. *TESOL Quarterly*. 17:3, 359–382.

Mackey, W. and V. N. Beebe. 1977. *Bilingual Schools for a Bicultural Community*. Rowley, MA: Newbury House.

McLaughlin, B. 1985. *Second-Language Acquisition in Childhood: Volume 2. School-Age Children*. Hillsdale, NJ: Lawrence Erlbaum Associates.

Milk, R. D. 1985. The changing role of ESL bilingual education. *TESOL Quarterly* 19:4, 657–672.

National Clearinghouse for Bilingual Education (NCBE) *Forum* 1986. 9:3 (March), 7.

Oller, J. W. 1976. Bilingual education: promises and paradoxes. In J. E. Alatis and K. Twaddell (eds.), *English as a Second Language in Bilingual Education*. Washington, D.C.: TESOL, 65–75.

Otheguy, R. and R. Otto. 1980. The myth of static maintenance in bilingual education. *Modern Language Journal* 64:3, 350–355.

Ovando, C. and V. Collier. 1985. *Bilingual and ESL classrooms*. New York: McGraw-Hill.

Parker, D. 1985. Sheltered English: Theory to practice. Paper presented at the NABE Annual Conference, San Francisco, CA.

Paulston, C. B. 1980. *Bilingual Education: Theories and Issues*. Rowley, MA: Newbury House.

Paulston, C. B. 1981. Bilingualism and education. In C. A. Ferguson and S. B. Heath (eds.), *Language in the USA*. Cambridge: Cambridge University Press, 469–485.

Philips, S. 1970. Acquisition of rules for appropriate speech usage. In J. E. Alatis (ed.), *Bilingualism and Language Contact*. 21st Annual Roundtable, Georgetown University.

President's Commission on Foreign Language and International Studies. 1979. *Strength through Wisdom: A Critique of U.S. Capability*. Washington D.C.: U.S. Government Printing Office.

Rotberg, I. 1984. Bilingual education policy in the United States. *Prospects* 14:1, 133–147.

Schumann, J. H. 1978. The acculturation model for second language acquisition. In R. Gingras (ed.), *Second Language Acquisition and Foreign Language Teaching*. Arlington, VA: Center for Applied Linguistics, 27–50.

Snow, C. E. and M. Hoefnagel-Hohle. 1978. The critical period for language acquisition: Evidence from second language learning. *Child Development* 49: 1114–1128.

Spolsky, B. 1972. The limits of language education. In B. Spolsky (ed.), *The Language Education of Minority Children*. Rowley, MA: Newbury House, 193–199.

Tsang, C. 1983. Code-switching strategies in bilingual instructional settings. In M. Chu-Chang and V. Rodriguez (eds.), *Asian and Pacific-American Perspectives in Bilingual Education: Comparative Research*. New York: Teachers College, Columbia University, 197–215.

Tzeng, O. 1983. Cognitive processing of various orthographies. In M. Chu-Chang and V. Rodriguez (eds.), *Asian and Pacific-American Perspectives in Bilingual Education: Comparative Research*. New York: Teachers College, Columbia University. 73–97.

Tucker, G. R. 1980. Implications for U.S. bilingual education: Evidence from Canadian research. *Focus* (National Clearinghouse for Bilingual Education) 2, 1–4.

Waggoner, D. 1979. Teacher resources in bilingual education: A national survey. *NABE Journal* 3:2, 53–60.

Waggoner, D. 1986. Estimates on the need for bilingual education and the proportion of children in need being served. *NABE News* 9:4 and 5, 6–9.

Wong, S. C. 1987. The language needs of school-age Asian immigrants and refugees in the United States. In *Ethnicity and Language*. W. A. Van Horne and T. V. Tonnesen (eds.). Milwaukee, WI: University of Wisconsin System Institute on Race and Ethnicity. 124–159.

Wong-Fillmore, L. 1976. *The Second Time Around: Cognitive and Social Strategies in Second Language Acquisition*. Ph.D. dissertation, Stanford University.

CHAPTER 13

Educational Rights of Language Minorities

Sau-ling Cynthia Wong

In the first two chapters of this section, McGroarty and McKay have examined the educational implications of language diversity from theoretical perspectives. By analyzing the second language acquisition theory of Cummins, Krashen, and Schumann, McGroarty shows various ways in which larger social forces may affect individual members of language minority groups as they attempt to function in a second language. A coherent understanding of psycholinguistic and sociolinguistic concepts would provide language educators with a sound basis for formulating promising approaches. McKay suggests some criteria for weighing available alternatives in language education, including theoretical assumptions, research evidence, administrative and pedagogical feasibility, and impact on students. Awareness of such criteria would help policy makers and concerned citizens to determine the suitability of an approach for a specific population.

While the above concerns are of utmost importance, we are still left with the unfortunate fact that given the nature of language as a potent symbol of identity, policy debates on the education of language minorities often take place with little reference to the considered opinions of researchers and language professionals. Rather, they readily become a battleground for opposing perspectives: language-as-problem and language-as-right (see Ruíz, this volume), and disputes often end up being resolved by appeal to law. Thus a survey of the educational implications of language diversity must return from the discussion of desiderata to that of mandates, of laws, of court decisions. This chapter attempts to clarify some major legal issues regarding the rights of language minorities to receive language education services.

(The phrase "language education services," which is not a legal term, I have coined to refer to publicly funded programs related to the language education of minorities. It is preferred over possible alternatives such as "language assistance," "language remediation," or "special language programs," which all connote something "extra" given to minorities. Since the very issue under discussion is what minority school children are entitled by law to receive, such connotations are to be avoided.)

Because of the virtually inevitable emotional component in exchanges over language issues, what a group feels to be its "rights" regarding language may bear only a tenuous relationship to the much more precise and technical concept of "language rights" upheld in law. Thus, in a sense, a clarification of the nature of educational rights for linguistic minorities will be useful only to those who, predisposed to take a more dispassionate view of the subject, already feel the need for such a clarification, which is to say that it will be of limited value in influencing the turn of larger political events. Still, responsible individual decisions concerning language issues cannot be made without knowledge of how language rights have been shaped by the evolving U.S. legal tradition. In particular, teachers and administrators charged with language education, if only out of concern for their livelihood, need to be informed about how their work fits into the overall language policy of this nation.[1]

The term language minorities covers groups with varied citizenship status, settlement history, and "track record" of language maintenance, all of which affect a group's precise degree of entitlement; the legal literature on language education services is voluminous and often inconclusive. In a chapter of this length, it would be difficult to give an in-depth review of all relevant aspects of educational rights. For the sake of simplicity, we will restrict the discussion to two main questions: *Is submersion justified by law? And if not, are language minorities entitled to bilingual education?*

Since submersion (see McKay, this volume; note particularly the distinction between "submersion" and "immersion") means simply placing language-minority children in regular classrooms with speakers of the majority language, the question is really another way of asking whether the children are entitled to any kind of language education service. The phrasing chosen here, however, has the advantage of drawing attention to the legality of a so-called "method," touted by many English-only proponents, that is in fact a "nonmethod." As for the second question, the chosen phrasing has the advantage of placing in the background many questions (e.g., on the pedagogical soundness or feasibility of various methods) that, although relevant, are not questions of entitlement. If a group is legally entitled to bilingual education, it has to be provided, however controversial or difficult the implementation. Only after the entitlement issue is settled can we begin to focus on the other questions.

SOME PRELIMINARY CLARIFICATIONS

Before focusing on the two major questions of entitlement concerning submersion and bilingual education, it might be helpful to examine some common perceptions of and arguments against the educational rights of language minorities in the United States.

Public debates on the educational rights of language minorities are often colored by an "us vs. them" tone: "foreigners" are those who "talk funny," "can't speak English properly," "don't belong in this country." One reason for this attitude is that for an ingroup intent on containing a perceived threat to its privileged status, language is a particularly felicitous device for targeting outsiders, since the ingroup members' acquisition of their first language is reassuringly unrelated to individual merit (the achievement of which can be used to support an outsider's demand for admission to the ingroup). On this point, it is important to remember that, as Waggoner's statistics (this volume) show, many language minorities are native-born citizens; that immigrants are legally admitted and are taxpayers just as much as citizens; and that, even for the children of illegal immigrants, there may be some legally guaranteed rights to receive a public education (see below). Without such an awareness, the issue would easily become clouded, turning into a pitting of the usurping, freeloading "foreigners" against the responsible but victimized "taxpayers."

In casual usage, the term "foreign student" is commonly used to refer to any student who is not native English-speaking; even legal scholars like Farrell (1983:70) use the term in this loose sense. The practice is unfortunate in that it creates confusion in the public's mind between students who are permanent members of this society—more appropriately designated as "immigrant students"—and "foreign students" proper: those temporarily in the United States on F-1 visas (student visas) for educational purposes only. The former group, when erroneously named "foreign," are often unjustly seen as rivals to "American children," siphoning away resources their parents supposedly did not pay for and allegedly lowering the quality of education for the latter. Actually, the everyday term "foreigner" is not precise enough to capture the various degrees of entitlement enjoyed by subgroups of linguistic minorities.

Awareness of the residency and citizenship status of language minorities is also important when one encounters attacks on immigrant language rights made in the form of what Kloss (1971:255–256) calls the "tacit compact" and "take-and-give" arguments, namely, that in deciding to emigrate, the immigrant has tacitly given up any claim to his or her language and has in effect agreed to exchange it for benefits obtained in the adopted land. It should be noted that, first, immigrants are already contributing to their new country by working, buying goods and services, and in particular paying taxes (which would make them taxpayers instead of "outsiders" or "foreigners" taking advantage of taxpayers). Second, in U.S. immigration laws, giving up one's language for English is not stipulated as a condition for immigration; it would not be reasonable, subsequent to admitting immigrants on some other bases, to accuse them of not having held up their end of the bargain when they cannot demonstrate English proficiency to the satisfaction of native English speakers (see the arguments in Beck 1975:6–7).

In addition to the "tacit compact" and "take-and-give"[2] theories referred to above, what may be called the "we were here first" argument has frequently been advanced to curtail ethnic language use or deny English-language assistance to groups perceived as "newcomers." The reasoning is that "newcomers" should conform to the long-time inhabitants of the land. As Molesky's historical overview (this volume) amply demonstrates, however, English speakers were *not* "here first" relative to a significant number of linguistic minorities.

Finally, we may attempt to understand the issue of entitlement using a well-known concept in the literature on language rights: "tolerance-oriented" vs. "promotion-oriented rights" (Kloss 1971). Since educational rights concerning language education services are specific instances of language rights, they too fall under the terms of Kloss's system. Proposing that the allocation of language rights be based on how successful a group has been in maintaining its ethnic language, he distinguishes two kinds of language rights: "tolerance-oriented rights" and "promotion-oriented rights." Briefly stated, the former are rights to use the minority language in home and communal life, such as attending private language schools or publishing commercial ethnic language newspapers, where public funding is not used. The latter involve government use of public resources for the benefit of those using the minority language, such as translation of laws, bilingual ballots, or purchase of ethnic language books in public libraries. Kloss argues that it would be reasonable to expect a group to have a strong "track record" in language maintenance, that is, to demonstrate the ability to maintain its language beyond the third generation, before granting it promotion-oriented rights. If language maintenance were a passing fancy or a doomed enterprise rather than a successful long-term commitment, it would not be sensible to allocate public resources for it.

Kloss's distinction of these two kinds of rights is a useful one in general. However, it may be problematic under certain circumstances. Given current U.S. immigration trends, certain long-standing ethnic groups will experience a constant influx of speakers of the ethnic languages; these, along with the native-born population, will be labeled as belonging to the same language minority. In such cases, while the group *taken as a whole* may show maintenance beyond the third generation, the success is due mainly to immigration and the precise status of its "track record" is obscured. As the case of Chinese language retentiveness shows (see Wong, "The Language Situation of Chinese Americans," this volume), even with massive empirical data it is not always easy to disentangle the effects of continued immigration from those of successful intergenerational transmission of the language (which seems to be Kloss's concept of maintenance).

Furthermore, the term "promotion" is not entirely satisfactory, since it connotes an active enhancement of the minority language's status or its speakers' influence. It is true that connotations do not affect how law is interpreted in the judicial system, but they do cloud the issue when the technical terminology, retaining only part of its meaning, is used in discussions among nonexperts in law. While language education services intended to ease transition into the English-speaking mainstream technically qualify as "promotion," in effect they may only serve to bring disadvantaged minorities up to par with speakers of the majority language and may have little long-term effect on the strength of the minority languages used. The current controversy over bilingual education for Spanish speakers stems partly from a perception that maintenance is the *aim* (rather than the unintended *effect*) of the programs, and that the presence of students who do maintain their ethnic language proves that it has been unfairly "promoted." In other words, any failures of transitional programs are cited as if they were the successes of maintenance programs. The case of immersion education (see McKay, this volume), which suggests that sometimes "maintenance" of the minority language is the best kind of "transition" into mainstream society, further complicates the issue. Thus the dividing line between "transition" and "maintenance" is not always clear. Without a firm definition of "maintenance," the question of what constitutes "promotion" itself becomes harder to answer. Still, Kloss's scheme is useful under most circumstances and is widely accepted in the literature on language policy.

With the above clarifications in mind, we may now take a closer look at educational rights for language minorities.

OVERVIEW OF ENTITLEMENT ISSUES IN LANGUAGE EDUCATION SERVICES FOR MINORITIES

Table 13.1 gives an overview of the various possible legal grounds on which language minorities may be able to claim language education services. Due to space limitation, we will cover only the more important level, the federal level (if federal and state laws conflict, the former overrides the latter; see Macías 1979:90). The legal grounds at the federal level are further divided into "constitutional" and "statutory" components. The three items in bold type, one constitutional and two statutory, with the exact texts of their relevant portions given, are the most frequently appealed-to principles on which claims to language education services are made. They are the equal protection clause of the Fourteenth Amendment (often abbreviated to "the equal protection clause"); Title VI of the Civil Rights Act of 1964 (often abbreviated to "Title VI"); and the Equal Educational Opportunities Act of 1974, Section 1703(f) (often abbreviated to "the EEOP"). Title VII of the Elementary and Secondary Education Act (ESEA), although frequently as-

Table 13.1. POSSIBLE LEGAL GROUNDS ON WHICH LANGUAGE MINORITIES MAY BE ABLE TO CLAIM LANGUAGE EDUCATION SERVICES

Federal

Constitutional

Equal protection clause of the Fourteenth Amendment

"No state shall . . . deny to any person within its jurisdiction the equal protection of the laws." (Section 1)

Related: Due process clause

"No state shall . . . deprive any person of life, liberty or property, without due process of law." (Section 1)

Statutory

Title VI of the Civil Rights Act of 1964

"No person in the United States shall, on the ground of race, color, or national origin, be excluded from participation in, be denied the benefits of, or be subjected to discrimination under any program or activity receiving Federal financial assistance." (Section 601)

Related: "May 25 Memorandum" of 1970

"Where inability to speak and understand the English language excludes national origin–minority group children from effective participation in the educational programs offered by a school district, the district must take affirmative steps to rectify the language deficiency in order to open its instructional programs to these students."

Related: "Lau Remedies" of 1975

The Equal Educational Opportunities Act (EEOA) of 1974

"No state shall deny equal educational opportunity to an individual on account of his or her race, color, sex, or national origin, by . . . the failure of an educational agency to take appropriate action to overcome language barriers that impede equal participation by its students in its instructional programs." (Section 1703(f))

Title VII of the Elementary and Secondary Education Act (ESEA), 1968, 1974, 1978, 1984

State

Certain state constitutions

Certain state statutes permitting or mandating language education services

sociated with bilingual education, will not apply if the state does not receive federal funds (Grubb 1974:62); it is more a piece of legislation to provide funding than entitlement. Thus it will not be discussed here. Interested readers are referred to Fernández (1987) for an overview of Title VII.

Table 13.2 summarizes entitlement issues concerning language education services for minorities, listing the legal bases cited, the legal concepts at stake, and key court decisions that have shaped answers to our two questions.

This chapter will not discuss language rights in terms of international law. Although several documents of international law do recognize the language rights of the minorities, the United States did not ratify some of them,

Table 13.2. **LANGUAGE EDUCATION SERVICES FOR LANGUAGE MINORITIES: ENTITLEMENT ISSUES: IS SUBMERSION JUSTIFIED BY LAW? IF NOT, ARE LANGUAGE MINORITIES ENTITLED TO BILINGUAL EDUCATION?**

Possible legal basis	Issues	Relevant major court cases
Constitutional		
Equal protection clause	Equality of access vs. outcome	*Brown* v. *Board of Education* 1954
	Discriminatory intent vs. impact	*Washington* v. *Davis* 1976
	Fundamental right	*San Antonio Indep. School District* v. *Rodriguez* 1973
	Suspect classification	*San Antonio Indep. School District* v. *Rodriguez* 1973
	Compelling state interest	*Plyler* v. *Doe* 1982
Statutory		
Title VI of Civil Rights Act 1964	Equality of access vs. outcome	*Lau* v. *Nichols* 1974
	Discriminatory intent vs. impact	*Lau* v. *Nichols* 1974
		Regents of U. of Cal. v. *Bakke* 1978
	Substantial numbers	*Lau* v. *Nichols* 1974
	Desegregation	*Keyes* v. *School District No. 1, Denver, Colorado* 1976
Section 1703(f) of Equal Educational Opportunities Act 1974	Equality of access vs. outcome	*Castaneda* v. *Pickard* 1981
	Discriminatory intent vs. impact	
	"Appropriate action"	*Castaneda* v. *Pickard* 1981

Conclusion: The law does not justify submersion, but neither does it create entitlement for bilingual education.

and there are also problems with interpretation and implementation (Macías 1979:86–91; Marshall 1986:18–19).

THE EQUAL PROTECTION CLAUSE OF THE FOURTEENTH AMENDMENT

The equal protection clause is the portion of the Constitution most frequently cited to establish claims for language education services for minorities. Some legal scholars have also appealed to the due process clause to argue that by compelling minority children to attend school without providing language education services, one is in effect depriving them of physical liberty as well as the liberty to acquire useful knowledge (based on the 1923 *Meyer* v. *Nebraska* Supreme Court decision) (Grubb 1974:88–91). However, traditionally these arguments have not been important in affecting court decisions.

The Concept of "Equality"

The equal protection clause applies only to "state action," not private action (Johnson 1974:957). The concept of "equality" has "never been adequately defined as a philosophical concept, much less as a legal concept" (Johnson 1974:965). In the area of education, "traditionally, the courts have found a denial of equal protection only where the state has made *different* provisions for similarly situated citizens without adequate justification" (Grubb 1974:71); the classic example of this principle is the 1954 *Brown* v. *Board of Education* Supreme Court decision that ended segregation. As we will see, however, in the case of language-minority children, if no language education services are provided (i.e., in a submersion situation), we would have a group receiving what is on the face similar treatment, but experiencing markedly different results (Grubb 1974:58). In such a case, a "proportional or consequential theory of equality" has been proposed (Grubb 1974:72); its criterion is whether a group has been denied equal protection because it bears a disproportionate share of the measure's impact. The main issues here are (1) equality of access vs. equality of outcome; and (2) discriminatory intent vs. discriminatory impact. Let us turn now to how the judiciary stands on these issues.

Discriminatory Intent?

It is, of course, impossible to run an educational system without distinguishing between and classifying students in some way; the question then arises of when a classificatory scheme is acceptable and when it becomes discriminatory against a particular group. In determining whether the equal protection clause has been violated, it has been customary to examine, first, to see if the classification is "rationally related" (i.e., not arbitrary) to the purpose of a formally neutral program. If that is the case, the judiciary will normally uphold the program even if its impact is discriminatory (Grubb 1974:81–82). The burden would be on the plaintiff to demonstrate that there has been discriminatory intent. The 1976 *Washington* v. *Davis* Supreme Court decision rules that even with disproportionate racial impact, discriminatory intent must be proven (Farrell 1983:75–76). In the context of minority language education, we might note that in trying to establish claims to language education services for children from a recent immigrant group, it would be difficult to demonstrate discriminatory intent because the group's history in this country is so short (Dobray 1984:269; McFadden 1983:25).

Judicial restraint normally prevails when a program is formally neutral. However, if the state action "either impairs a fundamental right or distinguishes a suspect class," the burden of justification would be on the state to show that a "compelling state interest" is at stake, so that it has been necessary to violate a "fundamental right" or distinguish a "suspect class" (Grubb 1974:83; Johnson 1974:958). In such instances, a merely rational relationship between purpose and classification has been insufficient to uphold the measure in question, and decision has been based on a balancing of societal benefit against individual harm (Grubb 1974:83).

Fundamental Right

What, then, is a fundamental right? And is the right to education a fundamental right? Fundamental rights have been variously defined as rights "implicit in a concept of ordered liberty" (Dobray 1984:258) or rights based on "natural law" (such as the rights to procreate and to travel) (Johnson 1974:960–1). For all practical purposes, a fundamental right is best defined as one "explicitly or implicitly guaranteed by the Constitution" (Johnson 1974:960–961). Although legal scholars have argued for education as a fundamental right because of its value to society and its importance for protecting other rights (e.g., free speech, voting), the courts thus far have explicitly ruled that the right to an education is *not* guaranteed by the Constitution.

The landmark case concerning the status of education as a right is *San Antonio Independent School District* v. *Rodriguez* (1973). In this case, the Texas system of financing public schools through local property taxes, which resulted in great disparities between school districts, was challenged (Farrell 1983:72). The Supreme Court upheld the system. While acknowledging the relationship of education to First Amendment freedoms and the franchise, the Court also stated: "Education . . . is not among the rights afforded explicit protection under our Federal Constitution. Nor do we find any basis for saying it is implicitly so protected'' (cited in Johnson 1974:975; see also Farrell 1983:72ff for details). If education itself is not a fundamental right, it follows that language education services are not constitutionally guaranteed. It would also follow that submersion would not violate a fundamental right. (Note that the 1974 *Lau* v. *Nichols* Supreme Court decision, one of the best known in the area of minority language education issues, was *not* decided on constitutional but on statutory grounds, specifically Title VI. See discussion below.)

Before we leave the question of fundamental right, however, two more points must be noted. In a dissenting opinion to the *San Antonio Independent School District* v. *Rodriguez* decision, Justice Marshall pointed out that ''the Constitution neither mentions nor implies the right to privacy, the right to interstate travel, the right to participate in state elections, the right to procreate, all of which have been held to be fundamental'' (cited in Johnson 1974:976). Thus, as the American legal tradition evolves, education may one day come to be regarded as a fundamental right. Moreover, an aside to the *San Antonio* case leaves the question open as to whether ''a system which failed to provide some identifiable quantum of education'' would in fact be denying its students a fundamental right (Farrell 1983:73; McFadden 1983:25; Dobray 1984:259). In other words, while education itself is not asserted to be a fundamental right, total denial of education may constitute the denial of a fundamental right. Non-English-speaking language-minority children in submersion classes may arguably be seen as suffering from a total denial of education. Again, since *Lau* v. *Nichols* avoided the constitutional issue altogether, at this point it is still unclear whether such an interpretation would hold. We may safely say, however, that the question of whether education is a fundamental right is far from closed.

Suspect Class

Suspect classification could be based on race, national origin, alienage (i.e., legal status as an alien) (Johnson 1974:961), as well as sex and illegitimacy (Johnson 1974:990–991), which are all characteristics beyond the choice and control of the individuals so classified. Classification on the basis of these characteristics has been struck down as reasons for discrimination. The question for the language education of minorities is whether a suspect class is involved. If so, the authorities responsible for a given program would have to demonstrate a state interest compelling enough to justify the classification. If not, the principle of judicial restraint would cause the courts to uphold a formally neutral educational program.

It is true that language, unlike characteristics such as race, is not immutable (Grubb 1974:84): language can be learned and changed. In this sense, limited-English-proficient (LEP) and non-English-proficient (NEP) students from a minority language group do not form a suspect class. On the other hand, in many cases language and race or national origin are intimately related (Johnson 1974:980); the relationship may be so close that "separation is meaningless in practice" (Grubb 1974:84). Moreover, being LEP or NEP involves "disabilities beyond [the children's] control" (Dobray 1984:265–266); "a bilingual child cannot select a language" (Johnson 1974:975). In addition, the *San Antonio Independent School District* v. *Rodriguez* decision further characterizes a suspect class as being saddled by disabilities, subjected to a history of purposeful unequal treatment, and politically powerless, to such an extent that "extraordinary protection from majoritarian political powers" is called for (cited in Johnson 1974:979). Language-minority children could fit such a description (Grubb 1974:79). Finally, from a second language acquisition perspective, language is really not as "mutable" as popularly believed; accents, morphological errors, and other features often persist in spite of the best efforts of the individual. Overall, a case may be made to challenge the denial of language education services by demonstrating suspect classification in the case of LEP and NEP children.

Compelling State Interest

Although education is not a fundamental right, the judicial system has come to recognize that it occupies a special status, so that failure to provide education must be subjected to more stringent demands for justification.

In the 1982 *Plyler* v. *Doe* Supreme Court decision, involving the question of whether the state of Texas had to give the children of illegal aliens an education, the Court reiterated that education is not a fundamental right. (Note that this is so even though the state was considering absolute denial of education.) At the same time, it also recognized that education is more than just another governmental benefit, because of its important role as socializing agent and sustainer of the nation's political and cultural heritage (Farrell 1983:80). As a result, rather than allowing the state to justify its classification by relating it rationally to a purpose, the Court required it to show a "compelling state interest" (Farrell 1983:80). In the *Plyler* v. *Doe* case, fiscal restraint, local autonomy, and the desire for a homogeneous society were all rejected as "compelling state interests" (Dobray 1984:276). The Court noted that denying an education to the children of illegal aliens has imposed "a lifetime hardship on a discrete class of children not accountable for their disabling status" (Dobray 1983:276), and ordered Texas to provide an education to the children of illegal aliens.

Because of the many parallels between the children of illegal aliens and LEP and NEP children from language-minority groups, such as disabilities beyond their control and disfavored status in American society (Dobray

1984:276), it is likely that a claim for language education services can be established based on arguments similar to those used in the *Plyler* v. *Doe* case. "A school district that failed to provide any remedial programs for language-deficient students would have a very difficult time finding state purposes sufficiently substantial to justify this exclusion from participation" (Farrell 1983:80). For example, an argument that submersion saves the school district money that can then be applied to benefit "everybody" will not carry weight in the courts.

TITLE VI OF THE CIVIL RIGHTS ACT OF 1964

Title VI, as Table 13.1 shows, prohibits discrimination on the basis of race, color, or national origin in federally funded programs. The so-called "May 25 Memorandum" extends protection to language-minority children, specifically barring assignment of such children to retarded classes and tracking or ability grouping based on language (Rotberg 1982:151). (As Johnson 1974:947 and McFadden 1983:8 point out, placement of Mexican American children in classes for the "educable mentally retarded" was once commonly practiced in the American school system.)

Lau *v*. Nichols (1974)

Title VI is the basis for a landmark decision, *Lau* v. *Nichols* (1974). In 1970, Kinney Kinmon Lau and 12 NEP Chinese American students—over half of whom were American-born—filed a class action suit on behalf of Chinese-speaking students in the San Francisco Unified School District, charging that they were being denied an education because of a lack of special English classes with bilingual teachers (Wang 1976:240–241). The case reached the Supreme Court, which in 1974 ruled in favor of the plaintiffs.

The Court noted: "Simple justice requires that public funds to which all taxpayers of all races contribute not be spent in any fashion which encourages, entrenches, subsidizes, or results in racial discrimination." Moreover,

> [T]here is no equality of treatment merely by providing students with the same facilities, textbooks, teachers, and curriculum; for students who do not understand English are effectively foreclosed from any meaningful education.
>
> Basic English skills are at the very core of what these public schools teach. Imposition of a requirement that, before a child can effectively participate in the educational program, he must already have acquired those basic skills is to make a mockery of public education. We know that those who do not understand English are certain to find their classroom experiences wholly incomprehensible and in no way meaningful.

The Court ordered "appropriate relief," although it did not specify a particular method (quotations from the *Lau* decision are from the summary in Leibowitz 1982:131–135).

Significance of the *Lau* Decision

The *Lau* decision, as Landry (1983:369) notes, is "just as important for what it did not say as for what it did say." It is therefore imperative to have a clear understanding of what the case implies on the issue of entitlement to language education services.

The *Lau* decision did not clarify the status of education in general, and language education services in particular, as a constitutionally guaranteed right. In fact, the Court scrupulously avoided a constitutional argument and instead relied on a statutory one (Title VI) to determine the plaintiff's claim to language education services. "It is tempting to say that somehow the *Lau* decision created some language rights for the plaintiffs, but it did not" (Macías 1979:92). Thus the question of whether education is a fundamental right is as yet unsettled.

The *Lau* decision did differentiate equality of access from equality of outcome. The Court rejected the defendant's argument that the Chinese-speaking students were treated equally because they were in the same classrooms, using the same books, being taught by the same teachers, etc. In other words, submersion was determined to be neutral on the surface but discriminatory in fact (Dobray 1984:266).

The *Lau* decision did not require showing of discriminatory intent and accepted disproportionate impact as sufficient proof of discrimination, stating: "discrimination is barred which has that *effect* even though no purposeful design is present" (Leibowitz 1982:133). In other words, it reflected the "proportional or consequential theory of equality" mentioned earlier. (But see below for recent developments on this issue.) However, two of the Justices emphasized that numbers were "at the heart of the case" (Macías 1979:92): "even if Title VI may be violated without the presence of a discriminatory intent, . . . remedial relief may be appropriate only when a significant number of limited English-speaking students are denied an equal opportunity" (Dobray 1984:283). The question of what constitutes a sufficiently substantial number to trigger relief is difficult to determine (Farrell 1983:106–107), and so far lower court decisions have given the concept conflicting interpretations (Dobray 1984:279).

The *Lau* decision did not create a right to receive bilingual education. Much of the confusion on this question arose from the so-called "Lau Remedies" or "Lau Guidelines," which were issued in 1975 on the basis of, but were *not* part of, the 1974 Supreme Court decision. Regarding appropriate relief, the Supreme Court simply stated: "Teaching English to the students of Chinese ancestry who did not speak the language is one choice. Giving instruction to this group in Chinese is another. There may be others" (cited in Rotberg 1982:151). The "Lau Remedies," in contrast, went further to call for bilingual education instead of English as a second language (ESL), maintenance of the minority language as a program goal, and cultural components (Rotberg 1982:152–154). These requirements were stringent, often unworkable (Rotberg 1982:152–154; Farrell 1983:85–86), and came under much criticism (Fernández 1987). It should be noted that the "Lau Remedies" had no statutory status (Dobray 1984:281–282) and could not, strictly speaking, prohibit ESL and require bilingual–bicultural education (Fernández 1987). Nevertheless, between 1975 and 1980, over 400 school districts negotiated "compliance agreements" with the Office of Civil Rights, many of which contained bilingual education provisions in the spirit of the "Lau Remedies" (Fernández 1987).

Ironically, in some cases, setting up bilingual education programs may conflict with another provision of the law protecting minorities: desegregation. "Whereas *Brown* v. *Board of Education* clearly forbids the maintenance of separate educational facilities for minority children, bilingual programs by their very nature tend to segregate language minority students during a large part of the school day" (McFadden 1983:17). In the 1976 *Keyes* v. *School District No. 1, Denver, Colorado* decision, a lower court ruled that desegregation should take precedence over bilingual education when the two conflict (McFadden 1983:17). Landry (1983:372) proposes that such conflicts be resolved by determining, in a given school community, whether protection of language rights or protection against racial discrimination is "the most pressing need"; in practice, however, assessing the relative urgency of the needs is problematic. The courts have by no means been unanimous on this issue, but "most courts have not seen the two philosophies as incompatible" (McFadden 1983:19).

Developments Since Lau

Diminishing Federal Role in Minority Language Education. In 1980, a new set of "Lau regulations" were proposed that would have had the force of law; however, they were withdrawn in 1981 (Rotberg 1982:154; Farrell 1983:86). Fernández (1987:102) notes:

> By 1981, any hope of enacting enforceable rules focussing on LEP students had vanished. The push for local control and decentralization meant that the federal government was relinquishing its more active pre-1981 role in the area of education. . . . The Department of Education reverted to the May 25 memorandum and to the language of the *Lau* decision . . . as the basis for enforcement by the OCR [Office of Civil Rights], a practice that continues to this day.

As Seidner and Seidner (1983) suggest, the 1980s are a period of conservatism when bilingual education will be viewed in an increasingly unfavorable light by the Administration. Choice of language education service programs is likely to be left more and more to the local school districts, yet on this matter the law has offered a confusing array of precedents, with some lower court decisions requiring bilingual education and some requiring ESL (see review in Farrell 1983:77–89).

Recent Emphasis on Discriminatory Intent. Since *Lau,* another landmark Supreme Court decision in the area of education has raised "serious doubts concerning the correctness of what appeared to be the premise of [the *Lau* decision]" (Farrell 1983:87). In its 1978 decision on the *Regents of the University of California* v. *Bakke* case, in which a white applicant to medical school sued the University of California claiming that affirmative action constituted "reverse discrimination," the Supreme Court ruled that the Constitution was coextensive with Title VI and that Title VI would prohibit only *intentional* discrimination (Farrell 1983:87). This might force a radical reassessment of the significance of the *Lau* decision. In the meantime, however, *Lau* still stands.

THE EQUAL EDUCATIONAL OPPORTUNITIES ACT OF 1974

Finally, claims to language education services may be based on Section 1703(f) of the EEOA. As Table 13.1 shows, the relevant portion of the EEOA text is very similar to that of Title VI, except for the inclusion of "sex" in the phrase prohibiting discrimination, and the term "appropriate action to overcome language barriers." The issues raised by EEOA are also very similar to those raised by both the equal protection clause and Title VI.

Again, equality of access vs. equality of outcome is one of the points of contention. Johnson, in clarifying these concepts, suggests that the latter is harder to measure and is not as useful as the former (1974:969). He adds, however, that access must not be taken to mean merely physical access, which is the bare minimum. Rather, citing a 1950 court decision, *Sweatt* v. *Painter,* he points out that students should have access to the "interplay of ideas and the exchange of views" (971). A language barrier can be said to occur "at the lower end of the access continuum, is readily recognizable, and is readily remedied" (971). It is thus a "justiciable issue."

Discriminatory intent vs. discriminatory effect is again an issue to consider in deciding whether the EEOA has been violated. In a 1981 decision on the *Castaneda* v. *Pickard* case (see Leibowitz 1982:192–218 for a summary), a lower court ruled that there was no need to prove discriminatory intent (Farrell 1983:94; McFadden 1983:15; Dobray 1984:284).

The EEOA is, nevertheless, not identical to other possible legal justifications for language education services because of its "appropriate action" clause. This clause proved to be important in the *Castaneda* case, where the court devised a three-prong test to determine whether the language education services then being provided constituted "appropriate action" (Dobray 1984:287–288; Farrell 1983:95–97): the challenged program must be informed by a sound educational theory, implemented effectively with sufficient resources, and, after a reasonable period of trial, evaluated as being able to overcome the students' language barrier. In other words, "[m]ere good faith efforts are insufficient" (Farrell 1983:96). Thus Section 1703(f) of the EEOA "has been generally interpreted by courts to require that school districts take *effective* action to overcome language barriers, whether or not there has been discriminatory intent on the part of school officials" (McFadden 1983:26; original italics).

"Appropriate action" is not specifically identified with bilingual education (Dobray 1984:285). ESL, for example, is also based on sound educational theory, can be adequately implemented, and can therefore satisfy the first two parts of the three-prong test. However, if it can be convincingly demonstrated that upon evaluation, ESL has not produced the desired results, a claim for bilingual education can be made (Farrell 1983:100). "Prevailing on the liability issue may be easier for plaintiffs under the EEOA than under the Constitution or Title VI" (Dobray 1984:285).

CONCLUSION

After the above review of the major possible legal bases on which claims to language education services for language minorities may be made, we are now ready to return to the two central questions of entitlement: Is submersion justified by law? And if not, are language minorities entitled to bilingual education?

The answer to the first question is "No." Although the legal tradition thus far has not considered education a fundamental right, and although the *Lau* decision avoids the constitutional issue, absence of language education services (i.e., submersion) approaches total denial of education and may constitute a violation of a fundamental right. Moreover, a suspect classification may be involved, and compelling state interest for it is difficult to establish. The *Lau* decision provides protection against submersion on the basis of Title VI. Even if *Lau* were someday to be overturned because of a post-*Bakke* emphasis on demonstration of discriminatory intent, the EEOA would still suggest an adequate basis for requiring effective "appropriate action" to remove the language barrier.

As for the second question on bilingual education, the answer is also "No." *Lau* did not specify the type of language education service the challenged school district was to supply. Neither did the EEOA. Bilingual education, like ESL, is, according to the law, only one possible kind of "appropriate action"; only when ESL can be shown to be ineffective upon evaluation can a claim for bilingual education be made. What needs to be borne in mind, however, is that submersion and bilingual education, though often portrayed in public debates as the only two alternatives, simply refer to absence of all language education service on the one hand, and a particular type of it on the other. There are other choices, such as ESL, to which language minority children *are* legally entitled. One should not be misled by the terms of the existing public debate into thinking that since bilingual education is not mandated by law, submersion is the only alternative.

A lower court judge, commenting on the *Lau* case, described LEP and NEP language-minority children as being "separated from their English-speaking peers" not by "walls of brick and mortar, but [by] the language barrier" (cited in Grubb 1974:52). The recent English-only movement, in promoting submersion as an allegedly effective, cheap, fair, and patriotic means of educating LEP and NEP students, is threatening to strengthen, not weaken, this invisible language barrier. To help protect the welfare of the nation's many language-minority children, it is important for all those concerned, language education professionals and ordinary citizens alike, to be acquainted with both the historical context and current status of language rights.

EXPLORING THE IDEAS

1. In her introduction, Wong suggests that language education professionals need to be informed about how their work fits into the overall language policy of the nation. In a footnote, she quotes Judd's statement that "ESOL teaching and teachers are not only affected by the political processes; we are also part of that process."

Think about ways in which language education professionals may be affected by the political process, as well as ways in which their work with language-minority children may be said to be political in nature.

2. Wong calls submersion a "nonmethod" rather than a method of teaching English to language minority children. On the other hand, many people do consider submersion (often referred to as "immersion" by laymen) as a method.

Which view do you find more acceptable? Why?

3. The issue of whether education (and, by implication, access to education through a meaningful language program) is a fundamental right has not been fully settled. So far, the Supreme Court has maintained that education is not constitutionally guaranteed; however, it has also left "room" for protecting minorities against absolute denial of education.

If you were a proponent of the view that education should be guaranteed by the Constitution, what arguments would you use to make your point? Conversely, if you were an opponent, how would you refute this view?

4. In providing language education services to linguistic minorities, there is much potential for conflict: on the one hand, one needs uniform and enforceable laws to ensure protection of language rights; on the other hand, one needs to be responsive to local conditions and flexible in implementing the regulations. These two needs have to be carefully balanced.

What might happen if one need prevails too strongly over the other? In concrete terms, how would language minority children be affected in each case?

APPLYING THE IDEAS

1. Wong refers to Kloss's discussion of arguments against the language rights of immigrant groups in his 1971 paper. She also mentions the "we were here first" argument.

Look up Kloss's article. Summarize his points; think of additional ones on both sides of the four "theories" cited as well as the "we were here first" argument. Make a list of the pros and cons.

2. Wong refers to Kloss's distinction between "tolerance-oriented" and "promotion-oriented" rights, and gives some examples of each type.

English-only proponents have made many suggestions concerning the language rights of minorities. Look up some examples of proposed legislation and try to determine which pertain to tolerance-oriented rights, which to promotion-oriented rights. According to Kloss's concept, which proposals are justified, which are not?

3. Wong observes that "foreign students" are different from "immigrant students," although the former term is frequently used to refer to both groups.

Investigate the legal differences between the status of foreign students and that of immigrant students. A good place to start is to check with the foreign student advisor of a nearby university.

4. Interview a local school administrator to find out how legislation affects language programs for minorities. Some suggested questions are: What types of programs (if any) are provided? Are they mandated or merely permitted by law? What are their funding sources? What are the entry and exit criteria for the program? Have legal requirements created problems, either in administration (e.g., conflict with desegregation requirements; teacher recruitment) or in classroom teaching?

NOTES

1. Judd (1987:15) notes: "ESOL instruction . . . is part of the country's general language policy. . . . ESOL teaching and teachers are not only affected by the political processes; we are also part of that process. . . . We may choose on an individual level to remain apart from partisan politics, but we cannot claim that we are above politics or beyond its grasp. As educators implementing approved governmental policies, we are a part of that system."

2. The two other commonly used arguments against the language rights of immigrant groups, examined and refuted in Kloss (1971), are the so-called "antighettoization" theory and "national unity" theory. The former states that imposition of the majority language is necessary for the good of the minorities, to enable them to escape the ethnic ghetto. The latter states that allowing immigrant language rights endangers national unity. Both these arguments overlook the fact that language is often merely an excuse for rationalizing or perpetuating existing inequities between the majority and the minorities.

ACKNOWLEDGMENTS. I would like to thank the following people for the generous help they have given me on the research for this chapter: Carolyn Patty Blum, Ray Frank, Paula Gillett, Rachel Moran, Jeff Numberg, Anne Okahana, John D. Trasvina, Evelyn P. Walters, Michael J. Wong, and the staff of the Asian Law Caucus in Oakland and the Immigrant Law Resource Center at the Stanford Law School.

REFERENCES

Beck, C. 1975. Is immigrant education only for immigrants? In A. Wolfgang (ed.), *Education for Immigrant Students: Issues and Answers*. Toronto: Ontario Institute for Studies in Education, 5–18.

Dobray, D. 1984. Constitutional and statutory rights to remedial language instruction: Variable degrees of uncertainty. *St. Mary's Law Journal* 15, 253–297.

Farrell, R. C. 1983. Bilingual education: The extent of an entitlement. *GMU [George Mason University] Law Review* 6:1, 69–110.

Fernández, R. R. 1987. Legislation, regulation, and litigation: The origins and evolution of public policy on bilingual education in the United States. In W. A. Van Horne and T. V. Tonnesen (eds.), *Ethnicity and Language*. Milwaukee WI: University of Wisconsin System Institute on Race and Ethnicity, 90–123.

Grubb, E. B. 1974. Breaking the language barrier: The right to bilingual education. *Harvard Civil Rights-Civil Liberties Law Review* 9, 52–94.

Johnson, W. E. 1974. The constitutional right of bilingual children to an equal educational opportunity. *Southern California Law Review* 47, 943–997.

Judd, E. 1987. Teaching English to speakers of other languages: A political act and a moral question. *TESOL Newsletter* (February), 15–16.

Kloss, H. 1971. The language rights of immigrant groups. *International Migration Review* 5, 250–268.

Landry, W. J. 1983. Future Lau regulations: Conflict between language rights and racial nondiscrimination. In R. V. Padilla (ed.), *Theory, Technology and Public Policy on Bilingual Education*. Rosslyn, VA: National Clearinghouse for Bilingual Education, 365–376.

Leibowitz, A. H. 1982. *Federal Recognition of the Rights of Minority Language Groups*. Rosslyn, VA: National Clearinghouse for Bilingual Education.

Macías, R. F. 1979. Language choice and human rights in the United States. In J. Alatis and G. R. Tucker, (eds.), *Language in Public Life: Georgetown Round Table on Languages and Linguistics 1979*. Washington, D.C.: Georgetown University Press, 86–101.

Marshall, D. F. 1986. The question of an official language: Language rights and the English Language Amendment. *International Journal of the Sociology of Language* 60, 7–75.

McFadden, B. J. 1983. Bilingual education and the law. *Journal of Law and Education* 12:1, 1–27.

Rotberg, I. C. 1982. Some legal and research considerations in establishing federal policy in bilingual education. *Harvard Educational Review* 52, 149–168.

Ruíz, R. 1984. Orientations in language planning. *NABE Journal* 8:2, 15–34. (See also this volume.)

Seidner, S. S. and Seidner, M. M. 1983. In the wake of conservative reaction: An analysis. In R. V. Padilla (ed.), *Theory, Technology and Public Policy in Bilingual Education*. Rosslyn, VA: National Clearinghouse for Bilingual Education, 327–349.

Wang, L. L.-C. 1876. *Lau v. Nichols:* History of a struggle for equal and quality education. In E. Gee (ed.), *Counterpoint: Perspectives on Asian America*. Los Angeles: Asian American Studies Center, University of California, Los Angeles.